The AIX Survival Guide

The AIX Survival Guide

Andreas Siegert

Addison-Wesley

An imprint of Pearson Education

Harlow, England · London · New York · Reading, Massachusetts · San Francisco
Toronto · Don Mills, Ontario · Sydney · Tokyo · Singapore · Hong Kong · Seoul
Taipei · Cape Town · Madrid · Mexico City · Amsterdam · Munich · Paris · Milan

PEARSON EDUCATION LIMITED

Edinburgh Gate
Harlow CM20 2JE
Tel: +44 (0)1279 623623
Fax: +44 (0)1279 431059
Website: *www.pearsoned.co.uk*

First published in Great Britain 1996

ISBN 0-201-59388-2

British Library Cataloguing in Publication Data
A CIP catalogue record for this book can be obtained from the British Library.

Library of Congress Cataloguing in Publication Data
Applied for.

10 9

Typeset by the author.
Printed and bound in Great Britain by Biddles Ltd, *www.biddles.co.uk*
Cover designed by Viva Design.

The Publishers' policy is to use paper manufactured from sustainable forests.

For Krümel

Preface

With the move toward open systems, interest in IBM's UNIX implementation is growing fast as users move up from PC-based systems, move down from mainframes, move over from proprietary solutions or switch to a more modern UNIX implementation. Most people learn about a standardized operating system, UNIX, during this process. Every UNIX system has its own features and advantages. This book is geared towards those users who have basic UNIX skills and want to know more about AIX. I do not intend to teach UNIX basics, abundant books on that topic are available elsewhere. Instead I will focus on AIX specifics. I want to help the reader to get the most out of AIX on IBM's RISC System /6000.

As a member of IBM Germany's AIX field support center since 1989, I have been confronted with questions from a wide range of users on nearly all aspects of AIX. These questions, together with several years of AIX experience, have shaped the contents of this book. It represents my view on daily life with AIX.

Andreas Siegert

afx@ibm.de

How to read this book

This book should help you to set up and maintain systems running AIX on the RISC System/6000. I assume that you have already a basic UNIX knowledge and thus focus on how things are done on AIX. If you have not yet worked with AIX, I suggest reading this book from front to back. If you already have some experience of AIX, then use the table of contents and the index to locate the items on which you want more information.

All of this applies to AIX versions 3.2.5 and 4.1 on the RISC System/6000. There are/were completely different AIX versions for PS/2s and the System/370 available which are not discussed in this book. Every time AIX is mentioned here the version for the RISC System/6000 is the one that is meant. Be sure to check the documentation that is supplied with the system when you try to apply the techniques shown in this book. Things might have changed slightly since the book was written as IBM is always active in keeping up with new technologies.

The introduction of the PowerPC chip-based PCs has resulted in a completely new class of machines capable of running AIX. Apart from booting and some device support details, these systems run standard AIX and the techniques described in this book should also be directly applicable to them.

Throughout the book, monospaced font is used for paragraphs of sample code listings as in

```
# ls -a /tmp
.X11-unix   .info-help  lost+found
```

Other typefaces used in the text are:

<CTRL-K>	Hold down the Ctrl key while pressing the K key.
info	The name of a command or other special item.
/.profile	The name of a file or directory.
ls -la	A command to be executed.

What is AIX?

AIX is UNIX, but what is UNIX? Long ago UNIX was defined by Bell Labs, then some said that UNIX is what the Berkeley Software Distribution (BSD) provides. Nowadays UNIX is what adheres to POSIX, X/Open and SPEC 1170 standards (or even FIPS for the US government).

AIX is first of all POSIX compliant everywhere a POSIX standard exists. It has XPG4 branding, complies with the OSF AES B (much of OSF/1 is based on AIX), it is compliant with SPEC 1170, and once all these official standards are covered it tries to adhere to System V standards as well as BSD.

Inside is a totally different kernel that is pageable and pre-emptable and which supports real-time processes with fixed priorities, interrupt handlers with guaranteed time slots, dynamically loadable kernel extensions, kernel processes (and on AIX 4 also kernel threads) and more.

The disk management of AIX was the first UNIX disk management that had on the fly extensible file systems and dynamic disk import/export. It was also the first UNIX to have a journaled file system, finally putting an end to the horror stories of lost file systems on UNIX.

Its system management interface, SMIT, makes it easy to control the system with menus without taking away command line access to system management. By storing configuration information in a database (ODM) instead of flat files it reduces the risks of editing errors while at the same time alienating experienced UNIX gurus.

AIX is also an operating system that scales from small laptops, such as the 850, to multiprocessor supercomputers such as the SP2 with up to hundreds of nodes.

A short history of AIX

AIX is not the first UNIX operating system from IBM. IBM had a long UNIX history internally, with very early installations of System III on mainframes. Commercially available UNIX versions from IBM included XENIX on the PC-AT, ix/370 on the mainframes, the TCF AIX with a single system image on PS/2s and mainframes as well as one of the first RISC-based machines, the RT or 6150, which was the little-known predecessor of the RISC System/6000 running AIX 2.

In 1990 IBM introduced the RISC System/6000 series with AIX 3.1. AIX 3.1 reached its peak in 1993 with AIX 3.1.5. However, there are still AIX 3.1 systems out there that run happily without problems. The majority of systems installed at the moment use AIX 3.2.5, which was introduced in 1992. The current version of AIX is 4.2. AIX 4 was introduced in 1994 but only started to take off in 1995 with the introduction of new IBM systems and PowerPC-based systems from other vendors that can run AIX but need at least version 4.1.

Acknowledgments

I would like to thank my colleagues at the AIX FSC in Munich for their patience with me and my questions. I would also like to thank everyone on the internal and external news groups who helped me build up my knowledge. Many people helped me to get the story straight. Thanks are due to Mickey Coggins, Glen (Tex!) Chalemin, Gunilla and John Easton, and many more. My sincere thanks also to Frank Kraemer, who took the pains to find many of my errors.

The staff of at Frame Technologies Ltd in Ireland helped me tremendously by making FrameMaker available to me for writing this book.

Trademark notice

DEC™ and VT100™ are trademarks of Digital Equipment Corporation

DCE™, Open Software Foundation™, OSF™ and Motif™ are trademarks of Open Software Foundation

Frame Technology Corporation® and FrameMaker® are registered trademarks of Frame Technology Corporation

IBM® is a registered trademark and AIX™, AIXwindows™, IBM RISC System/6000™ and Micro Channel™ are trademarks of International Busines Machines Corporation

Intel™ is a trademark of Intel Corporation

Interleaf® is a registered trademark of Interleaf Inc

PostScript® is a registered trademark of Adobe Systems Inc

Sun Microsystems® is a registered trademark and NIS™, NFS™, Sun™ and SunOS™ are trademarks of Sun Microsystems Inc

Transarc™ is a trademark of Transarc and AFS® is a registered trademark of Transarc

UNIX® is a registered trademark in the United States and other countries, licenced exclusively through X/Open Company Limited

X/Open™ and the X device are trademarks of X/Open Company Ltd

X Window System™ is a trademark of X Consortium Inc

All other company and product names may be trademarks of the organizations with which they are associated

Contents

Appendices

1

Installing AIX

Before you can do anything useful with AIX you need to install it. Even if you have ordered a machine with AIX pre-installed, you should read through this chapter as it also discusses some other initial set-up items. Installation on AIX is usually a two-step process. First the core of the base operating system (BOS) is installed and, secondly, optional components of the operating system and any licenced program products (LPPs) are installed.

1.1 Planning your installation

Installation planning involves several steps. First start a folder where you keep all information about the system such as README files, CPU id, layout of the hard disks, user contacts, paper copies of important profiles and whatever is useful for you. It pays to keep that information handy when a system is down. When you get AIX from IBM you should also receive a *Notice to Licencees*. Read this document first before you attempt any installation. It usually contains important hints.

The next thing you need to think about is the layout of the file systems. This depends on the applications you run and on the number of users you need to support on the system. Although AIX is more flexible than traditional UNIX systems insofar as you can extend file systems at runtime, you still cannot shrink them easily. You can spread your file systems over several hard disks, which is quite convenient but might also introduce a new maintenance headache if one of them gets damaged. Apart from the initial paging space, which usually will be at least 64MB and up to twice the size of the installed memory, all file systems will be kept very small by AIX during installation and most of them need to be extended later. If your system comes preloaded, then there might be an additional pitfall because of the amount of disk space that is used up by install images on the hard disk.

AIX will install the following initial file systems:

/home	**/dev/hd1**	The home file system for users, initially 4MB.
/usr	**/dev/hd2**	The /usr file system that stores all commands, the size varying depending on which components you install.
/tmp	**/dev/hd3**	The temporary file system, initially 8MB.
/	**/dev/hd4**	The root file system, initially 4MB.
Boot image	**/dev/hd5**	The boot area it needs 8MB.
Pagingspace	**/dev/hd6**	The paging space, at least 32MB, up to double the size of the installed memory or 20% of the available disk space at maximum.
Dumpdevice	**/dev/hd7**	The primary dump device on AIX 3, initially 8MB. AIX 4 will use the paging space as the default dump device.
JFS Log	**/dev/hd8**	The log area for the journaled file system, usually 4MB.
/var	**/dev/hd9var**	The var file system for spool data, initially 4MB.

The documentation that comes with the operating system tells you how much disk space the individual parts need so that you can calculate the space required for the /usr file system.

Additional applications might need their own file system or they may be installed directly in /usr/lpp like all the software IBM ships. During the initial installation you do not have many choices. As soon as you boot the system the first time you can rearrange things and give dedicated file systems or volume groups to applications. This is a chicken and egg problem. To learn about the logical volume manager you need to have a running system to gather experience. But first you need to install a system, and here knowing how AIX arranges file systems would help a lot. The following sections will guide you through the initial installation. They should be sufficient for most cases. If you want to set up an extremely customized system you might need to redo your installation once you find out how it all fits together. The only strict rule for the first installation is to keep the initial code all on one disk.

1.1.1 Installable options

After the initial base operating system is installed, there are numerous add-ons that can be installed. It may not be necessary to install everything supplied, depending on your needs. However, quite often people do not install crucial parts and complain later that they have received an incomplete system. The following lists should help you in deciding which optional parts you need to install. AIX 3 and AIX 4 differ greatly in their packaging. On AIX 3 it is easy to install too much, whereas on AIX 4 it is easy not to install enough. For example, AIX 3 will install many more device drivers than you need, whereas AIX 4 will only install the drivers you need on the system you are installing. This makes it very hard to clone the system later on. AIX 4 uses ISO code pages by default, whereas AIX 3 assumes PC850 code pages initially. Should you install too much on AIX 4, then you can easily remove it. AIX 3 makes this a bit more complicated (see Section 1.6 for a remedy).

AIX 3.2

The following LPP options are shipped with standard AIX 3.2.5:

bsl.en_US.aix.loc	US English locale for ISO code page.
bsl.en_US.pc.loc	US English locale for PC850 code page.
bsl.xx_XX.xxx.loc	There are many more locales of course. Install those that you need. For non-US English installations I suggest also installing the US locales as many people prefer to work in this locale when carrying out system maintenance. You should install the ISO locales for your country. The PC locales should only be installed if compatibility with PC code pages or older AIX systems (AIX 3.1 or AIX on the PS/2 or the 6150) is required.
bsl.lat-1.fnt.loc	The Latin-1 ISO fonts for the system. You should install those.
bsl.xxxx.fnt.loc	There are more fonts than Latin-1 available. Install them only if they are needed.

bsl.aix31.imk.loc	Old AIX 3.1 input method locales. These are only needed for compatibility with a few old software packages.
bsmEn_US.msg	All the externalized messages for the operating system. These are definitely needed.
bos.data	Data files for the base system, for example the *terminfo* database. Install them.
bos.obj.*	Additions to the base operating system. They should be installed in normal systems.
bssiEn_US.info	System InfoExplorer database. Do not install any InfoExplorer database from tape if you intend to get the InfoExplorer database from a CD.
bspiEn_US.info	Programming InfoExplorer database.
bseiEn_US.info	System Education InfoExplorer database.
INed.obj	The INed Editor; avoid it as it easily corrupts files when used for system management.
bosadt.*	The parts of the application developer's toolkit.
bosext1.*	Various extensions, such as the C-shell or the MH mail program and other useful commands.
bosext2.*	More extensions, including accounting, a terminal emulator and various network programming interfaces.
bosnet.tcpip.obj	TCP/IP and all the standard networking tools.
bosnet.ncs.obj	NCS (Network Computing System).
bosnet.nfs.obj	NFS (Network File System) and NIS (Network Information System).
bosnet.snmpd.obj	SNMP support.
txtfmt.*	Various parts of the text processing system. This is also needed for formatting traditional man pages. It contains the Adobe TypeScript utilities.
pci.obj	The host part of AIX access for DOS users.
xlccmp.obj	The C compiler.

You get the following parts if you have ordered AIXwindows 2D:

X11rte.obj	X runtime system.
X11rte.ext.*	X runtime extensions. This includes the desktop and other utilities.
X11dev.obj	X development support.
X11dev.src	X source samples and additional utilities.
X11mEn_US.msg	The externalized messages for X programs.
X11deviEn_US.info	InfoExplorer library for X.
X11fnt.*	Various fonts. I suggest loading ISO-1, coreX and oldX plus other ISO or kanji fonts if needed.

AIX 4.1

The AIX 4 shipment includes AIXwindows, but unfortunately no C compiler.

X11.Dt.*	AIXwindows desktop components (CDE).
X11.adt.*	AIXwindows application development toolkit; even for non-developers this contains many useful utilities.
X11.apps.*	Various AIXwindows applications.
X11.base.*	AIXwindows basic runtime environment.
X11.compat.*	AIXwindows options for backwards compatibility, not necessarily needed.
X11.fnt.*	AIXwindows fonts. Select the ones you need, all ISO Latin-1 fonts plus whatever you need for your language.
X11.fnt.fontServer	AIXwindows font server.
X11.fnt.util	AIXwindows font utilities (font editors and compilers).
X11.info.rte	AIXwindows InfoExplorer runtime environment.
X11.info.en_US.*	AIXwindows on-line documentation.
X11.loc.Xx_XX.*.*	AIXwindows locales.
X11.man.en_US.Dt.rte	AIXwindows desktop runtime man pages – US English.
X11.motif.lib	AIXwindows Motif libraries.
X11.motif.mwm	AIXwindows Motif window manager, not needed if you run only with the AIXwindows desktop.
X11.msg.En_US.*	AIXwindows messages.
X11.samples.*	AIXwindows samples; contains plenty of useful utilities.
X11.vsm.*	Visual system management, a graphical way of carrying out some of the system management tasks.
X11.x_st_mgr.*	Xstation manager, needed only for the IBM Xstations 120 and 130; newer models can work without it.
bos.INed	INed Editor. Avoid it!
bos.acct	Accounting services.
bos.adt.*	Base application development toolkit.
bos.compat.NetInstl	AIX 3.2 network installation tools.
bos.compat.cmds	AIX 3.2 compatibility commands; contains useful features such as the *li* command.
bos.compat.lan	LAN COMIO compatibility software and device entries
bos.compat.libs	AIX 3.2 compatibility libraries.
bos.compat.links	AIX 3.2 to 4.1 compatibility links, for those that still believe /etc is a directory for executables.
bos.compat.net	AIX 3.2 TCP/IP compatibility commands.
bos.compat.termcap	AIX 3.2 termcap source and library.
bos.compat.termcap.data	AIX 3.2 termcap source data.
bos.data	Base operating system data.
bos.diag.rte	Hardware diagnostics.
bos.dlc.*	Various data link control drivers.
bos.dosutil	DOS utilities.
bos.games	Games: contains the very important *fortune* command!

bos.iconv.*	Various language-to-language conversion utilities.
bos.ifor_ls.*	iFOR/LS licence system tools.
bos.info.en_US.*	Various on-line references for InfoExplorer.
bos.info.rte	Base system InfoExplorer.
bos.loc.adt.*	Language converter development toolkit.
bos.loc.com.*	Common locale support for various non-Latin languages.
bos.loc.iso.*	Various ISO code sets; install only those you need.
bos.loc.pc_compat.*	Various PC-compatible code sets; only needed when using the system as a PC server.
bos.mh	Mail handler.
bos.msg.*.*	Runtime messages for various languages and file sets.
bos.net.ate	Terminal emulator for serial lines.
bos.net.ncs	NCS (Network Computing System).
bos.net.nfs.*	NFS (Network File System) and NIS (Network Information System).
bos.net.nis.client	NIS client support.
bos.net.tcp	TCP/IP support.
bos.net.uucp	UNIX-to-UNIX copy program.
bos.pci	Server for use with AIX access for DOS users, do not install it unless really needed.
bos.perf.diag_tool	Performance diagnostic tool.
bos.perf.pmr	Performance PMR data collection tool.
bos.rcs	Remote customer support and services, not very useful outside the US.
bos.rte.mp	Base operating system multiprocessor runtime.
bos.rte.up	Base operating system uniprocessor runtime.
bos.som	SOM/DSOM support.
bos.sysmgt.*	Various system management tools. This should be installed as it contains features such as the *errpt* command.
bos.terminfo.*	Various terminal support files.
bos.txt.*	Parts of the text formatting system.
bos.txt.tfs	Needed for man page support.
devices.base.com	Common base system device software.
devices.base.rte	Uniprocessor base system device software.
devices.buc.*	Support for local graphics devices.
devices.graphics.com	Graphics adapter common software.
devices.isa.*	Support for ISA bus cards.
devices.mca.*	Support for Micro Channel cards.
devices.msg.*	Messages for device support.
devices.pci.*	Support for PCI cards.
devices.pcmcia.*	Support for PCMCIA cards.
devices.rs6ksmp.base.rte	Multiprocessor base system device software.
devices.rspc.*	RISC PC common base system device support.

devices.scsi.* Various SCSI support parts (drivers, diagnostics).
devices.sio.* Drivers for built-in I/O (keyboard, mouse, diskette).
devices.sys.* Various drivers for integrated devices.
devices.tty.rte TTY device driver support software.
printers.* Printer support.

1.2 Choosing an installation method

There are several methods of installing a system. You can use a tape, the network or on AIX 4 also a CD ROM (in the US there is also a CD for AIX 3). Or you might have ordered a preloaded, preinstalled or preconfigured system. If you have a preconfigured system continue with Section 1.3. If you are installing a system from scratch you should read about tape/CD installation and, if appropriate, the other installation methods.

1.2.1 Basic installation from tape or CD

My preferred method for initial installations is via tape or CD. You get a completely clean machine and can decide which disk to use for what purpose. But first you need to set up the system physically. Either connect a terminal to the serial port 1 and set it to 9600 BPS, eight data bits, no parity, one stop bit (9600 8N1) or connect a keyboard and a mouse to the system unit and a monitor to the graphics card in the system. Make sure that all attached SCSI devices have unique addresses and are powered on. There should be a *Notice to Licencees* or a *README* that comes with the operating system tape. Be sure to read and understand it before you continue.

Put the key in secure mode. Switch on the tape or CD drive if it is an external one and then switch on the system itself. As soon as the LED code reaches 200 put the tape or CD into the drive and turn the key to service mode. Follow the instructions on the screen that will appear after a while. PowerPC PCs without the key switch will boot off the CD automatically if a bootable CD is detected in the CD drive.

First you will be prompted for a console device. The device you select here will be the default console from now on until you change it explicitly. After a few more minutes you will be presented with the installation menu. It will give you several options but we are only interested in standard installation at the moment.

The installation menus on AIX 3 and AIX 4 are a bit different. AIX 4 allows more choices for the installation language and you can set up a mix of locale and language for the system at install time.

The menu will allow you to select the initial locale (locales and other international support is discussed in Chapter 20), the installation device, the hard disk(s) that are used for the installation and the disk that will be used as a boot device.

I suggest leaving the initial locale set to C (POSIX). It can be changed later on if necessary. The locale is used for the language of the system messages, the keyboard layout and data representation on AIX 3. On AIX 4 you can set those individually right from the start. Whereas an AIX 4 system will show you an installation menu in the selected language, AIX 3 will use only English. Once you have installed your AIX 3 system then you should adapt keyboard, fonts and other language-specific items. By selecting those features immediately on AIX 4 the proper language support will be installed automatically, removing one extra step later on.

The default installation device will be the tape/CD you booted from. If you have several hard disks in the machine then the system might offer an installation that uses more than one disk. All the disks that are used for the initial installation will be part of the root volume group (*rootvg*). Volume groups and other AIX disk management concepts are discussed in Section 6.1. I suggest changing this selection so that only one disk is used unless you have space problems (You need at least 400MB for the *rootvg* in a tight system). The default boot disk will be the first SCSI disk on the first SCSI adapter found.

On AIX 4 you can also decide whether you want to install the TCB (trusted computing base). If you have any security requirements at all, install the TCB. It cannot be added later on; a complete new installation would be required to get the TCB on the system. Use of the TCB is discussed on page 297.

When you are finished with this menu the system will install the minimum base operating system when installing AIX 3. When installing AIX 4 support for all devices found in the system will be installed as well. If the installation process detects a graphics card a basic AIXwindows runtime system will also be installed.

After a long coffee break the system is ready for rebooting. Reboot the machine according to the instructions on the screen and log in as root.

1.2.2 Installing options on AIX 3

If you are working on a direct attached monitor and not an ASCII terminal then you should execute the command **open ksh** first. This gives you a second console screen. You can toggle between them via <ALT-Action>. Run **smit install_latest**. Press <F4> and select the tape drive where the installation tape resides (usually /dev/rmt0.1). You will be presented with the menu shown in Figure 1.1.

Press <F4> on the field 'SOFTWARE to install'. SMIT will read a table of contents from the tape and you then can select individual parts by pressing <F7>. Select all the components you need and then press <ENTER>. Depending on what you have selected it will take a few minutes up to several hours until everything is loaded from tape. After the software has been loaded you are ready to proceed to Section 1.3.

```
                    Install Software Products at Latest Available Level

Type or select values in entry fields.
Press Enter AFTER making all desired changes.

                                                          [Entry Fields]
* INPUT device / directory for software                    /dev/rmt0.1
* SOFTWARE to install                                     []                  +
  Automatically install PREREQUISITE software?             yes                +
  COMMIT software?                                         yes                +
  SAVE replaced files?                                     no                 +
  VERIFY Software?                                         no                 +
  EXTEND file systems if space needed?                     yes                +
  REMOVE input file after installation?                    no                 +
  OVERWRITE existing version?                              no                 +
  ALTERNATE save directory                                 []

F1=Help             F2=Refresh          F3=Cancel           F4=List
F5=Undo             F6=Command          F7=Edit             F8=Image
F9=Shell            F10=Exit            Enter=Do
```

Figure 1.1 Installing with SMIT on AIX 3.

I have started to use a slightly faster method because I became tired of paging through the selection list. First I list the complete table of contents from the tape with **installp -qld /dev/rmt0.1 > /tmp/tape.contents**. It is necessary to specify a non-rewinding tape here, by adding '.1' to the tape name. Copy the list generated to a file called tape.run for example so that you have a backup copy. The list will look similar to that in Figure 1.2.

```
  Option Name                    Level                       I/U Q Content

===================================================================================
  txtfmt.tfs.obj                 03.02.0000.0000.U413301      S  N usr
#   Text Formatting Services
  pcsim.obj                      01.02.0000.0000.U409405      S  N usr
#   PC Simulator
  bosnet.tcpip.obj               03.02.0000.0000.U404378      S  Y usr
#   TCPIP Applications
  bos.obj                        03.02.0000.0000.U402381      C  N usr
#   Base Operating System
```

Figure 1.2 A sample list of files on an install tape.

Edit the tape.run file and remove anything you do not want to install. Then remove all comment lines and the location specifier at the end of the lines. In the end you should have a list that looks similar to Figure 1.3.

```
txtfmt.tfs.obj                03.02.0000.0000.U413301
pcsim.obj.all                 01.02.0000.0000
bosnet.tcpip.obj              03.02.0000.0000.U404378
bos.obj                       03.02.0000.0000.U445566
```

Figure 1.3 An input file for *installp.*

This file can now be used by *instafllp* to install all the software you want. Run *installp* with the following command line:

```
installp -aqgcXd /dev/rmt0.1 'cat /tmp/tape.run' 2>&1 |
tee /tmp/tape.run.out
```

The above command line will install the parts you select and their prerequisites, commit them and extend the file system if necessary. The output of *installp* will be written to the terminal and the file /tmp/tape.run.out. This is not something that I would recommend for total beginners as it commits (committed software is not easily de-installable on AIX 3; see page 261) the software immediately. Also sometimes software needs to be installed in a certain order. You should consult the *Notice To Licencees* that comes with the system first. If you have done several AIX installations already and it is beginning to get very boring, you may prefer this method.

1.2.3 Continuing the AIX 4 installation

AIX will start the install assistant (*install_assist*) when booting after the initial installation. This is either a SMIT-like ASCII application or a graphical program depending whether a graphics card was detected or not. Although this is basically a good idea, I am not convinced by its implementation. It starts with a time zone selector that still thinks the whole world uses the US switchover times for daylight savings and continues with other assumptions about a system that I do not share. I suggest configuring TCP/IP (because CDE needs the correct host name) and the basic local time with it. You can also use it to install additional software right away. I usually ignore it and work with the standard command line and SMIT tools. On the ASCII version get into a subshell with <F9> and on the X version use the right mouse button in the root window to get an *aixterm*. Now set the time zone in /etc/environment and in the current shell as described in Section 4.2.1. It is not essential to set the time and time zone immediately: it merely ensures that some file dates reflect the installation date.

AIX 4 installs a very small paging space initially. Depending on your disk layout you should increase the primary paging space now before the fast spots on the disk are used up by the software that will be installed. Check out the installed memory with **bootinfo -r** and then see how much disk space is still free in the root volume group with **lsvg rootvg**. You can then increase the primary paging space with **chps -s N hd6**, where *N* is the number of physical partitions that you want to add to the paging space. (Unless you have disks that are 4GB or larger, a physical partition will have a size of 4MB.) Assuming that there is enough disk space, a good formula is to use a paging space that is twice the size of the installed RAM, but at least 64MB. If you have more than 64MB of memory and several disks, you should try to allocate a paging space on each disk, so do not increase the initial paging space too much. The install assistant has the habit of creating a second paging space on the same disk, which is terrible for performance (see Section 6.5 for details). This is another reason why I believe that these tasks should be done manually.

The most important task is to install any components that you need but which are not included by the automatic installation. This can be done by running **smit install_latest**. Select the proper installation drive and then use <F4> to obtain a selection screen for the individual components. You will see a list like that in Figure 1.4.

```
4.1.0.0  X11.fnt                                                   ALL
  + 4.1.0.0  AIXwindows Cyrillic Fonts
  @ 4.1.0.0  AIXwindows Default Fonts
  + 4.1.0.0  AIXwindows Font Server

3.1.1.0  xlC.C                                                     ALL
  ! 3.1.1.0  C for AIX Compiler
  + 3.1.1.0  C for AIX Manual Pages
```

Figure 1.4 Selecting software to install on AIX 4.

Use <F7> to select the items that you need. Items that have the keyword ALL on the right are used to select complete groups of file sets. Items marked with an '@' are already installed, a '$' donates an item that needs a licence which is already installed and a '!' donates an item that needs a licence key that is not yet installed.

As AIX 4 tries to be very disk conservative, the initial installation is really minimal. Make sure you install all the components needed to avoid another install session later on. Once the installation is finished, reboot and continue with Section 1.3. Finally, tell the installation assistant that you have finished. If you do not, the next reboot will bring up the assistant again instead of a login prompt.

1.2.4 Installing from a preloaded system

A preloaded system is a system that has the base operating system already installed, but not the optional components, which can be found on the disk in /usr/sys/inst.images. I personally do not like this method of shipment as a great deal of disk space is used for these images and it is possible that there will not be enough space left over to install them if you have bought the system with a small hard drive. If you have enough space then simply select /usr/sys/inst.images as an installation device in SMIT (**smit install_latest**). This is the only difference in the second part of the installation from the installation from tape.

Regardless of whether or not you have enough space, I would back up this directory to a tape first. If you do not have enough space then you definitely need to do this. In addition, I suggest making a bootable image backup as well, as described in Section 1.4. Install the optional parts one by one and set the option to delete the input file after the installation. You may even need to delete some of the options and then restore them later from tape on a very tight system.

1.2.5 Installing from a clone tape

The installation of a clone tape is similar to normal tape installation with one big difference: you install the whole system in one step. Because the tape is a clone of an already installed machine there is no need for the extra LPP installation. The clone tape has all the code and configuration of the original machine. The interesting part here is the creation of the clone tape. This is done with the *mksysb* command. Before creating a clone tape you can modify many features that make it easier to work with the new clone. The creation of clone tapes is discussed in Section 13.1. Most people refer to clone tapes as *mksysb* tapes as they are generated with this command. AIX 4 adds a major pitfall to system cloning as it no longer installs all device drivers. Therefore you can clone a system only if you have installed all the device drivers and processor support needed on the target system.

1.2.6 Installing via the network

Network installation is very useful for larger sites. On older systems and PC-like machines without the key switch you can use floppies, a CD or a tape to boot the system and then select the network as the installation device. On newer systems you can get to the network boot screen by booting with the key in secure mode, waiting for LED 200, turning the key to service and then pressing the reset button. If you do not have a real RS/6000 with the three-digit LED display and a key lock, check the documentation that comes with the system.

You need to specify the address of the installation server and perhaps a gateway and the hardware parameters for the network (ring speed or type of Ethernet connector). Your machine will then contact the installation server and offer you a menu of the packages that you can install. Select one and go for lunch.

The set-up of an installation server is discussed in Chapter 14. You can also install from a remote tape. This method is described in Section 14.1.2. If you then select the 'tape image' you will get the code from a remote tape.

1.3 Finding important last minute notices

AIX comes with several README files on-line in various places. You should check them to make sure that you are not missing any important changes or warnings. The best way to find them all at once is via the *find* command:

```
find / -name "*README*" -print
```

After you have installed a printer you should print the ones that are important for you (you will not want to print all of the them as there may be very many if you installed a lot of software) and keep them for reference in case you need the information and the machine is not available. The most important file is /usr/lpp/bos/README. It has many hints and points to other files of interest.

In addition, you can use InfoExplorer to access most of the README files, just use *README* as a search argument.

1.4 Making the first backup

I am sure you heard this before, but here it comes again:

DO MAKE BACKUPS!

After you have installed your system it is still in a virgin configuration. If you make an installable backup now, you can recreate this state much faster than via a reinstallation from the distribution medium. So if you make a complete mess at customizing the system you will need much less time to recover. This type of backup is a special one, as it can be used to install machines completely directly off the tape.

Either go through the SMIT menus or use the direct road via **smit mksysb**, or just enter the command **mkszfile && mksysb /dev/rmt0** (on AIX 3) or **mksysb -i /dev/rmt0** (on AIX 4) to start a system backup on the *rmt0* tape device. It will take some time, depending on the amount of software installed and the speed of the tape drive.

After you have customized your system you should do the same backup again to another tape. Then you have an installable tape with all your site-specific customization done already, and you can use this tape for cloning systems.

1.5 Generating boot diskettes on AIX 3.2

Check out the README file in /usr/lpp/bos on AIX 3.2; it contains the correct steps to create boot diskettes for your AIX release. Four formatted diskettes are required. Formatting is done with the **format** command without any additional parameters. Then create a boot diskette via the **bosboot -a -d /dev/rfd0** command. Next is the display diskette with **mkdispdskt** followed by the display extension diskette with **mkextdskt**. Finally you need to generate a maintenance install diskette via **mkinstdskt**. After you have created the diskettes, shut down the system, put the key in service mode, put in the first diskette and try booting with the newly generated diskettes. Every time the system prompts you with an LED display of c07 you are requested to replace the diskette in the drive with the next one. If you reach the installation menu you can be sure that you have some working boot diskettes for emergencies. Store them in a safe place. Together with the system key they can be used to break into the system if the root password gets lost.

1.6 Getting rid of installed software

AIX 4 allows you to remove installed software easily with **installp -u lppname** or **smit install_remove** (you might want to use the *-p* flag on *installp* for a preview first). On AIX 3 it is not that easy. If the software is in the applied state, it can be rejected (**installp -r lppname**) and you are rid of it. If it is committed, you need to find out how the LPP is organized, remove all the files that the LPP installed and delete all ODM entries that refer to the LPP. The following script makes this easy, but be careful. The first time a *rmlpp* script was posted to the Internet, people found out that there were LPPs that claimed to own the /usr directory. Removing them removed /usr as well. As a consequence the following *rmlpp* script generates a script to remove the files that can be examined manually before letting it loose.

```
#!/usr/bin/ksh
#
# Permanently remove a product from disk and AIX databases
# based on rmlpp that was posted to comp.unix.aix by Mickey Coggins
#

export LANG=C
export ME=`basename $0`
export FilesToRemove=/tmp/remove.those.files
export TMPDIR=/tmp/$ME
export RMfilesTMP=$TMPDIR/ToBeRemoved.$$

errexit () {
	echo $*
	exit 123
}

[[ `uname -svr` != "AIX 2 3" ]] && errexit "$ME works only on AIX 3.2"

[[ $# -lt 1 ]] &&
	errexit "usage: $ME lppname [lppname ...]\n
	lppname is a string compatible with grep, ie 'X11' or 'PHIGS'\n
	typing '$0 PHIGS' will remove all LPPs with PHIGS in their name."

TMP_FREE=`df /tmp | awk '$3 != "KB" {print $3}'`
[[ "$TMP_FREE" -lt 1000 ]] &&
errexit "There is not enough room in your /tmp directory.\n
You need 1000 KB free, and you have only $TMP_FREE KB free.\n
Either remove some stuff from /tmp, or use chfs to make it bigger."
```

```
ODMDIRS="/etc/objrepos /usr/lib/objrepos /usr/share/lib/objrepos"

NAMES=$1
shift
while [[ $# -gt 0 ]] ; do
  NAMES="$NAMES|$1"
  shift
done
echo "Searching for lpps with egrep \"$NAMES\"...\c "

for ODMDIR in $ODMDIRS ; do
  if [[ ! -d $ODMDIR || ! -w $ODMDIR ]] ; then
     echo $ODMDIR is not writeable or is not a directory.
     echo I hope this is because you are a /usr client or diskless.
     echo If you are not a diskless or a /usr client, you should stop.
     echo "Enter y to continue ->\c"
     read answer
     if [ "$answer" != "y" ] ; then
       exit 0
     fi
  fi
  TMP='odmget lpp | awk -F\" '/name/ {print $2}' | egrep "$NAMES"'
  LPPS='echo $LPPS $TMP'
done

[[ -z "$LPPS" ]] &&
errexit "$ME failed.\nNo LPP with the name $NAMES detected."

echo "found them"

for ODMDIR in $ODMDIRS ; do
  mkdir -p $TMPDIR$ODMDIR > /dev/null 2>&1
done

> $RMfilesTMP# Make sure the temp file is clean
echo
echo This script is about to attempt to remove an LPP from your system.
echo I say attempt, because it could fail.  If it fails, you may have
echo to at least reload the LPP.  Use the \"lppchk\" command to make sure
echo all is well with your system.
echo
# Loop through all the LPP names found.
for LPP in $LPPS
do
  DESCR=none
  answer=""

 # find the LPP ids. They will be different in the three SWVPD databases.
  for ODMDIR in $ODMDIRS ; do
    # get the lpp id for this ODMDIR (yes, they are different)
    LPPID='odmget -q name=$LPP lpp | awk '/lpp_id/ {print $3}''

    # did we find the LPP?
```

```
    if [[ "$DESCR" = "none" && -n "$LPPID" ]] ; then
      # all the descriptions should be the same
      DESCR=`odmget -q name=$LPP lpp |
             awk -F\" '/description/ {print $2}'`
      echo "Delete $LPP, $DESCR?"
      echo "y or (n) ->\c"
      read answer
      if [[ "$answer" != "y" ]] ; then name
        continue 2       # jump back up to the next LPP
      fi
    fi
    # if there is no DESCR, then we didn't find the LPP.  Weird.
    if [[ "$DESCR" = "none" || "$LPPID" = "" ]] ; then
      continue
    fi
    # Optionally, save the ODM stuff we are about to remove,
    # in case something goes wrong.  The problem is it is difficult
    # to determine if something really did fail, since these commands
    # do not return any decent error return codes.
    odmget -q lpp_id=$LPPID history    > $TMPDIR/$ODMDIR/$LPP.history
    odmget -q name=$LPP lpp            > $TMPDIR/$ODMDIR/$LPP.lpp
    odmget -q lpp_name=$LPP product    > $TMPDIR/$ODMDIR/$LPP.product
    # Get the list of files and links to remove later....
    odmget -q lpp_id=$LPPID inventory > $TMPDIR/$ODMDIR/$LPP.inventory
    awk -F\" '/loc/ {print $2}' $TMPDIR/$ODMDIR/$LPP.inventory | \
      sed 's/,/ /g' >> $RMfilesTMP
    odmdelete -o history -q lpp_id=$LPPID   > /dev/null 2>&1
    odmdelete -o lpp -q name=$LPP           > /dev/null 2>&1
    odmdelete -o product -q lpp_name=$LPP   > /dev/null 2>&1
    odmdelete -o inventory -q lpp_id=$LPPID > /dev/null 2>&1
    SOMETHING_DONE_FLAG=true
  done
done

if [[ "$SOMETHING_DONE_FLAG" = "true" ]] ; then

  echo "ODM work is done.  Now, time to delete files...."

  # This could be catastrophic if there is a problem. For example,
  # if the ODM database for an application had /usr as one of its files.
  # You be the judge.  Here's your rope....
  cat $RMfilesTMP | sort -ur > $FilesToRemove

  rm -f $RMfilesTMP
  echo "Please check $FilesToRemove and then remove the files listed"
  echo "in there with \"rm -fr \`cat $FilesToRemove\`\""
fi

echo done.

# Activate the following one if you do not care about the saved ODM stuff
# rm -rf $TMPDIR

exit 0
```

The script queries the ODM to find the LPP id in each database that corresponds to a given LPP. Then it uses this id to scan the inventory for the files. After that it removes the ODM entries and generates a list of files to be removed.

2

Basic system management

Traditional UNIX system management involves editing cryptic configuration files, relinking the kernel, or even patching libraries. The average user who is not really interested in the low-level details of system configuration is easily intimidated by these chores. More modern systems usually have some menu-driven tool to take care of the most important system management topics. In the case of AIX it is called the system management interface tool (SMIT). SMIT is the preferred tool for system administration on the RISC System /6000. Nearly all system management activities on a RS/6000 can be handled via SMIT. SMIT itself is just a menu front end for the tasks: everything that SMIT does can also be achieved via the command line. In addition, SMIT can be customized to include your own menus and tasks. Even so, there are people who prefer icon-based system management. AIX includes a suite of visual system management (VSM) tools for them. They allow system management based on mouse clicks.

Not all tasks can be handled via SMIT or VSM; occasionally it is necessary to edit files or run some commands that are not yet integrated into SMIT. In contrast to other UNIX systems, AIX does not store its system configuration parameters in flat ASCII files; instead it uses a database called object data manger (ODM). This database is accessed either via dedicated configuration commands that know how to deal with the database or via the *odmget*, *odmput* and *odmdelete* commands. It is discussed in Chapter 18. I will use a mix of commands and SMIT actions in the examples in this book.

If you are an experienced BSD user working with an AIX 3 system, you will find the information in /usr/lpp/bos/bsdadm helpful. It explains the main differences between AIX system management and traditional BSD system management. Unfortunately, the text is somewhat outdated as it was written for AIX 3.1, but it is still helpful. For AIX 4 there is an equivalent InfoExplorer article. Search for 'AIX for BSD System managers Overview' or just 'BSD'.

2.1 Using SMIT

Two versions of SMIT are available on the system. One, called *smitty* (Figure 2.1), runs in character mode on any terminal. The other one is used under AIXwindows and is called *msmit* (Figure 2.2). By running the command **smit** the appropriate version will be used automatically. New users usually find that choices within the graphical version of SMIT are presented slightly more intuitively. As the graphical version does not offer more functionality than the ASCII version and is slightly slower I prefer to use the ASCII version only.

```
                              System Management

Move cursor to desired item and press Enter.

  Installation and Maintenance
  Devices
  Physical & Logical Storage
  Security & Users
  Diskless Workstation Management
  Communications Applications and Services
  Spooler (Print Jobs)
  Problem Determination
  Performance & Resource Scheduling
  System Environments
  Processes & Subsystems
  Applications
  Using SMIT (information only)

F1=Help                F2=Refresh             F3=Cancel              F8=Image
F9=Shell               F10=Exit               Enter=Do
```

Figure 2.1 The ASCII version of SMIT (*smitty*).

In the remainder of the book I will refer only to the ASCII version of SMIT. Everything that can be done via the ASCII version can be done with the mostly the same keystrokes in the Motif version. The only advantages of the Motif version are the selection of items via scroll bars and the visual indication of work in progress by a running man in the upper right corner. If you also prefer to use only the ASCII version, you might want to set up an alias in your .kshrc file such as

```
alias smit='/usr/bin/smitty'
```

so that you always get the ASCII version without having to remember to type *smitty* each time.

SMIT does not check your privileges. This means that you can still play around with SMIT menus even if the command that is to be executed cannot be run by you. You will fail if you try to execute a command for which you do not have permission.

SMIT is controlled via cursor and function keys. Whenever possible, a fill in the blanks approach is used together with lists of possible choices. Figure 2.3, which shows a screen for adding a user on AIX 3, will serve as an example.

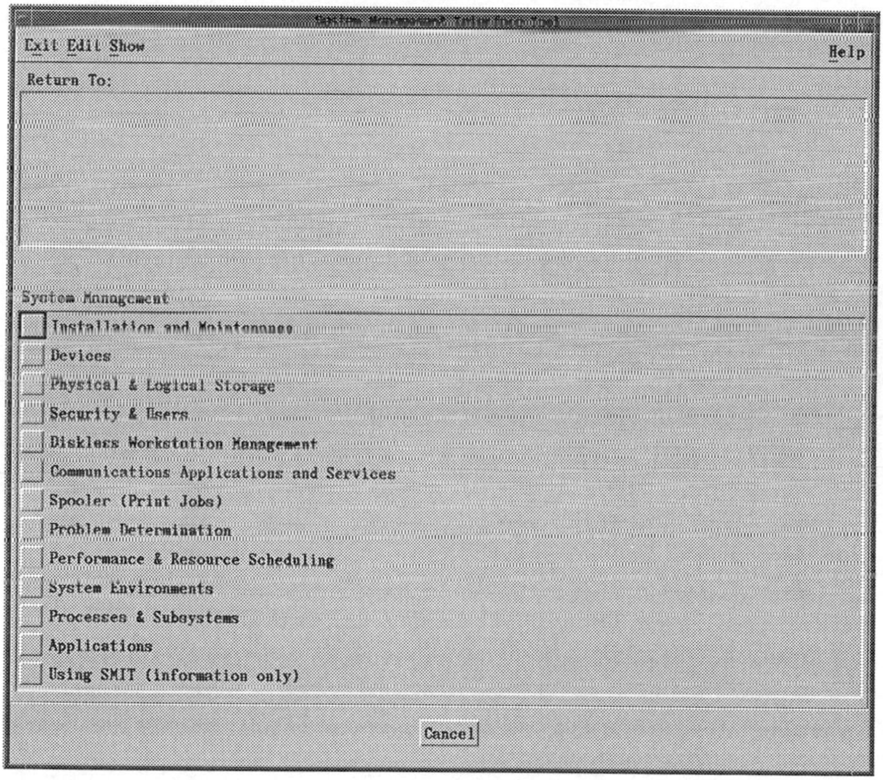

Figure 2.2 The Motif version of SMIT (*msmit*).

```
                              Create User

Type or select values in entry fields.
Press Enter AFTER making all desired changes.

[TOP]                                             [Entry Fields]
* User NAME                                      []
  ADMINISTRATIVE User?                            false                  +
  User ID                                        []                      #
  LOGIN user?                                     true                   +
  PRIMARY group                                  []                      +
  Group SET                                      []                      +
  ADMINISTRATIVE groups                          []                      +
  SU groups                                      [ALL]                   +
  HOME directory                                 []
  Initial PROGRAM                                []
  User INFORMATION                               []
  Another user can SU to user?                    true                   +
  User can RLOGIN?                                true                   +
  TRUSTED PATH?                                   nosak                  +
[MORE...12]

F1=Help              F2=Refresh           F3=Cancel            F4=List
F5=Undo              F6=Command           F7=Edit              F8=Image
F9=Shell             F10=Exit             Enter=Do
```

Figure 2.3 Creating an account via SMIT.

All editable fields are enclosed in square brackets '*[]*'. The brackets change to less than and greater than signs '<>' if the text is not completely displayed in the field. To the left of the fields where input is required, you will see an asterisk '*'. In the above example only the user name is required; filling in the other fields is optional. To the right of an input field you might find one of the following indicators: a plus sign '+', which tells you that you can select a value from a list of choices by pressing <F4>; a hash '*#*', which indicates that this is a numeric field like the user id in Figure 2.3, an '*X*' to indicate a field that requires hexadecimal input, or a '*/*' to indicate that a file-name is required. If the information does not fit onto one display page, indicators that there is more to see will appear at the top and bottom of the screen.

Then there are the function keys:

F1=Help Calls up help on the currently selected item if there is any help available.

F2=Refresh Refreshes the screen if a message from another program disrupted the display. The classic <CTRL-L> works as well.

F3=Cancel Cancels the command and/or takes you one level back in the menu tree.

F4=List Lists possible choices if SMIT knows about them. It is only active if a '+' is displayed to the right of the field. If multiple items in a list are selectable, then they must be marked via <F7> in the list.

F5=Undo Undoes changes in the current field.

F6=Command Shows you the command that SMIT will execute when you press <ENTER>.

F7=Edit Gives you a bigger editing field.

F8=Image Shows you the fastpath to this particular SMIT screen and optionally dumps the current screen into SMIT's log file.

F9=Shell Gives you a shell.

F10=Exit Quits SMIT without having to go back through the menus. <CTRL-C> will work as well.

Enter=Do Executes the underlying command with the current choices.

/ When present, the '/' key can be used to search for items in long lists.

My favorite of all these keys is <F6> as it helps the user to understand what SMIT does and it gives you a chance to check the command before execution if you are not sure what SMIT is going to do. On some ASCII terminals that do not have function keys or where the terminal definition database does not support the function keys you can use <ESC>Number to simulate the functions keys. The action of the <F1> key would be initiated by pressing <ESC>1 in this case.

The description of <F8> mentions fastpaths. Fastpaths are ways of accessing specific SMIT menus without going through all the others first. Thus, by using **smit tcpip**, for example, you go directly to the TCP/IP configuration menu.

2.2 Learning from SMIT

One of the best features of SMIT is the logging of all its actions. SMIT logs all activities it performs in $HOME/smit.log and all commands it finally executes in $HOME/smit.script. The script file is extremely helpful for repetitive tasks. Simply use an editor to generate a shell script out of the appropriate part of the SMIT script or use the complete script to perform the same actions on several machines without having to do all the work again manually.

For example, to add 30 users to the system via the SMIT menus might be somewhat tedious. Do it for one user and then generate a small script that will do the rest for you.

Run **smit mkuser** to generate one user, for example *tina*, then examine the $HOME/smit.script file. At the end you will find some lines like the following:

```
#
#     [Dec 24 1993, 17:07:23]
#
mkuser groups='staff ,usr' tina
```

With **tail $HOME/smit.script > /tmp/moreusers** the end of the SMIT script is copied to a new file. (Using *tail* will work only for short commands like this one of course.) Edit this file so that you have the following fragment in your editor:

```
mkuser groups='staff ,usr' tina
```

Now generate a shell function out of the invocation of the *mkuser* command:

```
for u in mick tex volker pat peter frank and whatever users you need
do
        mkuser groups='staff,usr' $u
done
```

Run this script via the command **ksh /tmp/moreusers**. Using this method, the editing also takes some time, but it is still a lot faster than creating 30 users manually and it serves as an easy example for this book. Depending on your particular needs you will soon find out when it makes more sense to work via scripts and commands and when to use the menus.

2.3 SMIT hints

Although it is nice to have a log of all SMIT actions, the log files create a major pitfall for new system administrators: they grow very fast. As the default root file system is only 4MB in size, it is easy for it to become full, which in turn leads to boot problems and other nasty situations. There are several ways around this:

(1) Enlarge the root file system as described in Section 4.1.

(2) Remove the log files automatically every time you log out or at some other regular interval.

(3) Set *$HOME* to some other directory such as /home/root in root's .profile, so that the log file is sent somewhere else rather than to the root file system. In this case it is necessary to create some symbolic links for files like .kshrc to ensure that they are accessible in both places.

(4) Use specific SMIT options to send the file to the /var file system (**smit -s /var/tmp/smit.script -l /var/tmp/smit.log**).

I use method 1 and 3 together. SMIT is not the only program that would clutter the root directory without this trick and I want to avoid problems that are caused by a full root file system.

When working with SMIT it is sometimes necessary to have more functionality when editing fields or browsing menus than is provided by the standard keyboard editing keys. In addition, you end up with a terminal that does not have a full working cursor pad. Although neither officially supported nor documented, there is a second way of controlling SMIT: by a subset of Emacs commands. Here are some of the commands that I have found helpful:

<ESC><<> Moves the cursor to the beginning of the text or menu.

<ESC><>> Moves the cursor to the end of the text or menu.

<CTRL-V> Moves the cursor one page forward.

<ESC><V> Moves the cursor one page backward. (If you used <CTRL-V> immediately before this then it will not work - in this case you need an extra <ESC> key, as in <ESC><ESC><V>.)

<CTRL-A> Moves the cursor to the beginning of the field.

<CTRL-P> Moves the cursor to the previous line.

<CTRL-N> Moves the cursor to the next line.

<CTRL-F> Moves the cursor forward one character.

<CTRL-B> Moves the cursor backward one character.

<CTRL-E> Moves the cursor to the end of the field.

<CTRL-K> Deletes all text from the cursor to the end of the field.

<CTRL-G> and <CTRL-C> Quits SMIT immediately.

<CTRL-X> Deletes the character under the cursor.

It is possible, but unlikely, that these commands will be removed from future releases. Many developers use Emacs for editing so you can find subsets of Emacs commands in various utilities, for example InfoExplorer, not just in SMIT.

Some people still believe that using the command line interface instead of SMIT will not handle the ODM correctly. Let me assure you that SMIT does nothing special with the ODM. It simply calls the same shell commands to configure things directly without wading through several layers of menus. Most experienced administrators use the command line to do routine work and resort to the SMIT menus only for less common tasks for which the command options are not easily memorized.

A few configuration files need to be synchronized with the ODM when changed manually, for example /etc/inetd.conf and /etc/services, but that is fortunately corrected in AIX 4. These cases are rare and I will point them out at the appropriate places in the book.

To get a good feel for what you can do with SMIT and how the menus are structured I suggest that you start it via **smit -x** so that it does not perform the real actions and that you play around with it for a while.

2.4 System management by icon: VSM

The VSM programs are graphical icon-oriented front-end programs to common system management tasks. They are an addition to SMIT and not a replacement: they cover only a subset SMIT's functionality. Although some of the VSM programs are available on AIX 3.2.5 they are not shipped with it by default.

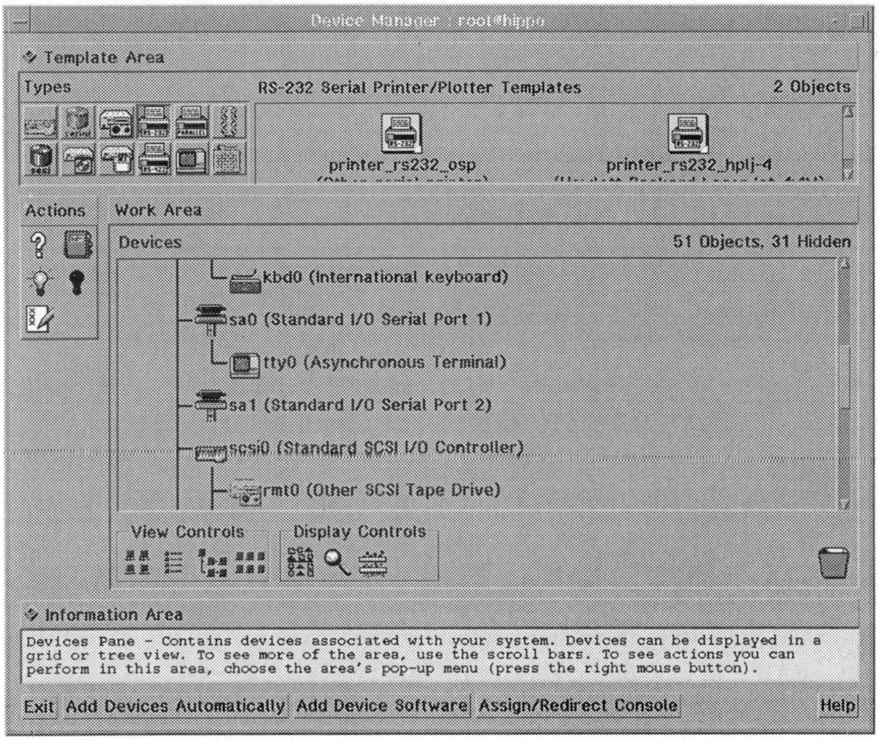

Figure 2.4 The VSM device manager (*xdevicem*).

On AIX 4 the following components are available:

xdevicem The device manager (Figure 2.4). It is used to configure adapter cards and SCSI and other devices.

xinstallm The install manager, with which you can install new software.

xmaintm The software maintenance manager. This is the counterpart of *xinstallm* for already installed software. It allows you to change the status of installed software or remove it from the system.

xlvm The LVM manager. This allows you to manage disks, volume groups and file systems.

xprintm The print manager. This allows simple printer management.

xuserm The user account manager allows you to add, delete or change accounts.

All of the above tools are supposed to make system management easier. I personally consider them to be marketingware as they are appealing on demos but are not very useful for daily professional system management. Although they make things easier for the casual user migrating from a PC to a UNIX workstation, they also hide even more of the system. To do something not included in the operations offered by the tools means going back to the command line, and in that case it is essential to understand what is going on. Each of these tools uses huge amounts of resources so that using them on a small machine (less than 48MB of memory on a 4.1 system) can be pretty cumbersome. Have a look at them yourself and see if they are useful for you.

2.5 Some more initial system management tools

As well as becoming familiar with SMIT you should have a look at a few configuration commands that SMIT uses which are very useful from the command line as well. Most of these commands list the contents of ODM entries or modify them. It is very easy to use them directly without working through layers of SMIT menus. If every time you use SMIT you check out the underlying command, quite often you will find it is one of the following:

lsdev Lists devices. Try out **lsdev -C** and **lsdev -Cc disk** (Figure 2.5). The *-C* option shows currently defined or available devices. Devices that are available are accessible. Devices that are only defined might be present but are not accessible, for example, a tape drive that was not switched on during system boot. The *-c* option limits the output to a specific class of devices. Using **lsdev -P** will give you a list of all predefined devices in the ODM that can be autoconfigured by AIX.

```
...
sys0        Available 00-00         System Object
sysplanar0  Available 00-00         CPU Planar
ioplanar0   Available 00-00         I/O Planar
bus0        Available 00-00         Microchannel Bus
sio0        Available 00-00         Standard I/O Planar
scsi0       Available 00-00-0S      Standard SCSI I/O Controller
rmt0        Defined   00-00-0S-60   2.3 GB 8mm Tape Drive
mem0        Available 00-0A         8 MB Memory SIMM
bbl0        Available 00-0J         GXT150 Graphics Adapter
siokb0      Available 00-00-0K      Keyboard Adapter
...
```

Figure 2.5 An abridged sample output from **lsdev -C**.

lsattr Lists device attributes. You can use it for all defined and available devices. For example, **lsattr -El sys0**, allows you to see the settings of the system device whereas **lsattr -El rmt0** (Figure 2.6) lists the current settings for the *rmt0* tape devices.

```
mode        yes  Use DEVICE BUFFERS during writes True
block_size  1024 BLOCK size (0=variable length)    True
extfm       no   Use EXTENDED file marks           True
```

Figure 2.6 The output of **lsattr -El rmt0** for an 8 mm tape.

If a line is terminated by the keyword *True*, then the setting of this attribute can be changed by the system administrator. If the last word is *False*, then the setting has been fixed by the system and cannot be changed manually. To find the ranges for one specific setting, use the *-R* option, for example **lsattr -Rl rmt0 -ablock_size** lists the range of allowed block sizes for the *rmt0* device.

chdev Changes those device attributes that are user configurable. All attributes that have the keyword *True* after the attribute description when listed via **lsattr -El** can be changed via chdev. For example, **chdev -l rmt0 -ablock_size=1024** changes the block size for tape rmt0 to 1024. Sometimes you cannot change device attributes because the device is busy. One solution is to use the *-P* flag on the command. This will change the attribute only in the database not in the real device. The device will then be changed at the next system boot. Alternatively, change the device when it is no longer busy. How this is done depends on the device.

Although I prefer to run my system with *LANG=C*, I have to set it to something else such as *en_US*, when trying to list devices. The names of devices and device attributes are not available to the programs directly but only via message catalogues. Be sure that your *$LANG* (or *$LC_MESSAGES*) is set to something other than C, otherwise you get 'N/A' instead of meaningful descriptions, for example when listing devices.

If you browse through /usr/bin and /usr/sbin you will find many commands that start with *mk*, *ch*, *rm* and *ls*. AIX tries to avoid having to edit files for configuration. Most of the configuration tasks can be done by these commands. Establish initial configurations via the *mk*something commands, change them via the *ch*something commands, list them via the *ls*something commands and finally remove them again through the *rm*something commands. The advantage of commands is their easier integration into automated tasks. It is much easier to write scripts that call commands than to write foolproof editing scripts for configuration files.

No matter what you want to use for your everyday editing tasks, you should always use an editor that understands tabulator characters and has no arbitrary margins for editing system files. This precludes INed (*e*) which comes with AIX, and some other commercially available editors. Using the wrong editor on some system files will result in strange problems that are difficult to diagnose. Even Emacs may give problems when using it on files that are hard links because of its backup mechanism. Stick to *vi* for system administration even if learning it drives you up the wall.

3

Explore the system with InfoExplorer

The complete documentation for AIX would take up nearly 2 m of shelf space. The largest part of which would become obsolete with every release change of the operating system. This wastes your money and environmental resources and creates update headaches. IBM offers on-line documentation on CD or tape as a remedy. Nearly all of the systems documentation is available in softcopy format via the InfoExplorer program. The documentation comes in a proprietary format and not as standard man pages. The reason behind this is the presentation of the information. All the documentation is cross-linked in a hypertext system. This allows you to select a reference in the text and jump to the referenced text and back. By using the hypertext links the documentation can be used more efficiently to resolve complex questions with many references.

The InfoExplorer database is available on either CD or tape. The CD is mounted onto /usr/lpp/info/lib/en_US (/usr/lpp/info/En_US on AIX 3) or the files are copied there from tape or CD for faster access. Some countries, for example Germany, offer users some of the on-line documentation in their native language. The mount point then changes to something like /usr/lpp/info/lib/de_DE. I suggest using only the English version or, if you order a translated version, keeping the English version on the system as well. People who are experienced with computers usually find it difficult to work with translated manuals, and those people who do not want to use the English manuals usually do not want to access the operating system anyway but only want to see their application and thus should be shielded from AIX.

If the base operating system is installed, then there is already a mini version of the database on the system if you are using AIX 3. You should delete it before you mount the CD as it is not used when you install the full version and it only wastes disk space. It can be found in /usr/lpp/info/En_US/aixmin.

To mount the CD permanently you can use the command line **crfs -vcdrfs -pro -dcd0 -Ayes -tno m/usr/lpp/info/lib/en_US** or the SMIT panel shown in Figure 3.1, which is obtained via **smit crcdrfs**.

```
                          Add a CDROM File System

Type or select values in entry fields.
Press Enter AFTER making all desired changes.

                                                         [Entry Fields]
* DEVICE name                                         cd0                  +
* MOUNT POINT                                         [/usr/lpp/info/lib/en_US]
  Mount AUTOMATICALLY at system restart?              yes                  +


F1=Help             F2=Refresh          F3=Cancel           F4=List
F5=Undo             F6=Command          F7=Edit             F8=Image
F9=Shell            F10=Exit            Enter=Do
```

Figure 3.1 Adding a CD ROM file system in SMIT.

To mount the CD only temporarily and copy the files to the hard disk, use the following commands:

```
mkdir /cdrom
mount -v cdrfs -p -r /dev/cd0 /cdrom
cd /cdrom
cp -r * /usr/lpp/info/lib/en_US
cd /usr/lpp/info/lib/en_US
chmod -R a+r .
find . -type d -exec chmod a+x {} \;
```

The above examples are for AIX 4. In AIX 3 the path for the info database is still /usr/lpp/info/En_US. After you have installed the database in one way or the other you need to tell InfoExplorer about it. The file /usr/lpp/info/data/ispaths contains the list of databases that the *info* command will find. Although this file is already complete on AIX 4, you might need to adapt it on AIX 3. In the

/usr/lpp/info/data directory you will find several sample ispaths files on AIX 3. Use the one that comes closest to your installation and modify it according to your needs. It is usually sufficient to copy the ispaths.full file to ispaths and, if necessary, to delete a few entries. A typical entry looks like the following excerpt:

```
id                      1
glossary                TRUE
name                    aix
title                   Using and Managing
sys                     /usr/lpp/info/%L/sys.sys
key                     /usr/lpp/info/%L/aix/aix.key
rom                     /usr/lpp/info/%L/aix/aix.rom
```

Each entry has an *id*; if you add your own simply number them continuously. If the database contains a glossary, then the *glossary* attribute is set to TRUE. The *name* of the database is usually the name of the directory where it resides. The *title* given here will show up in Info in search results windows. The *sys* entry is a constant that is required by the system. The *rom* and *key* entries finally point to the real database. The *%L* in the pathnames above will be replaced by the contents of *$LANG*. If there is no database to be found under the current *$LANG* setting, *info* defaults to the prime directory on AIX 3, which is usually a link to En_US. On AIX 4 the en_US directory is used as the default if nothing else is set.

On AIX 3 the /usr/lpp/info/data and /usr/lpp/info/En_US directories are in different directory trees, the data directory being only a symbolic link. For this reason, I usually do not keep the ispaths file in this directory but put it in /usr/lpp/info/En_US and create a symbolic link to it in /usr/lpp/info/data. The reason behind this is NFS. I copy the database files to the hard disk and then export them via NFS. If the ispaths file that is correct for the database is in another directory then either two mounts are needed or the file has to be adapted on each mounting machine after any additions to the database. By using a symbolic link I only need to maintain one file and everybody can access it easily via a symbolic link. The link is created by **ln -s /usr/lpp/info/En_US/ispaths /usr/lpp/info/data** after you have removed the original ispaths file on each machine that mounts /usr/lpp/info/En_US. On AIX 4 everything is accessible by mounting /usr/lpp/info.

As soon as you install additional software you may get more info databases in other locations. I suggest copying them onto the standard info directory tree. This will again make NFS export easier.

Of course, it is possible to mix databases on CD and on the hard disk simply by setting up the ispaths file so that it points to the right files. And there is no need to use the %L in the file name if you run with only one language. You can point directly to file names (AIX 4 does this by default). If disk space is tight and it is not possible to put all databases on disk try to keep at least *nav* and *aix* (AIX 3) or *cmds* (AIX 4) on disk and leave the rest on the CD. This will still give you a better response time as those are the biggest and most frequently used databases.

3.1 Reading the on-line documentation

The documentation can be read in three ways: first by using the X version of InfoExplorer (Figure 3.2), second by using its character-based instance and third at least partly by the *man* command.

If you start InfoExplorer via the *info* command it will check whether you run under X (is *$DISPLAY* set?) and start the X version; otherwise it will bring up the character version. The X version is usually the best way to access InfoExplorer. In this case you can use multiple windows to access the documentation that is cross-linked via hypertext links. The character version is severely limited by the capabilities of the ASCII screen.

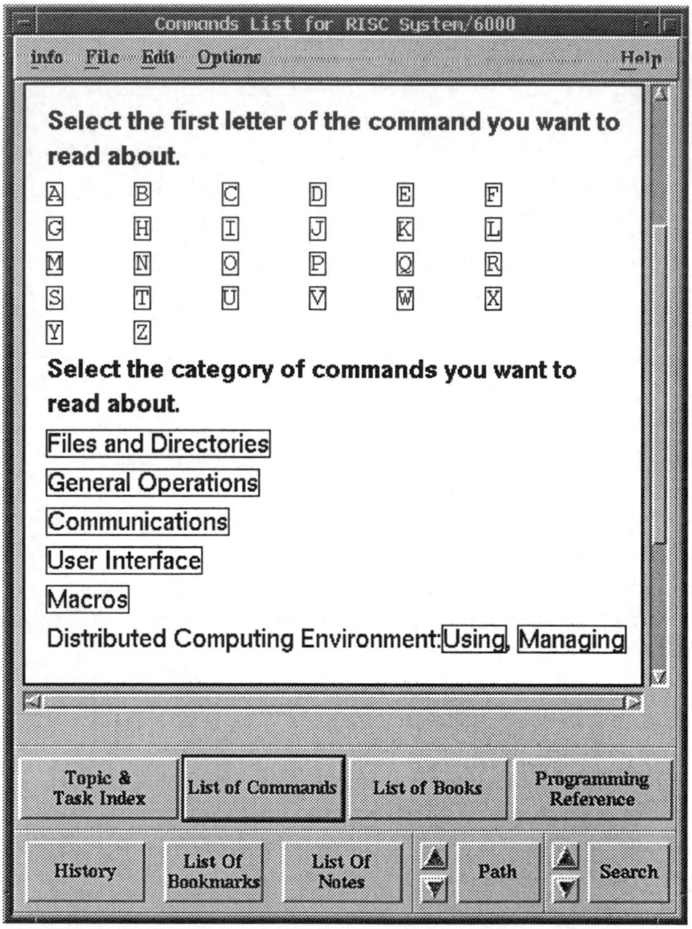

Figure 3.2 The X version of InfoExplorer.

On the X version it is easy to play around and learn how to maneuver through the windows. All the rectangles in Figure 3.2 are some form of link. Selecting a letter from the list will replace the contents of the window with the commands reference page for this letter. Alternatively, selecting the rectangle with the text 'Files and Directories' will open up a new window and show you a files reference.

The first thing you must know when using the character version is that <CTRL-O> brings the cursor to the top menu where you can select the next action with the cursor keys. The <ESC> key terminates menus. Hyperlinks in the text are accessed via the <TAB> key. To follow them just press <Enter>. When working on a keyboard without a cursor pad, <CTR-P> and <CTRL-N> can be used for page scrolling and <CTRL-F> and <CTRL-B> for item selection.

Regardless of which version you are using, take the time to experiment and become familiar with the menus and links. Choose *Help* from the menu bar and then *List of Helps* and let *info* guide you through its features. You will probably modify some of its defaults, for example window size, font size, printer or the default section displayed. In the X version try the *Customize* menu entry. In the ASCII version (Figure 3.3) you have to select *Info* and then *Preferences* and *Defaults*.

```
Info  Help  Display  History  Bookmarks  Notes  Search  Path  Exit
 About the Topic & Task Index                              o Document
 About the Topic & Task Index             Simple
                                          Compound
 The Topic & Task Index for the IBM RISC System/  Article Titles  nsive list
 of topics within the following high-level task  Glossary   Managing,
 Programming, and Problem Solving.  It is design  Files       as quickly
 as possible to the topic and tasks in which you

 The information for the RISC System/6000 is in an information base that is
 made up of many articles--almost like a very large encyclopedia.  There are
 four types of articles in the information base.  They are:

 Navigation      Navigation articles help you locate information in the
 information base.  These articles always stay in the navigation window to
 help you keep track of where you have been.  You may be led through a series
 of navigation articles until it is apparent which of the other types of
 information you should read.

 Procedure       Procedure articles tell you step by step how to do a task.

 Reference       Reference articles describe commands, subroutines, and other
 system functions.  When a task can be done by typing a single command, the
 task index will lead you directly to the examples of how to use the command.
```

Figure 3.3 The ASCII version of InfoExplorer.

3.2 InfoExplorer hints

If you have enough space, I would suggest installing InfoExplorer on the hard disk. You will be rewarded by much faster access. Even getting the data over NFS is faster from a hard disk than from a local CD. It is usually sufficient for one server to store the database and the other machines to get it over the network. Sometimes, however, NFS can be very slow, especially when there are many bridges and routers between the server and the user. There are cases where running the info program on the server and displaying it locally is much faster, as searching over several hundred megabytes via NFS is more time-consuming than remote display updates.

If the results of search operations are not what you expect, then you probably have a different idea about the search string from *info*. Non alphanumeric characters in strings may be interpreted as word separators. Try to search for the individual parts instead. Sometimes a string that you think will lead you to the desired information does not do so even though you know it has to be there. Try searching for similar items that should get you near the target and look at the "related" section of the articles you have found.

In the USA and some other countries an extended version of the InfoExplorer database is available on CD under the name TechLib. This CD is issued quarterly and has two additional databases. One is a collection of how-to questions and answers on AIX from an internal IBM support system called HONE. The other one contains bug reports and work-arounds that are found in IBM's RETAIN system. Anyone who seriously uses AIX should subscribe to this disk. It will pay for itself in time saved. If you cannot obtain it from your IBM representative then you should try to obtain it directly from the manufacturer (see Section 24.1.3 for details).

To integrate your own documentation into InfoExplorer you need the optional InfoCrafter program. It will take either Interleaf 5, FrameMaker or some SGML ASCII format as input to create the InfoExplorer database. With the advent of HTML as a standard for distributed hypermedia I think that putting your documentation into InfoExplorer is probably too much effort. The COSE-based desktop that comes with AIX 4 also includes an SGML browser that is fairly common and more widely used than InfoExplorer.

3.3 Where are the man pages?

Users who are familiar with other UNIX systems will miss the man pages on AIX. There is still a *man* command, but all the data comes from the InfoExplorer database. Not all items in the InfoExplorer database can be found via the *man* command and the *man* command cannot follow hyperlinks, but it should allow a quick check on a command. If you do not find the information you are looking for, it is necessary to resort to the *info* command as not all items in the InfoExplorer database are available to *man*. Of course, if you add your own man pages and set *$MANPATH* correctly it will find those pages. The *man* command searches first in the man directories, like the standard UNIX *man* command, then it checks the InfoExplorer database. If you are familiar with the *whatis* command you should execute **catman -w** as root to create the whatis database.

On AIX 3, there are some hints in /usr/lpp/bos/bsdadm that will tell you how to create man page files out of the InfoExplorer database. If you are really desperate for man pages this is currently the only way to get an approximation.

3.4 What about hardcopy?

All the information that you find in InfoExplorer can be ordered as real paper manuals. In my experience only books with the word 'concepts' in their title are of any use. These will give you an introduction or detailed guide to individual topics. After all, you may not be at your terminal when you want to learn something new. In addition, it is hard to get overviews out of InfoExplorer, which is more useful as a reference. I suggest you order all concepts manuals that are of interest to you as hardcopy: they make pleasant bedtime reading and you can be sure that you will quickly fall fast asleep. All the other useful reference documentation is easily accessed via *info*.

In addition, any individual article in InfoExplorer can be printed. To print more than raw text is is necessary to configure the printer in the *Customize/Defaults* menu entry. The data is piped to that printer command so you can use anything you want here. You could also *cat* the data to a file, by for example entering **cat >> $HOME/info.print** in the field for 'Simple Printer'. For quick and dirty prints I usually use **enscript -b "Info Explorer" -MA4 -dps0 -fCourier9**. For nicely printed articles you should set up the 'pretty printer' as in **psroff | lp -dps0** and set the default printer to pretty.

3.5 Multiple instances of InfoExplorer

InfoExplorer tries to run only once per user. This is accomplished by the info daemon *infod*. It tracks the invocations of the *info* program. If *info* is already running when you try to start a new invocation, *info* will detect this and it will not start anew. If you used search arguments as in **info -s ksh** then the search will be performed by the info version that is already running.

This feature is helpful when one wants to link InfoExplorer into an application on a single-screen system, but it can be confusing when running with multiple screens, multiple log ins or the virtual screens of the COSE desktop.

To avoid this feature, kill the info daemon (**stopsrc -s infod**) or remove its /etc/inittab entry. InfoExplorer will then complain that it cannot connect to socket 3, but you will be able to run multiple invocations per user id.

3.6 Using different libraries

InfoExplorer uses the library defined by the /usr/lpp/info/data/ispaths files as a default. But you can tell *info* to work on a totally different library by giving it the name of a directory that contains the ispaths file with the *-l* option. This is needed when accessing documentation in InfoExplorer format that was not supplied by IBM, for example.

4

Customizing the system

You can save a great deal of work if you customize your system properly. The suggestions in the following chapters are my ideas on initial customization. As your needs are probably different, your system will look different, but I hope that the following will give you a different or new view of the things to look at in addition to how and where to perform the customization.

4.1 Initial actions

The first step is to ensure that there is enough space in the root file system. It is shipped with a size of 4MB by default. As all system configuration and SMIT log files are stored there, care is required to avoid a full root file system. Since a full root file system prevents the system from booting and could introduce log-in problems, it should be avoided at all cost. Using the command **chfs -asize=+1 /** will increase the root file system by 4MB. This asks *chfs* for only an increase of one 512-byte block, but as file systems are allocated on a physical partition basis and we have already one full partition, *chfs* needs to add a complete new physical partition, which now gives us a root file system of 8MB. This assumes the standard default physical partition size of 4MB. Please see Chapter 6 for more details on disks.

4.2 System defaults

There are many default settings that need to be adapted to your needs to achieve a sound system. The following sections describe the most useful ones.

4.2.1 The environment

Most crucial initial environment variables are stored in /etc/environment. This file might look like a shell script, but that is not the case. You cannot put shell commands in there, only variable assignments. This is the place to set up all environment variables that are used by everything in the system. The file will be evaluated by the daemons that come with AIX as well as by the *login* program. If you change major items such as the time zone in this file then you should reboot the machine; otherwise there are inconsistencies between the environment for the system daemons and the user environment. The most important environment variables that are set up here are:

PATH The initial search path. Keep it short and do not include the current directory. As shipped, /etc is still in the path. Remove it, as all executable code in /etc is really symbolic links to other directories that are already in the path. Setting it to */usr/bin:/usr/sbin:/usr/bin/X11:/usr/dt/bin* is usually a good minimum.

TZ The time zone you are in and optionally the rules for daylight-saving time. Check out the documentation of environment in info to see the exact format. To select the time zone use **smit system**, which is the easiest way to find the right time zone. The time zones selected by SMIT might not work for daylight-saving time in non-US environments. In this case it is necessary to set the switch dates manually. In Germany a valid time zone would be CET-1CEST,M3.5.0,M10.5.0 which says that we have Central European Time here and that daylight-saving time starts on the last Sunday in March and ends on the last Sunday in October. Some other UNIX systems store time zone information in /usr/lib/zoneinfo. This does not exist on AIX, so you have to set *$TZ* manually.

LOCPATH Where locales are to be found. It defines the base directory for many national language support items such as keyboard maps and conversion tables.

NLSPATH This variable points to the message catalogues. All program messages are found via this path unless *$LANG* is set to C.

ODMDIR The directory where the ODM resides. See Chapter 18.

LANG The language environment in which the system is run. Because the POSIX environment C uses no message catalogues and does not support NLS sorting and string compares, setting this to C results in a slightly faster performance. This will cost you some NLS features in return. I suggest keeping it set to C in this file and setting it to the correct language for individual users in their profiles.

LC_FASTMSG On AIX 4 systems this controls whether programs running with the POSIC (C) locale use internal messages or message catalogs. Keep it at the default value of true to get the internal messages of the programs, which avoids additional file accesses for the catalogs.

Those are the standard variables that are set in /etc/environment. You can set other variables in here that you think should be available to all users. They will be set regardless of the shell used, for example:

MANPATH Where the system searches for man pages before it searches in the InfoExplorer database. A good choice would be /usr/local/man:/usr/share/man.

4.2.2 Kernel parameters

Unlike common UNIX configuration, the AIX kernel has only a few changeable parameters. And, since the AIX kernel is not re-linked when these parameters change, there are no /etc/system and /etc/master files that need to be changed. You can change some parameters via the submenus of **smit system** or the *chdev* command. Figure 4.1 shows how they might look like when checked via **lsattr -El sys0**.

```
dcache       8K        Size of data cache in bytes                          False
icache       8K        Size of instruction cache in bytes                   False
keylock      normal    State of system keylock at boot time                 False
maxbuf       20        Maximum number of pages in block I/O BUFFER CACHE True
maxmbuf      2048      Maximum Kbytes of real memory allowed for MBUFS      True
maxuproc     40        Maximum number of PROCESSES allowed per user         True
autorestart true       Automatically REBOOT system after a crash            True
iostat       true      Continuously maintain DISK I/O history               True
realmem      32768     Amount of usable physical memory in Kbytes           False
primary      /dev/hd7  Primary dump device                                  False
secondary    /dev/sysdumpnull Secondary dump device                         False
conslogin    enable    System Console Login                                 False
maxpout      0         HIGH water mark for pending write I/Os per file      True
minpout      0         LOW water mark for pending write I/Os per file       True
memscrub     false     Enable memory SCRUBBING                              True
logfilesize 1048576    Error log file size                                  False
```

Figure 4.1 Sample settings of the *sys0* device on an AIX 3 system.

Some of the entries are for information only and cannot be changed:

dcache The data cache of the processor.

icache The instruction cache of the processor.

keylock The position of the keylock at boot time.

realmem The amount of memory installed in the machine.

The following entries can be changed by means other than changing *sys0*:

primary The primary system dump device.

secondary The secondary system dump device.

To change the dump device options use *sysdumpdev*. The default dump device on AIX 4 is the paging space and not a separate logical volume as on AIX 3. If a dump exists at boot time it will be copied to a directory that can be specified, for example, by **sysdumpdev -D /tmp/dump**. The default directory is /var/adm/ras. This saves the disk space that was used for dumps on AIX 3.

conslogin The state of the system console log in. Although listed with the *sys0* device, this attribute is changed by the *chcons* command.

logfilesize The size of the error log on AIX 3 systems. It can be changed by the /usr/lib/errdemon command on both AIX versions. To display its size use **/usr/lib/errdemon -l**.

The following parameters are changeable either via the above SMIT path or via **chdev -l sys0 -aattribute=value**.

maxbuf The maximum number of 4KB pages allowed for block I/O buffer space. In contrast to other UNIX systems, this is not used for the file system, so leave it alone or else you might even decrease your performance by setting memory aside for the wrong purpose. Only users that run applications with direct disk access (using /dev/hdisk1 directly for example) might benefit from changing this paramaeter.

maxmbuf The size of the *mbuf* pool. As this sets only the inital value at boot time, I suggest changing it via the *no* utiltity instead. See Section 19.4 for more details.

maxuproc The maximum number of processes per user. Unfortunately, this cannot be set on an individual user basis but must be set to the maximum for the user that uses the most processes. The root user is the only user who is not limited by this setting.

autorestart If set to true the machine will reboot automatically after a crash.

iostat If set to true, then a continuous history of disk I/O is maintained for commands such as *iostat*. Set it to false if you are not tuning the machine.

maxpout The high water mark for pending I/O requests to a file.

minpout The low water mark for pending I/O requests to a file.

These two parameters can be used to tune the machine for high multiuser loads. They control how many writes to a file will be successful / blocked while there are still pending writes to the file. See Section 19.2.3 for more details.

memscrub When set to true this will try to correct memory errors on the fly in the running system. This only works on machines with the appropriate hardware. At the time of writing, models in the 2xx series as well as the C10 and PowerPC-PCs are the only machines not capable of this function because of their low-cost memory architecture.

All changes made to *sys0* are effective only after the next system restart.

If you are accustomed to configuring /etc/master and then rebuilding the kernel, then you probably notice that many parameters are missing. Don't worry; there are a few more changeable parameters in other places, but the default configuration of features such as maximum number of open files, maximum semaphores is such that the limits should never be reached. The tables in the system are very large, but because of the sparse memory allocation utilized by the virtual memory manager they do not take up space until used. To see these limits and other system constants of interest in a running system, the *sysconf()* subroutine can be used from C programs. Table 4.1 contains the current AIX system limits. Only the maximum file system size has been changed in AIX 4; all other values are the same.

Table 4.1 AIX system limits.

Pipes	Pipes per process	2000
	Bytes per pipe	32 KB
Message queues	Queue ids	4000
	Bytes per message	8 KB
	Bytes per queue	64 KB
	Messages per queue	8 KB
Shared memory segments	System-wide limit of segments	10 MB
	Per process limit of segments	4 KB
	Concurrently accessible segments per process	10
	Size of working segment	256 MB
Semaphores	Semaphore ids	4 KB
	Semaphores per id	64 KB
	Maximum semaphore value	32 KB
	Operations per semop call	1 KB
	Undo entries per process	1 KB
	Size of undo structure	8 KB
Files	System file table	200 000
	Process file table	2000
	Maximum file system size	2 GB (AIX 3) 64 GB (AIX 4)
	Maximum file size	2 GB

The above limits might change in future versions, but, if they do change, the chances are that they will be raised.

4.2.3 Configuring the high function terminal on AIX 3

The terminal that consists of a direct attached monitor and keyboard is called the high function terminal (HFT) in AIX 3. This is no longer available on AIX 4, which instead contains a low function terminal (LFT) (see Section 4.2.4).

To configure various HFT options use **smit hft,** which allows you to adapt the HFT according to your liking. When using the system in a non-US English environment you need to set the fonts for your locale as well as the keyboard map. The fast path for changing the keyboard map is **smit chkbd**. Select the appropriate map for your country.

Map names that start with a lower-case letter are for ISO code pages; those that start with an upper-case letter are for PC850 code pages. With **smit chfont_n** you can select the fonts for your system. Be sure to select fonts that use the same code page as the keyboard map. Font names without any ISO indication in the name are usually PC850 fonts. Several attributes of an HFT can be modified to your liking, for example the repeat rate of the keyboard. This can be accomplished by **chdev -l siokb0 -a typmatic_rate=30 -P** (to set the repeat rate to 30 characters per second). This change will be in effect permanently after you reboot. For a temporary change use *chhwkbd* or the SMITs hft menu.

AIX allows you to use virtual terminals when using an HFT. Up to 16 virtual terminals can be configured; the default is four. This can be changed by **chnumvt -nX**, where X is the maximum number of virtual terminals. Once logged in you can create virtual terminals by the *open* command or *xopen* when working under X. You switch forward between the terminals by using <ALT-CTRL>, or <ALT-Action> as it is called on the RS/6000 keyboards. You can go backward in this virtual terminal ring by using <SHIFT-Action>. Virtual terminals are quite convenient if you need to run several sessions without X, for example while doing maintenance work. You could also run several X servers of course and switch between them.

4.2.4 Configuring the low function terminal on AIX 4

The terminal that consists of a direct attached monitor and keyboard is called the low function terminal (LFT) in AIX 4. As the name implies, some functionality was removed when switching between AIX 3 and AIX 4. The cost of supporting multiple virtual terminals was considered too high compared with the benefits and available alternatives through CDE. Use **smit lft** to set up the keyboard mapping, default screen and fonts for the LFT terminal.

Because of the different way AIX 4 installs device drivers you might need to install additional keyboard maps or fonts from the distribution media if the ones you want to use do not match the keyboard that was used for the initial installation of the system.

4.3 User defaults

Each user gets a process environment and specific limits at log in time. The directory /etc/security stores the files that hold all user configuration and defaults in addition to the traditional files /etc/passwd and /etc/group. When using SMIT or the system commands to add, change or delete accounts, these files are updated by the correct commands automatically. Some of them, however, have additional features that need manual editing. AIX 4 contains the additional command *chsec* to change the attributes in this files from the command line. To force the user *joe* to change his password at the next log in one can use **chsec -f/etc/security/passwd -sjoe -aflags=ADMCHG**. Let us review what each file is used for.

4.3.1 /etc/security/group

This file stores administrative information about groups. Currently, there are only two valid attributes for the stanzas in this file: *adms* and *admin*. If *admin* is set to true than only the root user can change the group's other attributes. If set to false then not only the root user, but also members of the security group, can change attributes of the group. If *admin* is set to false and *adms* is set to a list of names, then those users can also modify the group. The commands to change this file together with /etc/group are *mkgroup*, *chgroup*, *rmgroup*, *lsgroup* and *chgrpmem*. The comment character in this file is a '*'.

Now what would you need all this for? AIX supports multiple concurrent groups per user, which allows you to control security very closely. You then can make normal users administrators of groups so that root privileges are not needed to change group membership. For example, someone who is responsible for the printers can be made not only a member but also the administrator of the printq group. The administrator of this group can then add or remove other users from the printq group in case a vacation backup is needed.

4.3.2 /etc/security/limits

This file stores user-specific system limits. There is one stanza for each user in this file. If an attribute is not set for a specific user, then the value is taken from the default stanza. Apart from the CPU limit, all values are expressed in 512-byte blocks.

fsize The maximum file size that the user can create.

core The biggest core dump file that the user can create.

cpu The maximum amount of CPU time in seconds that a user can consume.

data The maximum size of the data segment for the user.

stack The maximum size for the stack segment of the user.

rss The maximum amount of real memory the user can consume. Unfortunately, this limit is not enforced in either AIX 3 nor AIX 4.1.

For users that run large jobs and compiles the initial limits here might be too small. If you get error messages from the linker that ran out of memory either you don't have enough paging space or one of the limits mentioned here is too low. If you do not need any limits at all, set the values to 0. Comments in this file begin with a '*'.

4.3.3 /etc/security/login.cfg

Here you will find several stanzas that configure the behavior of the *login* program. There are some major differences between the use of this file in AIX 3 and 4. The '*' character is used to start comment lines in this file.

On AIX 3 systems you will find several port stanzas in this file. There is only one default stanza for AIX 4. However, the syntax for custom port settings is the same on AIX 3 and 4, with AIX 4 having more parameters. A port stanza can look as follows on AIX 3:

```
port:
        herald = "\n\rlogin:"
        sak_enabled = false
* comma-separated pathnames
        aliases =
```

First you can define the default heralds that are displayed as log in messages with the herald entry of a port stanza. You could include your machine name here for example. Usually the *defport* stanza is used unless one defines a specific stanza via the pathname of the device. The console is an example of a device that is explicitly configured here. If a terminal supports the secure attention key then this will also be defined here. The aliases section allows you to define one port setting that is used on several ports. This is used for the console, for example, which might be a link from /dev/console to /dev/tty0.

On an AIX 4 system you will find a default stanza like the following:

```
default:
    sak_enabled = false
    logintimes =
    logindisable = 0
    logininterval = 0
    loginreenable = 0
    logindelay = 0
```

No default herald is given here. It is read from the message catalogs of the locale for which the machine is configured. You can add your own if you want to. The other parts of the AIX 3 port stanza will still work as well. Most interesting, however, are the new ones, which allow a better control of the use of the port. By default there is no restriction active on those parameters. In addition to editing the file they can be set with **smit login_port**.

logintimes With this entry the times at which this port can be used for login are controlled. To allow a port to be used only during regular working hours such as Monday to Friday from 8.00 a.m. until 6.00 p.m. you could use 1-5:0800-1800. You can have several comma-separated entries. An entry that is preceded by an '!' disallows use of this port during the given time.

logindisable The number of failed login attempts on this port before the port will be disabled. Invalid login attempts on a port are recorded in the file /etc/security/portlog.

logininterval The number of invalid login attempts configured by *logindisable* that block the port need to occur within the time specified with *logininterval* (in seconds). If this is set to zero then the blocking of failed logins is deactivated.

loginreenable Defines the time in minutes after blocking a port that needs to pass before the port is enabled again. If set to zero the port is not automatically enabled again.

logindelay The delay multiplication factor between unsuccessful logins and the display of the new login prompt. If this is set to 4 seconds, then the second login prompt will appear after 4 seconds, the third one after another 8 seconds and the fourth after yet another 12 seconds.

The next important stanza is the *auth_method*. It is a placeholder for your own programs that will be run instead of, in addtion to or after the authentication method of the *login* program. It can be used to check a magnetic card reader at log in time for example. You will find more information on this in Chapter 16.

The *pw_restrictions* stanza defines the limits for acceptable passwords on AIX 3. On AIX 4 those limits have been made more flexible and are now user specific, therefore they are set in the /etc/security/users file instead.

maxage This is the maximum age for a password in weeks. Good values are from 8 to 26 weeks.

minage The minimum time in weeks before a password can be changed again. This rarely makes sense because it is sometimes necessary to keep out-of-date passwords or to beg the administrator (who is probably out for the day) for a change if someone has seen the brand new password and it cannot be immediately changed. Leave it at zero.

minalpha The minimum number of alphabetic characters in the password. I would use at least three.

minother The minimum number of non-alphabetic characters in the password. I would use at least one.

mindiff The minimum difference in characters between the old and the new password. It should be at least two.

maxrepeats The maximum number of total repetitions of one character in the password. It should not be more that two.

The last stanza is *usw.* I don't know why this German abbreviation is used rather than misc, but this is the catchall for a few more items:

maxlogins This can be set via the *chlicense* command. It defines the maximum number of concurrent log ins. It should be set according to your licence agreement.

shells This defines valid shells. If you want to change shells via system commands then they should be listed in here. All shells shipped by IBM are already included. If you install *bash* or *tcsh* you should include them here as well. Also, if you use UUCP you should include /usr/sbin/uucp/uucico. This stanza effects log in via *ftp* too; only if the user's shell is listed here can the user connect to the ftp server of this machine. It serves the same function as /etc/shells on other UNIX systems.

logintimeout This is an AIX 4 addition. It sets a timeout in seconds for the *login* program that controls the time between entering a user id and a password.

4.3.4 /etc/security/user

All user attributes are stored in this file. Apart from the default stanza they all are changed via SMIT or the *mkuser* or *chuser* commands. Whenever there is no attribute in the user-specific stanza, the attribute from the *default* stanza is used.

admin Usually set to false. If true, then the user's attributes can be changed only by the root user; otherwise they can be changed by anyone in the security group. The default is false.

auth1 Defines the primary authentication method. Usually this is 'SYSTEM', which translates to a standard password check by the *login* program. You can specify that the password for another user is checked or you can specify that passwords of multiple users are checked. Alternatively you can install your own log in check that has to be defined in /etc/security/login.cfg. If you want the root user to have to enter not only her or his own password but also the operator password, you could use *SYSTEM,SYSTEM;operator* for example in the root user's stanza. If you do not want any authentication it can be set to NONE. You will find more on authentication methods on page 280.

auth2 Defines a secondary authentication method that will be run if the primary succeeds. In contrast to the primary one, this method cannot be used to validate the user's log in. A failure of this method will not prevent log in. You could write your own audit information here or have the system activate some device for this user.

daemon If set to false, the user cannot start *cron* or *at* jobs. It defaults to true.

expires If non-zero it gives the expiration date for an account in MMDDhhmmYY format. This is quite useful for temporary users. If the field is empty or set to 0101000070 then the account is treated as if it has expired, which is another way of blocking accounts temporarily. When set to zero no expiration is active.

login The default allows all users to log in. You might want to set this to false for the root user. A simple audit trail via the *su* log then tells you who used the root account as all root access has to be done via *su* when direct log in for root is not available. The default for this field is true. One could also disable the login of an id by using a '*' in the password field of /etc/passwd.

rlogin Blocks remote log ins via the network (*telnet* and *rlogin*) when set to false. Initially it is true. It does not, however, block *ftp* access. You need to customize /etc/ftpusers if you want to restrict *ftp* access. On AIX 4 systems the *rlogin* attribute also controls remote XDM access. Only if it is set to true are remote XDM sessions enabled. XDM is discussed in Section 11.2.2.

su If set to true, then other users can use the *su* command to switch to this user. This is the default.

sugroups Lists all groups that are allowed or denied to *su* to this user. Denial is specified by preceding the group with a '!'. The default is 'ALL'.

ttys Specifies which terminals can be used to log in by this user. The default is 'ALL'. If 'ALL' is not specified here, then one needs to include /dev/pts to make network logins work. AIX 4 adds the capability to specify XDM-controlled X sessions here. According to the documentation, XDM creates a fake device entry like /dev/xdm/xterminal_your_domain_0 for remote connections (when using Xstations and domain names for example) or /dev/xdm/_0 for the local display. You can use those to specify allowed or prohibited XDM log in sessions. So far I have not been able to work with this feature. I have had to use a different syntax, for example simply _0, for the local display without the /dev/xdm part. Theoretically this should work also with the CDE login program, but I had no luck there either. Check the README files to determine whether this has been fixed in your AIX release.

tpath This is used to configure the trusted path facility. It is usually set to *NOSAK*. This is discussed further on page 297.

umask The standard file creation mask. This specifies which permissions you revoke in the permission bits when creating new files. For relaxed security use the default of 022; otherwise use 027, and if you don't trust your group 077 might be in order.

AIX 4 adds more attributes to the user stanzas in this file. The attributes *maxage*, *minage*, *minalpha*, *minother*, *mindiff* and *maxrepeats* for AIX 4 are the same as the ones for AIX 3 in /etc/security/login.cfg, as discussed on page 48.

account_locked If this is set to true then the account is locked (login is disabled). The normal state is false.

admgroups A list of comma-separated groups that are administered by this user.

dictionlist This is a list of dictionaries that a password is checked against before it is accepted by the passwd command. If you have the text formatting system installed use /usr/share/dict/words to disable all words in this dictionary as passwords. You can list several dictionaries separated by comas. Of course, when using the password rules to specify that there has to be at least one non-alpha character, this dictionary list no longer needs to include ordinary words as they are already disabled by the rule.

histexpire The number of weeks during which a password cannot be reused.

histsize The number of passwords that the system remembers for checks against new passwords to disallow reuse of older passwords. The old passwords are stored in encrypted form in /etc/security/passwd.{dir | pag}.

logintimes This lists the permissible times for log in on this account. It uses the same syntax as the *logintimes* entry in /etc/security/login.cf (see page 47).

loginretries The number of login attempts before an account is blocked and *account_locked* is set to true.

maxexpired If a password has not been changed after *maxage* weeks, then the user still has *maxexpired* weeks to log in and change the password. After this period of time the account is locked.

minlen Sets the minumum length for a password. Six is usally a good number.

pwdwarntime The system will warn the user *pwdwarntime* days before a password change is needed.

registry This is used when a remotely administered account (via DCE, the Distributed Computing Environment from the OSF) cannot be authenticated by the standard methods. It describes the repository where the user's authentication information is supposed to come from. It is not very useful on standard AIX systems as you only get a choice when installing DCE.

pwdchecks You can list external programs here that are used to check a password before it is accepted. Use full pathnames or the system will assume that they are relative /usr/lib. This program has to conform to the *pwdrestrict_method()* interface described in the AIX 4.1 technical reference.

SYSTEM Defines the way that system authentication works on AIX 4. AIX 3 type authentication is set by *compat*, which will use the local files and NIS (see Chapter 9). You can also use just the local files with the *files* keyword or you can use DCE authentication (if you have DCE installed).

4.3.5 /etc/security/passwd

This file acts as a shadow password file and stores some other dynamic user information. There is one stanza for each user in this file. The following attributes can be found here:

password The encrypted password. If set to just an asterisk '*', then the account is blocked for log in. This is the default, which also explains why the root user must give each user a password before the new account can be used. The password in this file is used only when /etc/passwd contains a '!' in the password field.

lastupdate The time of the last password change is stored here in seconds since epoch (1 January 1970).

flags If not blank, three values can be set, separated by commas: *ADMIN* if the password can be changed only by the root user; *ADMCHG* forces the user to chose a new password at the next log in, usually after the root user has changed the user's password; *NOCHECK* if the password restrictions in /etc/security/(login.cfg | user) should be ignored.

4.3.6 /etc/security/.ids

The next free default user id number is stored in /etc/security/.ids. This file stores four numbers, the next administrative uid, the next uid, the next administrative gid and the next gid. Unless you do something very strange you should not need to access this file directly.

4.3.7 /usr/lib/security/mkuser.default

On AIX 3 this file is a symbolic link to /usr/lib/security, and in here we are only dealing with a symbolic link. This is a useful feature for diskless/dataless clients. They will use the defaults from the server. If the link is removed and a copy of the file is created locally, then it can be customized for the particular machine instead of being uniform for all client machines. On AIX 4 the symbolic link is no longer included and the file is now only in /usr/lib/security.

If you want to use other defaults for the creation of users than the standard defaults listed in user, then you can set them in this file. There are two stanzas, one for normal users and one for administrative users that is selected when you call *mkuser* with *admin=true* or if you set administrative user to true in SMIT. The values that you set here are not shown in SMIT when you create a new account, but they will be used unless you override them with specific entries. You can use all attributes here that you can use for *mkuser* or *chuser*. On AIX 3 home directories are created in /u by default, which is a symbolic link to /home. You might want to change this to be really /home. This is already the default for AIX 4.

4.3.8 /usr/lib/security/mkuser.sys

Every time a new account is created, this shell script is run. Like mkuser.default, this is a symbolic link to the real file in /usr/lib/security on AIX 3. For AIX 4 you must use the file in /usr/lib/security. You should modify it according to your needs if you want to supply the new user with a reasonable set of default profiles. All the things that you need to do when setting up a new user id can be automated here. Larger installations will particularly benefit from a careful adaptation of this file.

The original shipped by IBM supports the Korn shell, the C shell in a limited way and takes care of creating the home directory for the new user. The following replacement script handles the Korn and C shells plus some other default configuration files. If you use another shell this sample should be sufficient to get you started. It assumes that some of the profiles described in the following chapters are present in /etc/security.

```
#!/usr/bin/ksh
# replacement for the IBM supplied mkuser.sys in /etc/security
# adapt it to your needs
# afx 1/93
#

# Check the number of arguments first
#
if [ $# -lt 4 ]
then
    echo "$0 called with less than four arguments!"
    echo "usage: mkuser.sys home user group shell"
    exit 1
fi
```

```
home=$1
usr=$2
grp=$3
shell=$4

#
# Create the home directory if it does not already exist
# and set the file ownership and permission
#
if [ ! -d $home ]
then
    mkdir $home
    chown $usr.$grp $home
    # change this to 700 if tighter security is required
    chmod 750 $home
fi

sh=`basename $shell`
src=/etc/security

# inital shell files for the new user
case $sh in
    ksh) shfiles=".profile .kshrc .kshexit"
        ;;
    csh) shfiles=".login .cshrc .logout"
        ;;
    *) : ;; # no default
esac    # end of case for shell

# give the new user some other helpful initial files as well
shfiles="$shfiles .mwmrc .xinitrc .Xdefaults"

# for each file check if we have a default file and if it doesn't
# already exist in the home directory.
# If ok, copy the file and change ownership and permissions.
if [ -n "$shfiles" ]
then
    for i in $shfiles
    do
        f=$home/$i
        if [ ! -f "$f" -a -f "$src/$i" ]
        then
            cp $src/$i $f
            chown $usr.$grp $f
           # modify the following chmod if you want a more open system
            chmod u+rwx,go-rwx $f
        fi
    done
fi

exit 0
```

4.4 Default user profiles

Although the old Bourne shell and the C shell are shipped with the system, the Korn shell is the default. It has better programming and interactive usage support than its predecessors. Today the C shell is used mostly by experienced old timers or people who grew up on BSD systems. In the following I focus on the Korn shell as it is the default shell for AIX and I must admit I gave up using the C shell as soon as I discovered the Korn shell. It is easier to use and program in my opinion. If you want to use the C shell, then you probably already know how your profiles should look. And Bourne shell users will immediately feel comfortable with the Korn shell. So lets focus on the Korn shell. Here are some sample profiles.

4.4.1 /etc/profile

In /etc/profile you can set environment variables for Korn and Bourne shell users and run commands for them. It is executed by those shells at log in time. As it is not used by the C shell it is not always the best place to do things for all users. I usually just keep the file as shipped and never modify it. Your needs might be different, so have a look at it and see what it does in the shipped version. It will set some environment variables like *LOGNAME, MAIL*, *MAILMSG*, and *TERM*.

4.4.2 ~/.profile

This file is read at log in time by the Korn shell. You should put all commands in here that you want to have executed once when you log in. Do not set aliases or functions in here. Another place, the environment file, is better suited for this task. The environment file is specified by the *ENV* environment variable. If *$ENV* is set, then the Korn shell reads the commands in the file to which *$ENV* points. This happens for every instance of the shell, not just for the login shell.

```
# ksh profile
# afx 1/93

# execute logout script when terminating session for cleanup
trap '$HOME/.kshexit' EXIT

# ignore CTRL-D when in login shell
set -o ignoreeof

# pointer to environment file
export ENV=$HOME/.kshrc

# search path for executables, remove the :~/bin:. at the end
# for a more security concerned environment
export PATH=/usr/bin:/usr/sbin:/usr/ucb:/usr/local/bin:/usr/bin/X11:\
/usr/lpp/X11/Xamples/bin:~/bin:.
```

```
# get the machine name for the prompt
export NODE=`hostname -s`

# set a prompt that shows the return code of the last command, the
# machine name, the current directory and the command history count
export PS1='($?)$NODE:$PWD !$ '

# set up some form of command line editing
export VISUAL=emacs

# set the default editor
export EDITOR=/usr/bin/vi

# set the editor for fullscreen command editing
export FCEDIT=$EDITOR

# the default pager
export PAGER=/usr/bin/more

# how many commands do we store in our command history?
export HISTSIZE=100

# make vi more endurable, overrides ~/.exrc
export EXINIT="set ic smd noslow"

# any good news from the system administrator?
if [ `news -n|wc -l` -gt 0 ]
then news | $PAGER
fi

# I want my cookie! (If you have the games installed)
/usr/games/fortune

# check for mail
if [ -s "$MAIL" ]
then echo "$MAILMSG"
fi
```

Let's look at some of the more interesting things that happen in the above .profile. The *trap* instruction at the beginning tells the shell to execute the $HOME/.kshexit script when it receives the exit signal. This way we can clean up when we log out. The subsequent *set* command tells the shell to ignore the <CTRL-D> key and not terminate if the user presses the key. This prevents accidental logout. Instead, *exit* must be typed explicitly. Options activated with *set* are active only in the current shell, so the log out check is only done in the login shell. Next we set up a pointer to our environment file that will be executed for every instance of the Korn shell. The *$PATH* assumes that users have their own bin directory, but this is not essential. If you work in a multimachine environment, the name of the machine in the prompt is quite helpful, so that will be considered next. After the prompt is set up the command line editor is set to Emacs. You could set it also to vi, but I consider the Emacs commands easier, and in Emacs mode you can also map the cursor keys to the basic functions (this will be done in the .kshrc file). The other variable settings are quite obvious I hope; set anything else you need here. In the end we check for mail, get a fortune cookie and check for system news.

4.4.3 ~/.kshrc

This is the file that is executed by every invocation of the Korn shell if *$ENV* is set correctly. Where I use .kshrc any name can be used. The InfoExplorer examples use .env for this file.

```
# Korn shell startup file
# afx 1/93

# check for interactive usage
case $- in
*i*)  # Options for interactive shells

    # each terminal should have it's own history file, so get rid of
    # the file name and the next shell will create a new one.
    rm -f $HOME/.sh_history

    # I want the window title to show where I am
    if [ -n "$WINDOWID" -a -n "$NODE" ]
    then
        if [ "$TERM" = "aixterm" ]
        then
            echo "\033]P$USER@$NODE: $PWD\007\c"
        elif [ "$TERM" = "xterm" ]
        then
            echo "\033]2;$USER@$NODE: $PWD\007\c"
        fi
    fi

    # Some aliases to make life easier
    alias cls='tput clear'
    alias dir='ls -al'
    alias ll='ls -al'
    alias la='ls -a'
    alias dird='li -la -Od'
    alias dirx='li -la -Ox'
    alias lld='li -la -Od'
    alias llx='li -la -Ox'
    alias h='fc -l'
    alias j='jobs'
    alias md='mkdir'
    alias rd='rmdir'
    alias pg="pg -cnsp[%d]"

    # enable cursor keys for command line editing
    # works only for ksh in emacs mode
    # ^P means the CTRL-P character is really entered in the file!
```

```
    # use CTRL-V in vi to do this.
    # This maps up, down, right, left, home and delete.
    alias __A='^P'
    alias __B='^N'
    alias __C='^F'
    alias __D='^B'
    alias __H='^A'
    alias __P='^D'

    # everytime we cd somewhere the window title shows the new
    # directory
    unalias cd
    _cd() {
        unalias cd
        cd $1
        if [ -n "$WINDOWID" -a -n "$NODE" ]
        then
            if [ "$TERM" = "aixterm" ]
            then
                echo "\033]P$USER@$NODE: $PWD\007\c"
            elif [ "$TERM" = "xterm" ]
            then
                echo "\033]2;$USER@$NODE: $PWD\007\c"
            fi
        fi
        alias cd="_cd"
    }
    alias cd="_cd"

    ;;      # end -- options for interactive shells

*) : ;;     # no default

esac    # end of case for interactive shells
```

One needs to check for interactive use of the shell, otherwise background jobs might abort because of commands executed in here. If you work in a window system you probably do not want your windows to share the same command history, so create a different history file for each running shell. This is done by removing the current history file. This will not remove the file, as the shell is still accessing it, only its directory entry. When a new shell is started, it will create a new file, which will also be removed. This ensures that all shell invocations have their private history. The disadvantage of this method is that you cannot access the history as a file. You have to use the *fc* command instead. If the shell is executed in a window, we also want it to show the complete current directory in the window title, together with user id and machine name. To make sure that the window title is changed while we change the current directory, the Korn shell built-in *cd* command is changed to our own. Apart from some aliases for frequently used commands, we define some of the cursor keys on the HFT keyboard as command retrieval keys. This works only in *emacs* command line editing mode and only for keys that return only two character escape sequences. All the possible keys are defined here; the other cursor keys return up to six characters. The characters shown as '^X' are real control characters. You have to use <CTRL-V> <CTRL-A> in *vi* to enter a '^A' for example.

In Section 23.4 you will find a few shell functions that you might want to add to your .kshrc.

4.4.4 ~/.kshexit

This file is executed when the log in shell exits and is a useful way to clean up when you leave. This works only if the *trap* instruction in .profile sets it up. You could remove backup files and other temporary items here or display a farewell fortune cookie.

```
# my logout file
# clean up smit and other logs
rm -f $HOME/smit.*
```

4.5 Adding users

Now that you have the initial profiles and user defaults in place you can add users to the system. The easy way is via **smit mkuser**, but you can also use the *mkuser* command directly, as in **mkuser zaphod**. Note that you do not need to specify a user id for the new account. *Mkuser* will automatically use the next available number from /etc/security/.ids if you do not specify one explicitly.

When adding users you should set their full name in the GECOS field ('User information' in SMIT), for example

```
afx:!:4711:1:Andreas Siegert:/u/afx:/usr/bin/ksh
```

Apart from making the real name known on the system, this also allows you to receive mail not only with the account name but also with the full name. Without any further aliases, the mail name *Andreas.Siegert* will be accepted in addition to *afx*.

If you want to migrate a large number of users over from a non-AIX system, then you can use a trick to get the necessary information into the system. Create backup copies of /etc/passwd, /etc/group, /etc/security/group and /etc/security/user in case the commands in the following steps are too strict with their changes. Add the /etc/passwd entries of the old system to the /etc/passwd file in the new system. Do the same for /etc/group. Then run the command **grpck -y ALL**. It will fix some problems with the new groups and tell you about others that you need to fix manually. Once the groups are all right you can generate the necessary information in the /etc/security files by running **usrck -y ALL** and **pwdck -y ALL**. This will integrate the accounts into the system. If the imported /etc/passwd file contains encrypted passwords then they will be migrated to the shadow password file /etc/security/passwd. The new ids will be expired. You can change the expiration date to never by executing **chuser expires=0 UserName**.

The method has one problem however. The user ids *nobody* and *guest* will be lost. Losing *guest* is not a problem, but losing *nobody* is. It is needed for NFS and some daemons. Recreate the entries for *nobody* from the backup files manually after you have run the **ck* commands.

If you have a large number of users on the system (>100), then the login process is slowed down by the sequential look-up in /etc/passwd. By executing the command **mkpasswd /etc/passwd** you can create a hashed user database that will speed up password look-ups. The *login* program uses the database automatically if it exists. You have to execute *mkpasswd* each time you create new users to update the hashed database, so it might be a good idea to add it to /etc/security/mkuser.sys.

Once you have created a new user on the system you need to allocate the user a password to allow her or him log in. This can be done via the *passwd* command. Execute **passwd username** to give the new user a password. Every time the root user changes the password for another user the *ADMCHG* flag is set in /etc/security/passwd for this user. When this flag is set the user is forced to change the password at the next log in. If you have a user for whom you do not want that to happen, remove the *ADMCHG* flag from the user's stanza in /etc/security/passwd after you have changed the password. You can use *pwdadm* if you do not want to edit the file directly.

4.6 Getting organized

One thing one should do for a cleanly structured system is create the directory tree /usr/local. It pays to keep homegrown utilities separate from the system-supplied commands. I suggest putting all local things in here, using a directory structure like the following:

/usr/local	all homegrown things
/usr/local/bin	commands
/usr/local/etc	configuration files
/usr/local/lib	invariant local data
/usr/local/src	sources for local commands
/usr/local/doc	local system documentation
/usr/local/man	man pages for local stuff

Use **chown -R bin.bin /usr/local** and **chmod -R 755 /usr/local** to set the correct ownership and permissions for that tree.

If you keep the /usr/local tree in a separate file system it will survive preservation installations in case you need to reinstall or upgrade the operating system. I suggest keeping it in the root volume group but in its own file system. This will ensure that your local commands will be backed up by the SMIT system backup (*mksysb*) and you will have fewer hassles in getting the system reinstalled or cloned together with your own additions. If you expect your local file system to be very large it might be better to put it in its own volume group (see Section 6.6).

While we are creating directories let's create /var/log. The /var file system exists mainly for storing log and spool files. This is the obvious place to store logs from the syslog daemon and other log files. The permissions you give this directory depend on what type of logs you store in there and who you want to give access to the logs. I suggest using **chown root.adm** and **chmod 2750 /var/log**. This will give root full access and change the default group membership of all files created in there to *adm* so that anyone in the *adm* group can read it. The rest of the world has no access. Users with a BSD background might want to use /var/adm instead of /var/log for history's sake.

As shipped, the /var file system might be too small for your needs. Monitor it closely and increase its size when needed. Beware that the /usr/tmp directory is in reality /var/tmp and the /usr/spool tree is also just a link to /var/spool. It is not uncommon to have /var file systems of more than 250MB on larger servers; single workstations often can get by with 8 - 12MB.

4.6.1 rc.local

Some installations need to run initial commands after the system has booted. A good place to store those commands is /usr/local/etc/rc.local. You tell the system to execute this script by putting it into the /etc/inittab file with the *mkitab* command:

```
mkitab "rclocal:2:once:/usr/local/etc/rc.local"
```

The *init* process will execute the rc.local command once when it boots in multiuser mode. Now what would you want to put into rc.local? You could, for example, switch the console to a file so that whenever something is sent to the console it is logged to file instead. This ensures that you do not lose any warnings that show up on the console if it is turned off or while you are running X. This is what our initial rc.local file looks like:

```
#!/usr/bin/ksh
# /usr/local/etc/rc.local
# Executes local commands to be executed at system boot time
# afx 1/93

echo "starting $0"

export PATH=/usr/sbin:/usr/bin:/usr/local/bin

function OldLog {
# maximum number of logfiles before warning
  maxlogs=5
  d=`dirname $1`
  n=`basename $1`
```

```
  f=$1
  df=$f.`date +"%y%m%d.%H%M"`    # file name with current date
  # get rid of logfile. We still have the version with the date.
  rm -f $f
  touch $f                       # create new logfile
  ln $f $df                      # alias new file with filename.date
  typeset -i x=`ls $f.*|wc -l`   # how many are there already?
  if [ $x -gt $maxlogs ] # if too much sent mail to root
  then
      files=`cd $d;ls $n.*`
      mail -s "Too many $n log files in $d" root <<- EOF
      Warning, there are more than $maxlogs instances of $n in $d.
      Time to clean up!
      $d:
      $files
EOF
  fi
}

# Switch console to log file:
OldLog /var/log/console
swcons /var/log/console

# Now sent the log also to the console terminal
tail -f /var/log/console > /dev/tty0 2>&1 &
# Use /dev/hft/0 or /dev/lft instead of /dev/tty0 if you run
# a direcly attached monitor and not an ASCII terminal.

echo "finished $0"
exit 0
```

First we make sure we have a clean *$PATH* so that we do not search in too many directories. Then we create a function that saves old log files for reference. This ensures that we have a new one for each system start and still have a copy of the one from the previous run. The current log file is always available under two names: the name of the log file itself and the name with the creation date appended. This makes it easy to keep several log files on line. The version of the *OldLog* function shown here only mails root if there are too many old log files. One could also erase them automatically in this function or mail the most recent log file to the administrator. A function is introduced here because there might be more log files that need to be handled in this file than just the console. By using *swcons* the console output is switched to the file /var/log/console and anything sent to the file is continuously sent to the console terminal as well by the *tail* command. There will be other commands put into rc.local in the remainder of this book. Do not forget to make it executable with **chmod 744 /usr/local/etc/rc.local**.

As soon as the root user uses the *swcons* command to switch the console output to a window the whole set-up is broken unfortunately. Instead of using the *swcons* command, it would be better to use the *tail* command. If you put **alias tailcons='tail -f /var/log/console &'** in the .kshrc file for root then you have a simple command to see everything sent to the console in the current window.

If you run a machine continuously then it might be useful to have fresh log files at more frequent intervals than reboots. You could put the above logic in another shell script and run it via cron every Sunday night, for example. Be sure to kill any old *tail* processes running on log files that you remove. If you forget to do so, then after a while you will have plenty of them sitting in your process table.

4.7 Using *cron* for housekeeping

The *cron* command is very useful for repetitive housekeeping chores. It runs commands unattended at predefined times. Typical tasks include removing old temporary files, accounting and performing automated security checks or unattended file transfer via UUCP. The timetable for *cron* should not be directly modified: this is the task of the **crontab -e** command.

When the root user executes **crontab -e** then the cron table for root is put into the editor specified by *$EDITOR*. Let's have a look at the initial cron configuration:

```
#0 3 * * * /etc/skulker
#45 2 * * 0 /usr/lib/spell/compress
#45 23 * * * ulimit 5000; /usr/lib/smdemon.cleanu > /dev/null
0 11 * * * /usr/bin/errclear -d S,O 30
0 12 * * * /usr/bin/errclear -d H 90
# The following two lines are not present in the default AIX 4 crontab
01 4 * * * /etc/lpp/diagnostics/bin/test_batt 1>/dev/null 2>/dev/null
01 3 * * * /etc/lpp/diagnostics/bin/run_ela 1>/dev/null 2>/dev/null
```

As an example we will activate the automatic house cleaner, *skulker*. Remove the comment char '#' at the beginning of the *skulker* entry. This will tell cron to run *skulker* every night at 03.00 hours. If you look at /etc/skulker (it is really /usr/sbin/skulker) you will find that this is a shell script to remove old files from temporary directories as well as old backup files. This will ensure that you do not keep too many old files that have not been used on the system for several days. Modify /etc/skulker according to your needs if you want more or fewer actions performed during cleanup. But be careful: if you remove too much you might regret it. In particular, log files that are still used by application should be treated with care: they cannot just be removed.

When you save the cron table it will replace the previous cron table. If you have used other systems in which the cron files in /usr/spool/cron/crontabs must be edited directly, then note that you need to *kill cron* that it picks up the changes. By using the *crontab* command you can be sure that *cron* is notified of the changes immediately without having to send a signal. Another difference from some older systems is that each user has a private cron table. There is no need to use *su* in crontab to change to another user id.

For those that are new to *cron*, here is the general syntax of cron table entries:

```
Minute(0-59) Hour(0-23) Day(1-31) Month(1-12) Weekday(0-6) Command
```

Day 0 in the weekday entry is Sunday; the '*' is a wildcard for all times. Ranges can be given by hyphens, as in 9-17; lists of values are separated by comas.

If a command that is executed via cron has some output that is not redirected to a file, then it will be mailed to the user, in this case root.

Some other commands are listed in the system-supplied cron table. The entry for /usr/lib/spell/compress should be activated if you use the standard *spell* command frequently. It compresses the *spell* history file. If you run *sendmail* for mail processing then smdemon.cleanu will ensure that your log files do not grow too big: you will get daily log files instead for the last 4 days. If you need more, modify the /usr/lib/smdemon.cleanu script. The *errclear* lines remove old entries from the system error log. Software errors are thrown away after 30 days, hardware errors after 90 days. The two entries out of the diagnostics directory check whether the battery for the CMOS RAM is still good and run diagnostics on the hard disks.

In the example for the /usr/local/etc/rc.local file we create fresh log files for each system restart. For example, one could use a cron script to create new log files for every week to make housekeeping easier. If you find yourself repeating tasks at regular intervals then it is time to think about a shell script that does this via *cron*.

Occasionally one does want different default *nice values* or queue limits for *cron* jobs. Check out the /var/adm/cron/queuedefs file. This defines how many parallel *cron* or *at* jobs can be run at any given time and their priority.

5

Device management

Device management on AIX is slightly different from on other UNIX systems. Drivers are loaded dynamically instead of being bound statically into the kernel and configuration parameters for devices are stored in a database (the ODM). Most users will never have to deal with device configuration because of the automatic customization built into the system, but occasionally it cannot be avoided. Should you need to add your own driver or tweak an existing one, you can get the necessary information out of (*AIX Version 3.2 Writing a Device Driver*, 9) or (*AIX Version 4.1 Writing a Device Driver*, 10) and (*AIX Version 4.1 Kernel Extensions and Device Support Programming Concepts*, 7).

5.1 Configuring devices

On AIX 3 all the available drivers are installed automatically. If you need a driver that was not available when you bought the system you will need to install the appropriate update. On AIX 4, which is a bit more space conservative, it is necessary to install the drivers that you need selectively. The system will install only the drivers for devices that are available when the system is installed initially. Any drivers that you need for printers or other additional devices will have to be installed in an extra step via the normal installation methods (use **smit devinst** to install additional drivers).

All device configuration on AIX can be done with the submenus of **smit devices**. The device attributes can also be changed and examined from the command line as well. Use **lsdev -C** to see all configured devices. The ones that are marked *Available* are active and can be used. The ones that are marked *Defined* are known to the system and device configuration commands can be used on them but they are not usable. To restrict the output of *lsdev* one can add a class, as in **lsdev -Ccadapter**, which would only list adapter cards but not disks or tapes for example. To see the available classes use **lsdev -P**.

The configuration of individual devices can be listed with *lsattr*, as in **lsattr -El rmt0**. To change device attributes the command *chdev* is used, as in **chdev -l rmt0 -ablock_size=1024**. Should you get an error message that the device is busy, then you need either to bring the device to a state where it is not in use or to change only the database entry (with *-P*) and the changes will be activated at the next reboot. To get rid of a device use *rmdev* like in **rmdev -l rmt0**. This will still keep the device in the ODM. To remove it from the ODM as well, use **rmdev -l rmt0 -d**. Deleting a device but keeping it in the database can be quite helpful in the case of external disks or tape drives that are not always available.

When listing devices with **lsdev -C**, strings such as 00-00-0D-00 appear in the third column. Those are device location codes. They are dependent on the hardware platform. On the 2xx machines the integrated SCSI adapter shows up as 00-00-0S, whereas the devices connected to it have codes such as 00-00-0S-20, where the last digits denote the SCSI address. On AIX 4 you can see the device hierarchy graphically using the **xdevicem** command.

5.2 Adding SCSI devices

Each time the system boots, it checks all its device connections for known devices. Known devices are automatically configured into the system when they are found. If a device has a different configuration from the default, the changes will be applied at boot time. All of this is done through the configuration manager, which is discussed in Section 18.4. Some devices can be dynamically added to a running system. To configure them one can either try to set up the connection manually or leave the work to the configuration manager, which can also be used in a running system. Simply run **cfgmgr** to activate new disks or tapes.

Running *cfgmgr* has one disadvantage, however: each device it looks at will be unavailable during that time. The system appears to hang for a brief moment. If you know how your device is connected, then you can use SMIT to configure it directly.

Let's assume you have hooked a new tape drive to the SCSI bus and that it has the SCSI id 6. This can be done in a running system, although no one will guarantee you that the fuse on the SCSI card will not blow while you open the bus. I usually *sync* the system, remove the terminator, hook up the new device and then terminate the SCSI chain again. So far I have had no problems with this method (and I use it quite often), IBM service engineers are not particularly keen on it. After the tape has been hooked up, power it on and run **smit maktpe**. This will offer you a list of known tape drives to choose from. If yours is not on the list, choose the *ost* driver. The *o*ther *S*CSI *t*ape driver allows you to connect most of the tape drives on the market to the system. SMIT will show you a panel in which you can enter the tapes parameters (Figure 5.1).

```
  Tape Drive type                                    ost
  Tape Drive interface                               scsi
  Description                                        Other SCSI Tape Drive
  Parent adapter                                     scsi0
* CONNECTION address                                []                     +
  BLOCK size (0=variable length)                    [512]                  +#
  Use DEVICE BUFFERS during writes                   yes                   +
  Use EXTENDED file marks                            yes                   +
  RESERVE/RELEASE support                            no                    +
  BLOCK SIZE for variable length support            [0]                    +#
  DENSITY setting #1                                [0]                    +#
  DENSITY setting #2                                [0]                    +#
  Set delay after a FAILED command                  [45]                   +#
  Set maximum delay for the READ/WRITE command      [144]                  +#
```

Figure 5.1 Adding an unknown tape drive to the system.

The only thing you need to enter is the connection address, which is the SCSI id and which is displayed as a two-digit number on AIX 3 and as a two digits separated by a comma on AIX 4. The first of the digits is the SCSI id and the second is the SCSI unit number, which is zero in most cases. For our sample tape it would be "60" or "6,0" respectively.

All other parameters are device dependent. Most tape drives will work with a block size of 512 bytes, but the optimum size depends on the tape drive. This value can also be changed later. Normally one should use device buffers for optimum speed. Extended file marks are needed when one wants to create a tape with multiple images on it so that the driver can find the start and stop of the data blocks on the tape. But they are much larger than normal EOF marks on the tape. Unless you have a twin-tailed SCSI configuration you should not need to worry about the RESERVE/RELEASE support. Tape drives that support variable length records usually use block size zero for this. The density settings depend on the drive you want to connect. Most tapes support more than one density. Density setting 1 is mapped to /dev/rmX, whereas density setting 2 is mapped to /dev/rmtX.4. The time settings depend very much on the tape drive and should be set according to the documentation that comes with the tape. More information on the tape driver that comes with AIX can be found by searching for the *rmt* special file in InfoExplorer.

The mechanism used for a tape drive can be used for other devices as well. SCSI disks that are unknown to the system can usually be used with the *osdisk* driver, foreign CD ROM drives are addressable via the *oscd* driver and there is a *osomd* driver for unknown optical drives. When adding non IBM or IBM OEM disk drives, some driver parameters are not set to their optimum values by default. See Section 6.1.2 for details.

5.3 Playing dirty tricks

There are always a few cases where the standard device support is not sufficient. For example, some adapter cards insist on using specific interrupts. In some rare cases the configuration manager cannot resolve the resulting conflicts. The system will not configure one of the contending adapter cards. To get around this you can patch the ODM. Check out Chapter 18 before you start to fiddle with the ODM. The following example assumes that a Token-Ring card configuration conflicts with some vendor card as they both want the same interrupt level. In addition, the OEM card cannot be changed, therefore we need to work on the Token-Ring adapter configuration.

(1) To find out the default value for the interrupt level of the Token-Ring adapter you could use

```
odmget -q "uniquetype = adapter/mca/tokenring and attribute =
bus_intr_lvl" PdAt
```

which would report

```
PdAt:
        uniquetype = "adapter/mca/tokenring"
        attribute = "bus_intr_lvl"
        deflt = "3"
        values = "3,4,5,7,9,10,11,12"
        width = ""
        type = "N"
        generic = "D"
        rep = "nl"
        nls_index = 4
```

This tells us that the default value is 3. If there is another adapter that will be configured later than this adapter but needs interrupt 3, then there might be a fight for interrupt 3. One can patch the ODM to use a different default value. You should save the above *odmget* output in a file; call it /tmp/tr.intr.

(2) Edit this file and change the *deflt* line to read:

```
deflt = "4"
```

to get a default interrupt level of 4 instead of 3. You could use any of the values shown in the *values* line.

(3) Delete the current definition from the ODM with **odmdelete -o PdAt -q "uniquetype= adapter/mca/tokenring and attribute = bus_intr_lvl"**.

(4) Add the new definition with **odmadd /tmp/tr.intr**.

At the next reboot the configuration manager will try to use interrupt level 4 instead of interrupt level 3 for the Token-Ring adapter. It is rarely necessary to resort to such tricks, but they are occasionally required because some OEM adapters insist on certain interrupt levels not willing to share the interrupt.

The above method can be used for other device defaults as well. Just *grep* through the output of **odmget PdAt** to find the key strings for the device you want to modify and then use the outlined steps.

6

Disk management

One of the biggest differences between older UNIX systems and AIX is the logical volume manager (LVM) for disk management. Disk and file system management in a standard UNIX system is tedious. File systems have a fixed size; to increase it, it is necessary to back up the file system, delete it, recreate it and finally restore it from the backup. During this period the file system or even the whole machine is unavailable and it requires to have enough space on one disk to do so. Mirroring for higher availability requires expensive disk controllers that support it. With the introduction of the LVM all of this is history. The LVM allows you to do mirroring, spread file systems over disks, dynamically expand file systems, bad block reallocation and more. Although AIX was the first operating system to have the LVM, others are now getting it too because it has become part of OSF/1, the operating system from the Open Software Foundation. All disk activity on the system is done through the LVM so one should know how it works to make optimal use of it.

The other highlight in AIX disk management is the journaled file system (JFS), which ensures the integrity of the file system meta data in case of system crashes, a common problem with classical UNIX file systems.

6.1 The logical volume manager

The LVM was designed to overcome the limitations of classical UNIX file system management. Disks (physical volumes) are grouped together in volume groups. Volume groups in turn contain logical volumes, which are the equivalent of partitions or mini disks in other UNIX systems. A logical volume can be spread out over several disks when they belong to the same volume group. Figure 6.1 shows the relationships.

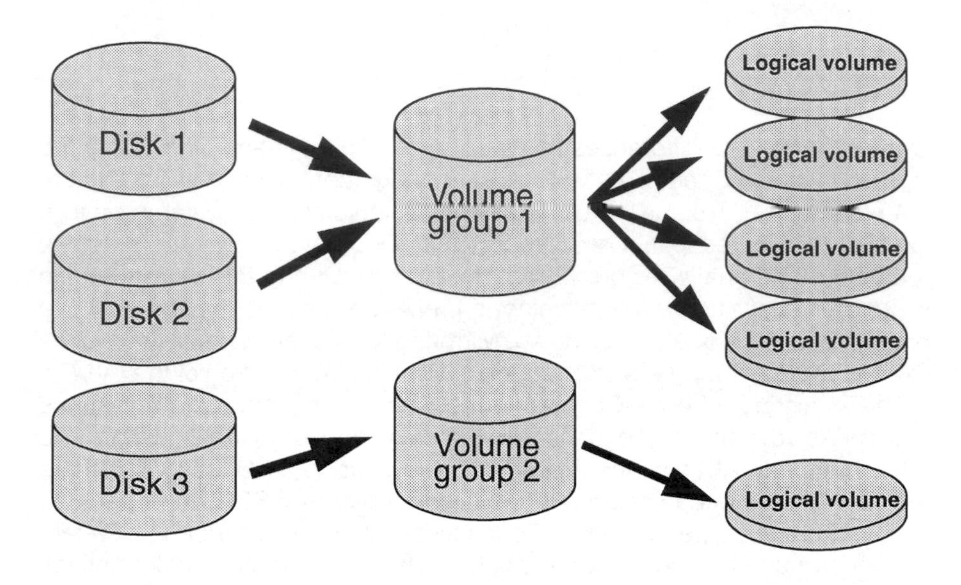

Figure 6.1 Logical volumes.

Logical volumes are the entities in which file systems reside. They are like disk partitions in traditional UNIX systems. To manage disk space in convenient pieces, physical and logical partitions are introduced. A physical partition is a fixed-size chunk of real disk space, by default 4MB. A logical partition is the abstraction for the physical partition. A logical partition can contain up to three physical partitions when mirroring is used, but usually one logical partition maps onto exactly one physical partition. The size of a physical partition is configurable. One could achieve a slightly better use of disk space on small disks with several file systems when using a physical partition size of 2MB for example, but those cases where this is needed are usually rare.

Some sites will have very specific needs for disk storage that cannot be covered in this book. There are two IBM publications that should be considered: (*AIX Storage Management*, 15) and (*Keeping Your RISC System/6000 Up in a Down Economy / Managing AIX V3 for Availability*, 16). The first one is the best reference on AIX disk management internals that I have found so far and the second one is indispensable for those who are interested in high availability without wanting to invest in a cluster solution.

6.1.1 LVM terminology and limits

Much of the functionality of the LVM is geared towards mirroring. The discussion of the following terms reflects this.

Physical volume (PV)

One physical disk. It has one system-wide unique name, the physical volume id (PVID). New disks will get their PVID when *mkdev* is used to integrate them into the system. A physical volume can be accessed as /dev/hdisk0 for example.

Volume group (VG)

A collection of physical volumes of varying sizes and types. A volume group looks like one single disk to the user. It may be created, dynamically expanded, activated, deactivated, reorganized and synchronized.

Physical partition (PP)

A contiguous set of bytes on a physical volume (low-level bad block management might spread this out over several disk blocks, but it is still seen as one allocation unit by the system), the allocation unit of disk space that is assignable to a logical volume. There is only one physical partition size in a volume group. All disks in one volume group share the same physical partition size, which is set when creating a volume group. It defaults to 4MB unless a volume group has an initial size larger than 4GB, in which case it becomes 8MB.

Logical partition (LP)

Matches one to three physical partitions depending on mirroring. Without mirroring there is one physical partition per logical partition. When using mirroring there will be two or three physical partitions for one logical partition depending on the number of copies.

Logical volume (LV)

A collection of logical partitions within one volume group. It may be dynamically extended in increments of one logical partition as long as there is space in the volume group. It can contain file systems, a JFS log, boot data, paging space, dump space or a raw disk space for a database. A typical example of a logical volume is /dev/hd2.

Volume group descriptor area (VGDA)

An area of reserved space at the beginning of each physical volume that contains information describing all the logical volumes and the physical volumes that belong to the volume group. By using a header and trailer time stamp, the most recent copy of the VGDA in a volume group can be identified. This is used when the volume group is activated via *varyonvg* to select a correct and non corrupted VGDA. A VGDA is only considered valid when header and trailer time stamps match. This mechanism ensures that the LVM does not use a VGDA with partially written data. A quorum (majority) of VGDAs is needed to ensure the integrity of the meta data of a volume group. Thus, a VG has several VGDAs, which are spread over its disks. A volume group with a single disk contains two VGDAs, with two disks there is one with one VGDA and one with two VGDAs. When using three or more disks each has a single VGDA. In addition, the VGDA also contains a physical partition map with a list of physical partitions allocated to the logical volumes within the volume group, a list of all physical partitions allocated to logical partitions and the status of all physical partitions. The VGDA makes a volume group self-describing by including all the relevant data in the volume group itself. This, in turn, allows the volume group to be exchanged between systems and makes it possible to transport disks from one system to another with the data intact. The management of the VGDA is done by the LVM library. It is updated by most of the LVM commands and subroutines that access the volume group.

Volume group status area (VGSA)

This is similar to the VGDA but contains additional state data about physical partitions. Here the information about which physical partitions are stale or incorrect and which physical volumes that belong to the volume group are missing is maintained. Like the VGDA, a quorum is needed to ensure data integrity when using a logical volume with several copies. The management of the VGSA is done by the kernel part of the LVM.

Quorum

To make sure that the system uses correct information about a volume group, a quorum (or majority) of VGDAs or VGSAs is needed. Depending on the volume group, a disk belongs to, it contains a different number of VGDAs. There are two VGDAs if the disk is the single physical volume in a volume group. If the disk is one of two in a volume group then there are two VGDAs on the first disk and one on the second. If there are three or more physical volumes in a volume group than each disk has only one VGDA. To reach a reliable quorum one usually needs more than 50% of the VGDAs of a volume group. Thus, a mirrored system should use always three disks so that in all cases of failure a quorum can be maintained. Mirroring can also be done by two disks, but in this case the reliability of the VGDA data is not as high.

The LVM on AIX has the following limits for managing disk space:

Maximum number of physical volumes per volume group	32
Maximum number of volume groups	255
Minimum number of physical volumes per volume group	1
Maximum number of physical partitions per physical volume	1016
Minimum number of physical partitions per logical partition.	1
Maximum number of physical partitions per logical partition	3
Minimum size for a physical partition	1 MB
Default size for a physical partition	4 MB
Maximum size for one physical partition	256 MB
Maximum number of physical partitions per volume group	max PPs per PV * max PVs per VG
Maximum logical partitions per logical volume	65535
Maximum number of logical volumes per volume group	256

The data for the management of logical volumes is spread all over the system. First there are the VGDA and VGSA at the beginning of the physical volume. Each logical volume has a logical volume control block (LVCB) at the beginning. You can have a look at it via **getlvcb -ATl lvdevice**, where *lvdevice* stands for any logical volume, such as hd2. There is also a corresponding *putlvcb*, which should not be used unless you really know what you are doing. Additional or duplicated data about volume groups is also kept in the ODM, and some data about logical volumes is kept in /etc/filesystems.

6.1.2 Working with physical volumes

You cannot do much about disks. Simply set the proper SCSI address, hook them up to the SCSI bus and power the system on (or run **cfgmgr** if you are working on a running system).

Of course, using non IBM-supplied disks might require a bit more jumper setting. AIX wants the disks to spin up on command, not on power on. Apart from this setting problems usually arise only with foreign disks when the SCSI controller chip of the disk and the RS/6000 are incompatible. In this case, contact your disk supplier.

When using non IBM or IBM OEM disks on AIX 4 one should check the queuing parameters of the disk. Usually IBM disks have a queue depth of 3 and a simple queuing policy. Any disk not shipped by IBM for the RS/6000 will not have the queuing parameters set, therefore losing performance. Use **lsattr -El hdisk0** to see the parameters. If you run an IBM OEM disk then it is fairly safe to assume that a queue depth of 3 and a simple queuing policy will give better performance. This can be set with **chdev -l hdisk0 -aqueue_depth=3 -aq_type=simple -P**. It will be active after the next reboot. Ask your disk supplier about the best parameters for the disk; it depends very much on the disk architecture and its controller electronics. When using SCSI-2 there is another parameter that might not be optimally set for non IBM drives, *extended_rw*. Set this to true to activate the 10-byte read option of SCSI-2.

The system will find the disk automatically and assign a name such as *hdisk0* to each disk (you could integrate it explicitly with **smit makdsk**). The disk is then known and can be used by the LVM. Once the disk is integrated you can list it via **lspv diskname** (Figure 6.2).

```
$ lspv hdisk0
PHYSICAL VOLUME:    hdisk0               VOLUME GROUP:     rootvg
PV IDENTIFIER:      00013909450ae6e7     VG IDENTIFIER     0001390965b18389
PV STATE:           active               VG STATE:         active/complete
STALE PARTITIONS:   0                    ALLOCATABLE:      yes
PP SIZE:            4 megabyte(s)        LOGICAL VOLUMES:  9
TOTAL PPs:          239 (956 megabytes)VG DESCRIPTORS:   2
FREE PPs:           12 (48 megabytes)
USED PPs:           227 (908 megabytes)
FREE DISTRIBUTION:  00..10..02..00..00
USED DISTRIBUTION:  48..38..45..48..48
```

Figure 6.2 Listing a disk's contents with **lspv diskname**.

Lspv tells you a great deal about the disk: how much disk space is already allocated to logical volumes, the physical partition size, to which volume group the disk belongs, how many VGDAs it has, where the free and used physical partitions are on the disk and so on. Both distributions fields show you the number of physical partitions on the inner edge, inner middle, center, outer middle and outer edge of the disk. The disk in Figure 6.2 is active and has no stale partitions. Allocation of the available free partitions is allowed and there are nine logical volumes on this disk. On AIX 4 the VG state is not displayed.

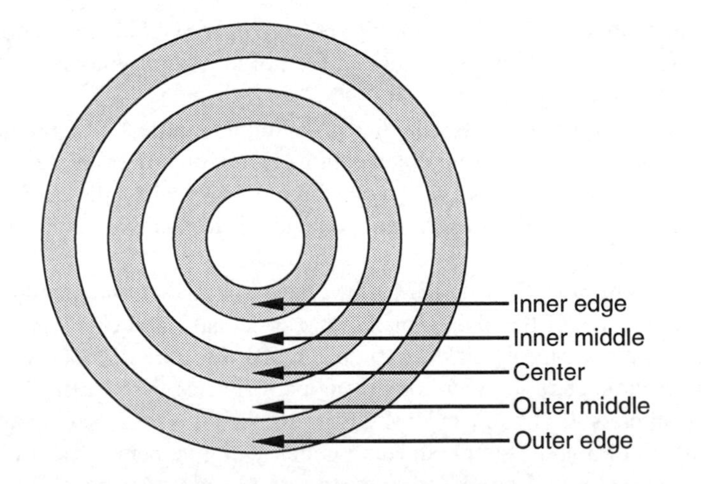

Figure 6.3 The distribution of the physical partitions on a disk.

Each disk has five different areas that can be used when allocating disk space to a logical volume (Figure 6.3). These areas have different access speeds. The fastest area is the one in the middle between the disk edges, called center. The further away from this center an area is, the slower is the access as the maximum seek distance is half of the disk's radius no matter where the head is at any time. One should try to keep the paging space and the JFS log in the center area.

You can obtain more details about the logical volumes on this disk with **lspv -l diskname**, which will show you how they are allocated on the disk (Figure 6.4).

```
$ lspv -l hdisk0
hdisk0:
LV NAME              LPs     PPs     DISTRIBUTION            MOUNT POINT
hd5                  2       2       02..00..00..00..00      /blv
hd7                  2       2       02..00..00..00..00      /mnt
hd2                  175     175     44..27..10..46..48      /usr
hd3                  3       3       00..03..00..00..00      /tmp
hd1                  21      21      00..08..13..00..00      /home
hd6                  20      20      00..00..20..00..00      N/A
hd8                  1       1       00..00..01..00..00      N/A
hd9var               1       1       00..00..01..00..00      /var
hd4                  2       2       00..00..00..02..00      /
```

Figure 6.4 Listing a disk's contents with **lspv -l**.

The interesting part of the above listing is the distribution. It tells you where on the disk the physical partitions are. The left column of the distribution represents the inner edge and the other columns continue to the outer edge. The output in Figure 6.4 tells us that the paging space (hd6) and the log logical volume (hd8) are on the center of the disk, where they should be for optimum performance. An even more detailed view is available via **lspv -p hdisk0**. The placement of the other file systems is less important, although one should always try to have the data that is accessed most as close as possible to the center. See the discussion of *reorgvg* on page 90.

There is not much that can be changed on an active physical volume, although you could block further allocation of physical partitions to logical volumes, for example, via **chpv -a n hdisk1**. To allow allocation again, use **chpv -a y hdisk1**. If you are about to remove a physical volume from the system you should make it unavailable via **chpv -v r hdisk1**. This ensures that all VGDAs and VGSAs are removed from the ODM and that the physical volume is no longer accessed by the LVM. If you attempt to make the physical volume unavailable while it is still needed for an open volume group the command will fail. To restore the physical volume to an available state use **chpv -v a hdisk1**. The *chpv* command can also be executed via SMIT. Use **smit chpv** to access the correct menu.

6.1.3 Creating volume groups

A standard AIX system has at least one volume group, the root volume group or *rootvg* (dataless systems use *vg00* instead of *rootvg*). It contains the root (/) file system, /usr, and some other logical volumes that are needed by the system. It and the default logical volumes it contains are generated automatically at install time. Many installations work only with the root volume group and never create another one even if they have several disks. This is quite convenient. There is only one volume group to worry about and the system backup via *mksysb* will back up the whole system automatically.

This method is not without drawbacks however. Should one of the disks in the volume group fail and the file system placement was such that its physical volumes were spread over several disks, the file system might become unusable. This is a situation that I never want to encounter. However, when confining file systems to single disks one loses one of the major advantages of the LVM. You should weigh your availability needs, backup policies and needs for large file systems carefully against each other and then decide whether or not you want to spread file systems over disks.

Most of the systems I administer have several disks. I usually have one disk for the root volume group with all the essentials for a smooth operation. This makes installation on a single disk a prerequisite. You should always try to keep the initial installation on one disk if possible. It is much easier to extend volume groups and file systems than to shrink them. I must admit I prefer the maintenance advantages of single-disk volume groups over the convenience of multidisk volume groups. The first disk with its own volume group is used for the /home file system (I call it *homevg*) and then there are others for application data and so on. When using your own disk for the home file system you should delete the /home file system on the *rootvg* to save space first (but keep the mount point). This separation gives more control and the data in the *rootvg* does not need to be backed up so often. Instead of using huge amounts of tape space and time to back up everything via *mksysb* I back up only the user data from the *homevg* and any additional data from other volume groups if needed (see Chapter 13). You should separate disks into volume groups that fits the organization of your data. You will gain more flexibility, better disaster recovery, easier upgrade ability and often better performance out of a well-laid-out system of volume groups. When using external removable disks it is best to keep each of them in a separate volume group to make import and export easier.

How does one create a volume group? Simple, use **smit mkvg** (Figure 6.5). You can choose any descriptive name you want for the volume group; if you do not specify one, the system generates something boring and non descriptive, such as *vg00*, for you. It is particularly important to have a meaningful name when working with portable disks that are exchanged between systems. If the system already has an internal volume group called *vg00* and you want to integrate a portable volume group with the same name you are in trouble if you depend on the name as the system will allocate another one. If you have a very small disk or want to create several very small file systems you might want to use a smaller physical partition size than

4MB; otherwise leave it at the default. If you press <F4> on the line for physical volumes you can choose from the unallocated disks that are available to you. The system will not allow you to create a volume group on disks that are already allocated to a volume group. When exchanging disks between systems you might want to assign a specific major number to avoid duplicate volume group ids.

```
  VOLUME GROUP name                                  []
  Physical partition SIZE in megabytes               4             +
* PHYSICAL VOLUME names                              []            +
  Activate volume group AUTOMATICALLY                yes           +
    at system restart?
* ACTIVATE volume group after it is                  yes           +
    created?
  Volume Group MAJOR NUMBER                          []            +#
```

Figure 6.5 Creating a volume group with **smit mkvg**.

The creation of a volume group via the SMIT menu has one drawback however. It assumes that you want to integrate up to 32 physical volumes into this volume group. This, in turn, creates a large VGDA and wastes some space on the disk and in /etc/vg (about 1MB per disk!). This is reason enough to create the volume group manually. You can claim some of that space, which might be useful if disk space is very tight. To create a volume group called *homevg* on the hard disks *hdisk1* and *hdisk2* with space for two more disks in the VGDA use **mkvg -y homevg -d 4 hdisk1 hdisk2**. The default for *mkvg* is to set the automatic vary on flag. If you do not want the disk to be varied on automatically at system restart use the *-n* flag. If you want to integrate an old disk that still has a VGDA from a previous volume group of which it was a member, use the *f* flag to force the integration. The creation of a volume group via SMIT does this by default. When using *mkvg* directly, you have to use **varyonvg vgname** to activate the volume group. If you do it via SMIT, this command is executed by SMIT automatically.

Once the volume group is created, the only characteristic that can be changed is whether it is automatically activated at boot time. Use **chvg -a y vgname** to set the automatic activation and **chvg -a n vgname** to deactivate it. Of course, you can add or delete physical volumes (disks) from it. On AIX 4 you can also unlock it with the *-u* flag of *chvg*. This can be useful when a LVM command has terminated abnormally and you need to access the VG again.

Once you have a volume group to play with you can have a closer look via *lsvg* (Figure 6.6). This tells you how much space you have used up already and how much is still unallocated in the volume group. Unallocated space on a disk only shows up here and not with the *df* command, which reports free space on already allocated physical space. The number of VGDAs and how many are available to reach a quorum are also shown. Any stale partitions or disks would also be displayed here. Should you have several disks in the volume group then **lsvg -n hdiskn** would give you the same output but specific for the disk. To find out about all active volume groups in the system use **lsvg -o**, which returns a list of volume groups that are on-line. To see the distribution of data over the physical volumes in the volume group use **lsvg -l vgname** and **lsvg -p vgname**, which will show logical and physical volume information respectively.

```
$ lsvg rootvg
VOLUME GROUP:     rootvg              VG IDENTIFIER:   0001390965b18389
VG STATE:         active/complete     PP SIZE:         4 megabyte(s)
VG PERMISSION:    read/write          TOTAL PPs:       239 (956 megabytes)
MAX LVs:          256                 FREE PPs:        12 (48 megabytes)
LVs:              9                   USED PPs:        227 (908 megabytes)
OPEN LVs:         8                   QUORUM:          2
TOTAL PVs:        1                   VG DESCRIPTORS:  2
STALE PVs:        0                   STALE PPs        0
ACTIVE PVs:       1                   AUTO ON:         yes
```

Figure 6.6 Listing a volume group via **lsvg vgname**.

6.1.4 Activating and deactivating a volume group

When a volume group is activated via *varyonvg* the following steps are executed:

(1) The VGDA of each physical volume is read.
(2) The header and trailer time stamps of each VGDA are compared. If they match the VGDA is accepted as valid.
(3) If the number of the usable VGDAs reaches the quorum value the volume group is varied on; otherwise *varyonvg* fails.
(4) The most recent VGDA is used to update the other VGDAs.

Should mirroring be active for one of the logical volumes in this volume group, the *syncvg* command is executed to synchronize all copies of the mirrored logical volume. This can be suppressed by the *-n* flag for *varyonvg*.

The activation of volume groups usually happens automatically at boot time, but occasionally it is necessary to run *varyonvg* manually, for example when in maintenance mode or importing a portable disk.

If the above fails and you are desperate to access the volume group, you might want to run *varyonvg* with the force flag (*-f*). However, make sure that you have checked every other troublespot first as it is very easy to lose data this way. There might be inconsistencies between the ODM and the VGDA. By using the *-m* flag the contents of the VGDA is used to update the ODM. When *-m1* is specified then the update is forced. To update the ODM only if errors are detected, use *-m2*.

When a volume group is no longer needed on-line it can be deactivated via **varyoffvg vgname**. This assumes that all file systems on it are unmounted already; it will fail if file systems from this volume group are still mounted.

Both the *varyonvg* and *varyoffvg* command support the *-s* flag to put the volume group into maintenance mode. In this mode the logical volume commands work on the volume group but file systems from it cannot be mounted.

6.1.5 Extending and shrinking volume groups

Volume groups are extensible in the running system via either **extendvg vgname hdiskn** or **smit extendvg**. The only difference is that SMIT uses the *-f* flag by default, which forces the inclusion of the disk even if it still has an old VGDA from its former life. After the extension the additional space is immediately available. If you choose a hard disk that contains data but which is not in a currently active volume group, the disk will be integrated and your data will be lost. Be sure to select the correct disk.

The *reducevg* command or **smit reducevg** works the other way. As soon as there are no more physical volumes in a volume group the volume group ceases to exist. When used with the *-d* flag the *reducevg* command will remove all logical volumes that are still on the physical volume. This is dangerous. You should only use it if those logical volumes are no longer active. Be careful with logical volumes that are distributed over several physical volumes. By also specifying the *-f* flag the system proceeds without any questions and forces the removal.

6.1.6 The import/export business

When working with portable disks or for performing major surgery on the system you might want to import or export volume groups. This is a clean way to tell the system about volume groups that should be integrated into the system or that are no longer available.

The import of a volume group tells the system about a new volume group by getting the volume group data from a disk. This is as simple as **importvg hdiskn**. The *importvg* command reads the disk's VGDA to find out about the volume group. You therefore need to specify only one physical volume even if the volume group you are importing contains several disks. In addition to importing the volume group, all logical volumes in it are also imported and made known to the system and the appropriate changes are added to /etc/filesystems. Should the system encounter duplicate names for either the volume group or the logical volumes, it will automatically create new names to avoid any clashes. This still might cuase problems as there might be dependencies on the names. By using the *-y* flag you can specify a different name for the imported volume group. To activate the disk, you then need to run *varyonvg*.

Volume groups that are to be removed from the system but used again elsewhere should be exported via **exportvg vgname**. All that actually happens is that the definition of the volume group in the ODM and the entry in /etc/vgs are removed. This is very important for volume groups that are moved among systems. It ensures that there are no clashes when a volume group that has been used on another system comes back. In particular, when the definition of logical volumes in the volume group is changed on the remote system, the *exportvg* command will avoid many problems. Both commands can be run from SMIT as **smit importvg** and **smit exportvg** respectively.

6.1.7 Working with logical volumes

Logical volumes are created via the *mklv* command. If you are not interested in raw logical volumes and you only want to create file systems, then use *crfs*, which will run *mklv* under the covers for you. When using *crfs*, many of the options of *mklv* are not available; for more control first use *mklv* and then create the file system with *crfs* in it.

If you want to access raw logical volumes you should be aware that there is a logical volume control block (LVCB) at the beginning of the disk. Data bases quite often want to write to raw logical volumes. Overwriting the LVCB should not be too harmful unless you want to use mirroring, in which case an overwritten LVCB will render it useless.

The *mklv* command has so many options and is used so rarely that you will run it mostly from SMIT via **smit mklv**. If you are only interested in standard file systems you can ignore this completely and just use **smit jfs**, the front end to the *crfs* command, which will give you only the subset of options that is needed for journaled file systems. This is discussed in Section 6.2. The menu that is associated with *mklv* is shown in Figure 6.7.

```
  Logical volume NAME                           []
* VOLUME GROUP name                              rootvg
* Number of LOGICAL PARTITIONS                  []                     #
  PHYSICAL VOLUME names                         []                     +
  Logical volume TYPE                           []
  POSITION on physical volume                    midway                +
  RANGE of physical volumes                      minimum               +
  MAXIMUM NUMBER of PHYSICAL VOLUMES            []                     #
    to use for allocation
  Number of COPIES of each logical               1                     +
    partition
  Mirror Write Consistency?                      yes                   +
  Allocate each logical partition copy           yes                   +
    on a SEPARATE physical volume?
  RELOCATE the logical volume during             yes                   +
    reorganization?
  Logical volume LABEL                          []
  MAXIMUM NUMBER of LOGICAL PARTITIONS          [128]
  Enable BAD BLOCK relocation?                   yes                   +
  SCHEDULING POLICY for writing logical          parallel              +
    partition copies
  Enable WRITE VERIFY?                           no                    +
  File containing ALLOCATION MAP                []
  Stripe Size?                                  [Not Striped]          +
```

Figure 6.7 Creating a logical volume with **smit mklv**.

If you create a logical volume manually then you probably want to give it a special name, otherwise the system will use something non descriptive, such as *lv00*, for it. The initial size is given in physical partitions and you can tell the system on which physical volumes the logical volume should be created when the volume group contains several disks. If you do not specify a volume type it defaults to JFS. Other types are paging, sysdump, boot or jfslog.

An important point is the position on the physical volume. The center of the disk is faster than the inner or outer edge because the average seek time to it is the shortest. As you cannot have all data in the center you have to decide where to put what. You can set the range of physical volumes to minimum, which enhances the reliability in case of disk failures. The other option is maximum, which will give you better performance because the data is spread over several disks that can be accessed in parallel. If you want to mirror the data you can specify the number of copies here. Allocating each copy on a separate physical volume is a default that you should accept otherwise usefulness of mirroring is greatly reduced.

The relocation attribute is needed when reorganizing volume groups. If it is set, then the logical volume can be moved on the volume group. This allows you to change the placement of logical volumes by specifying different positions and then running *reorgvg*. Or, in other words, should you discover that the initial placement of file systems on the disks is not right for optimal performance you can rearrange it later on when this attribute is set. It can be set and reset later via **chlv -r y yourlv**. The logical volume label specified in this menu is usually a mount point or the name of the file system. A standard troublespot is the maximum number of logical partitions. When creating large logical volumes the default of 128 is too small. It gives you only 512MB with the default physical partition size of 4MB. You will need to increase this attribute for larger file systems. You can do so at a later time via **chlv -x maxpv yourlv**.

The LVM can reallocate bad blocks automatically under the covers even if your disk subsystem cannot. I have yet to find a SCSI disk on the RS/6000 that does not do so. Leave the reallocation attribute at its default yes value. Should the LVM do any reallocation you will get a notice in the error log. If this happens often you may need a replacement disk if it is not recoverable by a format through diagnostics. The options that are especially interesting for mirrored logical volumes are discussed in Section 6.1.8. For some special cases it might make sense to manually specify an allocation map. You could specify exact physical partitions to be used for this logical volume in the map file.

On AIX 4 systems you also can specify a stripe size. When entering a stripe size you activate striping. Striping allows you actively to spread out logical volumes over several disks in such a way that the system will uses several disks at the same time per access, should the access be large enough. When using large sequential reads and writes striping can increase performance quite a bit. For other cases it is not very useful.

For a file with several blocks that needs to be written to disk and a logical volume that is striped across three real disks, you will have three write accesses in parallel, one to each disk writing blocks 1, 2, and 3 (Figure 6.8). The next write will write the next three blocks again to three disks simultaneously. As the disks are usually slower then the CPU issuing the write request, the system can theoretically triple the write speed in this case. Of course, there is some overhead involved so using three disks will not really triple the speed, but it will increase it significantly. The same applies to reading from a striped logical volume. Striping is not available when you use mirroring. You have to choose between availability and speed. The default is not to use striping. For optimum performance, all disks used in a striped logical volume should be connected to different SCSI adapters.

Block allocation for unstriped logical volumes

1	2	3	4	5
6	7	8	9	10
11	12	13	14	15

16	17	18	19	20
21	22	23	24	25
26	27	28	29	30

31	32	33	34	35
36	37	38	39	40
41	42	43	44	45

Block allocation for striped logical volumes

1	4	7	10	13
16	19	22	25	28
31	35	38	41	44

2	5	8	11	14
17	20	23	26	29
32	36	39	42	45

3	6	9	12	15
18	21	24	27	30
34	37	40	43	46

Figure 6.8 Striping on AIX 4 with a logical volume that is spread over three disks.

To create a striped logical volume named *stripedlv* on the hard disks hdisk1 to 3 with a size of 120 physical partitions and a stripe size of 32 KB use:

```
mklv -ystripedlv -S32K datavg 120 hdisk1 hdisk2 hdisk3
```

The file system /stripedfs is then created on the previously defined *stripedlv* with

```
crfs -vjfs -dstripedlv -m/stripedfs -Ayes -prw -tno -a frag=4096
-a nbpi=4096 -a compress=no
```

Mount it and you are ready to go.

Access to the disk on non striped LVs is via logical disk blocks. On striped volumes access is done by stripe units. A stripe consists of a stripe unit per allocated disk. The stripe unit size is specified at logical volume creation time and can be any power of two ranging from 4 KB to 128 KB.

Most of the things you can set with *mklv* can be changed later on with *chlv*. Extension of logical volumes is done with *extendlv*. Should the maximum number of logical partitions for this logical volume be too small, a new maximum can be specified with the *extendlv* command as well. For example, **extendlv -x 200 mylv 20** would increase *mylv* by 20 logical partitions and at the same time set the upper boundary for logical partitions to 200. This will not, however, extend the file system on this logical volume. The extension of file systems should be done directly by *chfs*, which will do everything in one step.

To monitor logical volumes the *lslv* command can be used (Figure 6.9). Use it either as **lslv lvname** to give you an overview of the characteristics or as **lslv -l lvname** to show you the physical partitions that are allocated and whether the distribution of the physical volumes on the disk matches what you specified when setting the characteristics for the logical volume.

```
$ lslv hd2
LOGICAL VOLUME:     hd2                    VOLUME GROUP:   rootvg
LV IDENTIFIER:      00013909 65b18389.6    PERMISSION:     read/write
VG STATE:           active/complete        LV STATE:       opened/syncd
TYPE:               jfs                    WRITE VERIFY:   off
MAX LPs:            190                    PP SIZE:        4 megabyte(s)
COPIES:             1                      SCHED POLICY:   parallel
LPs:                175                    PPs:            175
STALE PPs:          0                      BB POLICY:      relocatable
INTER-POLICY:       minimum                RELOCATABLE:    yes
INTRA-POLICY:       center                 UPPER BOUND     32
MOUNT POINT:        /usr                   LABEL:          /usr
MIRROR WRITE CONSISTENCY: on
EACH LP COPY ON A SEPARATE PV ?: yes
$ lslv -l hd2
hd2:/usr
PV                COPIES         IN BAND      DISTRIBUTION
hdisk0            175:000:000    5%           044:027:010:046:048
```

Figure 6.9 Listing logical volumes with *lslv*.

The output of *lslv* in Figure 6.9 is somewhat disturbing. The intra-disk allocation policy is center but it is achived by only 5%; most of the data is spread all over the disk, which is not a very good solution for the /usr file system that stores all the commands the system uses. If possible, one should set the reallocatable flag for all moveable file systems in this volume group and run **reorgvg rootvg** to allow the system to try to move the physical partitions to places that fit better with the specified intra-disk policy.

If you use a striped logical volume, then *lslv* will also tell you the stripe width and size. Whereas **lslv vgname** will give you the information stored in the ODM, the VGDA information is obtained by using *lslv* with the disk name, as in **lslv -n hdisk0 hd2**.

6.1.8 Mirroring and other safety nets

Mirroring works by associating two or three physical partitions with each logical partition of a logical volume. This means that mirroring can be done on a file system basis rather than on a disk or volume group basis. Mirroring can be established for a logical volume at any time, not only when creating it.

When you want to use mirroring it is necessary to select a scheduling policy for disk access. Write operations on copies can be either sequential or parallel and there are two more options to make the system more reliable.

Sequential write When using sequential write the copies are updated in order. The system waits for the first write to be completed before it continues to write the next copy. Reading is always done from the primary copy; only if the read operation fails is the next copy tried. The primary copy is then fixed by writing the data from the secondary copy to the first disk while at the same time reallocating the disk block.

Parallel write Writes are all started together. The write operation is finished when the last copy is written and can therefore take longer than sequential writing. Reads are done from the next available copy. This speeds up read operations on mirrored data. If the read fails, the same reallocation as with the sequential write policy happens.

Mirror write consistency (MWC)

The LVM ensures that the mirrored data is consistent across all the copies during normal operation. But what happens in case of a crash or another malfunction? The LVM needs to know which copies are correct and which copies are not yet up to date. Information about the state of the writes is kept in the mirror write consistency record, which is basically just a special sector on disk. The information in the MWC record is used when the volume group is synchronized or varied on to make the information for a logical partition consistent again. Use of the MWC record is off by default, you have to set it yourself when creating a mirrored JFS.

Write verify A third means of protecting your data is the write verify option. This also needs to be set explicitly when creating the mirrored file system and can also be set for non mirrored logical volumes. When activated, each write to the logical volume is checked by a read immediately following the write. Because of the additional read operation from disk, this option has a large impact on performance.

The SMIT fastpath to add a copy to a logical volume is **smit mklvcopy**, or you could specify that the logical volume has mirrored copies when creating a logical volume via **smit mklv**. To start mirroring for a logical volume from the command line, use **mklvcopy yourlv 1 hdiskn**. This would add one copy on *hdiskn* to each logical partition in *yourlv*. The reverse command is *rmlvcopy* with the same syntax. Any time you change the number of copies you should run **syncvg vgname** to resynchronize the copies. But you have to be aware that *syncvg* will take some time to complete its job. On AIX 4 it can happen that *syncvg* returns but the task is not finished. Use *lsvg* to see whether there are still stale physical partitions in the volume group. Proceed only after *lsvg* no longer shows stale physical volumes.

Here is a more complete example that assumes that the volume group where your data resides (*datavg*) has three hard disks (*hdisk1*, *hdisk2* and *hdisk3*) and two mirrored file systems (*datalv1* and *datalv2*) with 100 and 150 logical partitions respectively. Mirror write consistency is switched on, we use three copies and the maximum size for the logical volumes is set to 150 logical partitions on both file systems. To create this setup use:

```
mkvg -y datavg hdisk1 hdisk2 hdisk3
mklv -y datalv1 -u 3 -w y -x 150 -c 3 datavg 100 hdisk1 hdisk2 hdisk3
mklv -y datalv2 -u 3 -w y -x 150 -c 3 datavg 150 hdisk1 hdisk2 hdisk3
crfs -v jfs -d datlv1 -m /data/one -A
crfs -v jfs -d datlv2 -m /data/two -A
mklvcopy fsloglv00 hdisk2 hdisk3
```

The last step assumes you have not yet created other volume groups since *fsloglv00* is the default name for the first JFS log that is generated. This is generated by default on the first physical volume of the volume group and you need to tell the LVM that you want this to be mirrored as well. If you do not mirror it, your write performance will be better but the reliability will be greatly reduced.

Now that you have mirroring active, what can you do if one copy goes bad to get in synch again? Usually a physical partition is marked valid in normal operation. Should access to it fail it will be marked stale and the system knows it cannot be accessed or trusted. There are two ways to get it back to the valid state: resynchronizing the logical volume in the running system via **syncvg vgname** or activating a volume group via *varyonvg*. This is all very easy when the drive failed because of a failing power supply or other reasons that do not make it necessary physically to replace the drive. But what if you really need to replace the drive?

If it is still possible to access the old disk (I use the definitions from above for the example, assuming *hdisk3* went bad) then use the following sequence of actions:

(1) Do make a backup if you do not have one yet.

(2) Make the physical volume inaccessible for normal file system operation by **chpv -v r hdisk3**.

(3) Use **rmlvcopy datalv1 2 hdisk3** to remove the copies for *datalv1* from *hdisk3*. Do the same for *datalv2*.

(4) If you have any non mirrored logical volumes on this physical volume that are not spread over several disks, remove them via *rmlv*.

(5) If you have data in the volume group that is spread over several disks including *hdisk3* then use *migratepv* to move the data off the disk. You might get errors if there are problems accessing the disk, but this is the only way to make sure that the spread file system is at least consistent on the remaining disks even if you lose data.

(6) Remove the physical volume from the volume group by **reducevg datavg hdisk3**.

(7) Use **rmdev -l hdisk3 -d** to remove the disk from the ODM and deactivate it.

(8) Remove the disk from the SCSI bus. As long as the SCSI bus is terminated you can do this even in a running system.

(9) Add the new SCSI disk. Be sure that the SCSI address is right.

(10) If you have done the previous two steps with a running system then either run **cfgmgr** or add the disk manually via **smit makdsk**, otherwise the system will add the disk automatically at boot time. Because we removed *hdisk3* in step 6 the system will probably reuse the name for the new disk. If not, use the name the system has assigned to the new drive in the remaining steps.

(11) Add the disk via **extendvg datavg hdisk3** to the volume group.

(12) Now run **mklvcopy datalv1 hdisk3 ; mklvcopy datalv2 hdisk3 ; mklvcopy fsloglv00 hdisk3**. This will add the new copies to the new disk.

(13) Finally, run **syncvg datavg**.

If you are particularly interested in high reliability you should test such disaster recovery procedures before going into production mode.

Unfortunately, the process of getting data in and out of volume groups and using it elsewhere is somewhat complicated. This precludes mirroring from a snapshot backup strategy. Otherwise, one might use a mirrored copy, remove it from the volume group and move it to another, make a backup of it and then reintegrate it into the original volume group.

Special logical volumes

There are some logical volumes that are special for the system.

/dev/hd5 The boot logical volume contains a stripped down version of AIX that is used to boot the system. Without this the system does not come up. The boot logical volume is created and updated via the *bosboot* command. If you have several disks in your root volume group then you should create a boot logical volume on each of them so that the system can boot even if the boot logical volume on the first disk is not available. This is done via **bosboot -d hdiskn -a**, where *hdiskn* stands for the disk on which you want to create the boot image. After you have done this for all disks in the root volume group you also need to tell the system to look for a boot image not only on *hdisk0* but on the other ones as well. You can do so via the *bootlist* command. To tell the system that it should try booting from *hdisk0 hdisk1* and *hdisk2* in that order use **bootlist -m normal hdisk0 hdisk1 hdisk2**. You are still in trouble when the system chooses an alternate boot volume, but at least the system comes up and you can try to repair the damage. This logical volume should never be moved when reorganizing a volume group. Make sure it has its reorganize attribute set to false by **chlv -rn hd5**.

/dev/hd6 The standard paging space, which is automatically created at installation time. Paging space is not manipulated via the logical volume commands. There is a separate family of commands for it - *mkps, rmps, chps* and *lsps* - which are discussed in Section 6.5.

/dev/hd7 This logical volume is used to store system dumps in case of a crash on AIX 3. It does not exist on AIX 4 as AIX 4 uses the paging space (usually /dev/hd6) for dumps. It is created at installation time in the root volume group. Sometimes this is too small for dumps, but for most users this logical volume is of no concern. To see the size needed for a complete system dump run **sysdumpdev -e**. It can be used by developers to analyze dumps via the *crash* command.

This logical volume should never be moved when reorganizing a volume group. Make sure it does not have its reorganize attribute set by **chlv -r n hd7**.

/dev/hd8 The log logical volume for JFS. It is created at boot time and stores the transaction log for the JFS file systems on the rootvg or the first physical volume. The function of the log logical volume is discussed in Section 6.2.

6.1.9 Working with the LVM

Moving logical volumes

You may sometimes want to move logical volumes, for example to clean up and make a disk free, prepare for mirroring, or to spread your data for better performance. The *migratepv* command can help with this. If you want to move all data from one disk to another within a volume group, simply entering **migratepv sourcepv targetpv** will do it for you. If you want to move only a specific logical volume then **migratepv -l yourlv sourcepv targetpv** can be used. You need to be sure that this is the only activity of the LVM on those physical volumes when using *migratepv*. This should not be a problem when you are the only one logged in. If you really want to make sure that no other LVM activity interferes you should run **stopsrc -a** and **killall** first or go into maintenance mode by **shutdown -m**. Migrating data in the root volume group has some potential pitfalls. Some things required for booting and for the dump device are directly accessed without the retranslation of the LVM. You need to recreate this information after the move. And to be absolutely sure that we do not run into problems programs during the move should a crash occur we also need to tell the system about a different dump device during the move. The placement of the dump device is another thing that is 'hard coded' once it is there and needs some special commands to move it. Assuming that you have two disks in the root volume group, *hdisk0* and *hdisk1*, with *hdisk0* containing all the boot logical volume and other essentials, you can migrate all the data from *hdisk0* to *hdisk1* via the following commands:

```
sysdumpdev -p /dev/sysdumpnull
migratepv hdisk0 hdisk1
bosboot -a -d /dev/hdisk1
sysdumpdev -P -p /dev/hd7
```

On AIX 4 you would use /dev/hd6 instead of /dev/hd7. If you then want to remove *hdisk0* from the root volume group you can do so via:

```
reducevg rootvg hdisk0
```

Reorganizing volume groups

The *reorgvg* command can be used to redistribute the physical partitions in a volume group so that they better correspond to the placement policies specified for the logical volumes. The *reorgvg* command will move only logical volumes for which the relocation attribute is set to true. This can be done via **chlv -r y lvname**. There are some logical volumes that should not be moved: the boot logical volume and the system dump device on AIX 3. To make sure that they are not moved, use **chlv -r n hd5** and **chlv -r n hd7**. On AIX 4 you do not need to worry about *hd7*. When reorganizing volume groups you should be sure that no other activity is interfering with the process. Use **shutdown -m** to go into maintenance mode so that you can be sure you are the only one working with the system. After you have set your allocation policies with either *chlv* or **smit chlv**, you then can run *reorgvg*. To move only *hd2* and *hd1* in the root volume group while also favoring *hd2* use **reorgvg rootvg hd2 hd1**. You can now go for a coffee break or lunch depending on the size of the logical volumes that you want to have reorganized as the process will take some time. For each logical volume that has been reorganized the program prints a message indicating its progress.

If you do not specify any logical volumes on the *reorgvg* command line then all logical volumes where the reallocate attribute is set are considered. You can limit the reorganization to specific physical volumes by entering their names on *reorgvg*'s *stdin* and specifying the *-i* flag: **echo hdisk1 | reorgvg -i rootvg hd2 hd1** would reallocate only the parts of *hd2* and *hd1* which are on *hdisk1*. You might need several runs of *reorgvg* to achieve the distribution you want as there is no way of ranking the file systems. In particular, when working with only one disk and not many free partitions it takes some time to achieve the desired results as the system needs plenty of spare partitions to do a reallocation fast.

There are two logical volumes that should always be in the center for good performance: the paging space and the JFS log. If you have a disk that has those types of logical volumes, be sure that you move them to the center and then lock them there by disallowing reallocation (**chlv -r n hd8** for example).

Reorganizing volume groups to move file systems into faster disk regions will not necessarily make file access faster. LVM does not know about files, so that logical partitions that stored a file in sequence might now be separated. You would need to dump the files to a tape, remove the contents of the file system and then restore the files to get them onto disk in an unfragmented form.

Beware of moving hard disks

Owing to the automatic configuration of devices, the names of physical volumes are not constant between reinstallations if drives have been added to the system after the installation. Using a clone tape to reinstall a system without having changed a bit in the configuration can still result in different hard disk names as the order in which they are integrated into the system is defined by their placement on the SCSI bus and not on the sequence in which they where originally added to the system.

6.1.10 The LVM and large disks

With the increasing popularity of large disks (4GB and greater), one can easily run into problems with the LVM limit of 1016 physical partitions per physical volume. With the default physical partition size of 4MB the maximum logical volume is 4064MB. Newer AIX releases will automatically use a bigger physical partition size at install time if a large installation disk is detected, but if one creates additional volume groups one needs to be aware of that limit.

6.2 The journaled file system

The journaled file system is one of the major advantages of AIX over other UNIX systems. At the time of writing only one vendor on the market has a similar function for PC-based UNIX systems as an option. However, with the advent of DCE/DFS this functionality should become more widespread. Even so, AIX is the only operating system that is shipped with a complete journaled file system by default.

After one paragraph of bragging about it I should probably explain the advantage of the JFS over traditional UNIX file systems (or the OS/2 HPFS, which is in any case nothing more than a UNIX-like file system). The major drawback of UNIX file systems is their vulnerability to crashes. Because file system data and meta data is cached in dynamic memory, changes to the file system structure might be in memory and not yet on disk. Should a power outage or some other form of crash occur at that instant then the file system structure on the disk is inconsistent. In very bad cases the file system might be completely lost. The minimum penalty is usually a lengthy *fsck* run to get the file system back. The JFS is the solution to this problem. It provides a transaction-oriented access and recovery mechanism for file system meta data. Or, in other words, it is very hard to corrupt the file system on AIX and the days of endless *fsck* runs during the boot phase are gone forever. Whenever a change to the file system meta data of the file system is started this change is recorded in a transaction log, the JFS log. When the change is finished another entry in the log is made. If there is only one entry the system knows that the last action failed because of a crash and cleans up anything that happened after the last correct check point.

I have been working with AIX on the RISC System/6000 since before its introduction and have a habit of playing with beta code. For me it is quite normal to crash machines or switch them off without a proper shutdown. I have never had to run *fsck* because of this and I have never had any file system problems due to a non proper shutdown. This does not imply that the data is always safe however. The JFS protects only itself, not the user data. Just imagine the size of the transaction log if it were also to log all changes to the file data. Investment in mirroring and other means is necessary to achieve data protection. So do not switch your machines off while your database application is still running!

The JFS is the only native file system type that AIX supports (not counting CD ROM support and NFS). It always does journaling; this cannot be turned off. A JFS is just one type of logical volume, so all the logical volume management commands from the previous sections can be used on it. However, they use the device name of the logical volume and not the mount point name for specifying the victim. When using the file system commands you can usually use both names.

6.2.1 Working with journaled file systems

Journaled file systems are created via *crfs* or **smit crfs**. If you want to add the file system /usr/local to the root volume group you could do so via **crfs -v jfs -g rootvg -m /usr/local -A yes -asize=200000**. This creates a logical volume with some default name, such as *lv00*, with a size of 100MB in the root volume group and which is mounted automatically at system restart; the mount point is /usr/local. The size of the file system is specified with 512-byte blocks to make life more confusing. The size you get is the size you specified rounded up to the nearest logical partition boundary. In other words, file systems are like logical volumes allocated with a granularity of logical partitions.

By default, a JFS is created with a fragment size of 4KB. This means that even a tiny one-screen E-mail message of less than 2KB takes up 4KB of disk space. When you create a file system on AIX 4 you can change the fragment size to 512, 1024 or 2048 bytes if 4KB is too large for your needs. This is done with the

-a frag=1024 parameters to *crfs*. You should use a different fragment size only if you do not want to exchange the disk between AIX 3 and AIX 4 systems as only the 4KB fragment size on AIX 4 allows that. The file systems /home and /var are created with a fragment size of 512 bytes initially on AIX 4 to be more space efficient. Small fragments work only for files that are less than 32KB in size. Files that are 32KB or larger will always use a 4KB fragment size. The larger a file is, the less it will profit from fragments. The overhead of managing fragments would become very costly for those files, therefore they are not used. If optimum throughput is your goal, leave the fragment size for new file systems at the default value of 4KB. Once you start to use fragments you should occasionally check the overall disk fragmentation of those file systems. This can be done with **defragfs -r /home**. To defragment the file system use **defragfs /home**. As AIX needs to allocate fragments in a continuous way, fragmentation will not only reduce performance but also decrease the available disk space over time. When defragmenting a file system, the number of available contiguous fragments is increased.

In addition to the fragment size, you can specify the ratio i-nodes to file system size on AIX 4. With the availability of fragments, one needs to be able to accommodate much larger numbers of files per file system than before. The number of bytes per i-node (NBPI) value allows you to specify the number of i-nodes in a file system (*-a nbpi=1024*). As files systems can be dynamically extended, this value gives a ratio and not a fixed number. For each NBPI bytes in the file system an i-node is allocated. The NBPI values range from 512 to 16384. If you anticipate a large number of small files in a file system you would use a fragment size of 512 or 1024 together with an NBPI value of 512 or 1024. Unless you mostly have one-fragment-sized files, you should use a NBPI value higher than the fragment size to avoid wasting disk space on i-nodes. On a file system with only a few large files a NBPI value of 16384 makes the most sense.

The NBPI value also defines the maximum size of a file system, as follows:

NBPI	Maximum size in GB	Maximum size in blocks
512	8	16777216
1024	16	33554432
2048	32	67108864
4096	64	134217728

Another addition on AIX 4 is the support of compressed file systems. Current CPU speeds often allow compression on file systems without major performance hits (use *crfs* with *-acompress=LZ*). Consider any type of on-line archive for example. If you store large scientific data files or have a collection of PostScript files in a separate file system then compression can be a huge space (and therefore money) saver. As the compression happens transparently you do not need to worry about the compress/decompress steps yourself, it is done by the system. Compression happens at quite a low level; you can even NFS export compressed file systems.

Compression happens at logical block level. If one does not use fragments then it will not save any space. Thus *crfs* refuses to create compressed file systems if the fragment size is 4 KB: the fragment size has to be less than 4 KB. The performance impact of a compressed file system is about 50 cycles per byte written and 10 cycles per byte read.

As the output of **df -k** and **du-k** in Figure 6.10 shows, using compressed file systems presents a few pitfalls. Backup/restore between compressed and uncompressed file systems (or file systems with compression and different fragment sizes) might bring surprises as the real disk space requirements differ.

```
$ du -k /uncompressed /lz-compressed
1993     /uncompressed
1287     /lz-compressed
$ df -k /uncompressed /lz-compressed
Filesystem 1024-blocks    Free %Used Iused %Iused  Mounted on
/dev/lv01          12288    9732   20%    17     0%  /uncompressed
/dev/lv00          12288   10440   15%    17     0%  /lz-compressed
$ ls -l /uncompressed /lz-compressed
/lz-compressed:
total 2572
-r-xr-xr-x   1 root      sys        2038417 Aug  7 13:59 unix
/uncompressed:
total 3984
-r-xr-xr-x   1 root      sys        2038417 Aug  7 13:59 unix
```

Figure 6.10 The impact of compression.

The *crfs* command does not mount the new file system at creation time: you still have to use the *mount* command yourself. Should you be unhappy with the default name for the logical volume assigned by *crfs*, you can change it via either **smit chlv2** or **chlv -n newname oldname**. The SMIT version has the advantage that you can select the old name from a list. You can get a list of file systems via *lsfs* yourself if you are not using SMIT.

To change attributes of an existing file system use *chfs* or **smit chfs**. Most of the options for *crfs* are available here as well. Most of the time you will find yourself typing something like **chfs -asize=+100000 /home** to increase the size of a file system, but you could also change the log logical volume (jfslog) to some other logical volume by specifying *-alogname=someloglv*. Why would you want to do this? For performance reasons. Writing to the log takes some time. If the log is on the same disk then you need a seek inbetween. If the log is on another disk then the seek can happen in parallel with the original write operation. A standard performance tip is to have the logs for several disks on a different disk. This, of course, reduces the overall reliability, but you cannot have both speed and high availability. For extreme performance requirements you could buy a solid-state disk to put the log on.

Another way of increasing performance is to place the most used file systems in the center of the disk and spread file systems over disks to minimize seek times (see page 90).

If you want to get rid of a file system use **rmfs /filesystem** after you have unmounted it. This will remove the associated logical volume and, if you specify the *-r* flag, also the mount point.

6.2.2 Changing the size of file systems

Why have a section on changing the size of file systems when all it takes is a **chfs -asize=+N filesystem** to make it bigger? Well, first there are limits to file system sizes and second the *chfs* command can only increases the size not reduce it. The size of a file system or, rather, logical volume has a limit of 128 logical partitions by default, which usually means you can have only 512MB in a file system. That limit can be changed however. Either use **smit chlv1** to get to the right menu or use **chlv -xN hdx**, where *N* is the new maximum number of logical partitions and *hdx* stands for the logical volume you want to change. You can then use *chfs* again to extend the file system up the new limit.

A much more interesting problem is decreasing the size of a file system. Basically you are back to the old times:

(1) Back up the data with you favorite backup command.

(2) Delete the file system. Use **umount /whatever && rmfs /whatever**.

(3) Create a new file system either via **smit crfs** or by **crfs -v jfs -g volumegroup -asize=SizeIn512ByteBlocks -mMountPoint -Ayes -prw -tno**.

(4) Restore the data from tape.

Easy but tedious. Now what about decreasing the size of a file system that cannot be deleted, such as /usr? This is very difficult. The easiest way is to create a bootable backup tape that will use a different size for the /usr file system. Here are the steps for AIX 3.2:

(1) Create a complete image backup via **mkszfile && mksysb /dev/rmt0** so that you can recover in case something goes wrong in the following steps.

(2) Edit the /.fs.size file that you created with the above *mkszfile* command. It contains information about all normal file systems within the root volume group which are backed up by *mksysb*.

(3) Modify /.fs.size so that it has the new size for the /usr file system. The file will look something like Figure 6.11.

```
imageinstall
rootvg 4 hd4 / 2 8 jfs
rootvg 4 hd2 /usr 134 536 jfs
rootvg 4 hd9var /var 2 8 jfs
rootvg 4 hd3 /tmp 3 12 jfs
rootvg 4 hd1 /home 14 56 jfs
```

Figure 6.11 The contents of /.fs.size.

Each record contains the volume group, the logical partition size in MB, the name of the logical volume, the name of the file system, the size in physical partitions, the size in MB, and the type of the logical volume. You now have to change the size values for /usr to reflect your new size. Be sure that you have at least 8MB free on the new /usr file system. You also should have at least 8MB free in /tmp. If you do not have enough free space then the install will fail. Be sure to specify a size that leaves enough room for your files and the installation process.

(4) Run **mksysb /dev/rmt0**. The newly created tape contains an image of your system that will have a smaller /usr file system when installed again.

(5) Boot from this tape and install the new image.

On AIX 4 the steps are similar. Instead of editing /.fs.size you will have to modify the /image.data file.

(1) Create a complete image backup via **mksysb -i /dev/rmt0** so that you can recover in case something goes wrong in the following steps.

(2) Edit the /image.data file that you created with the above *mkszfile* command. It contains information about all normal file systems within the root volume group which are backed up by *mksysb*.

(3) Modify /image.data so that it has the new size for the /usr file system. In the file you will find a stanza for the /usr file system. Modify the points that you need (Figure 6.12).

There is a stanza like that in Figure 6.12 for each logical volume. The lines marked in boldface are the ones of interest here. Change the value for *LPs* to match your new size. Be sure that this is a size above or equal to the one listed for *LV_MIN_LPS* because the system needs those logical partitions at minimum to restore /usr.

```
lv_data:
        VOLUME_GROUP= rootvg
        LV_SOURCE_DISK_LIST= hdisk0
        LV_IDENTIFIER= 00001798685c50c8.5
        LOGICAL_VOLUME= hd2
        VG_STAT= active/complete
        TYPE= jfs
        MAX_LPS= 512
        COPIES= 1
        LPs= 120
        STALE_PPs= 0
        INTER_POLICY= minimum
        INTRA_POLICY= center
        MOUNT_POINT= /usr
        MIRROR_WRITE_CONSISTENCY= on
        LV_SEPARATE_PV= yes
        PERMISSION= read/write
        LV_STATE= opened/syncd
        WRITE_VERIFY= off
        PP_SIZE= 4
        SCHED_POLICY= parallel
        PP= 120
        BB_POLICY= relocatable
        RELOCATABLE= yes
        UPPER_BOUND= 32
        LABEL= /usr
        MAPFILE=
        LV_MIN_LPS= 114
```

Figure 6.12 The contents of /image.data.

(4) Run **mksysb /dev/rmt0**. The newly created tape contains an image of your system that will have a smaller /usr file system when installed again.

(5) Boot from this tape and install the new image.

On AIX 4 there is an easier way however. When installing from an image backup, you can ask the system to shrink all file systems to their minimum size.

6.3 Using *fsck*

Occasionally one still needs to use *fsck* on file systems to fix minor problems. There are two problems however. First, one cannot run *fsck* on mounted file systems, it will always report errors; second, one cannot unmount /usr to fix it in normal operation. On any file system that you can unmount in normal operation you can use *fsck* directly after unmounting it.

All the file systems that cannot be unmounted in normal operation can be checked from the maintenance mode. Use a bootable tape, CD or floppies to boot the system. On AIX 4 you should then follow the menus to access the root volume group but without mounting the file systems. On AIX 3 get into a maintenance shell and execute **getroofs hdisk0 sh**, where hdisk0 stands for your boot disk. Then run *fsck* on the file system in question, **sync** twice and reboot.

6.4 Files that grow

AIX keeps several log files for various subsystems. You should keep an eye on them as some of them grow until their file system is full. You could modify /usr/sbin/skulker to delete some of them automatically, but this only works for files that are not constantly accessed, such as smit.log files. It will not work for files that *syslogd* uses, as *syslogd* keeps its log files open all the time. Those files that are kept open all time can be truncated from the shell with the command > **filename**. On AIX 4 you can use the performance diagnostic tool to monitor those files and directories (see page 347). Here is a list of places and files that you should check regularly.

/var/spool This directory and its subdirectories are the prime locations for spool files which will vary in size and can grow extremely fast.

/var/spool/mail All the mail for users ends up in this directory. You should check it regularly for mail to users that no longer exist or mail to ids that are not used.

/var/spool/lpd Here you find temporary files of the printer subsystem, such as the queue status.

/var/spool/mqueue Outgoing mail that has not yet been delivered is spooled in here.

/var/spool/qdaemon When the queuing daemon copies file into a temporary directory then this one is used.

/var/spool/rwho The home directory for the *rwho* daemon. Usually this daemon is not run as it is mostly a waste of resources without any real benefits.

/var/spool/uucp UUCP status and spool files are stored in here.

/var/tmp The large temporary space that is also known as /usr/tmp. Quite a few programs use this directory for temporary files rather than /tmp. It is also used by daemons for debug log files.

/var/log If you followed the recommendations in Section 4.6, then *syslogd* output and other log files will end up here.

/tmp Much of temporary data from the pagers and other utilities ends up here and needs to be cleaned out regularly. Some update and installation commands need at least 8 MB of free space in here. Use *skulker* (page 63) to keep the /tmp directory clean.

/var/adm There are various log files stored in the subdirectories of /var/adm. Particularly AIX 4 uses this one frequently.

/var/adm/cron/log Logs cron starts and other activities. The file should be deleted from time to time.

/var/adm/sulog Here all successful and unsuccessful runs of the *su* command are logged.

/var/adm/wtmp This files stores the data for the *who* program. It contains much more than what you see by simply running *who*. Check out the *who* command line options to find out what you can get out of this file. The file grows quite quickly.

/var/adm/ras/errlog The data for the error report (*errpt*) command is stored here. You can truncate this file with **errclear 0** if you no longer need it.

/etc/utmp This is a snapshot of the current system activity. Use it with the *who* command.

/etc/security/failedlogin This file logs failed log ins. Unfortunately, it resides in the root file system. You might want to replace it with a symbolic link to /var/log/failedlogin. Be sure to check it regularly with **who /etc/security/failedlogin**.

/audit Depending on how you configure auditing there might be growing files in here. You should configure it differently from the default and put the auditing information to some subdirectory of /var.

~/smit.script This file can be a growing menace, especially for the root user. On the other hand, it can provide you with a log of all actions performed through SMIT.

~/smit.log This file grows even faster than smit.script as it logs more information.

/dev/* Quite often a simple typing error leads to huge files in the /dev directory. Using /dev/rmt instead of /dev/rmt0 is very typical. Should your root file system run out of space, check here as well.

6.5 Paging space

Although AIX is quite good in file system management it is somewhat lacking in the handling of paging space. There is no way of using a normal file for paging space as you can do in some other UNIX versions. All paging space has to be allocated as such.

Executables on AIX are never paged out to paging space. They are already on disk, so they only need to be paged in from the normal file system. Any normal file

I/O is done through the memory management subsystem as all file I/O is memory mapped in AIX.

If you have more memory than paging space then this memory is not used for your programs; it is as if there is no memory above the paging space limit. The best way to think of paging space on AIX is to think of memory. And the RAM chips in the machine are just some form of cache for this memory. Any memory above the size of the paging space is used as file cache by the system and so is not totally lost.

When modifying the paging space you should keep in mind that seeking on a disk takes a long time. You should never therefore have more than one paging space per disk, and it should never be fragmented. Try to keep it in the center region of the disk for optimum performance. If you have several disks, then put one paging space on each disk so that the individual paging spaces can be accessed in parallel. To understand better the use of paging space in AIX have a look at Chapter 21.

6.5.1 Working with paging space

Adding paging space is done via *mkps* or **smit mkps**. Here the size is specified in logical partitions. To add a paging space of 20 logical partitions (which translates to 80MB when the default partition size of 4MB is used) on your data volume group, for example, use **mkps -s20 -n -a datavg**. The *-n* flag will activate the paging space now and the *-a* flag will activate it at subsequent reboots as well. You could also add the name of the disk at the end of the command line if the volume group contains more than one disk. The system will try to allocate the new paging space on the center of the disk. If this space is already in use, then it is necessary to reorganize the volume group manually later for optimum performance.

When adding paging spaces, remember never to allocate more than one per disk. Seeking between different paging spaces on the same disk is a real performance killer.

The characteristics of an already allocated paging space can be modified via *chps*. You cannot deactivate an active paging space in the running system. You can only tell the system not to activate it at the next reboot via **chps -a n yourps**. You can, however, increase a paging space in a running system via the *-s* flag and the number of additional logical partitions. To see all your paging spaces use **lsps -a**.

Paging space is removed via *rmps* after it first has been deactivated. Thus, you need to run **chps -a n yourps**, then reboot the machine; you can now run **rmps yourps**.

Now how do you make a paging space smaller? If it is not the primary paging space on *hd6*, simply deactivate it for the next reboot, reboot the machine and then delete it and create a new one that takes up less space. This method will not work for the primary paging space however. Its activation is hard coded in the boot scripts and you need to perform some additional actions to change the size of the primary paging space. The following method works only on AIX 3.2. For AIX 4 you need a different procedure as AIX 4 will refuse to boot without a paging space.

(1) Deactivate the primary paging space with **chps -a n hd6**.

(2) Edit /sbin/rc.boot and comment the line that reads *swapon /dev/hd6*.

(3) Build a new boot image with **bosboot -a -d/dev/hdisk0** or whatever your boot disk is. This boot image will not have the default paging space. If you have no other paging spaces the system will come up without any paging space after the next reboot. It still works however.

(4) Reboot the system with **shutdown -Fr**. Now the paging space *hd6* is no longer active.

(5) Remove *hd6* via **rmps hd6**.

(6) Create a new paging space via **mkps -snewsize -a rootvg hdisk0**. It should be in the root volume group and it should be at least the size of your memory. The exact size depends on your needs. Do not make the paging space active immediately.

(7) Rename the new paging space, which is probably called *paging00*, to *hd6* with **chlv -n hd6 paging00**.

(8) Edit /etc/swapspaces and remove any references to the old name of the new paging space (probably *paging00*). Make sure that *hd6* is listed in there.

(9) Edit /sbin/rc.boot and remove the comment from the *swapon /dev/hd6* line.

(10) Rebuild your boot logical volume to include the activation of the paging space: **bosboot -a -d/dev/hdisk0**.

(11) Reboot the machine with **shutdown -Fr**.

On AIX 4 you need at least some free space in the root volume group to generate a temporary paging space while the standard paging space will be unavailable. Then you can use the above method with the addition of a few more steps.

(1) Create a temporary paging space with **mkps -a -n -s10 rootvg**. This will create a paging space of 40MB. The size should be at least 32MB, but can be anything above that depending on your free disk space. For the example we assume the system has assigned the name *paging00* to the new paging space.

(2) Deactivate the primary paging space with **chps -a n hd6**.

(3) Edit /sbin/rc.boot and comment the line that contains *swapon /dev/hd6*. Instead insert a line like:

```
[ ! -f /needcopydump ] && swapon /dev/paging00
```

(4) Build a new boot image with **bosboot -a -l/dev/hd5 -d/dev/hdisk0**. This boot image will now use the new temporary paging space.

(5) Make sure the dump device no longer points to *hd6* by using **sysdumpdev -Pp /dev/sysdumpnull**.

(6) Reboot the system with **shutdown -Fr**. Now the paging space *hd6* is no longer active.

(7) Remove *hd6* via **rmps hd6**.

(8) Create a new paging space via **mkps -snewsize -a rootvg hdisk0**. It should be in the root volume group and it should be at least the size of your memory. The exact size depends on your needs. Do not make the paging space active immediately.

(9) Rename the new paging space, which is probably called *paging01*, to *hd6* with **chlv -n hd6 paging01**.

(10) Edit /etc/swapspaces to reflect the change made in the previous step as this file will still try to activate something like *paging01* instead of *hd6*.

(11) Edit /sbin/rc.boot, reactivate the *swapon* command that we commented out in step 3 and remove the activation of the *paging00* paging space. Now the line should read

```
[ ! -f /needcopydump ] && swapon /dev/hd6
```

(12) Rebuild your boot logical volume again to include the activation of the paging space: **bosboot -a -l/dev/hd5 -d/dev/hdisk0**.

(13) Deactivate the temporary paging space with **chps -a n paging00**. This will be active after the reboot.

(14) Reboot the machine with **shutdown -Fr**.

(15) Remove the temporary paging space with **rmps paging00**.

(16) Reset the dump device with **sysdumpdev -Pp /dev/hd6** if you want to have the default dump to paging space again.

If this method sounds a bit convoluted or you do not have enough space in the root volume group for a temporary paging space then you might like the following one better. Use the same method that is used to shrink /usr on AIX 4 as described in Section 6.2.2, but instead of shrinking /usr shrink the paging space.

6.6 Custom file systems

Although I have hinted at it already in previous chapters, I want to reiterate the advantage of organizing your data in specific file systems. The better you can adapt the layout of your file system to the organization of your data the easier it is to manage.

I usually have /usr/local and /home not only in their own logical volume but also in their own volume group. This makes it much easier to upgrade the operating system, to do backups and to keep problems with file systems isolated. Here is a brief overview of how to create your own /home file system in your own volume group with a meaningful name.

(1) Save the contents of /home with *tar*, *pax* or *backup*, for example **cd /home ; tar -cf /dev/rmt0 .**.

(2) Remove the current /home file system: **umount /home && rmfs /home**. Using *rmfs* without the *-r* option will leave the mount point intact.

(3) Create a new volume group on, for example, *hdisk3* either with **smit mkvg** or, perferably, by executing **mkvg -d 3 -f -y homevg hdisk3** and then activate it with **varyonvg homevg**. With the *-d 3* option you allow only three disks in this volume group, which will save plenty of space in /etc/vg.

(4) Then create a new file system on this volume group. Use **smit crfs** or **crfs -v jfs -ghomevg -a size=200000 -m /home -Ayes -prw -tno**.

(5) Rename the logical volume. For the example I assume that the system has created the new file system on *lv01*. Use either **smit chlv** or **chlv -n homelv lv01**. Use *lsfs* to see the name that was created initially by the LVM for this file system.

(6) Mount the file system with **mount /home**. In the future it will be automatically mounted at system restart.

(7) Restore the previous contents of /home from tape.

Typical candidates for custom files systems are:

/export
/home
/tftpboot
/usr/local
/usr/lpp/info/En_US on AIX 3
/usr/lpp/info on AIX 4
/usr/sys/inst.images
/var/spool/news
/your/application

6.7 File systems on diskettes

AIX does not support file systems on floppy disks as the overhead of the JFS logging would make it unbearably slow. Creating a custom file system for diskettes was not considered to be in demand. However, one still can have a file system on the floppy disk as long as it is readonly. AIX can create a file system image from a directory, and this mechanism can be used to place a read-only file system on a floppy disk. This can be useful to keep tamperproof reference files on-line for example.

(1) To create the floppy file system, use a clean directory and copy all the files and directories that you want on the diskette into it.

(2) Use the *proto* command to generate a prototype file:

```
proto /tmp/fdfs > /tmp/fd.p
```

(3) The header of the file needs to be adjusted:

```
echo '<noboot> 0 0' > /tmp/fd.proto
sed '1d' < /tmp/fd.p >> /tmp/fd.proto
```

(4) Now you can use *mkfs* to generate the file system (on a previously formatted diskette):

```
mkfs -p /tmp/fd.proto -V jfs /dev/fd0
```

(5) Now the floppy can be mounted like any other file system. You only need to specify that it is readonly and removable:

```
mount -p -r /dev/fd0 /mnt
```

This method can be useful to store things like the TCB database (see 'TCB and TCP' on page 297) or other security-relevant files that need to be stored on direct accessible media without being vulnerable to tampering.

7

Networking with TCP/IP

AIX supports the full range of TCP/IP connectivity facilities. However, if you move to AIX from other UNIX versions you might notice some differences. First, AIX TCP/IP is based on the BSD 4.3 Reno code, in which BSD introduced some changes, most of which, fortunately, are of no concern to the user. Secondly, although AIX TCP/IP can be configured via the usual files, the preferred method is via specific commands that define the operations of the TCP/IP subsystem. I suggest using the AIX method for the basic TCP/IP configuration as it is usually easier. If you really want to use BSD-style rc file configuration use **smit setbootup_option** to reach the selection menu for the type of network configuration.

7.1 Some thoughts on network addresses

Skip this chapter if you know what subnets and legal addresses are. After watching many people installing networks that caused them trouble I think a short explanation is needed here. In addition, there are several good books on TCP/IP on the Market: (*TCP/IP Illustrated, Vol. 1*, 38) and (*TCP/IP Running a Successful Network*, 40) have been very helpful to me. Although a bit Sun centric, (*TCP/IP Network Administration*, 39) is also a good reference.

TCP/IP uses 4-byte addresses to identify hosts and networks. Those addresses are mapped automagically by the address resolution protocol (ARP) to hardware addresses of the LAN adapters, which are of no concern in this discussion. The 4-byte addresses cannot be chosen at random as some people believe. First, there are a few reserved combinations, such as 0.0.0.0 and 255.255.255.255, which are old- and new-style broadcast addresses. When using new-style broadcast addresses, which is the default on AIX, then any address that contains 255 should be avoided. Then there is the loopback address 127.0.0.1, which is also reserved; this actually reserves any address starting with 127. This still leaves many free combinations, but there are more constraints.

Currently there are three classes of network addresses in use: A, B and C. These classes are implicit and are recognized by the range in which the first of the four bytes of the address lies.

1-127.h.h.h	Class A
128-191.n.h.h	Class B
192-223.n.n.h	Class C
224-239.x.x.x	Class D, multicast addresses
240.x.x.x - 255.x.x.x	Reserved for the IAB

There is a class D for multicasting, but that is not common yet. It is supported only on AIX 4, but those addresses are not used to configure network adapters directly. Addresses above 240 are reserved for the Internet Activities Board. This leaves us with the first three classes. In the above list the letter n represents another number for the network, the letter h represents a number for a host. Or, in other words, you can have 127 class A networks with 245^3 hosts, 15256 class B networks with 254^2 hosts and 2129028 class C networks with 254 hosts each. To make matters worse, subnets are introduced. Subnets are means of dividing large networks into smaller networks by telling TCP/IP to use more bits of the address for the network and fewer for the host than implicitly given by the class.

001.hhh.hhh.hhh	Class A address
255.255.255.0	Subnet mask
001.nnn.nnn.hhh	New network addresses with a different network / host ratio, in this example we now have 64516 networks with 254 hosts each instead of one network with 254^3 hosts.

Each bit in the address where the corresponding bit in the subnet mask is set is considered part of the network part of the address. By using subnet masks you can define arbitrary subnets within a larger network. The subnet mask does not have to end on a byte boundary, but because of sloppy implementations it should not have holes as in 255.255.10 (FF.FF.$0A_H$ or $11111111.11111111.00001010_B$) when working in a heterogeneous environment. Another restriction comes from the fact that broadcast addresses are defined to be all bits set (or all bits not set on very old systems). Therefore you cannot use subnet masks that use only one bit for the subnet part. You have to use at least two bits. This translates to 255.255.255.128 (FF.FF.FF.80_H or $11111111.11111111.10000000_B$) being an illegal subnet mask for a class C address. For example, you have to use at least two bits in the last byte, as in 255.255.255.192 (FF.FF.FF.$C0_H$ or $11111111.11111111.11000000_B$), if you want to divide a C range into subnets, which will give you two usable subnets with 63 hosts each.

As soon as you have more than one physical or logical network and need routing, these classes and subnets might get you in trouble if you are not aware of their implications.

The problem can be greatly reduced by deciding what you want to achieve and what your constraints are before you start to implement your network. If you are connected to the real Internet or you obtain your network numbers from some central point in your organization you have no choice but use the addresses you are given. Those people who give you the addresses should be able to set up the right addressing and subnetting for you. If you are not yet connected to the Internet but see a remote chance of being connected to it in the distant future, get official addresses now! If you have to change them later it will cost you at least a weekend for the reorganization. There are some recommended addresses (according to RFC 1918) that can be used for those who want to be sure that they might not get into conflicts later on. These are addresses that will never be routed on the Internet. If you need a class A range, use network 10. This is used by the US military (MIlnet) and will never be connected. Similar networks in the B range are 172.16 – 172.31. And there are also plenty of C networks: 192.168.0 – 192.168.254. Of course, if two companies try to connect directly and both use addresses in those ranges the problem resurfaces.

If you are the one who suddenly has to invent an addressing scheme or map a given class B address into the needs of your organization you have to invest some time in thinking through the setup. The key points to remember are:

(1) Each network interface can talk to only one network or subnet directly. For more connectivity you need routing or interface aliases. A machine on 200.1.1. cannot reach a machine on 200.1.2 without routing because those are distinct networks even if you implement them on the same physical wire.

(2) A saturated network does not perform well. The less load you have on a physical network the better. A Token-Ring network is slightly better in this respect than an Ethernet as the load can be increased linearly.

(3) The more routers and bridges you have in a communications link the more the performance suffers, so try to keep traffic local. You have to balance this constraint against the previous point.

(4) Subnets are not recognized outside of their network. Or, in other words, if you route to the subnet 9.23.4 from 129.2 then the machines on 129.2 think all traffic to 9 can be routed via this interface as the standard IP routing mechanisms do not provide the means to distinguish subnets outside of the network that is subnetted. This might change with the advent of the OSPF routing protocol, but currently you have to be careful about this special feature.

Unless you need large numbers of hosts on a physical network I suggest selecting some addresses out of the class C range. Start with 192.168.1 and add from there on. Staying in the class C range will free you from the hassles of subnet masks unless you have some very specific requirements.

7.2 Base TCP/IP customization

Initial TCP/IP configuration on AIX is easy; simply select the interface and fill in one screen and you are up and running. Call up **smit tcpip** and select "Minimum Configuration & Startup". Depending on the network interface cards you have installed, SMIT will prompt you for one:

en0 Standard Ethernet. Still the most common one.

et0 IEEE 802.3 Ethernet. Use this for Ethernet if you start your whole new network from scratch.

tr0 The Token-Ring interface.

There are more possible interfaces, for example FDDI, X.25 or the serial optical channel. You can select them as well if the right cards are installed. Now fill in the form (Figure 7.1).

```
* HOSTNAME                                         [host.your.do.main]
* Internet Address (dotted decimal)                [192.168.1.13]
  Network MASK (dotted decimal)                    []
* Network INTERFACE                                 en0
  NAMESERVER
           Internet ADDRESS (dotted decimal)       [192.168.1.1]
           DOMAIN Name                             [your.do.main]
  Default GATEWAY Address                          [192.168.1.1]
         (dotted decimal or symbolic name)
  Your CABLE Type                                   N/A                  +
  START TCP/IP daemons Now                          yes                  +
```

Figure 7.1 Initial TCP/IP configuration.

If you use the domain name system enter the host name, including the full domain; otherwise just enter the host name. Next comes the internet address. If you have to use subnet masks, enter it here, otherwise you can ignore the field. The network interface has been selected by the previous menu. When using a name server you should enter its address here and the full name of the domain you are in. If you do not know what a name server is, then read Section 7.3.3 on naming machines. If you have only a default gateway where all traffic that is not for the local net should be sent, enter its address as the default gateway. Should you have more elaborate routing needs, leave this field empty and use the *route* command later. If you need good performance for NFS or other protocols that transfer large amounts of data I suggest not using the route entry here but always using the *route* command (see Section 7.3.2).

If you have one of the Ethernet adapters that sits on the Micro Channel you can select the cable type here. In the 3xx machines with the built-in Ethernet adapter you have to jumper the right interface on the riser card in the machine; ISA Bus machines will need the proper jumper settings. On machines with both BNC and DIX interfaces be sure to remove the wrap terminator that comes on the card from the unused connector. Those are for testing only. The 2xx models and the M20 have only thick wire (AUI/DIX) so you cannot choose anyway. When using Token-Ring you can set the ring speed here. Be sure to use the right one otherwise the network administrator and the other users will be very upset with you. Set the start option to yes and hit <ENTER>. You should be up and running.

Now what happens when you hit <ENTER>? SMIT will run the command *mktcpip* for you. This, in turn, will change several ODM classes and files; it also will dynamically load the TCP/IP support into the kernel. If DNS is used then /etc/resolv.conf will be created and contain your domain name and the name server address. The file /etc/hosts will be updated with your own address. In the *CuAt* ODM class the following items will be modified: inet0, which contains host name and routing information; en0 (or tr0), which contains the network address and netmask; and ent0 (or tok0), which can contain the cable type or ring speed. You can see all the items that get changed for a device by executing **odmget -q"name=en0" CuAt**, for example.

Use this initial configuration screen only once for the initial interface. You will get error messages if you try to use it again because some things are already defined. For all other TCP/IP configuration use the 'Further Configuration' submenus that you reach with **smit tcpip**.

For example, if you want to define another network interface because your machine is a router, select 'Network Interfaces' in the 'Further Configuration' subsection and configure another network interface.

As shipped, the AIX 3 kernel acts as a router, so you do not have to configure that if you want to run a router. This, unfortunately, might lead to problems such as ICMP broadcast storms, if you do not act as a router but the kernel thinks it is a router and some misconfigured machines are on the net. To configure the kernel so that it no longer acts as a router you should modify the file /etc/rc.net. It is here that the low-level network services are started. At the end you will find lines that look like the following:

```
if [ -f /usr/sbin/no ] ; then
        /usr/sbin/no -o tcp_sendspace=16384
        /usr/sbin/no -o tcp_recvspace=16384
fi
```

Add three commands in the *if* construct:

```
if [ -f /usr/sbin/no ] ; then
        /usr/sbin/no -o tcp_sendspace=16384
        /usr/sbin/no -o tcp_recvspace=16384
        # We do not act as a router:
        /usr/sbin/no -o ipsendredirects=0
        /usr/sbin/no -o ipforwarding=0
        # and we do not do IP source routing
        /usr/sbin/no -o nonlocsrcroute=0
fi
```

An AIX 4 system, in contrast, will have the routing function disabled by default so you need to enable it with the *no* command on those systems that act as routers.

The *no* utility changes network options in the running system. Use **no -a** to see the current values. Section 19.4 will tell you more about it.

7.3 More TCP/IP services

The TCP/IP daemons that are not controlled by *inetd* (they are not configured in /etc/inetd.conf) are started out of /etc/rc.tcpip, which is invoked by its *inittab* entry. Most daemons can be configured via SMIT, but you can also change the appropriate lines in rc.tcpip.

7.3.1 The system resource controller

To make it easier to control a group of processes that form a subsystem, AIX has a program that acts as a process manager, the system resource controller, SRC. It controls the complete execution environment of the daemons in the subsystem. To stop a daemon that is under the control of the SRC you do not need to find its process number and then kill it. The command **stopsrc -s daemonname** will stop the daemon. Daemons that are run under the SRC are started via the *startsrc* command. To tell those daemons to reconfigure, the command **refresh -s daemonname** is used. If you want to know which subsystems operate under SRC control use **lssrc -a**. To see which daemons for the *tcpip* group are active, use **lssrc -g tcpip**. Most TCP/IP-related daemons run under SRC control. The SRC is started out of /etc/inittab before TCP/IP is started.

If you want to integrate your own programs into the SRC check out the documentation on SRC. There is a full API for the integration.

There are several defaults for each subsystem that are stored in the ODM. For example, the priority, standard out and standard in. You can change them by modifying the *SRCsubsys* ODM class (Section 18.3).

7.3.2 Routing

As soon as you have more than one network, routing becomes an issue. Systems that are not on the same network and which want to communicate need to know via which gateways they can connect.

Figure 7.2 shows four machines in three networks. Two of the machines have multiple network interfaces and act as routers (rhino and lion). There are two basic principles for routing: dynamic routing via some routing protocol or static routing. To make things more confusing, they can be mixed.

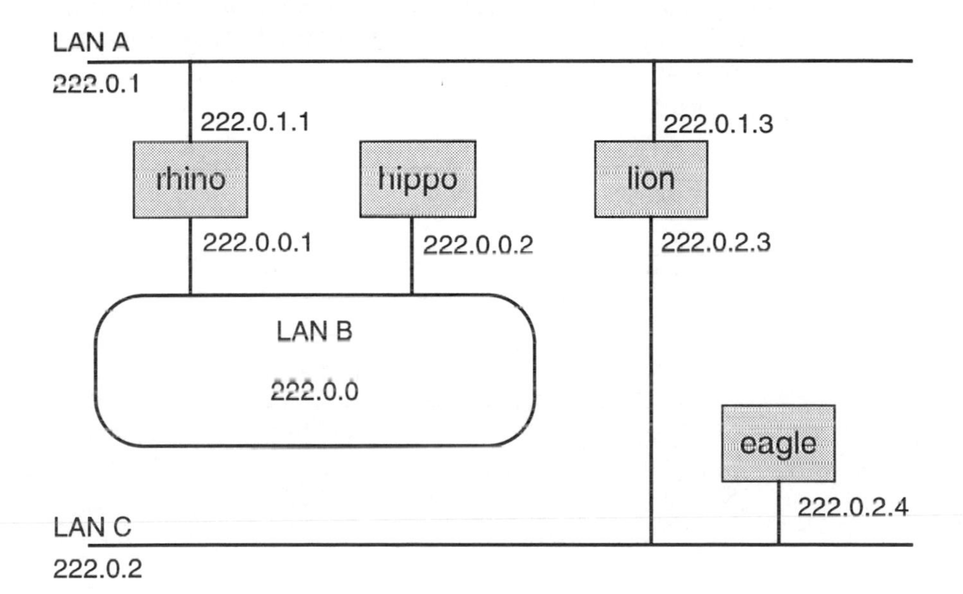

Figure 7.2 A sample network.

Static routing
Let us first look at static routing and how this is configured under AIX. If we use only static routing in the above setup then we need to add routes on each machine. There are two ways of adding static routes on AIX. One is via **smit mkroute,** which will use **chdev -l inet0 -a route=dest,source** to add the routes and save them in the

ODM. They will be available immediately as well as after the next system reboot. The other way is via the standard *route* command. If you want to make those permanent you would have to add the *route* statements in /etc/rc.net. When querying routes via the **netstat -rn** command you do not see how routes were added, just that they are there. To delete routes from the ODM you can use the **chdev -l inet0 -a delroute=dest,gateway** command. Those will be deleted permanently. To delete routes that exist only in the currently running system you can use the command **route delete -net destination gateway**. If you do not remember which of the routes you set up in ODM, you can query them via **odmget -q"attribute=route" CuAt**. This will get all route attributes out of the database for *cu*rrently defined *at*tributes. It will not show the routes that are present in the kernel only. Overall, I prefer not to use SMIT or the *chdev* command to changes routes. The *route* command offers more functionality with additional options that are not supported through the ODM configuration and it is easier to work with the routing information in the kernel via the *route* command. The route can be used to specify packet sizes, hop counts and other details for remote connections, if you need more than simple routes look up the *route* command in *info* for all its details. To simply add a route to another network the following command is used: **route add -net DestNet Gateway**. When you have only one default route for everything, then the route in the ODM that is added via SMIT is usually easier.

Here are the routes that need to be added to the systems:

Machine	Destination	Gateway
rhino	222.0.2	222.0.1.3
hippo	222.0.2	222.0.0.1
	222.0.1	222.0.0.1
	or	
	0	222.0.0.1
lion	222.0.0	222.0.1.1
eagle	222.0.1	222.0.2.3
	222.0.0	222.0.2.3
	or	
	0	222.0.2.3

For each route we specify a machine that is directly reachable as the gateway. The case of a destination 0 is special. This means route everything where no direct path is known to that gateway address. If your machine has only one other system that can act as a gateway for it, then this is the simplest solution.

AIX 3.2 as well as AIX 4 uses a default remote message transfer unit (MTU) of 576. This means that any packet sent via a route is only 576 bytes long. That has a dramatic impact on the performance of large data transfers with NFS or FTP. You can use the *-mtu* option of the *route* command to tell AIX to use a different MTU when using a specific route. I strongly suggest using this feature on LAN routes. I am working in an environment where the MTUs range from 1492 (4MB Token-Ring) through 1500 (Ethernet) to 4096 (16MB Token-Ring). To make sure I get the best throughput without fragmentation (which would cost performance) I always use an MTU of 1492 on my routes.

Dynamic routing

Now what about dynamic routing? For a network that is only connected via a few non-redundant links, dynamic routing is not necessary. However, as soon as you have redundant links so that packets can travel different ways to reach the destination dynamic routing becomes a viable solution. With dynamic routing the gateways exchange information about their routing capabilities, and if one gateway is down the others will automatically learn about it. Dynamic routing has the advantage of self-reconfiguration, so that alternatives are used automatically should one route die. Our mini network does not need dynamic routing, but we will configure it for the sake of an example. To configure dynamic routing in the above network you would start an dynamic routing daemon on rhino and on lion. The other two machines start quiet routing daemons. This is done via **smit routed** and then you just select "Start using the routed subsystem." For dynamic routers we need to do a bit more. First we set up an /etc/gateways file so that the daemons know some initial routes. The format of this file is:

Destination `gateway` *Gateway* `metric` *Metric value Type*.

On rhino /etc/gateways looks like this:

```
222.0.2   gateway  222.0.1.3   metric  1  active
```

On lion the /etc/gateways file has the following contents:

```
222.0.0   gateway  222.0.1.1   metric  1  active
```

This tells the *routed* on those systems where to find initial routes to the network that is not directly visible. Then we need to start a dynamic *routed* here. This is done via **smit chrouted**. When you fill in the fields and press <ENTER>, the corresponding entry in /etc/rc.tcpip will be changed. You should set the fields in Figure 7.3.

```
                                                                 Change it to:
* LOG DEBUGGING information                              no
* This host is acting as a GATEWAY                       no          yes
* SUPPRESS sending routing information                   yes         no
* DO supply routing information                          no          yes
* Write all packets sent and received to STDOUT          no
  Write all PACKETS to LOGFILE                           []
```

Figure 7.3 Setting up *routed*.

This will tell *routed* to inform others about the routes it knows. The machines with the quiet *routed* daemon learn about the routes from the systems with active routing daemons that broadcast the routing information.

Sometimes strange routes get inserted into the routing table when running with the *routed* daemon. You can clean it up quickly by executing **route -nf**, which flushes the routing table. If you then execute **refresh -s routed** the daemon will be reinitialized and will start checking for routes from scratch. The *routed* daemon only supports RIP (routing information protocol) for exchanging routing information. Further routing protocols are supported by the *gated* daemon. Usually the other protocols that this daemon supports are used only in very large networks or on gateways to the Internet.

However, even when you only run RIP the *gated* daemon is more versatile than the *routed* daemon. It allows you to specify static routes together with hosts that you want to listen to for routing table updates. Here is a simple gated configuration file (/etc/gated.conf) for a machine running AIX 3.2 that is a gateway and listens to one other gateway and has a default static route:

```
interface 222.0.1.2 passive ;
rip supplier {
    trustedgateways 222.0.1.3 ;
} ;

static {
    default gateway 222.0.1.7 ;
} ;

propagate proto rip metric 1 {
    proto direct {
        announce all;
    };
    proto static {
        announce all;
    };
    proto rip {
        noannounce all;
    };
};
```

The *interface* keyword above specifies local interfaces that should be kept in the routing table even if there is no traffic over them. The *rip* keyword defines the use of RIP. If you where to specify *quiet* after the *rip* keyword instead of *supplier*, then this machine would not supply routing information. Use this when running *gated* on a non-gateway machine. The *trustedgateways* keyword informs *gated* about other systems that we trust to deliver correct routing information. Any static routes that have to be present initially can be specified with the *static* statement. The *propagate* statement specifies the routing protocols that the daemon uses to supply routing information. Here all direct routes (routes to the machines interfaces) and all statically defined routes are propagated. Routes learned via RIP from other daemons are not propagated to avoid routing loops.

AIX 4 uses a newer version of *gated* and the syntax of the statements in the configuration file has changed. The same functionality as in the above example is achieved with the following file:

```
interfaces {
        interface 9.23.7.4 passive ;
} ;

rip yes {
    broadcast ;
    trustedgateways 9.23.7.1 ;
} ;

static {
    default gateway 9.23.7.1 ;
} ;

export proto rip metric 1 {
    proto rip {
        all restrict;
    };
};
```

You can start *gated* via SMIT with **smit gated**. Unless you want to run it in debug mode you do not need to change any parameters.

Although the configuration of *gated* looks complicated at first (especially when you look at the shipped sample configuration file), it is usually less problematic than running *routed,* which is much more vulnerable to routing problems. I have been running *routed* for a long time and have always had problems because of strange routes. When I switched to *gated* all routing problems went away.

I suggest running *gated* daemons on all your gateways. On your normal machines you then need only a static default route to the nearest of the gateways.

If you are linking several LANs via a WAN, check out BGP or OSPF (AIX 4 only), which are routing protocols that do not need broadcasts, which makes much more sense on WAN connections than the broadcast traffic of RIP updates. When moving from AIX 3 to AIX 4 you will find that *gated* supports more options in the configuration file, but that the syntax has also changed. *Gated* sends syntax errors to *syslog*, so check your logs while configuring *gated.* One common problem is the order dependency of the statements in the configuration file. It is essential to use the order specified in the documentation. The configuration parser in *gated* is not good enough for free-form configuration files.

Analyzing routes

Routing can be very complex and you should be familiar with some tools for analyzing routing problems. First there is **netstat -rn** (Figure 7.4), which will display the contents of the routing table.

```
Routing tables
Destination        Gateway              Flags  Refcnt Use      Interface
default            9.23.2.24            UG          0        0  en0
9.23.2             9.23.2.12            U           5      452  en0
9.23.4             9.23.4.120           U           9    29339  tr0
9.23.10.30         9.23.2.5             UGHD        0        7  en0
127                127.0.0.1            U           1        0  lo0
```

Figure 7.4 Sample **netstat -rn** output.

Figure 7.4 shows some typical output of **netstat -rn**. When you execute **netstat -rn** on your system you will obtain some additional information about netmasks and other protocol families that is of no relevance for this example. The above sample tells us that the default gateway is 9.23.2.24 and the route is up and points to a gateway but that it has not been used since system start. It is reachable via the en0 interface of the machine. The next entry is the route to 9.23.2 via 9.23.2.12, which is a local interface as the flags field does not contain G for gateway. There are five TCP connections active via this interface, and 452 packets have been sent so far. The next entry is similar but for a Token-Ring interface (tr0). Then we have a host route to the machine 9.23.10.30, which is reachable via the gateway 9.23.2.5 on the ethernet. We know that it is a host route because it is a full address and not only a network and the H flag is set, which indicates a host route. The D flag also tells us that the route was created dynamically via a redirect message from some gateway. The last entry is the ever-present line for the loopback interface.

Finally, *ping* tests the connection to another host. In the simplest case *ping* will tell you if you get through or not and at what speed.

If the connection works and you want to know which way the packets went you might find out via the *-R* option. Unfortunately, all the machines involved must support route records otherwise this will give you incorrect results. Another limitation of the *-R* option is that it only records up to nine routes because of the size limitation of the IP header.

The routing history in Figure 7.5 is quite strange. It is a real-life example, but the names have been changed to protect the innocent. The machine from which the ping comes is *barolo*. It is on a Token-Ring and also has an Ethernet interface under the name *baroloe*. Apart from the target machine, all other machines are also on the Token-Ring (222.23.4) as well as the Ethernet (222.23.2). There are far too many hosts in this picture. There should have been only three machines in the route record. The sending machine *barolo* was on Token-Ring; it should have sent the packet directly to *filou* which is the gateway between 222.23.4 and 222.23.10, but instead it went on a journey through some more machines and came back on the Ethernet interface of the machine. If you see too many hops, as in this example, you should check your routing tables. They are probably wrong. In this case a broken *routed* daemon had inserted bogus routes in the tables.

```
# ping -R dl340a.acct.beverages.com -c 1
PING dl340a.acct.beverages.com (222.23.10.30): 56 data bytes
64 bytes from 222.23.10.30: icmp_seq=0 ttl=253 time=6 ms
RR:     bct930.wines.beverages.com (222.23.4.5)
        filou.acct.beverages.com (222.23.10.198)
        dl340a.acct.beverages.com (222.23.10.30)
        filou.wines.beverages.com (222.23.4.198)
        chablise.wines.beverages.com (222.23.2.2)
        baroloe.wines.beverages.com (222.23.2.12)
64 bytes from 222.23.10.30: icmp_seq=1 ttl=253 time=6 ms  (same route)
--- dl340a.acct.beverages.com ping statistics ---
4 packets transmitted, 4 packets received, 0% packet loss
round-trip min/avg/max = 6/6/6 ms
```

Figure 7.5 Sample *ping -R* output.

The most important tool for checking routes is *traceroute*. It utilizes some tricks with ICMP messages to show you exactly how a packet travels or where your route ends in case of problems. Figure 7.6 shows a trace from an Internet site in Germany to *www.ibm.com* on the Internet.

```
$ traceroute www.ibm.com
traceroute to www.ibm.com (165.87.194.133), 30 hops max, 40 byte packets
 1  proseccog (192.54.74.1)  8 ms  7 ms  6 ms
 2  isdngate2.Munich.Germany.EU.net (139.4.74.1)  46 ms  53 ms  44 ms
 3  Munich.DE.EU.net (139.4.6.2)  51 ms  53 ms  62 ms
 4  Dortmund.DE.EU.net (139.4.4.1)  94 ms  87 ms  98 ms
 5  Amsterdam2.NL.EU.net (134.222.1.1)  120 ms  113 ms  112 ms
 6  Vienna3.VA.ALTER.NET (134.222.5.2)  252 ms  261 ms  412 ms
 7  Vienna1.VA.ALTER.NET (137.39.11.1)  233 ms  240 ms  313 ms
 8  Dallas1.TX.ALTER.NET (137.39.128.7)  305 ms  404 ms  347 ms
 9  Advantis-gw.ALTER.NET (137.39.226.66)  335 ms  460 ms  319 ms
10  dallas1-br2.tx.us.ibm.net (165.87.6.2)  373 ms  395 ms  308 ms
11  chi1-br2.il.us.ibm.net (165.87.7.2)  369 ms  375 ms  386 ms
12  wp1-cr2-mf0.ny.us.ibm.net (165.87.194.193)  357 ms  359 ms  622 ms
13  www.ibm.com (165.87.194.133)  453 ms  377 ms  447 ms
```

Figure 7.6 Sample *traceroute* output.

For each host you can see the reply times for the three messages that were sent back to the machine. If you see either asterisks '*' or exclamation marks '!' instead of a clean picture you know that something is wrong.

7.3.3 Naming machines

When naming machines there are two problems: what names to choose and how is the name database maintained. You can name machines any way you like, but the following guidelines have helped me quite a lot.

(1) Do choose names you can remember. A name like d0815r1 is harder to remember than gorilla, for example, although it might contain the information that this is RISC machine number 1 in department 0815.

(2) Choose names for groups of machines that also belong to a group, such as cars, animals, stars, Greek gods, wines or whatever appeals to you.

(3) Do not name machines after functions or machine types. Use aliases instead. If the function or type of machine changes you only have to change the alias and nothing else. Your users will thank you if you change a server and they can still reference it by the same alias even although it now points to a different machine.

(4) When using a domain name system you should try to use domain names that last longer than the next organizational change. You do not want to change all domain and machine names whenever your organization is restructured. Unfortunately, there is no ideal rule for this: no matter which way you attack this problem, you will run into domain name changes or you will run with obsolete domain names. The less frequently you separate your domain into subdomains the less vulnerable you are to domain changes. However, this, in turn, demands central domain name service which might not fit your organization.

7.3.4 Setting up a name server

For a small number of machines you can keep the /etc/hosts file up to date manually. But what about larger installations? In this case another mechanism is required, the domain name system (DNS). The best documentation I have ever seen on managing a name server environment can be found in (*DNS and Bind*, 30). If you want to set up a DNS server for a non-trivial installation this book is a must.

The name server (often called *bind* for Berkeley Internet Name Domain) is a daemon that supplies other machines with mapping information about machine names and addresses. In SMIT and InfoExplorer you will find hints on how to set up a simple name server that manages one domain and one network address. This works reasonably well. But what if you have several domains, several networks or a connection to the Internet? The system-supplied *awk* scripts to convert /etc/hosts files into name server configuration files are not made for that. (You can find them in /usr/samples/tcpip (AIX 4) or /usr/lpp/tcpip/samples (AIX 3)). I suggest staying away from them as the configuration files that they produce are illegal, which results in massive problems if you are connected to any other network. To help you get started I will describe the setup of a primary name server for one domain that governs two networks and is also a shadow of another domain and network. You should still read the InfoExplorer articles on configuring a name server. The sample here does not list all possible variations but focuses on one common configuration. A name server is configured by /etc/named.boot. Here all the domains it governs are listed, as well as the places where it gets the data. Our name server, named *barolo*, is in the domain *wines.beverages.com*, and it maintains this domain as well as the networks 222.0.1 and 222.0.2. In addition, it serves as a secondary server for *soft.beverages.com* and the network 222.1.1.

The following /etc/hosts file is used as a basis:

```
222.0.1.1     barolo.wines.beverages.com barolo nameserver printer
222.0.1.2     soda.soft.beverages.com soda wines
222.0.1.11    merlot.wines.beverages.com merlot
222.0.1.12    chablis.wines.beverages.com chablis

222.0.2.1     barolo2.wines.beverages.com barolo2
222.0.2.111   chianti.wines.beverages.com chianti
222.0.2.112   barbera.wines.beverages.com barbera
```

Barolo.wines.beverages.com has the address 222.0.1.1. The other server, *soda.soft.beverages.com* has the address 222.0.1.2. How does our /etc/named.boot look?

```
; /etc/named.boot for the server of wines.beverages
;
; Keep all files for named in their own directory
directory     /var/named
; where are we
domain        wines.beverages.com

primary       wines.beverages.com                      wines.hosts
primary       1.0.222.in-addr.arpa                     222.0.1.rev
primary       2.0.222.in-addr.arpa                     222.0.2.rev

secondary     soft.beverages.com         222.0.1.2     soft.hosts
secondary     1.1.222.in-addr.arpa       222.0.1.2     soft.hosts

primary       0.0.127.in-addr.arpa                     named.local
```

The above file tells *named* that all configuration files apart from named.boot are to be found in /var/named. This ensures that when *named* gets data from other zones all the data is in a non-root file system and is grouped together. We then tell *named* that we are in the *wines.beverages.com* domain. This line is not used in other UNIX implementations of the name server daemon. You can skip it if you set up a full /etc/resolv.conf file, which is usually not needed for AIX. For each domain and network over which this server has authority, a primary statement is used. The addresses are specified in reverse and end with *in-addr.arpa* domain. This is not very intuitive; the reverse name resolution seems to be something the designers of *named* thought about very late in the design stage. So, for each domain and each network, we have one file. The domains and networks for which this server acts as a secondary are listed with the secondary keyword. In addition to the file name where the data will be stored, the address of the server where the data comes from is listed. One could list multiple servers here to have a backup if there are multiple servers for this domain. A secondary server gets the information from the primary server and stores it in a file. This file acts as a backup in case the primary is not accessible. You should have at least two name servers in your network to ensure that one is always available. A name server can be a primary, secondary or a mix of both, as in our example. When setting up a secondary the information that is fetched from the primary is stored in a file so that when the secondary starts without being able to access the primary it can fall back on the files.

Now we need to set up the data files in /var/named.

wines.hosts

```
; Name table for the hosts in wines.beverages.com domain

@ IN SOA barolo.wines.beverages.com. root.barolo.wines.beverages.com. (
            93021001      ; serial number YYMMDDvv
            86400         ; refresh daily
            3600          ; retry every hour
            3600000       ; expire after 1000 hours
            36000         ; default ttl for cache entries is 10 hours
            )
; name servers for this domain
            IN     NS     barolo.wines.beverages.com.
            IN     NS     barolo2.wines.beverages.com.
            IN     NS     soda.soft.beverages.com.
; useful aliases
nameserver  IN     CNAME  barolo.wines.beverages.com.
; our print server
printer     IN     CNAME  barolo.wines.beverages.com.

; Machines in our domain
localhost   IN     A      127.0.0.1
loopback    IN     CNAME  localhost.wines.beverages.com.

; Machines on the 222.0.2 net
barolo      IN     A      222.0.1.1
            HINFO  "RS530 Room 0815" "Arthur Dent"
merlot      IN     A      222.0.1.11
            HINFO  "RS580 Room 0817" "Zaphod Beeblebrox"
chablis     IN     A      222.0.1.12
            HINFO  "RS220 Room 4711" "John Clerk"
; Machines on the 222.0.2 net
barolo2     IN     A      222.0.2.1
            HINFO  "RS530 Room 0815" "Arthur Dent"
chianti     IN     A      222.0.2.111
            HINFO  "RS560 Room 0077" "Joe Random Hacker"
barbera     IN     A      222.0.2.112
            HINFO  "RS32H Room 0047" "Ford Prefect"
```

We start the data in this file by an @. This tells the *named* daemon that all the data in this file is relative to the domain that was specified in named.boot for this file. The first entry in a name server data file is the statement of authority (SOA). It defines for which domain the data is authoritative and who is the contact for this domain. The SOA contains some timer values that determine for how long entries are valid and how often other servers should check for updates. All the times are given in seconds. The first number is the *serial number*. It should be changed any time the file is changed so that other servers will know about the change. When servers check for changes they only compare the serial number, not the actual data. This number is a 32-bit integer. Therefore one cannot use a YYYYMMDDhhmm notation, which does not fit into 32 bits. But YYYYMMDDvv with a daily version number appended works quite well. If the number is too large, the name server silently truncates it, which generates problems that are difficult to diagnose. The next number is the *refresh* time for this zone. When another server gets the data from this server it will check for changes every refresh time in seconds. If it cannot contact this server it will retry every *retry* seconds. The data for this zone *expires* after some time, and this is set with the fourth number. The final number is the default time to live for entries in this file. If no other time is specified for the individual entries then this time is used. After the SOA one usually lists name servers for this domain that also keep a copy of this file (secondary servers). They are identified by the NS records in the file. Aliases for specific machines are next and are defined with CNAME (canonical name) records, in this case, for example, for the print server. With this entry users need only specify *printer* as the hosts for remote print jobs. Whenever the real print server changes, the administrator needs only to change this alias: users do not need to change anything. Note that all domain names end in a dot. If they do not end with a dot, then the domain would be appended to them. To make absolutely clear what is meant, one should always list complete names and terminate them with a dot. To ensure that when using the name server the localhost or loopback interface is still available, we include it here as well. Then the real machines are listed. There are two lines or records for each machine: one that specifies the address of the machine with the A record and one that sets the host information with the HINFO record. Initially this was meant for machine type and operating system, but it is far more useful to include your own information in here, such as the location type and owner of the machine. TXT records could also be used, but support for them is less common.

222.0.1.rev

```
; Address table for the hosts in 222.0.1

@ IN SOA barolo.wines.beverages.com. root.barolo.wines.beverages.com. (
              93021001        ; serial number YYMMDDvv
              86400           ; refresh daily
              3600            ; retry every hour
              3600000         ; expire after 1000 hours
              36000           ; default ttl for cache entries is 10 hours
              )
; name servers
              IN     NS      barolo.wines.beverages.com.
              IN     NS      barolo2.wines.beverages.com.
              IN     NS      soda.soft.beverages.com.
; addresses:
1             IN     PTR     barolo.wines.beverages.com.
```

```
2            IN     PTR    soda.soft.beverages.com.
11           IN     PTR    merlot.wines.beverages.com.
12           IN     PTR    chablis.wines.beverages.com.
```

As for the names file, we start off with an SOA record and the name servers that know about this domain. Then all hosts are listed by host number. The IP address of the machine is built out of the reversed numeric *in-add.arpa* domain and the host number listed here. Given 1.0.222.in-addr.arpa and the host number 12 the complete address of chablis would be 222.0.1.12.

222.0.2.rev

```
; Address table for the hosts in 222.0.2

@ IN SOA barolo2.wines.beverages.com. root.barolo2.wines.beverages.com. (
             93021001       ; serial number YYMMDDvv
             86400          ; refresh daily
             3600           ; retry every hour
             3600000        ; expire after 1000 hours
             36000          ; default ttl for cache entries is 10 hours
             )
; name servers and other important machines
             IN     NS     barolo.wines.beverages.com.
             IN     NS     barolo2.wines.beverages.com.
             IN     NS     soda.soft.beverages.com.
; addresses:
1            IN     PTR    barolo2.wines.beverages.com.
111          IN     PTR    chianti.wines.beverages.com.
112          IN     PTR    barbera.wines.beverages.com.
```

This file is similar to the reverse mapping file for the 222.0.1 network.

named.local

```
; named.local for reverse name resolution of the localhost/loopback
interface

@ IN SOA barolo2.wines.beverages.com. root.barolo2.wines.beverages.com. (
             1              ; serial number
             86400          ; refresh
             3600           ; retry
             3600000        ; expire
             36000          ; ttl
             )
; name servers and other important machines
             IN     NS     barolo.wines.beverages.com.
             IN     NS     barolo2.wines.beverages.com.
             IN     NS     soda.soft.beverages.com.
;
1            IN     PTR    localhost.
```

The named.local file is used to provide correct reverse name resolution for the loopback interface.

Once you have configured all the files, use either **smit named** or **startsrc -s named** to activate the name server daemon. Have a look at the *syslog* output while working with the name server configuration. Major errors are often shown there.

Connecting your network to the Internet

The above name server setup works fine as long as you live on a small island. But what happens if you are connected to a larger network such as the Internet? You cannot be the secondary name server for all the other domains on the Internet. The following is true not only for real Internet connections but also for connections to any large network. To tell your name server that there is more than it knows directly, use a hints file, commonly called the cache file named.ca. Tell the name server about this file by including the following line in /etc/named.boot:

```
cache                   named.ca
```

The cache file stores the addresses of the root name servers that are contacted by the local server if it does not know how to resolve an address. They are the authoritative name servers that are supposed to know everything, or more correctly, know the domain servers that serve the top level domains. They will tell your name server whom to contact for the top level domains. Those servers will then tell you about their subdomains and so on until the whole domain name is resolved.The exact contents of the cache file depends on the network to which you are connected. The following sample could be used for an Internet connection as it lists real Internet root name servers:

```
; A current vresion of this files is available on
; ftp://FTP.RS.INTERNIC.NET/domain/named.root
.                      3600000     IN  NS    A.ROOT-SERVERS.NET.
A.ROOT-SERVERS.NET.    3600000     IN  A     198.41.0.4
.                      3600000     IN  NS    B.ROOT-SERVERS.NET
B.ROOT-SERVERS.NET.    3600000     IN  A     128.9.0.107
.                      3600000     IN  NS    C.ROOT-SERVERS.NET.
C.ROOT-SERVERS.NET.    3600000     IN  A     192.33.4.12
.                      3600000     IN  NS    D.ROOT-SERVERS.NET.
D.ROOT-SERVERS.NET.    3600000     IN  A     128.8.10.90
.                      3600000     IN  NS    E.ROOT-SERVERS.NET.
E.ROOT-SERVERS.NET.    3600000     IN  A     192.203.230.10
.                      3600000     IN  NS    F.ROOT-SERVERS.NET.
F.ROOT-SERVERS.NET.    3600000     IN  A     39.13.229.241
.                      3600000     IN  NS    G.ROOT-SERVERS.NET.
G.ROOT-SERVERS.NET.    3600000     IN  A     192.112.36.4
.                      3600000     IN  NS    H.ROOT-SERVERS.NET.
H.ROOT-SERVERS.NET.    3600000     IN  A     128.63.2.53
.                      3600000     IN  NS    I.ROOT-SERVERS.NET.
I.ROOT-SERVERS.NET.    3600000     IN  A     192.36.148.17
```

The entries here are for the root domain (donated by the '.') and they have a very long Time To Live (3600000 seconds), which is proper for a root name-server. For each server the address must also be specified.

The mechanism of a cached name server can be also used for other purposes. Suppose a machine on the network makes many name server queries. Instead of always asking a name server for the information, it could be configured to be itself a caching only name server. Its named.boot file will not list any data files, just the cache file. All queries will be cached and the number of remote name server accesses will be greatly reduced.

A variation of this theme works by telling the name server to forward all queries that it cannot handle to specific servers instead of directly contacting the root servers. The *forwarders* directive can be used in named.boot to tell the daemon that the servers listed should be queried if a name cannot be resolved directly. On an Internet gateway one would typically list the name server of the service provider there as follows:

```
forwarders        192.76.144.66
```

Even if you have a *forwarders* statement, you need the cache file to make it work. And a machine that has a *forwarders* statement will not be able to query any servers directly. It will resolve all queries via the specified forwarding hosts, not by querying any other servers.

Using a name server

The use of a name server is configured through the file /etc/resolv.conf. If /etc/resolv.conf is empty, then the local machine is assumed to be a name server and all queries are sent to the name server daemon on the local machine. If it is not empty, the servers listed in this file are used for name resolution.

You should always list several name servers in /etc/resolv.conf so that there is a backup. In addition, the file stores the name of the domain that the machine is in. For a client in the wines.beverages.com domain on network 222.0.1 a sample /etc/resolv.conf file would look like:

```
domain wines.beverages.com
nameserver 222.0.1.1
nameserver 222.0.1.2
```

In case 222.0.1.1 is not available the local resolver will try to use the name server at 222.0.1.2. If that fails, /etc/hosts is checked.

It might take a while until the information or failure is returned, as any query is usually sent out several times with increased delays inbetween, and this happens for every server listed until some answer is found. Thus, it does not make sense to have too many servers listed in here.

Starting with AIX 4.1.4, the *domain* keyword can be substituted by the *search* keyword which defines a searchlist for name resolution for up to six domains. Prior to that change, a name server query would always query the name of a machine with the current domains appended. Now the domains that will be appended to simple host names (actually any name that does not end in a dot) can be configured. The old search mechanism can be reconstructed easily, for example when in *wines.beverages.com* one would set up the following search list:

```
search wines.beverages.com beverages.com
```

This tells the resolver to first try *host.wines.beverages.com* and then *host.beverages.com* when trying to resolve a host name through DNS.

The complete name resolution search order is DNS first, NIS second and /etc/hosts last. On AIX 4 a different search order for name resolution can be specified with either /etc/netsvc.conf or the environment variable *NSORDER*. The following /etc/netsvc.conf file will search /etc/hosts first and then DNS:

```
hosts=local,bind
```

$NSORDER takes the same parameters as the *hosts* statement in the file, as in *NSORDER="local,DNS"*.

local	The /etc/hosts file
bind	DNS (Berkeley Internet Name Daemon)
nis	Network Information Services

Each of the services can be made authoritative, which would exclude the remaining services from being queried. For example, *hosts = bind=auth,local* would specify that if DNS returns a negative answer the /etc/hosts file is not checked. For normal use only DNS would be used and only if DNS is not available would the /etc/hosts file be consulted.

The configurable search mechanism can even be augmented with your own host registry. See InfoExplorer for details; search for "name resolution".

Checking a name server

The simplest name server debugging tool is the *host* command. **Host machinename** should always return the same as **host machineaddress**; if they do not match there is a problem with the name server, usually a wrong setup for reverse name resolution. For example see Figure 7.7.

```
$ host rhino.game.safari.com
rhino.game.safari.com is 222.23.13.11
$ host 222.23.13.11
rhino.game.safari.com is 222.23.13.11
```

Figure 7.7 Using the *host* command.

An exception to this rule are aliases or CNAME records. In this case it is necessary to follow the alias to the real name before the comparison is valid (Figure 7.8).

```
$ host www
zebra.game.safari.com is 222.23.13.33, Aliases: www.game.safari.com
$ host 9.23.4.2
zebra.game.safari.com is 222.23.13.33
```

Figure 7.8 Using the *host* command with aliased names.

AIX 4.1.4 comes with a newer version of the *host* command: *hostnew.* It has additional flags that allow you to query all name server information (Figure 7.9).

```
$ hostnew -a www
Trying domain "game.safari.com"
rcode = 0 (Success), ancount=1
The following answer is not authoritative:
www.game.safari.com is        zebra.game.safari.com
Trying null domain
rcode = 0 (Success), ancount=2
The following answer is not authoritative:
zebra.game.safari.com is    Server R121  RS560
zebra.game.safari.com is    100 mailhub.game.safari.com
zebra.game.safari.com is    222.23.13.33
```

Figure 7.9 Using **hostnew -a** on AIX 4.1.4

The *hostnew* command when used with the *-a* flag as in Figure 7.9 will show you which domains are searched through the searchlist. In addition, it will tell you about any resource records for this particular system. In Figure 7.9 there is a HINFO record and a MX record for the host name which is an alias.

When the *-n* flag is added to *hostnew,* the output will look like the entries in a domain name configuration file (Figure 7.10).

```
$ hostnew -a -n rhino
Trying domain "game.safari.com"
rcode = 0 (Success), ancount=3
The following answer is not authoritative:
rhino.game.safari.com       2419200IN    HINFO   afx r131        RS520
rhino.game.safari.com       2419200IN    A       222.23.13.44
rhino.game.safari.com       2419200IN    MX      100 mailhub.game.safari.com
Additional information:
mailhub.game.safari.com     2419200IN    A       222.23.13.33
```

Figure 7.10 Using **hostnew -a -n** on AIX 4.1.4

A more sophisticated name server checking tool is *nslookup*. The example in Figure 7.11 shows a *nslookup* query: apart from trivial queries like that, *nslookup* can be used to request any type of information from a name server up to complete domain listings. Have a look at its InfoExplorer entry for details. It is especially useful to find out about the SOA and additional name server database entries such as MX records.

```
$ nslookup
Default Server:  hippo.game.safari.com
Address:  222.23.4.2
> set type=any
> rhino
Server:  hippo.game.safari.com
Address:  222.23.4.2
rhino.game.safari.com internet address = 222.23.13.11
rhino.game.safari.com CPU = afx test box      OS = RS220
> game.safari.ibm.com
Server:  hippo.game.safari.com
Address:  222.23.4.2
game.safari.com  origin = hippo.game.safari.com
     mail addr = afx.game.safari.com
     serial=94062001, refresh=21600, retry=3600, expire=3600000,
     min=2419200
game.safari.com nameserver = hippo.game.safari.com
game.safari.com nameserver = cheeta.game.safari.com
game.safari.com preference = 0, mail exchanger = hippo.game.safari.com
hippo.game.safari.com           inet address = 222.23.4.2
cheeta.game.safari.com          inet address = 222.23.4.3
```

Figure 7.11 Using *nslookup*.

If those tools report nothing useful for you, you might need to start *named* in debug mode. The easiest way to do so is via **smit chnamed**. There you can set debugging levels from 1 to 9. In debug mode all actions of *named* are recorded in /var/tmp/named.run. This will restart the daemon. When you want to start debugging with a running daemon you should send the signal USR1 to the daemon. Each signal increases the debugging level by 1. To stop debugging use the USR2 signal. You can also force a dump of the current *named* database by sending an INT signal to the *named* daemon, which will produce /var/tmp/named.dump. In addition, you might find entries in the *syslog* files from *named* depending on your configuration.

When users complain about slow network log ins or that the *rup* command does not work or that errors occur in remote printing, check the name server first. Either it is down or reverse name resolution is broken. Quite often when people switch to a name server the *rsh* and *rlogin* commands stop working. This is because either reverse name resolution is not set up properly or the names used in .rhosts files do not include the domain, which is required when using DNS.

7.3.5 Remote printing

If your machine has to act as a print server then two things must be done after you have configured the printers. First, use **smit lpd** to start the line printer daemon (*lpd*). This daemon speaks the Berkeley LPD protocol, and any modern version of UNIX should be able to connect to it to print on the AIX machine. Secondly, set up

/etc/hosts.lpd. In here you should list the complete host names, including the domain of all other machines that are allowed to print on this host. Simply putting a '+' character in the file allows any other machine on the network to print via this server.

Setting up a printer client is discussed in Section 10.6. It amounts to filling in one SMIT screen that you get with **smit mkrque**.

7.3.6 Configuring pseudoterminals

Pseudoterminals (PTYs) are used for network connections (*rlogin*, *telnet*) or terminal windows under X (*aixterm*). Standard Berkeley PTYs are available under AIX as well as a multiplexed AIX PTY driver. In contrast to Berkeley PTYs, in which the number of available PTYs is limited by the entries in /dev, the AIX 3 PTY driver offers unlimited PTYs. On AIX 4 the number of multiplexed PTYs is also configurable. AIX PTYs are accessed via the /dev/ptc and /dev/pts control and slave parts of the PTY driver. This will then allocate the next free pseudoterminal, such as /dev/pts/3, without the need to look for a free PTY. BSD-style PTYs are offered for compatibility, but their number is limited and might need to be increased if many applications (like the vanilla MIT *xterm*) want to access the old-style PTYs. On AIX 4 use **smit pty** to increase the number of available multiplexed and BSD-compatible PTYs.

Up to 64 old-style PTYs can be configured on AIX 3 (the system is shipped with 16 initially). You can increase this number via **chdev -l pty -anum=X**, where X can be up to 64. The limit of 64 PTYs comes from the predefined device attribute object class in the ODM (PdAt). If you want to be able to configure more than 64 old-style PTYs you have to modify this class.

(1) Get the current definition out of the ODM:

```
odmget -q "uniquetype=pty/pty/pty and attribute=num" PdAt >
/tmp/odm.ptys
```

(2) Delete the current definition from the ODM:

```
odmdelete -o PdAt -q "uniquetype=pty/pty/pty and attribute=num"
```

(3) Edit the stanza in /tmp/odm.ptys so that you can configure a wider range:

```
PdAt:
  uniquetype = "pty/pty/pty"
  attribute = "num"
  deflt = "16"
  values = "0-64,1"
  width = ""
  type = "R"
  generic = "DU"
  rep = "nr"
  nls_index = 2
```

Change the values field to "0-128,1" for example. This will change the allowable values to the range 0 – 128. All values in this range can be chosen with a granularity of 1. Then execute:

```
odmadd /tmp/odm.ptys
```

(4) Now you can configure up to 128 PTYs with SMIT or **chdev -l pty -anum=128**.

7.3.7 Adding services to *inetd*

If you are running the internet daemon under the control of the SRC on AIX 3 then adding lines to /etc/inetd.conf to install new services will not configure these services for *inetd*. The information is obtained from the ODM class *InetServ* instead. After changing /etc/inetd.conf you should execute **inetimp ; refresh -s inetd** to tell *inetd* about the new configuration. The same also applies for changes to /etc/services: you need to run *inetimp* after changing this file as well. This works the other way round too: every time the *InetServ* class is changed (via the *inetserv* command), **inetexp** should be run to sync /etc/services and /etc/inetd.conf with the ODM.

AIX 4 does not replicate the information of /etc/services and /etc/inetd.conf in the ODM. You only need to run **refresh -s inetd** or send a *SIGHUP* signal to the daemon to activate your changes.

7.3.8 Configuring *syslogd*

Although it is started via /etc/rc.tcpip, this daemon is useful even when you are not networked. It receives information from other daemons and sends it to files, terminals, users or even other machines. Depending on its configuration it only logs critical errors or loads of debugging output. The daemon is configured via /etc/syslog.conf, in which the priority of the information, its source and where it should be sent to are specified. Priorities are classes of messages ranging from debug to emergency, and are described in the *syslogd* man page. *Syslogd* will log all messages of the priority you specify and all messages of a higher priority. To get all messages you have to use the debug priority. The available facilities can be found in the man page for the *syslog* system call. There are some standard facilities as well as free slots for your own programs. If a message should be sent to a file, then the file has to exist before *syslogd* is started; it will not create the file itself. When you specify user names as recipients of the messages then the messages will be sent to all terminals where those users are logged in: a '*' sends the message to all logged in users. If you have to maintain a network of machines then the facility of sending the messages to a *syslogd* on another machine is quite helpful to keep the administrator informed without the need to check other machines manually.

Experiment to find the best configuration for your system. I suggest using the following entries in /etc/syslogd.conf initially:

```
# Log all warnings
*.warn              /var/log/warnings
# Log debug messages
*.debug             /var/log/debug.all
# Log all security relevant messages
auth.debug          /var/log/security.messages
# send all interesting security events to the syslog daemon on bigserver
auth.notice         @bigserver
# notify everyone in case of real problems
*.alert             *
*.alert             @bigserver
# log all messages but mail messages to /var/log/debug
*.debug;mail.none   /var/log/debug
```

The **.debug* entry will log everything. You probably do not really want to keep it, but it will give you an idea of what messages can be expected. The last entry will also log all debug messages but exclude anything from the mail system.

I also suggest adding the following entries to our /usr/local/etc/rc.local script (page 60) to get new log files at every system reboot:

```
# Take care of syslog files
OldLog /var/log/warnings
OldLog /var/log/debug.all
OldLog /var/log/security.messages
OldLog /var/log/debug
refresh -s syslogd
```

This way you can be sure that there is always a fresh log file for each system restart, which is good housekeeping.

If you log at a very low priority such as debug, then you may receive very many messages, depending on your system configuration. This is a good chance to practice your *awk* or *Perl* skill to analyze the messages automatically (see Section 16.3.4).

In addition to the messages generated from programs you also can log your own messages from the command line using the *logger* utility.

7.3.9 Linking *syslog* and the AIX error log

An AIX addition to the traditional *syslog* facilities is the ability to log messages in the systems error log. When specifying the keyword *errorlog* instead of a file name, the messages are logged in the system error log and can be displayed with **errpt** or **errpt -a**. The reverse is also possible. If you want an entry in *syslog* for every entry in the error log you can add an error notification method to the error logging system. Create the file /tmp/errlog:

```
errnotify:
  en_pid = 0
  en_name = "syslog"
  en_persistenceflg = 1
  en_label = ""
  en_crcid = 0
  en_class = ""
  en_type = ""
  en_alertflg = ""
  en_resource = ""
  en_rtype = ""
  en_rclass = ""
   en_method = "/usr/bin/errpt -l $1|/usr/bin/tail -1|/usr/bin/logger
-t errpt -p daemon.notice"
```

This stanza defines an error notification method that is called for every entry in the error log. The parameters available to the method do not include the one-line error description that one usually sees with the **errpt** command. Thus, the method extracts this message (the message sequence number is in *$1*) with the *errpt* command and then pipes it into the *logger* command. To activate this error notification method run **odmadd /tmp/errlog**. Test it with **errlogger testing**. You should see a message in the *syslog* log file.

7.4 Setting up SLIP

SLIP (serial line internet protocol) is a simple way of connecting two machines via serial lines and optionally modems inbetween. It is not as easy as the newer point to point protocol (PPP), but it comes free with AIX. In the following the address 192.168.1.1 will be used for system rhino and 192.168.1.2 for system hippo. To set up SLIP on an AIX machine you need to do the following on system rhino (and the appropriate counterpart on hippo):

(1) Set up the serial ports. This is done by running **smit mktty**. The serial port that you use needs to support modem control signals if you run SLIP over a modem. You need to set login to disable as SLIP manages the port itself and does not need *getty*. Use the right speed for the modem. If you have a modem that supports variable speeds, select the highest speed that the modem supports. Set XON-XOFF to no. If the SMIT menu still does not allow you to configure RTS/CTS handshake ask your IBM support center for a work-around; you will need RTS/CTS handshake for the modem connection.

(2) Configure the file /etc/uucp/Devices:

```
Direct tty1 - 9600 hayes
```

This assumes you are using tty1, that the modem understands the Hayes command set and that the speed is 9600bps.

(3) Configure the modems to use RTS/CTS handshake (hardware flow control). The modem should be set to track DTR and hang up when it changes as *slattach* will bring up DTR. The CD line should also be set up.

(4) Configure SLIP on this port with **ifconfig sl0 192.168.1.1 up**. Now **ifconfig sl0** should report that the SLIP port is up.

(5) On the remote system (hippo) use **slattach tty1** to attach the interface to a tty.

(6) On the local system (rhino) run

```
slattach tty1 9600 ' "" AT OK ATDTHipposPhoneNumber CONNECT "" '
```

This will tell TCP/IP to use tty1 for the previously defined slip interface, connect at 9600 bps with the modem and exchange a short dialog with the modem. The modem dialog is as follows: First the modem gets an AT command for which it should respond with OK. Then it gets a dial string and after successful dialing it should respond with CONNECT.

(7) Now try to ping the remote system.

If the above method worked you are ready to set up a more permanent configuration via **smit mkinet1sl**. Before you do this first bring down the current slip interface: Kill the slattach process on the tty with **kill -HUP** not **kill -9**! Then use **ifconfig sl0 down** to bring the interface down and then detach it with **ifconfig sl0 detach**.

When running a direct connection without modems you can skip the DIAL string in the above instructions. Be aware that you cannot ping yourself with a SLIP interface as it is a point to point interface.

Should you have problems with a SLIP connection try finding the problem with the following checklist:

- Are you using the right modem cable?
- Is the tty set to disable (no *getty* running)?
- Do the tty and the modem have the same settings?
- Is XON/XOFF disabled and RTS/CTS enabled on the modem and the tty?
- Can you talk to the modem via **cu -lm tty1**?
- Do you see the modem light flicker when you try a ping?
- Do you have the same MTU on both sides?
- Are you using the right addresses and subnet masks?

7.5 Taming *sendmail*

Although most programs that people use today for sending mail (mail user agents, MUAs) are easy to use, the underlying sendmail program (mail transfer agent,

MTA) that does the actual sending on most systems is still a nightmare to configure for most people.

There are two levels of sendmail configuration: standard and wizardry. Standard configuration is easy but wizardry can also be achieved with a little help. Let's look at standard first.

7.5.1 Standard *sendmail* configuration

You need to specify your host name, your domain and perhaps some gateways, and to tell sendmail about the changes you have made. The sendmail configuration file /etc/sendmail.cf looks very strange but the simple things can be done easily – it is only as large as because of the comments that try to guide you through the file. All configurations settings start at the beginning of the line, although some are initially commented out. Do not use an editor such as INed (the editor you get with the *e* command) that does not preserve tab characters to edit this file as it will interfere with the tabulators in the file. Use *vi* or some other editor that understands tabs. You can also use the **/usr/lib/edconfig** command for these simple editing tasks if you do not need to specify any gateways. For the following example I assume a machine called barolo in the domain wines.beverages.com with a second interface that is reachable under the name barolo2. Here are the things that most frequently need to be changed:

Dw
: Set this to your host name without a domain, as in *Dwbarolo*.

Cw
: Set this to your host name and any aliases you have, as in
`Cwbarolo barolo2`

: You can also use complete domain names here if this host has to react to different domains. Any name that this machine should recognize as a local name when mail is delivered needs to be included here.

DD
: Set this to your full domain name, as in
`DDwines.beverages.com`

Cd
: If you have domain aliases then set this to something like
`Cd $D your.other.domain`

: Together with the *Cw* definition you can use this to set up a mail relay on a firewall that reacts to different domains. If you have multilevel company domains then this should include your top company domain (in my case *ibm.com*). Otherwise all mail to machines outside the local domain will sent via the mail relay (see below).

OK
: If you are using a name server set this to *OK MX MB MR*. As indicated in the comments in sendmail.cf do not use *OK ANY* when you have wildcard MX records for your domain as this might lead to some strange problems.

After executing **sendmail -bz ; refresh -s sendmail** you are ready to send mail. If you have a system that is known by only one name and you have defined a complete host name for your machine (name.your.domain) then you do not need to modify the default Dw, Cw, DD and Cd settings. They are usually used only if the host name and domain cannot be completely resolved from the host name of the machine that was defined with the *hostname* command.

Some other things that might need to be defined if you have specific mail gateways follow:

DV and CV Define these if you have some mainframe that will relay mail to a RSCS network. You then can use *user@machine.rscs*, for example, to mail from the LAN to a System/370 without any further trickery.

DU You need to define this if you have a UUCP mail gateway. All mail that has a bang address (the one with the '!') will be sent there.

DX This needs to be defined if you have an X.400 gateway somewhere.

DR All mail whose address cannot be resolved will be sent to the gateway specified here. Use this for your Internet link for example.

DL Some sites have a central mail server and individual workstations will not receive mail themselves but mount a mail spool directory from the mail server. If you use such a setup, define DL to point to your mail server. This reduces the chances of mail corruption as a result of locking problems, especially in a heterogeneous environment.

DZ Do not forget to update the version number if you change more than just the host name.

O-, O+ Those two options will disable alias expansion with the *VRFY* and *EXPN* commands and log all attempts to use them. This is very useful on security critical mail servers to hide internal mail aliases.

Almost everything else belongs to the wizardry department :-}. But some things are easy even for an apprentice if you know where to look.

7.5.2 Changing the rules

The following sections describe some typical things that people do with sendmail in larger installations. Usually this is done on gateways or mail servers and the normal machines use this machine as the default gateway if they cannot send the mail directly. Each vendor might have a different way of handling sendmail rules, and each vendor usually has some other uses for macros, so using the modifications that you made to one vendor's sendmail file might not work on another installation. The following examples are for the IBM-delivered sendmail.cf file. If you use a stock sendmail version the rules might be slightly different.

Changing the sender address

You might want to use different internal domain names from the ones that you use externally because you are an international company or just because you want to hide some internal details. If you have only one external gateway and want any replies to your mail to be delivered to this address, the following is also an appropriate solution. At IBM Germany everyone uses sub-domains of *ibm.com* internally because all of IBM is in this domain. However, for an external Internet connection in Germany one has to use a German domain name as the *.com* ending is usually used only in the US. (There are a few exceptions of course.) Externally IBM Germany is known as *ibm.de*. So all addresses that are on external mail need to be rewritten or else the recipient might get into trouble replying. This can be done in sendmail's ruleset 1, which is initially empty. Add the following line to the ruleset for S1 on your gateway machine. (Search for S1 in /etc/sendmail.cf and put the lines after the S1 line.)

```
# change all sender addresses from something.ibm.com to ibm.de.
R$+<@$+.ibm.com>    <TAB> $@$1<@ibm.de>
```

Do not use INed for this modification. There must be a <TAB> character between the pattern and the rule! When dissected the rule looks as follows:

R — This is a rule.

$+ — Any number of tokens. We accept multitoken sender names as well; otherwise it would be $- for explicitly one token. The tokens found here will be token number 1 in the right-hand side of the rule.

< — Start of the network part of the address.

@ — The at character that separates name and address.

$+ — Any number of tokens in the domain name

.ibm.com — The trailing part of the domain.

> — End of the network part of the address.

<TAB> — The separating tabulator character.

$@ — This tells sendmail to execute this rule only once. Without this statement it would loop over ruleset 1 for ever.

$1 — The first token that was found on the left-hand side rule, which is the name part of the sender address.

<@ibm.de> — The new domain address that will be used in the mail.

With this rule any sender address from *somewhere.ibm.com* would be translated to come from *ibm.de*. This mechanism also hides multipart domains as *sub.domain.ibm.com* is always translated to *ibm.de* no matter what the *sub.domain* is.

Checking incoming mail against the alias database

If you run a gateway or mail server you might want to hide the internal recipient addresses and publicize only the gateway or server address. The previous section provided you with half of that setup, rewriting of outgoing mail. Now you want to check incoming mail against the local aliases database. This can be done in ruleset 0. You should include the following lines after the part of ruleset 0 that handles local delivery and before the UUCP section.

```
R$+<@ibm.de>          <TAB>       $#local$:$1
R$+<@$+.ibm.de>       <TAB>       $#local$:$1
```

Let's dissect these two rulesets. The first one says hand everything that is sent to *ibm.de* to the local mailer, which in turn will use the /etc/aliases database to look up the name before delivery. The second does basically the same but for subdomains of *ibm.de*.

R — Introduces a rule.

$+ — Any tokens.

<@ibm.de> — The *ibm.de* domain. The enclosing brackets are a speciality of IBM's sendmail rule file. Others might not use it.

<TAB> — The separating tabulator character.

$#local$: — Send to local mailer.

$1 — The first token from the left-hand side, which is the receiver's mail name without the address.

The second rule is different only on the left-hand side. By specifying *<$+.ibm.de>*, all sub-domains are caught in addition to the first rule that matches only *ibm.de*.

Making sure any in-house mail stays in-house

If you set up DR on your machines, then anything that is not in the local domain or cannot be resolved is sent to the gateway. The gateway should then figure out where to deliver it. For an organization that uses multiple domains this might not be what you want, as mail outside of your sub-domain is then sent via the gateway instead of being delivered directly to the other subdomain in your company.

The official way to get around this is to set up Cd as described above. Or you use the brute force solution: an addition to ruleset 0 that blindly tries to send anything within the main company domain via the TCP/IP mailer. If that does not succeed then there is something wrong anyway. The following rule should be included in ruleset 0 before the check for the DR macro is made.

```
R$+<@$+.ibm.com>$* <TAB> $#tcp$@$2.ibm.com$:$1<@$2.ibm.com>$3
```

Sendmail rule symbols

Sendmail understands more rule set symbols than the ones used in the above example. If you need to dig deeper, then the following list might be helpful. First the LHS (left-hand side) tokens that sendmail understands in rule sets:

$*	Matches zero or more tokens.
$+	Matches one or more tokens.
$-	Matches exactly one token.
$=X	Matches tokens in class X.
$X	Matches tokens that are not in class X.

Tokens are parseable parts of an address as defined with *Do* in the sendmail.cf file. On the right-hand side of the rules (RHS) the following symbols are understood:

$n	Use the nth token from the left-hand side ($1 is the first one found).
$>n	Call ruleset n.
$#mailer	Send through the mailer specified.
$@host	Tell the mailer to use a specific host via which the mail is transferred.
$:user	Specifies the user id part of the address for the mailer.
$[hosts$]	Resolve host name via the resolver (usually DNS).
$@	Terminate rule set.
$:	Terminate current rule.

7.5.3 Debugging *sendmail*

If you have problems with sendmail you should look at its debug mode, not a pleasant task but one that might save you a lot of work. With sendmail in debug mode you can test all the rewriting that was shown in the previous sections.

You can invoke sendmail with other than the default configuration file and test it without interfering with the running system. The following example assumes a test sendmail.cf file in /tmp. Use **sendmail -bz -C/tmp/sendmail.cf && sendmail -C/tmp/sendmail.cf -bt -d21.19** to digest the sendmail configuration file and start sendmail in debug mode. The *-bt* flag tells sendmail to start up in interactive address test mode and the *-d* flag specifies the debug level. You can use different levels here, but all have to start with 21. The higher the level, the more debugging output you get.

All addresses are usually passed through rule 3 first. So you should specify 3,1 if you want to know what sendmail does with an address in rule set 1. To get a complete picture you should specify 3,1,4 because ruleset 4 removes some internal information from a mail address that is added in ruleset 3. Sender addresses are modified in rule set 1 whereas recipient addresses are handled in rule set 2. Rule set 0 handles the delivery.

At the prompt enter the rules that you want to check separated by colons and then the address that you want to check. The following is a sample dialog used on a sendmail configuration file that has the above modifications:

```
# sendmail -bz -C /tmp/sendmail.cf && sendmail -C /tmp/sendmail.cf -bt -d 21.99

Version AIX 3.2/UCB 5.64.
Address Test Mode:
Enter <ruleset> <address>
> 3,1 afx@barolo.munich.ibm.com
rewrite: ruleset 3   input: "afx" "@" "barolo" "." "munich" "." "ibm"
"." "com"
rewrite: ruleset 3 returns: "afx" "<" "@" "barolo" "." "munich" "."
"ibm" "." "com" ">"
rewrite: ruleset 1   input: "afx" "<" "@" "barolo" "." "munich" "."
"ibm" "." "com" ">"
rewrite: ruleset 1 returns: "afx" "<" "@" "ibm" "." "de" ">"
```

The rules we specified above told *sendmail* that anything within *ibm.com* should be modified to look like *ibm.de* in rule set 1 so the above output is quite correct.

```
> 3,1 zaphod@guide.altair.com
rewrite: ruleset 3   input: "zaphod" "@" "guide" "." "altair" "." "com"
rewrite: ruleset 3 returns: "zaphod" "<" "@" "guide" "." "altair" "."
"com" ">"
rewrite: ruleset 1   input: "zaphod" "<" "@" "guide" "." "altair" "."
"com" ">"
rewrite: ruleset 1 returns: "zaphod" "<" "@" "guide" "." "altair" "."
"com" ">"
```

As the address we test here is not within *ibm.com* it passed rule set 1 without any modification.

```
> 3,0 afx
rewrite: ruleset 3   input: "afx"
rewrite: ruleset 3 returns: "afx"
rewrite: ruleset 0   input: "afx"
rewrite: ruleset 0 returns: "^V" "local" "^X" "afx"
```

An address without any domain is usually treated as local. The *^V* tells us the mailer that sendmail is using; in this case it delivers the mail locally. The recipient is specified by the *^X*.

\> **3,0 zaphod@guide.altair.com**

```
rewrite: ruleset 3   input: "zaphod" "@" "guide" "." "altair" "." "com"
rewrite: ruleset 3 returns: "zaphod" "<" "@" "guide" "." "altair" "."
"com" ">"
rewrite: ruleset 0   input: "zaphod" "<" "@" "guide" "." "altair" "."
"com" ">"
rewrite: ruleset 0 returns: "^V" "tcp" "^W" "mail" "." "germany" "."
"eu" "." "net" "^X" "zaphod" "<" "@" "guide" "." "altair" "." "com" ">"
```

In the above rule we have a target address that is not within our domain (*ibm.com*) so it is sent off to the relay host, which is *mail.germany.eu.net* in this case, as specified by *DR* in the sendmail.cf file. The mailer used is TCP and the target address stays the same.

\> **3,0 afx@ibm.de**

```
rewrite: ruleset 3   input: "afx" "@" "ibm" "." "de"
rewrite: ruleset 3 returns: "afx" "<" "@" "ibm" "." "de" ">"
rewrite: ruleset 0   input: "afx" "<" "@" "ibm" "." "de" ">"
rewrite: ruleset 0 returns: "^V" "local" "^X" "afx"
```

If the machine receives mail addressed to *afx@ibm.de* it would treat it as local as specified in the sample rewrite rule above.

The address test mode is terminated by a <CTRL-D>.

You can also try to talk to the sendmail daemon directly. Use *telnet* on the SMTP port to see how the *sendmail* daemon reacts to connection attempts. You can specify any port when using *telnet* after the host name, for example **telnet localhost smtp**. This can be used to verify addresses and aliases unless you have set *O-* and *O+*. Just type *help* to see what commands are available to you.

7.6 Setting up anonymous FTP

Anonymous FTP is quite convenient if you want to make information available to others without NFS exports or guest accounts. AIX 3 comes with a shell script in /usr/lpp/tcpip/samples/anon.ftp to set up anonymous FTP. On AIX 4 you will find this script in /usr/samples/tcpip. Just run this script as root user and it will create the user id *ftp* as well as the id anonymou(s). It will then set up the correct directory structure in *ftp*'s $HOME. If you want to have a different directory for the anonymous FTP server create the *ftp* user yourself and set the directory you desire. The script will then use this directory. After the script has finished there will be some subdirectories in the home directory of *ftp* that are necessary for the operation of the FTP commands in a *chroot*ed environment. (The FTP daemon will use *chroot* under the hood to put the anonymous user in a restricted environment; without this precaution anonymous FTP would be a gigantic security hole.)

You might want to check the permissions of the created directories and modify them as they are still fairly liberal: the ~ftp/pub directory is writable by everyone. This could transform your server into an anonymous exchange site where anyone can store data for anyone. Thus, files or directories in the ~ftp directory tree should not be writable by *ftp*. It is best to make them owned by *root* and remove write access for all files/directories in the *ftp* home tree. The creation of the *ftp* user id will also run /etc/security/mkuser.sys. You might need to undo some things that are done in there after running *anon.ftp*, for example remove all the profiles.

In the ~ ftp/etc directory you can install a fake group file and assign any names to groups, otherwise the *dir* sub-command of *ftp* will list numerical group ids. You should also install a fake passwd file there. Do not use your real passwd file as it can be accessed via *ftp* and might reveal information about your user ids that helps crackers attack your system.

If you want to log all data import and export that happens via anonymous FTP then you should configure logging for *ftpd*. Modify /etc/inetd.conf and change the ftp configuration line from

```
ftp   stream   tcp   nowait   root   /etc/ftpd   ftpd
```

to

```
ftp   stream   tcp   nowait   root   /usr/sbin/ftpd   ftpd -l
```

then execute **inetimp** (only on AIX 3) and **refresh -s inetd**. This will update the internet daemon and further invocations of the FTP daemon will log all requests via *syslogd*. If you have not done so, configure *syslogd* as shown in Section 7.3.8. The FTP daemon will log all import and exports with the debug priority.

8

Using NFS

Network file system (NFS) was developed as a simple solution to the problem of file sharing in a small work group. Unfortunately, it is now used for campus-wide file sharing and other huge networks for which it was never designed. Its basic stateless design for easy crash recovery could not support all the needs of the users, so status information was added as an afterthought with additional daemons. This leaves us with NFS as it is now, with all the disadvantages of a stateless design as well as the disadvantages of a statefull design. In addition, NFS does not provide a mapping of the user ids between machines. Another suite of protocols is required for this, NIS (Network Information System, see Chapter 9). NFS is based on a high-level remote procedure call interface that uses UDP for data exchange. This makes the protocol in itself quite inefficient compared with a simple file transfer with FTP. As NFS mandates real writes to disk before a write call returns to the client, any caching performed by the operating system on the server is ignored, reducing the NFS write performance even further. Despite this, it is one of the easiest ways to share files in a department as long as one is aware of the limitations.

8.1 Configuring NFS services

Configuring an NFS server or client amounts to starting some daemons and either exporting or importing some directories. Run **smit mknfs** or just **/usr/sbin/mknfs -B** to activate NFS on the machine. This will put the start of /etc/rc.nfs into /etc/inittab and run rc.nfs to active the daemons. In rc.nfs the *biod*, *lockd* and *statd* daemons are started automatically. If the file /etc/exports exists then the *nfsd* and *mountd* daemons will also be started, because the system is considered to be a server. As NFS is based on remote procedure calls it needs the portmapper daemon to function. The portmapper daemon is started out of /etc/rc.tcpip. Sometimes it is not configured by default. Make sure that it is active by uncommenting its invocation in rc.tcpip.

Although the default number of *biod* and *nfsd* daemons is usually sufficient, you might want to adjust their number on machines with a very high NFS load. This can be done with the **smit nfsconfigure** menu or the *chnfs* command.

AIX already has one *biod* daemon built into the kernel (*kbiod*). This is needed to support diskless machines and you can therefore mount and access file systems without having *biod* daemons running. For normal performance, however, one needs the standard *biod* daemons are necessary.

8.2 Exporting file systems

Run **smit mknfsexp** to get to the exports menu (Figure 8.1).

```
* PATHNAME of directory to export                   []              /
* MODE to export directory                           read-write     +
  HOSTNAME list. If exported read-mostly            []
  Anonymous UID                                     [-2]
  HOSTS allowed root access                         []
  HOSTS & NETGROUPS allowed client access           []
  Use SECURE option?                                 no             +
* EXPORT directory now, system restart or both       both           +
  PATHNAME of Exports file if using HA-NFS          []
```

Figure 8.1 Exporting a file system with SMIT.

Use the export mode with the fewest privileges, preferably read only. If possible, restrict the access to a few machines, especially for write access. The read-mostly export is useful when most machines are allowed to read the file system but only a few have the privilege to write. Enter those in the host name list for read mostly.

The anonymous user id is the one that will be used for remote users trying to access this file system as root unless the remote machine has been granted root access. The default of -2 maps this type of access to the user id nobody. If you want to use Secure NFS (an oxymoron in my opinion) you can activate it for this file system as well.

For users of HANFS a different pathname for the exports file can be entered. This is of no concern for normal NFS exports.

When you press <ENTER> SMIT will run the command *mknfsexp* for you. This command will put the directory name in the file /etc/exports together with the appropriate options and run *exportfs* to tell the NFS daemons that there is another file system available for export. If you are familiar with NFS you can edit /etc/exports yourself and then run **exportfs -a** to update the daemons. If you do so, be aware that this file has a line length limit of 1024 characters.

8.3 Configuring NFS clients

NFS mounts are configured with **smit mknfsmnt** or the *mknfsmnt* command (Figure 8.2).

```
* PATHNAME of mount point                               []           /
* PATHNAME of remote directory                          []
* HOST where remote directory resides                   []
  Mount type NAME                                       []
* Use SECURE mount option?                               no          +
* MOUNT now, add entry to /etc/filesystems or both? now              +
* /etc/filesystems entry will mount the directory       no           +
   on system RESTART.
* MODE for this NFS file system                          read-write  +
* ATTEMPT mount in foreground or background              background  +
  NUMBER of times to attempt mount                      []           #
  Buffer SIZE for read                                  []           #
  Buffer SIZE for writes                                []           #
  NFS TIMEOUT. In tenths of a second                    []           #
  Internet port NUMBER for server                       []           #
* Mount file system soft or hard                         hard        +
  Allow keyboard INTERRUPTS on hard mounts?              yes         +
  Minimum TIME, in seconds, for holding                 [3]          #
   attribute cache after file modification
  Maximum TIME, in seconds, for holding                 [60]         #
   attribute cache after file modification
  Minimum TIME, in seconds, for holding                 [30]         #
   attribute cache after directory modification
  Maximum TIME, in seconds, for holding                 [60]         #
   attribute cache after directory modification
  Minimum & Maximum TIME, in seconds, for               []           #
   holding attribute cache after any modification
  The Maximum NUMBER of biod daemons allowed            [6]          #
   to work on this file system
* Allow execution of SUID and sgid programs              yes         +
   in this file system?
* Allow DEVICE access via this mount?                    yes         +
* Server supports long DEVICE NUMBERS?                   yes         +
```

Figure 8.2 Importing file systems with SMIT.

The mount type can be used to group several file systems. You can then unmount or mount them with one command. I usually keep all NFS mounted file systems in the mount group *nfs* so that I can run **mount -t nfs** to mount them all at once. You might want to group your mounted file systems for tasks or servers with this label.

If you want to mount the file system not only now but also in future sessions, you should add it to /etc/filesystems. If you tell the system to mount the directory on system restart it will be available automatically after the next boot. This has some drawbacks however. When using DNS the name service will not be available at the time the system tries to mount the remote file system. This, in turn, will delay the boot process for a long time while the system tries to find the IP address for the remote host. I suggest using a mount type and then mounting the file systems later from rc.local instead of setting the mount on restart option to yes. If you really need the file system mounted early so that you cannot mount it in rc.local you should have entries for the remote hosts in /etc/hosts so that the system can find the IP address even without the name server, at least after a timeout. On AIX 4 you can work around the timeout by configuring the resolver, see page 124.

If the server exports a file system in read–write mode you still can set read only in this menu if needed.

By default file systems are mounted in the foreground. The *mount* command will block until the file system is mounted. When background is specified then the *mount* command will fork off a child that retries the mount in the background after the initial attempt to mount the file system has failed. If you mount essential file systems at boot time you should stick to the default of foreground mounts.

Initially the number of retries for a mount attempt is 1000. This may seem to be high, but it is not if you consider that NFS tries to survive server crashes. Within 1000 mount attempts a server might be completely rebooted and the mount will eventually succeed.

The read and write buffer sizes define a cache for NFS reads and writes. Their default of 8 KB is usually sufficient. When writing many small data chucks to widely separate locations of a file then the write buffer size might be too big for an efficient operation. A very loaded server also might benefit from smaller client write buffers. Experiment in your environment to find the optimal sizes. Although not recommended, people still try to use NFS over WANs. If you are among those or if you have a really shaky network, you should consider making the buffer sizes much smaller, for example 2 KB, to ensure that the data is transferable over the network within the timeout periods.

The NFS timeout is the initial timout value for NFS requests in tenths of a second. After the first timeout the value is doubled and the access is tried again. This is repeated until the maximum number of retries is reached. Unfortunately, this maximum number cannot be set with this SMIT screen. You have to modify /etc/filesystems manually and add the *retrans* option to the stanza of the file system in question. The default is *retrans=3*. Together with the default timeout option (*timeo=7*) the first major timeout occurs after 4.9 seconds (0.7s+1.4s+2.8s). Now the initial timeout value (*timeo*) is doubled and the cycle starts again, the next major timeout will be after 9.8 seconds. These cycles are repeated until the maximum timeout for the call is reached, which is a minute. By changing the values of *timeo* and *retrans* you are specifying how often retries are attempted before the call finally fails. This has a direct influence on the server, assuming that the server is still available. If a loaded server gets too many retries its performance will be degraded even more.

Should you use some non standard server you can specify a different port number for accessing the server's daemons. Usually this is not needed.

A major decision is the type of mount, hard or soft. Hard mounts are the only choice for file systems with write access as the integrity of files written to via a soft mount cannot be guaranteed. For all essential file systems that are used to load executables or data you should choose hard mounts. The advantage of soft mounts is that an access attempt with a crashed server does not hang for ages. However, it is unfortunately not possible to make soft mounts that guarantee data integrity so they are not used in most cases.

When using hard mounts one should allow keyboard interrupts; otherwise there is no way to terminate a hung program that tries to access an NFS file system. Even with this option enabled it might take a while for the process to respond to the interrupt.

The cache options are used by clients that write to the server. Instead of rereading status information from a server after writing to a file, the information out of the cache is used. This information might be invalid because another client has modified the file meanwhile. On the other hand, the longer one keeps this information in the cache the less traffic for status information is sent over the network, which improves performance greatly. I suggest leaving these options at their default values.

The maximum number of *biods* that can be set here defines how many of the system's *biods* can be used concurrently for this particular file system. The more you allow, the more data can be processed in parallel. This parameter can be used to favor one mounted file system over others as all file systems share the available *biod* daemons.

When mounting executables from a server you can neutralize SUID and SGID bits on them. Any setuid (setgid) program accessed via this mount is just a normal program when this option is activated.

If you do not allow device access via this mount you do not allow programs that are mounted to access devices on your system.

Usually all modern NFS servers support long device numbers; so you can leave this option at the default setting of yes.

Assuming that you want to mount the read-only file system /usr/local from *chablis* onto /usr/local with the default options, a label of *nfs* and automatic mount at boot time. You can fill in the values in Figure 8.2 or run **/usr/sbin/mknfsmnt -f/usr/local -d/usr/local -h chablis -m nfs -A -w bg -t ro -H**. Either way you will get the following entry in /etc/filesystems:

```
/usr/local:
        dev             = /usr/local
        vfs             = nfs
        nodename        = chablis
        mount           = true
        type            = nfs
        options         = bg,hard,intr,ro
        account         = false
```

You could also add this entry manually, but I suggest using *mknfsmnt* or SMIT instead: finding typos in stanza files can be time consuming.

Since one does not always want to mount a file system permanently and filling in a SMIT menu for a quick temporary mount is somewhat tedious, you can do the mount on the command line instead. All the options of the SMIT menu are available for the mount command line, but one usually does not need them. For example, when accessing the directory /test on the server *grappa* read only as /mnt on the local machine you can use **mount -oro grappa:/test /mnt**.

8.4 Using the automounter

The automounter is a daemon that mounts file systems dynamically when necessary to avoid having all remote file systems mounted all the time. In addition, it can provide support for load balancing and backup servers by checking several possible servers until it receives an answer. When mounting remote file systems, the automounter uses /tmp_mnt for the mount points and then creates a symbolic link to it while the file system is being accessed. If the file system is no longer needed the mount and the symbolic link are removed.

There are several ways to invoke the automount daemon, but they all require manual work; the automounter can be started with SMIT, but there is no configuration menu. The simplest case for using the automounter is to list file systems to be mounted in a direct map. Direct maps map remotely exported file systems directly to local file systems, as in Figure 8.3.

```
/usr/local/rhino          -rw,hard,intr    rhino:/usr/local
/home/afx/rhino           -rw,hard,intr    rhino:/home/afx
/usr/lpp/info/En_US       -ro,soft,intr    rhino:/usr/lpp/info/En_US
/usr/frame4.0             -ro,hard,intr    rhino:/usr/frame4.0
/var/spool/news           -ro,soft,intr    hippo:/var/spool/news
```

Figure 8.3 A direct automounter map /etc/auto.direct.

The directory on the left-hand side is the local mount point. It is followed by the mount options and the source machine and directory. Instead of having all these file systems mounted via entries in /etc/filesystems, they are now mounted automatically when they are accessed. If they are not accessed for a while (the default is 5 minutes) they are unmounted again. To load this direct map the command **automount -m /- /etc/auto.direct** is used. The options tell the automount daemon to ignore NIS maps (*-m*) and load a direct map (*/-*) from the file /etc/auto.direct. If you check the mounted file system after starting the daemon you will see an output similar to that in Figure 8.4.

```
# mount
  node       mounted          mounted over    vfs        date         options
-------- --------------- --------------- ------ ------------ ---------------
         /dev/hd4        /               jfs    Mar 21 16:01 rw,log=/dev/hd8
         /dev/hd9var     /var            jfs    Mar 21 16:01 rw,log=/dev/hd8
         /dev/hd2        /usr            jfs    Mar 21 16:01 rw,log=/dev/hd8
         /dev/hd3        /tmp            jfs    Mar 21 16:01 rw,log=/dev/hd8
        /dev/homelv     /home          jfs    Mar 21 16:03 rw,log=/dev/loglv00
lion (pid25650/usr/local/rhino) /usr/local/rhino nfs    Apr 05 15:09 ro,ignore
lion (pid25650/home/afx/rhino) /home/afx/rhino nfs    Apr 05 15:09 ro,ignore
lion (pid25650/usr/frame4.0) /usr/frame4.0    nfs    Apr 05 15:09 ro,ignore
lion (pid25650/var/spool/news) /var/spool/news  nfs    Apr 05 15:09 ro,ignore
```

Figure 8.4 **mount** output when using the automounter.

When checking with *df* you will see only the file systems that are currently mounted, and not necessarily all of those displayed with the *mount* command. I suggest starting the automounter either from rc.local or directly from inittab. There is no standard place to start it in AIX as shipped. To see what the automounter is doing you can use the *-T* option multiple times on the command line, which will activate a trace to standard out in case you have problems.

Never use **kill -9** to terminate the automounter; always use **kill -15** (the default signal). When receiving SIGTERM the automounter can remove its entries from the mount table otherwise you will end up with entries in the mount table that do not work. The automounter will not unmount file systems that are still in use when it is being terminated.

If you only mount a few file systems from singular servers without backup then the automounter has few advantages over standard mounts, although it does give you a a less cluttered *df* output. However, there are other ways of using the automounter, for example the maps could be controlled by NIS so that the NIS administrator can substitute it without the need for the users to change anything.

8.5 NFS kernel parameters

NFS performance is heavily influenced by device, IP and socket buffers. Most of those values can be modified with the *nfso* utility at runtime. Please read Section 19.4 for more information on *nfso* and other utilities that will allow you to modifiy the low-level NFS characteristics.

8.6 PC-NFS

PC-NFS is an extension to NFS that allows PCs to access NFS servers. It deals with the missing concept of user and group ids on PCs. It also provides a spooling function other than through *lpd* for PCs when properly configured.

On AIX 3 the entry in /etc/inetd.conf sets up the daemon in such a way that it reacts only to version 1 of the PC-NFS protocol. AIX 4 automatically supports versions 1 and 2. To enable support for version 2 on AIX 3 edit the entry for *pcnfsd* in /etc/inetd.conf so that it looks as follows:

```
pcnfsd sunrpc_udp udp wait root /usr/sbin/rpc.pcnfsd pcnfsd 150001 1-2
```

9

Running with NIS

NIS, formerly known as YP or yellow pages, is an attempt to create a simple distributed environment together with NFS. It works quite well in small installations where the security requirements are not very high. Anywhere else it creates more problems than it solves; nevertheless it is widely used. If you need a more serious distributed environment you should look at DCE. NIS clients either access configuration files no longer directly but via maps that are maintained on a NIS server or their local files are extended with data from the NIS server. Like other distributed services, NIS has some form of redundancy built in via slave servers that replicate the information of a master server. On AIX you can control NIS painlessly via SMIT without the need to touch any of its more intricate configuration details as long as you don't want anything out of the ordinary.

9.1 Configuring NIS

NIS can be configured on AIX in the same way as on any other UNIX system, but using SMIT for standard activation is very easy. Fill in one form and off you go. However, before you do so you have to decide on how your NIS setup will look and how it will be managed. If you are serious about using NIS, check out (*Managing NFS and NIS*, 34), it is the most complete reference for NIS administration.

Administrative data is grouped into domains when using NIS. Each domain is a group of machines that shares the same configuration data. A NIS domain has nothing in common with a DNS domain, but quite often people match them with each other. A NIS domain could be all machines in the research group, all of which would have access to the same administrative information. A NIS client can also access other domains when needed. A domain has one master server, and it should also have a few slave servers for enhanced reliability. All configuration changes need to be done on the master server, and are then replicated on the slave servers. Clients always get the data directly from a server without keeping any data locally.

9.1.1 Files controlled by NIS

Table 9.1 Files under NIS control.

File	Map names	Alias	Data source
/etc/aliases	mail.aliases mail.byaddr		local/NIS
/etc/passwd	passwd.byname passwd.byuid		local/NIS
/etc/group	group.bygid group.byname		local/NIS
/etc/hosts	hosts.byaddr hosts.byname	*hosts*	NIS
/etc/services	services.byname	*services*	NIS
/etc/protocols	protocols.byname protocols.bynumber	*protocols*	NIS
/etc/rpc	rpc.bynumber		NIS
/etc/netgroup, on the server only	netgroup.byname netgroup.byhost	*netgroup*	NIS
	netid.byname		NIS
	ypservers		NIS

The files that are controlled by NIS are stored in maps, which are really just one-key databases. For each key there is one database. For example, hosts.byname is the database that is used for host name lookup. The database hosts.byaddr is its counterpart for address – name mapping. Unless you start to include your own files in NIS you do not need to worry about those details. The default files that are managed by NIS on AIX are listed in Table 9.1.

NIS is set up to manage even more files, as mentioned in InfoExplorer, but the other files are not used on AIX. When NIS is active, the client systems do not access files directly. NIS modifies system library services so that calls that would normally get their data out of those files get it via NIS. If you access the files manually on the clients you will still access the local file, not the NIS-managed database. If you need access to the NIS-managed files, use the *ypcat* command to get the data. The *ypcat* command accesses not the centrally administered files but the map database files generated from them. You can use **ypcat passwd** because it knows that *passwd* is an alias for the map *passwd.byname*. However, if you try **ypcat rpc** you will get nothing; you have to use **ypcat rpc.bynumber**.

In the case of /etc/passwd, /etc/group and /etc/aliases the local files are still consulted before the NIS database is queried. When you start to use NIS on a client machine, then an entry such as *+::0:0:::* will be appended to the /etc/passwd file. The plus is a hint to the system to start looking for NIS-supplied entries. Entries before the plus sign override the NIS database so you can have a locally administered root id for example. A proper /etc/passwd file for a NIS client could look like

```
root:!:0:0::/:/bin/ksh
daemon:!:1:1::/etc:
bin:!:2:2::/bin:
sys:!:3:3::/usr/sys:
adm:!:4:4::/var/adm:
uucp:!:5:5::/usr/lib/uucp:
guest:!:100:100::/home/guest:
nobody:!:4294967294:4294967294::/:
lpd:!:9:4294967294::/:
+::0:0:::
```

This would configure a locally administered root user. If NIS is not available, system maintenance still can be done this way, but one needs to maintain a local root password. If you do not want locally administered accounts at all, move the *+::0:0:::* entry to the beginning of the file. Beware that this might lead to maintenance problems in case of a missing NIS server.

On other UNIX systems the *+::0:0:::* entry in /etc/passwd can be very harmful. Should NIS be unavailable when the system boots, you can then log in as the user '+' without a password. This does not happen on AIX as one also needs a corresponding entry in /etc/security/passwd to activate a user id when NIS is not running.

Although the comments in /etc/sendmail.cf say that you need to activate the *Op* option to access NIS aliases, they worked even without it on the AIX releases on which I have tried it. Sendmail searches first /etc/aliases and then the NIS map *mail.byname* to resolve mail aliases.

When NIS is active, the /etc/hosts files on clients are no longer used (apart from the boot phase before the NIS daemons are up). However, if DNS name service is also active, then it overrides the NIS-supplied host name database. The search order can be configured on AIX 4 (see page 124 for details).

9.1.2 Setting up a NIS server

On not only the server but all NIS-controlled machines you need to set a NIS domain name. This can be dome with the menus that you reach with **smit yp** or directly with **chypdom -B yourNISdomain**. No matter how you do it, it will change /etc/rc.nfs and activate the *domainname* command there. All the NIS daemons can be configured manually in /etc/rc.nfs if you are accustomed to that method. With **smit mkmaster** you reach the configuration screen to set up a NIS master (Figure 9.1).

```
  HOSTS that will be slave servers                  []
* Can existing MAPS for the domain be overwritten?  yes        +
* EXIT on errors, when creating master server?      yes        +
* START the yppasswdd daemon?                       yes        +
* START the ypupdated daemon?                       yes        +
* START the ypbind daemon?                          yes        +
* START the master server now,                      both       +
   at system restart, or both?
```

Figure 9.1 Setting up a NIS master server.

Your NIS slave servers can be added later if you do not know which ones you will use (see page 153). If you set up a new server, you can overwrite the existing maps. You should terminate the server on errors so that you will not start up a new server with broken configuration files. The *yppasswdd* daemon should be run so that remote users can change their password on the server with the *yppasswd* command without needing to log in to the server. The local *passwd* command will not work for NIS-only administered machines. The *ypupdated* daemon should be activated in case you run slave servers as well. If you start the *ypbind* process, then the NIS master will also be an NIS client. This is highly recommended to ensure that the clients and the master always use the same information base. After you hit <ENTER> the system will run the *mkmaster* command for you. This, in turn, will run *ypinit* to build the maps out of the master's configuration files, will start the necessary daemons and will activate NIS in the /etc/rc.nfs file.

Unless you have very relaxed security requirements you should also configure the file /var/yp/securenets, which defines the systems and networks that can access NIS on this server. The example below would allow access from the machine 192.168.10.15 and the net 192.168.1. Do not forget to include the local host.

```
255.0.0.0         127.0.0.1
255.255.255.255 192.168.10.15
255.255.255.0     192.168.1.0
```

9.1.3 Setting up a NIS client

Activating a NIS client is even easier than activating the server. Simply run **mkclient -B** and your system will be a NIS client (you can also use **smit mkclient**). The activation of *ypbind* will be done out of /etc/rc.nfs. If you need to change the options of *ypbind* you have to do so manually in the /etc/rc.nfs file. The master server or a slave server needs to be up and running before you can activate NIS client functions. You will get a hanging system should you try to run a client without any reachable servers.

NIS clients use broadcasts to find their NIS servers. If you have an NIS client on a different subnet where it cannot reach the NIS servers, you can use the *ypset* command, as in **ypset YourServer**, to tell *ypbind* about a server that is not reachable by broadcasts. For security reasons, one should run *ypind* without the *-s* and *-ypsetme* options. This will make it harder for remote systems to tell your system to listen to another server: *ypset* requests will only work from the local system. Without the *-ypsetme* option, no *ypset* requests at all will be accepted.

9.1.4 Setting up a NIS slave server

Each NIS domain should have at least one slave server for backup reasons. Having several servers also reduces the load on the main server. As much NIS traffic is done in broadcasts, there should be a slave server for each subnet. Configure a slave server with **smit mkslave** after you have configured this machine as a client. Simply tell it the name of the master. If the master server does not yet know about this slave, you need to tell it now with **smit chmaster**. If the master server is running *ypupdated* then the slave servers will be automatically updated from the master.

9.2 Working with netgroups

NIS adds a special management object to the standard UNIX users, groups and machines. Netgroups are formed out of objects that are a combination of host, user and domain, though not all of the parts of a netgroup are used in all circumstances. They are only available via NIS servers and can be used in various places, such as /etc/exports or /etc/hosts.lpd. They are configured with the file /etc/netgroup. Netgroups are formed out of the following triples:

```
groupname (host, user, domain) {,(host, user, domain)]}
```

Blank entries are regarded as wildcards. A '-' donates a field that can take no value. A group of developers where only the user ids are used could be:

```
dev (-,tex,-),(-,peter,-),(-,mickey,-)
```

The netgroup *dev* defines only users, whereas the following group also includes machines:

```
admin (blackice,afx,-), (cpunk,nick,-), (pengo,tex,-)

all (,,research)
```

The above netgroup *all* would be a placeholder for all machines in the research domain as it defines any host (the first field is empty) in the research NIS domain. This is a very useful feature of netgroups as it can be used in NFS exports, just like a host name, to restrict the export to a specific domain. If you use a netgroup for NFS exports, the user part of the group specification is ignored.

These netgroups can be used wherever they would make management of user and host data more convenient. In /etc/hosts.equiv as well as /etc/hosts.lpd or ~/.rhosts one can use either +@*netgroupname* or -@*netgroupname* to specify access or denial of access for all the machines and/or users that are in a given netgroup. To deny access to all the users in the group *bad-guys*, no matter from which machine they come from, you could use :

```
+   -@bad.guys
```

This would take all NIS registered hosts and deny access to all users that are in the netgroup *bad-guys*. The host and domain part of the *bad-guys* netgroup is ignored.

In /etc/groups and /etc/passwd you can also use netgroups to specify which users or groups should be managed via NIS and which ids via local files. If you put

```
root:!:0:0:The Boss:/:/usr/bin/ksh
-@dev
+@admin
```

in your /etc/passwd file, then the root user is administered locally, the members of *dev* netgroup are excluded and the members of the *admin* netgroup are managed via NIS. In this case only the user ids in the netgroups are considered; the domain and host entries are ignored.

9.3 Custom NIS databases

You can manage not only the system-supplied databases with NIS, but your own additions as well. Typical examples are company phone books or other items of local interest, such as the canteen's lunch menu. We have the following menu this week (in /usr/local/etc/lunch.menu):

```
Monday:     Burgers and fries
Tuesday:    Lasagna al forno
Wednesday:  Pizza mare
Thursday:   Fajitas
Friday:     Sushi platter
```

This file needs to be converted to something that the NIS database mechanism can handle. In this case we convert it to a simple database that is keyed by weekday. The resulting database input file will have the following format:

```
Day<whitespace>ThisDaysEntry
```

To create it we use a little *awk* script (/var/yp/lunch.awk):

```
#!/usr/bin/awk -f
BEGIN {FS=":" }
{   printf("%s\t%s\n",$1,$0);
}
```

This script modifies the lunch.menu file to be a suitable input to the *makedbm* command, which creates the database. The NIS server controls the map file generation via /var/yp/Makefile. We need to change this file. Near the beginning of the file you will find an entry that looks as follows:

```
all: passwd group hosts ethers networks rpc services protocols \
        netgroup bootparams aliases publickey netid netmasks
```

It defines the first target for *make*. We append lunch to this entry:

```
all: passwd group hosts ethers networks rpc services protocols \
        netgroup bootparams aliases publickey netid netmasks lunch
```

Then we need to tell *make* how to create lunch. We add a dependency line:

```
lunch: lunch.time
```

and

```
/usr/local/etc/lunch.menu:
```

to the other entries at the end of the file. Finally we need to add the commands to generate the maps to the file:

```
lunch.time: /usr/local/etc/lunch.menu
    -@if [ -f /usr/local/etc/lunch.menu ]; then \
      /var/yp/lunch.awk < $? | $(MAKEDBM) - $(YPDBDIR)/$(DOM)/lunch.byday; \
        touch lunch.time; \
        echo "updated lunch\n"; \
        if [ ! $(NOPUSH) ]; then \
            $(YPPUSH) lunch.byday; \
            echo "pushed lunch\n"; \
            fi \
    else \
        echo "couldn't find /usr/local/etc/lunch.menu\n"; \
    fi
```

This entry generates the DBM files from the lunch.menu file. To generate the DBM file initially, *NOPUSH* needs to be defined. This will skip the *yppush* step that normally updates the slave servers. If you try to push the new map to slave servers then they will not accept it because they do not know it yet. Therefore execute:

```
cd /var/yp
make NOPUSH=TRUE lunch
```

You then need to execute the following steps on all slave servers to tell them about the new database:

```
cd /var/yp
ypxfr -h YourMaster lunch.byday
```

The *-h* option is needed only if you have multiple masters or domains. Future updates will then be handled automatically when you execute **make lunch** on the server.

To find out what the lunch for a given day is, use **ypmatch Monday lunch.byday**, which would return:

```
Monday:       Burgers and fries
```

To see the week's menu use **ypcat lunch.byday**. Or, if you are lazy, you could define yourself an alias such as:

```
alias lunch='ypmatch `date +%A` lunch.byday'
```

Unfortunately, *ypmatch* is not very flexible: it returns only exact matches of a key. You cannot search for a weekday given in lower case in this example. To perform a more flexible search you would need to *ypcat* the map and then *grep* through it, which of course can transfer much larger amounts of data over the net.

9.4 Synchronizing NIS hosts

Any NIS data change on the master host must be made known to the clients explicitly. This is done by **cd /var/yp ; make**. The only exceptions to this rule are password changes. Once the *ypbind* process is running, the *passwd* command will run *yppasswd* under the hood to change the password on the server directly.

All clients will know about server updates immediately as they get their data only from the master, but this is no longer true when running slave servers. If the slave server is known to the master, running *make* will also send the updated maps to the slaves via *yppush*. As the previous example pointed out, slaves need to be told explicitly about new maps with the *ypxfr* command, which has to be run on the slave. Should the server try to *yppush* a map to a slave that does not know this map yet the *yppush* command will hang.

9.5 Password management with NIS

One of the major drawbacks of NIS on AIX is its lack of integration with the standard password management tools. Users need to change their passwords with either *passwd* or the *yppasswd* command, both of which ignore the AIX password configuration completely once *ypbind* is running. Even in AIX 4.1 there is no provision to integrate NIS password management and the more elaborate native AIX facilities.

10

Printing on AIX

Although everyone talks about the paperless office I have the impression that we create more paper by the use of computers than before. Check out *xpreview* and *showps* to avoid excessive preview printing. Printing on AIX is performed through the queuing system which has many features you will find usefull once you understand how it works. You can use the usual BSD and System V commands such as *lp*, *lpr*, *cancel*, *lprm*, *lpstat* and *lpq*. These commands are front ends to the AIX queuing system, which uses *enq* for everything under the hood, or you can use the AIX queuing facilities directly and access its more advanced features. The inner workings of the queuing system are fully exposed on AIX 3, whereas AIX 4 tries to conceal most things. Although the underlying mechanisms are the same in both releases, AIX 4 is more user friendly as one does not need to dive deep to get the job done.

10.1 The queuing subsystem

AIX has a general-purpose queuing subsystem (Figure 10.1) that is used mainly for printing. I would think that most people would use it only for printing, though it can also be used for batch jobs as well. All printing is done through virtual printers that optionally modify the data before it is sent to the printer.

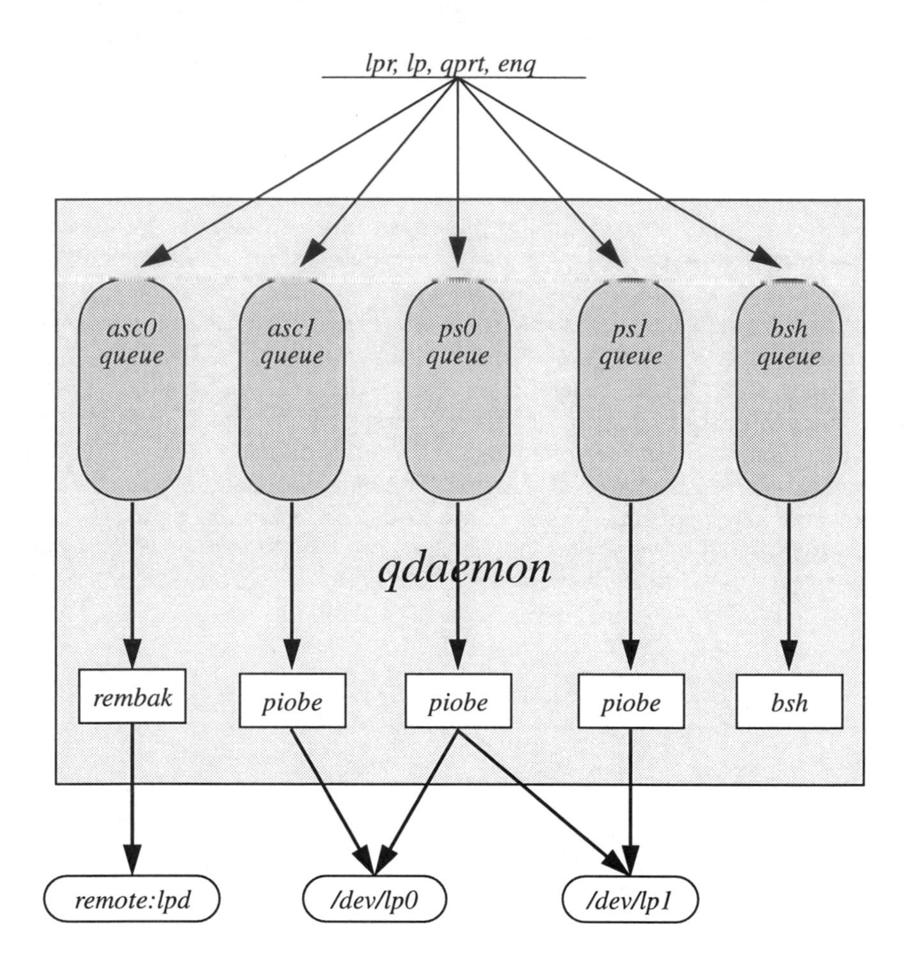

Figure 10.1 The queuing system.

A virtual printer queue is what you usually access when submitting a print job. It is composed out of a queue and a device with associated formatting capabilities. A virtual printer defines the queue to which the job is submitted. The queue then sends the job to a backend program (typically *rembak* or *piobe*), which in turn sends it to the real printer after optionally having modified the data stream. A queue can have several printers and a printer can have several queues. If you install backend programs other than printer drivers, then you can use the queueing system for batch jobs; in fact, AIX 3 already comes with such a queue, the *bsh* queue (Born shell queue).

The process that controls the queuing system is *qdaemon*. It is configured via /etc/qconfig. Here you will find stanzas such as

```
lp0:
          device = lp0
lp0:
          file = /dev/lp0
          header = never
          trailer = never
          access = both
          backend = /usr/lib/lpd/piobe
```

which defines a queue *lp0* to access a local printer on /dev/lp0 that will be driven by the *piobe* printer I/O backend program. A queue has one or more devices associated with it and may have attributes defined. A device usually points to a file and to a program that handles the request. It also can have more attributes defined. The generic form would look as follows:

```
queue:
          device = dev1{,devn}
          {attribute = value}
dev1:
          backend = /usr/lib/lpd/piobe
          {attribute = value}
dev2:
          backend = /usr/lib/lpd/piobe
          {attribute = value}
```

where programs other than *piobe* could also be listed. The following attributes, listed here with their default values are available:

acctfile=FALSE If this is set to a file name, then the file stores the accounting information for this queue. In my opinion printer accounting is useless as there is no accurate method of determining the number of pages printed out of arbitrary print jobs, especially when complex page description languages such as PostScript are used.

discipline=fcfs Sets the serving algorithm. An alternative to the default 'first comes, first served' is *sjn*, which means 'shortest job next'. The algorithm uses the file size to determine the job size.

up=TRUE Determines if the queue accepts jobs. Usually the attribute is not even present and the default TRUE is used. It can be used to disable the queue temporarily as it will not accept any jobs if up is set to FALSE. You can change it via **chque -qQueueName -s"up = FALSE"**. Note that the spaces around the = sign are significant.

If an attribute is not present, its default value is assumed. When using remote print queues the following attributes are also available:

host The host for the remote printer.

s_statfilter The short status filter for obtaining remote printer status reports. Filters are available for other AIX machines (aixshort), old AIX version 2 machines (aixv2short) like the RT, BSD systems (bsdshort) and System V systems (attshort). They can be found in /usr/lib/lpd.

l_statfilter The long status filter for obtaining remote printer status reports. Filters are available for other AIX machines (aixlong), old AIX version 2 machines (aixv2long) like the RT, BSD systems (bsdlong) and System V systems (attlong). They can be found in /usr/lib/lpd.

rq The name of the queue on the remote machine.

For the device there is also a host of attributes:

access=write If set to *both*, then the device can communicate with the queue. If set to *FALSE* it will be ignored. If you want to get PostScript error messages back from a serially connected PostScript printer you need to set this to *both*.

align=TRUE Sends a form feed in between jobs if there has been a pause.

feed=NEVER Specifies the number of separator pages between jobs.

file=/dev/null The output file for this device, which is usually set to something like /dev/lp0. On pseudoprinter devices (for example when writing your own backend) this file is often used to synchronize jobs via locking, even if data is never sent to it.

header=NEVER You can specify GROUP to get only one header page for each group of files printed by one user or ALWAYS to get a header page for each job. For remote access the default is ALWAYS.

trailer=NEVER This is like header, but it defaults to NEVER for remote jobs.

Is is not usually necessary to edit this file manually: all the information in here can be changed via SMIT or the associated commands, although in this case you have to create the queue via **mkque -q name** first. You can then use **mkquedev -q qname -d qdevice** to add devices to the queue. Both commands accept the *-a* option to set initial attributes. To complement those commands there are also *chque*, *chquedev*, *rmque* and *rmquedev* commands. Generating queues is usually easier via SMIT, but is necessary so rarely that one tends to forget all the command options. Use **smit lprint** to access the right menus.

The *qdaemon* uses not /etc/qconfig but a digested binary version – /etc/qconfig.bin – to read its configuration. The *enq* command does the conversion automatically whenever /etc/qconfig is newer than /etc/qconfig.bin. As *enq* is called by all other queueing commands, one can easily edit the file without bothering about updates. Simply running **lpstat** will do the conversion.

10.1.1 Controlling the queueing system.

The following commands can be used to control the queuing system:

lp, lpr, qprt These all send jobs to the queueing system. The first two can also be found on other UNIX systems, whereas the last is AIX specific. Note that *lpr* will always print a header page unless you use the *-h* flag. Look them up in InfoExplorer and use the one that suits you. In particular, *qprt* has more options than one can remember. Whereas *lp* and *qprt* only queue the file by default, *lpr* copies it to a spooling directory. This prevents problems with accidentally deleted files that are still in the queue but means that a bigger /var space is required for all the copies.

cancel, lprm, qcan These are commands to remove jobs from queues. The *qcan* is an AIX addition, but the other two can also be found elsewhere.

qadm This is used to changed the status of a queue; it replaces BSD's *lpc*.

lpstat, lpq, qstat These query the status of the print queue. Here *qstat* is an AIX addition.

qpri Changes the priority of a job in the queue.

qhld This AIX 4 addition allows you to put queued jobs on hold.

qmov Allows you to move queued jobs between queues on AIX 4.

lsallq, lsque These offer quick ways of listing queue configuration instead of reading /etc/qconfig.

enq This command is the one that performs the actual work for most of the above commands. The others *exec* it to access the queueing system. You can use *enq* directly instead of using the above commands.

Note that all the queuing commands that affect not only the jobs of the executing user but other jobs or the queue itself need root authority or the user needs to be in the *printq* group. Commands that try to change a job or queue will only work locally. There is no way to control a remote queue, you have to log in on the print server and do the work there. The only exception is cancelling jobs. This can be done for remote queues as well, but you always need to specify the device manually when cancelling jobs on remote queues.

When *$LPDEST* is set, all commands that do not reference a specific printer are executed for the printer that is specified in this environment variable. If *$LPD-*

EST is not set, then *$PRINTER* is checked. If this variable is also not set, the first queue in /etc/qconfig is used.

If a queue has more than one device, you can specify the device by appending *:devname* to the queue name in all places where a queue needs to be specified. If you do not specify a device then the first one that is available is used. Using several devices on one queue helps to distribute heavy printing requirements without the need for several access points.

10.1.2 How *qdaemon* works

For each queue the *qdaemon* sets up a status file. The status file resides in /var/spool/lpd/stat and has a name such as s.ps.lp0 or s.queue.queue-device. It is used to pass information between *qdaemon* and the backend program. The backend program gets some information about the job from this file, for example whether header pages are wanted, job title and so on. The backend, in turn, provides *qdaemon* with status information, such as the percentage of the job completed. This is a binary file that is not meant for humans to read.

When a job is received, the *qdaemon* queues the necessary information in a job description file. The job description file (Figure 10.2) is stored in /var/spool/lpd/qdir as *NNuser:queue*. This file is mostly readable ASCII text and can be used to analyze queueing problems.

```
207
#@%!: 0 0 15 0 740064883
1 1 3 3
afx 0
REAL_USER=afx\0LOGIN_USER=root\0REAL_GROUP=staff\0GROUPS=staff,printq,audit\0A
UDIT_CLASSES=\0RLIMIT_CPU=2147483647\0RLIMIT_FSIZE=2097151\0RLIMIT_DATA=419430
3\0RLIMIT_STACK=65536\0RLIMIT_CORE=2048\0RLIMIT_RSS=65536\0UMASK=22\0\0
USRENVIRON:\0_=/usr/bin/lp\0MANPATH=/usr/local/man:/usr/share/man\0LANG=en_US
\0NLSPATH=/usr/lib/nls/msg/%L/%N:/usr/lib/nls/msg/prime/%N\0PAGER=/usr/local/
bin/less\0ENSCRIPT=-dps -MA4\0VISUAL=emacs\0PATH=/u/afx/bin:/usr/bin:/usr/ucb:
/usr/sbin:/usr/local/bin:/usr/bin/X11:/usr/lpp/X11/Xamples/bin:.:/usr/Xframe/
bin\0COLUMNS=80\0CDPATH=:/u/afx:/usr:/usr/local\0WINDOWID=12582920\0EXINIT=se
t sw=4 ts=4 ai ic smd noslow\0EDITOR=/usr/bin/vi\0LOGNAME=afx\0MAIL=/usr/spool
/mail/afx\0LOCPATH=/usr/lib/nls/loc\0PS1=($?)$NODE:$PWD !\$ \0USER=afx\0
RDISPLAY=rhino:0.0\0DISPLAY=:0.0\0SHELL=/usr/bin/ksh\0ODMDIR=/etc/objrepos\0
NODE=rhino\0HISTSIZE=100\0HOME=/u/afx\0FCEDIT=/usr/bin/vi\0TERM=aixterm\0
MAILMSG=[YOU HAVE NEW MAIL]\0FMHOME=/usr/Xframe\0PWD=/var/spool/lpd\0TZ=CET-
1CEST,M3.5.0,M9.5.0\0ENV=/u/afx/.kshrc\0LESS=-icqM\0LINES=25\0A__z=!
 LOGNAME\0SYSENVIRON:\0NAME=root\0TTY=\0\0
-Ppclm
\0
/u/afx/.profile
afx
rhino
0
/u/afx/.profile 0
```

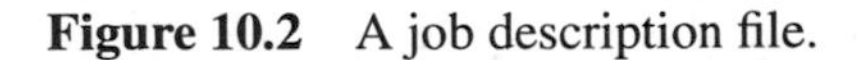

Figure 10.2 A job description file.

The first line in Figure 10.2 shows the job number. After the environment section you will find the options that were used to print the file, in this case *-Ppclm*, the file name, the user and the submitting host. Depending on the options you use, other information might be given as well. As this file is not meant to be an official interface, it is not documented. The "\0"s in the file are inserted for readability. The real file has ASCII 0 in their place, and some editors will not read this file.

For each job that is ready to be printed *qdaemon* prepares the necessary entries in the status file and then *execs* the backend. The backend is executed with the uid of the user that submitted the job and has access to a copy of the user's environment.

Should an error occur in the printing process then *qdaemon* sends a message to the user's log in terminal or the first log in window found in /etc/utmp. The last error message is also available as /var/spool/lpd/pio/msg1.queue:device on AIX 3.2. Unfortunately, there is no way to inhibit or redirect those messages in AIX.

If you want to see how the queueing system was invoked there are other methods, for example replace the backend in the /etc/qconfig stanza with a shell script that echoes its arguments to a file. If you want to know how another command used *enq* to print you could mount a similar script over the *enq* command to see the flags passed to *enq*.

The output that is sent to the printing device can easily be captured in a file should you need to. Create a file with **touch /tmp/printer.out; chmod 666 /tmp/printer.out**. Then replace the *file* attribute of the printer queue with this file. Now every file printed will be appended to this file and you can see any changes made to the original data.

10.1.3 Cleaning up the spool directories

Should you ever need to clean up the queueing system manually, execute the following steps:

(1) Kill all current print jobs with **qcan -X**.

(2) Stop *qdaemon* with **stopsrc -s qdaemon**.

(3) If there are still *qdaemon* processes or children of it (any *pio* processes) kill them with **kill -9 <pid>** manually.

(4) If you need to save print jobs copy the spooled files from /var/spool/qdaemon and /var/spool/lpd to /tmp.

(5) Remove the contents of the spool and control directories:

```
rm /var/spool/lpd/*
rm /var/spool/qdaemon/*
rm /var/spool/lpd/qdir/*
rm /var/spool/lpd/stat/*
```

(6) Activate the queueing daemon again with **startsrc -s qdaemon**.

(7) Now you can use your favorite print command to print the saved spool files.

10.1.4 Queue status information

The *lpstat* command will tell you about the queue status. Here is a quick rundown of the status entries and why they appear.

CONNECT You should rarely see it, as a CONNECT status is displayed only briefly to indicate that a connection to a remote printer has been established. It is quickly replaced by the SENDING status.

DEV_BUSY This indicates that the printer is in use either by another job in a different queue that refers to the same printer or by any other process that currently accesses the printer device.

DEV_WAIT The printer has problems (for example out of paper, paper jam, defective cabling). When working with a serial printer for the first time, the handshake might not be correct. Use **qadm -D queue** to stop the queue and correct the printer problem, then use **qadm -U queue** to start it up again.

DOWN This stage is reached after a timeout period in which the printer was in the DEV_WAIT state. Alternatively, if the system cannot communicate at all with the printer, then this state is reached immediately. Use **qadm -U queue** to get it back into a working state once you have fixed the printer problem.

GET_HOST This state is briefly displayed when the spooler tries to contact the remote host.

INITING This is displayed when a contact with the remote host is being established.

OPR_WAIT This will appear on queues where one needs to change the paper type manually or other programmed printer interventions are required. This status is accompanied by a terminal message for the operator.

QUEUED The standard status for queue jobs waiting to be processed.

READY Idle queues display this status.

RUNNING Displayed while a job is printing.

SENDING Displayed while the data for the job is being sent to a remote host.

UNKNOWN Displayed when the queueing system cannot determine the status of a device. This happens, for example, if you create a new queue on a device that is printing concurrently. Running **lpstat** after the job has finished will display a normal status.

10.1.5 Using the queuing system for batch services

The queueing system works not only for print queues but also for any kind of batch job. AIX 3.2 comes with one batch queue configured. This queue, *bsh*, runs shell scripts that are sent to it. If you have long-running jobs then you can send them to this shell via **lp -dbsh /your/long/job**.

On AIX 4 you would have to add the queue yourself. Use the following definitions in /etc/qconfig:

```
bsh:
        device = bshdev
        discipline = fcfs
bshdev:
        backend = /usr/bin/ksh
```

What is the function of this facility? You could, for example, use it to limit CPU-intensive jobs to be executed only one at a time. In contrast to *at* and *cron* jobs the queueing system is not bound to a specific execution time. One could easily bring the queue down during daytime and still send jobs to it. At night when the system load is low the queue is activated and the jobs run sequentially. A queue with currently executing jobs can be brought down if the system load is too high and restarted at a more convenient time. The jobs in the queue will then start again from scratch. Alternatively, if you have many batch jobs you could define a queue with a number of 'shell devices.' The number of devices limits the number of batch jobs executing simultaneously. And if you want to run jobs on other machines you can also do this via the queueing system.

This simple queueing facility is not meant to compete with UniJES, Loadleveler or NQS but works nicely for simple batch work that does not need much load balancing.

10.2 Local printers

Unless you want to print to a printer directly without the spooling system you do not need to configure a local printer on AIX 4 since it will be done automatically for you when configuring a printer queue (**smit mkpq**). On AIX 3 you need to configure a printer first before you can add a queue.

To configure a local printer the easiest route is to use **smit pdp**, which will take you to the "Printer/Plotter Devices" menu. To determine if the printer you want to use is directly supported by AIX you should first check the list of supported printers and plotters. If the printer you want to use is not directly supported and no compatible printer is supported, you can use the drivers for 'other serial printer' *osp* or 'other parallel printer' *opp*. AIX 3 comes with many printer drivers by default. AIX 4 is more space efficient. You need to install the drivers for your printers explicitly. This can be done directly from the **smit pdp** menu or via the standard installation procedures.

If you then add a printer, you will be prompted for the printer port. When you are in the printer configuration menu you should increase the timeout value to at least 600 (this is in seconds) if you are using a PostScript printer, which sometimes tend to respond late when processing complex PostScript files. You should also set the option 'send all characters unmodified' to YES even if you do not intend to use the port directly as it helps to debug problems when the driver never touches the data stream.

If you add a serial printer I suggest not using the XON/XOFF protocol as it has a high latency compared with hardware flow control. You should use the DTR protocol, which uses hardware lines for a reliable handshake, if your printer supports it. On AIX you will also have the alternative of using RTS/CTS, which is, however, less common with printers. After pressing <ENTER> SMIT will call the right invocation of *mkdev* for you.

If you have a lot of complex data to print, such as pictures in PostScript or large plot files, you should invest in network-attached printers. This can be done with any printer via the 4033 LAN connection or with printers that are available with network interfaces such as the Lexmark 4039 or the HP printers with JetDirect cards. The parallel port hardware and driver on the older RS/6000 models are not implemented very efficiently. It costs a lot of CPU time and offers only low throughput. Using a serial port at 38400 bps is usually better in terms of CPU utilization than the parallel port but still slow compared with a network-attached printer.

Some applications will not use the queuing subsystem but will print directly to the device. To modify the device settings on the fly, use the *splp* command to change some of the device characteristics temporarily, for example pass through. When checking those options, the output of *splp* without parameters will tell you what is really set for the device, no matter what the ODM says.

To test a printer you can *cat* files directly to the device. Use the *lptest* command to generate dummy test data, as in **lptest 80 70> /dev/lp0,** which would write 70 lines each 80 characters wide to *lp0*. Should you have trouble writing to the device use *splp* to check it, this is the most accurate way.

10.3 Generating print queues and virtual printers

On AIX 4 you create a printer queue and the rest is done automatically for you. On AIX 3 the process amounts to setting up local printers and virtual printers manually. The resulting printer queues are the same in the end only AIX 4 hides the internals better (Figure 10.3).

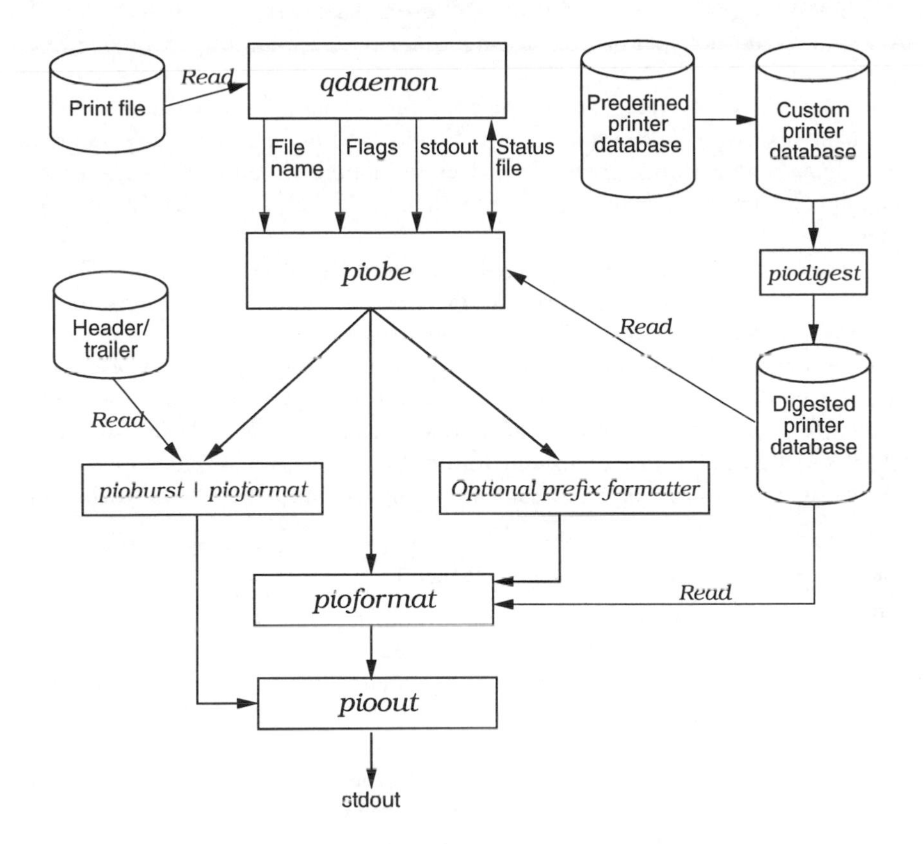

Figure 10.3 The innards of a virtual printer.

A virtual printer is accessed via a queue and sends the data on to the printing device after some possible modifications of the data stream. Code page translations, formatting and printer initialization can all be managed by the virtual printer. Once *enq* has told *qdaemon* about the print job, *qdaemon* takes over and hands the job to a virtual printer, which in turn will run several programs controlled by *piobe* to accomplish its task.

A virtual printer is generated via the *mkvirprt* command. This command uses the predefined printer database to generate a customized version for your printer. When exiting this program it will automatically call *piodigest* to generate a binary database from the customized printer definition. The printer backend *piobe* and its subprograms will then use this database to complete their job. If you access this command via SMIT on AIX 3 you are suddenly in a different world of menu guidance from SMIT. So do not bother going there via SMIT: instead run the command directly from the command line. It will prompt you for the necessary data. The *mkvirprt* command prompts you only for the absolute minimum configuration data. For printers that support multiple data streams such as the Lexmark 4039 or the HP

LaserJet IV you will be asked for different queue names for each data stream. On AIX 4 the **smit mkvirprt** fastpath is a true SMIT interface for the generation of virtual printers.

The next step is to adapt the printer driver to your specific needs. On AIX 4 you can do so with **smit chpq**, which will guide you through the configuration of the printer options (fonts, pitch, paper sizes and more). If you need to adapt more than the options shown here, use the same steps as on AIX 3 with the *lsvirprt* command.

Even for simple changes you need to use *lsvirprt* on AIX 3. Use the '*' command to list all attributes. You will then be put in the *pg* command. Use "**s /tmp/attributes**" to save this list as a reference then use the '~v' command to edit the printer colon file. In contrast to the previous listing, there is no description of the attributes, but this is the fastest method for modifying attributes if you want to modify several at once. Most of the attributes can be left at their default values. Check out the articles 'Printer Specific Information' and 'Virtual Printer Definitions and Attributes' in InfoExplorer. Each entry in the colon file has the following format:

```
:Description number:tag:reserved:value
:123:_u::1
```

The description number refers to messages in a message catalog that is defined with the *mD* tag. The tag is either a command line flag (those that start with an underscore '_'), a variable, a command, or an escape sequence. The colon file is really a programming language in disguise. Instead of having only static capabilities defined here, as in the classical printcap file, you can do anything to adapt the printer data stream according to your needs and control it by command line flags. A colon file has several sections that are started with tags that begin with two underscores '__':

__FLG Command line flag default values. Although all letters are listed here, not all of them might be used in a particular driver, individual drivers may ignore some flags.

__SYS System administrator attributes that define features such as the pipeline for creating header and trailer pages.

__IDS The main processing filter commands. The pipelines defined here take care of data stream translation. If you send ASCII data to a PostScript queue, for example, then the conversion pipe for encapsulating the ASCII data in PostScript is defined here. You could add a filter for DVI files here if needed.

__HTP The commands to generate header and trailer pages are stored here on AIX 4.

__PFL Prohibited flags. Command line flags that should be prohibited for certain data streams should be listed here so that the printing command can reject the job.

__FIL Preprocessing filter flags. This section stores pipelines for additional filters such as the *pr* command. You could add a preprocessing filter for the DVI format of TeX here for example. By default only filters for *ditroff* and *pr* are present.

__DIR Stores the names of directories.

__MIS Miscellaneous things.

__TRN Translation tables for the printer code pages on AIX 3.

__CTL Control characters. Here printer-specific control characters are stored. A PostScript driver would have '*showpage*' for the form feed attribute.

__WKV Internal work variables and defaults.

__CAG Miscellaneous commands, for example initialization and reset sequences for the printer.

__ESC Various escape sequences

__HIR Hierarchical file attributes that reference other printer colon files.

The colon file (Figure 10.4) contains features that need to be adapted for some printers. The attributes in the following list are those that are most often changed:

_l Page length in lines when using a line printer.

_w Page width in characters when using a line printer.

_u The default paper source for page printers.

_s[0-7] The paper size for different drawers on non-PostScript page printers.

_X The default input data stream on AIX 3. Set this to the code page that you use in the system, usually ISO8859-1 or IBM-850. On AIX 4 this is a more complex command that sets the default input code page automatically.

_O The default output data stream on AIX 3. Set this to the code page that your printer uses, usually ISO8859-1 or IBM-850. On AIX 4 the correct default is generated automatically.

si If you do not want users to receive printer messages you can specify the mail address of a printer operator. However, some types of error messages will go to the console no matter what you set here.

ci The initialization sequence for the printer.

_j Specifies whether the initialization sequence is sent.

cr The restore sequence for the printer.

_J Specifies whether the restore sequence is sent.

```
:056:__FLG::
:046:_X::ISO8859-1
:048:_Y::0
:050:_Z::+
:076:_j::1
:078:_k::
:459:_l::68
:083:_p::10
:321:sh::%Ide/pioburst %F[H] %Idb/H.ascii | %Ide/pioformat -@%Idd/%Imm
-!%Idf/piofpcl -J!
:322:si::
:323:sp::
:324:st::%Ide/pioburst %F[H] %Idb/T.ascii | %Ide/pioformat -@%Idd/%Imm
-!%Idf/piofpcl -t%o%G_1%r%{14}%-%d
:325:sw::78
:057:__IDS::
:274:ia::%Ide/pioformat -@%Idd/%Imm -!%Idf/piofpcl -l%IwL -w%IwW
 %f[bgijpqstuvxzIJLOQXZ]
:275:ic::%Ide/pioformat -@%Idd/%Imm -!%Idf/piofpcl -l%IwL -w%IwW -X ''
 %f[bgijpstuvxzIJLOQXZ]
:465:in::/usr/bin/hplj | %Iip
:277:ip::%Ide/pioformat -@%Idd/%Imm -!%Idf/piofpcl -#+ -x0 -l%IwL -w%IwW
 %f[jpuvxzIJUQZ]
```

Figure 10.4 Excerpts from a colon file.

Documentation for all of these codes can be found in several InfoExplorer articles. In addition, there are driver-specific codes that are only relevant for the driver itself. Currently, the only way to learn about the inner details is by exploring what *info* has to offer when searching for 'Printer Colon File' and its references. There you will find a description of how to add new printer drivers and the relationship between all these files. Fortunately, this is not necessary for most users. If your printer is not directly supported, simply use a virtual printer that comes closest to the printer you have and then modify a few of the attributes.

10.3.1 Some sample driver modifications

To understand the following two driver modifications you should first read the article 'Printer Colon File Escape Sequences' in InfoExplorer. Without having done so the following command sequences in the colon files look even more unreadable than they really are.

HP Laserjet IV M

When I started to write this chapter, AIX did not include a driver for the HP-IVM. There is one now of course. The following are my modifications to the HP LaserJet III driver. I used it to drive an HP-IVM printer. Theoretically this can be done immediately as these printers are very similar from the driver side. However, there are some features that one might want to add. The modifications are not very extensive, but they should help you by showing the principal way of attacking the problem.

Before adaptating the colon file a small change to the driver is needed for this printer. When driving the printer serially the HP-III driver is somewhat limited, since it supports only 19200bps at most. As the IV printer and my 250 can go faster I needed to patch the ODM entry for the driver so that I could configure 38400bps. This is done by modifying the PdAt entry for the HP-III driver.

(1) List the current default definition for the printer speed:

```
odmget -q "uniquetype = printer/rs232/hplj 3 and attribute =
speed" PdAt
```

This will result in output that looks as follows:

```
PdAt:
        uniquetype = "printer/rs232/hplj-3"
        attribute = "speed"
        deflt = "9600"
        values = "300,600,1200,2400,4800,9600,19200"
        width = ""
        type = "R"
        generic = "DU"
        rep = "nl"
        nls_index = 15
```

You should save this output in a file, call it /tmp/newspeed.

(2) Edit this file and change the values line to read:

```
values = "300,600,1200,2400,4800,9600,19200,38400"
```

(3) Delete the current definition from the ODM with **odmdelete -o PdAt -q "uniquetype = printer/rs232/hplj 3 and attribute = speed"**.

(4) Add the new definition with **odmadd /tmp/newspeed**.

Now you can configure the printer as shown in Section 10.2. You can also use the above method if you need to change defaults for other devices if you are using a superset of that device. To find out which entries in *PdAt* you need to change I suggest using **odmget PdAt | egrep yourkeyword** and then narrowing down the search with specific search criteria for *odmget* until you have the exact stanza that you want to modify. I found the speed entry above by first grepping for hplj and then narrowing down my search by searching explicitly for 'uniquetype = printer/rs232/hplj-3'. See Section 18.3 for more details.

A virtual printer on this printer device can then be generated via *mkvirprt*. Now you have a virtual printer that can be modified according to your needs. There are two queues available for the HP-III driver, PostScript and PCL. All the defaults on the PCL queue were what I wanted except from the page size, which I set by modifying *s0* and *s1*. PostScript drivers usually need little adaption although I found one thing that I needed to change in the PostScript queue: I wanted to be able to specify the paper source on the command line. The driver as shipped does not allow this. There are three entries in the colon file that need to be modified. The *-u* flag for *qprt* that sets the paper drawer is something the driver does not know about, so you need to activate it and set it to some usable default. To make sure that the paper tray is selected when the job is printed a sequence of commands needs to be sent to the printer. Using *lsvirprt* and then the edit command (*~v*) will show you the complete colon file. The following entries are the ones that I changed from the shipped default.

_j The activation of the initialization sequence is done by setting the *_j* attribute to '+'. If this is not set, then the initialization sequence is never sent to the printer.

_u The *_u* attribute, which is the default for the *-u* command line flag of *qprt*, needs to be set for the correct paper tray, which is 0 in this case. (When using the *lp* command you can specify this option as *-o -uX*, where X is the number of the drawer.)

is The formatter needs to know that there is an *-u* command line flag, otherwise it will abort with an error message. This is done by setting the *is* attribute so that it includes the *-u* command line flag. Change it from

```
%Ide/pioformat -@%Idd/%Imm -!%Idf/piofpt %f[jJ]
```

to

```
%Ide/pioformat -@%Idd/%Imm -!%Idf/piofpt %f[juJ]
```

The *%f* command at the end lists the valid command line flags. As PostScript jobs are usually created by applications that know how to drive the printer there are not many options active.

ci Finally, you need to include the paper tray selection in the initialization sequence for the printer. Change the *ci* attribute to look like

```
statusdict begin %G_u%d setpapertray end
```

This sends a PostScript command to the printer, which selects the paper source specified with the *-u* command line flag. Here the *%G* pushes the contents of *_u* on the stack and then *%d* pops it off as an integer.

In the case of an HP-IVM the following values for *-u* are accepted by the printer: 0 for the standard paper drawer, 1 for the 500 sheet feeder, and 3 for the manual feed.

The above modifications have been done on AIX 3.2.3. From release 3.2.5 AIX comes with an HP-IV driver so that there is no longer any need to follow this setup. The basic method used to customize a driver from a shipped driver remains the same however, even on AIX 4.

NEC P6 plus

To demonstrate how to configure a standard ASCII printer for more comfort I changed some definitions of the ASCII colon file for my old NEC P6 plus (a 24-pin noise generator). First I defined it as other ASCII printer and then I adapted the colon files. One could also start by defining it as an IBM Proprinter and then modify it. The printers have much in common so this would have probably been easier, but then I would have had less to show you in this example. The following modifications will allow you to select pitch and print quality. All the attributes presented here have to be set in the colon file, which you edit with *lsvirprt*.

_l German fanfold paper usually has 72 lines so I set *_l* to 72.

_q The print quality is controlled via the *-q* command line flag so the *_q* attribute needs to be set to some default, in this case 0.

_p The pitch also needs to be set to some default. The standard ASCII printer colon file already has *_p* set to 10.

ia The *ia* attribute that holds the *%f* command needs to be modified so that the printer backend understands that *-q* and *-p* are legal flags. Change it from

```
%Ide/pioformat -@%Idd/%Imm -!%Idf/piofasci -l%IwL
 -w%IwW%f[0bgijtxJLXZ]
```

to

```
%Ide/pioformat -@%Idd/%Imm -!%Idf/piofasci -l%IwL
 -w%IwW%f[0bgijpqtxJLXZ]
```

Note that both of the above lines are written as one line in the colon file; they have been split only for readability.

wz For the implementation of the *-q* flag we use an internal variable called *z* which has to be defined in the __WKV section of the colon file. It is initialized to 0, as in:

```
:000:wz::0
```

ci Next we need to set the initialization sequence *'ci'* to execute the right commands for what we specify with the command line flags.

```
:144:ci::\34\100%Zz%I[ep,eq,ei]
```

The sequence here first sends a reset to the printer '\34\100' (this is the octal sequence for a printer reset on a NEC P6), then zeroes the work variable *z* '%Zz', and finally includes the other command sequences: '%I[ep,eq,ei]'. The three included sequences are used to process the command line flags. They are executed in the sequence in which they are specified here, otherwise the following set up would not work as I am using only one command in *ei* to print the final ESC sequence and the *ep* and *eq* attributes are used to set up the right parameters for it in the work variable *z*.

cr To make sure the printer is in a known state after a print job, *cr* is set to '\34\100'.

ei The *ei* attribute in the __ESC section of the colon file that finally sets the printer looks as follows:

```
:000:ei::\33!%gz%c
```

It is an ESC sequence that sends the escape character, an exclamation mark and then the byte value of the variable *z*. The value of the byte sent after the exclamation mark is a bitmask of print characteristics. There are certainly easier ways to set some of the printers features, but demonstrating how to make several statements of the colon file work together is very simple with this one.

ep The pitch is set by the *ep* sequence, which sets the appropriate bit value in *z*.

```
:000:ep::%?%G_p%{10}%=%t%gz%{254}%&%Pz%e%G_p
%{12}%=%t%gz%{1}%|%Pz%;%;
```

The above sequence is one line in the colon file. It is an if-then-else sequence, no matter how awkward it might look. If the value of *_p* is 10 then a bitwise AND is performed on the variable *z*. Else if the value of *_p* is 12 then a bitwise OR is performed on *z* with the value of 16.

eq The definition of *eq* is a little more complex as it contains a nested if-then-else construct. It is spread over three lines for printing reasons.

```
:000:eq::%?%G_q%{0}%=%t%gz%{253}%&%Pz%e%?%G_q
%{1}%=%t%gz%{253}%&%Pz%e%G_q%{3}%=%t%gz%{2}
%|%Pz%e%G_q%{2}%=%t\33x\1%;%;%;%;
```

If *_q* is 0 then *z* is ANDed with 253. Else if *_q* equals 1 then *z* is also ANDed with 253. If *_q* is 3 then *z* is ORed with 2 and should *_q* be 2 then the ESC sequence escape x 1 is sent.

This utilizes *-q1* and *-q2* for draft quality and *-q2* and *-q3* for two types of letter quality.

It takes a while to read this terse notation, and it is even more complex when one is not accustomed to using a stack-oriented language. However, colon files are a very powerful means of interfacing all types of printers and if you have greater than average printer adaptation requirements then you should have a closer look at the colon files.

10.4 Making up your own backend

If the above facilities are not sufficient or too complex for your printing needs you might need to set up your own queue manually. When I started to write this book I had only an old dot matrix printer but occasionally needed to print PostScript files. Thanks to the Free Software Foundation I was able to obtain GhostScript, a freely available PostScript interpreter, via FTP from some server on the Internet. See Section 24.2 if you are interested in getting software off the Internet. GhostScript included a driver for my NEC P6 plus. Now how is the converter set up so that it all works automatically in the queuing system?

First I created a standard printer device for the NEC printer and an associated virtual printer and queue, all via SMIT. I used the *opp* driver and the generic ASCII queue device as AIX does not directly support this printer. Then I had to create a new printer backend that would perform the conversion. This is the new backend in /usr/local/bin/gs2nec.

```
#!/usr/bin/ksh
# printer backend to convert PostScript into something suitable
# for a NEC P6 plus and spool it on to lp0.
cat $* | nice -20 gs -q -sDEVICE=necp6 -sOutFile="|enq -P lp0" -
```

The backend takes the name of the file to be printed as a parameter. This file will be *cat*ed to GhostScript, which will pipe it to another queue, *lp0*. I used the **nice -20** here because GhostScript consumes a great deal of CPU time and I do not want printing jobs to interfere with the rest of the system too much. You can do anything you want here, for example send a file to a terminal for pass-through printing or to some totally exotic device. Do not forget to make it executable by **chmod 755 gs2nec**.

The next step was to install this new backend together with a new queue. I added the following manually to /etc/qconfig.

```
necps:
    device = necpsd
necpsd:
    header = never
    trailer = never
    backend = /usr/local/bin/gs2nec
```

The version of AIX I tested this on had a problem with the virtual printer definitions. Although I configured it to send the data to the printer unmodified, it tried to change things in the data stream. The operating system was configured for ISO code pages and the printer used PC code pages. The queueing system wanted to do character translation for me, which of course is nonsense when printing binary data. By changing the backend of *lp0* this was easily fixed. I simply told the backend program to use pass-through mode. This is how the /etc/qconfig stanza for *lp0* looked:

```
lp0:
    device = lp0
lp0:
    file = /dev/lp0
    header = never
    trailer = never
    access = both
    backend = /usr/lib/lpd/piobe -dp
```

After that, printing PostScript files to the matrix printer was a simple matter of entering **lp -dnecps file.ps**. So that I could still print a normal ASCII file with NLS characters I then created another virtual printer (*lp1*) on the *lp0* device that had formatting enabled so that character translation and line feed adaptation would occur automatically. This gave me in total three queues:

lp0 Sends data directly to the printer without any modification.

lp1 Does all necessary adaptations to print ASCII files correctly on the printer, including NLS conversions.

necps Prints PostScript data on the printer.

Of course this is the quick and dirty solution. One could also integrate the PostScript converter in the printer definitions in a colon file, but in most cases this is unnecessary.

10.5 Installing custom header pages

When one printer is used by several people you probably want to separate print jobs by header pages so that the owner of a stack of paper that comes out of the printer is easier identified. If you activate header pages by setting *header=group* in /etc/qconfig for a device you will get the system default header page, which tells you about the owner of the print job, where it came from, the flags used, and the date. However, it is all printed in a fairly small font. The job submitter, at least, should be printed in a larger font so that it is easier to identify the owner of the job. Alternatively, you might want to include your company or department name on the title page.

There are two way to do this: either by modifying the pipeline for printing the header in the colon file that defines the virtual printer or by modifying the header page template itself. The templates are in /usr/lib/lpd/pio/burst. There you will find header (H.*) and trailer pages (T.*) for different data streams. It is very simple to modify the PostScript header page to print the job delivery name in a larger font. The following is a slightly modified version of the standard H.ps file.

```
/LM 20 def
/ypos 725 def
/lineheight 12 def
/cr   { LM ypos moveto } def
/crlf { ypos lineheight sub
      /ypos exch def
      cr } def
/godown { ypos 50 sub
         /ypos exch def
         cr } def
0 rotate
/Courier findfont 12 scalefont setfont
cr
godown
/Helvetica-Bold findfont 30 scalefont setfont
( Deliver to: ) show crlf
godown
godown
/Helvetica-Bold findfont 70 scalefont setfont
( %D ) show crlf
/Courier findfont 12 scalefont setfont
godown
godown
(%t  %T ) show crlf
crlf
(%p  %P ) show crlf
crlf
(%q  %Q ) show crlf
crlf
(%h  %H ) show crlf
crlf
(%s  %S ) show crlf
crlf
(%d  =====> %D <===== ) show crlf
godown
(%a ) show crlf
(%A ) show crlf
showpage
```

When using this header page template you will get a header page that clearly identifies the delivery address, usually just the log in name of the job submitter. The % variables used in the file are documented with the *pioburst* command, which will expand them. On AIX 4 you will find a bullH.ps file in this directory. This prints the job information in large letters by default, but it omits the flag information.

For ASCII printers you might put escape sequences in the file to print a banner page with a large font, but this is very printer specific. A more generic way is to modify the *sh* attribute in the virtual printer definition. Run *lsvirprt* and select the ASCII printer for which you want to modify the header page. Then edit the *sh* attribute. It probably looks like:

```
%Ide/pioburst %F[H] %Idb/H.ascii | %Ide/pioformat -@%Idd/%Imm -
!%Idf/piofasci -J!
```

Replace the string before the first pipe symbol with a more elaborate pipeline:

```
USR=`echo "$PIOTO" | sed "s/@.*$//"`; USR=`/usr/bin/banner "$USR"`;
HDR1=`%Ide/pioburst %F[H] %Idb/H1.ascii`; HDR2=`%Ide/pioburst %F[H]
%Idb/H2.ascii`; echo "$HDR1\\n\\n$USR\\n\\n$HDR2" | %Ide/pioformat -
@%Idd/%Imm -!%Idf/piofasci -J!
```

The environment variable *$PIOTO* is set to the delivery address. This and other interesting variables can be found in the documentation for the *pioburst* command. Next create two header templates in /usr/lpd/pio/burst, H1.ascii and H2.ascii. H1.ascii is very simple:

```
*##############################################################################*
*##############################################################################*
```

This file is sent first. Then the name for the job delivery is sent via the *banner* command, followed by the second part of the title page, H2.ascci:

```
********************************************************************************
********************************************************************************


%t  %T

%p  %P

%q  %Q

%h  %H

%s  %S

%d  =====> %D <=====

********************************************************************************
********************************************************************************

%a
%A

********************************************************************************
********************************************************************************
```

Those two parts are just the original H.ascii file split into two pieces. Trailer pages can be modified in the same way of course. If you feel adventurous you might want to include graphics in the PostScript version.

10.6 Remote printers

To print on a remote machine it must be able to accept print requests, in which case it is necessary to configure the *lpd* daemon and the /etc/hosts.lpd file on the print server. See Section 7.3.5 for setting up a print server.

Whereas AIX 3 only allows direct printing to remote *lpd* daemons without any local formatting, AIX 4 gives you a choice of standard *lpd* printing, local formatting and then *lpd* printing and finally remote printing via *lpd* but with access to the remote printer definitions via NFS. Access to the remote printer definitions via NFS allows validation of printer flags at job submission time instead of receiving error messages later when the job has been sent to the remote system. The local formatting capability before jobs are sent to a remote system is very helpful in heterogeneous environments in which the remote print server does not have the necessary formatting capabilities.

On the client side you define a remote printer via **smit mkrque**. Simply fill in the form and it will create the right entries in /etc/qconfig for you. Be sure to specify the full domain name of the remote host when using domain names. Once you have defined the remote printer you will have an /etc/qconfig stanza similar to the following:

```
rlp0:
        device = rlp0d
        host = printserver
        s_statfilter = /usr/lib/lpd/aixshort
        l_statfilter = /usr/lib/lpd/aixlong
        rq = lp0
rlp0d:
        backend = /usr/lib/lpd/rembak
```

This stanza will send all print request to *rlp0* to the *lp0* queue on the machine print server, which is an AIX 3 or 4 host in this example.

As soon as a print job has left your machine you no longer have control over it from your local machine. The only thing you can do remotely is cancelling jobs via **qcan -x JobNumber -P Queue**. Changing the priority or halting the queue is only possible on the machine that has the job.

When using *lpstat* to check on the queue you will see that a remote printer has a two-line entry, one for local processing and the other for the remote status. On long jobs you might actually see the job first in the local queue while it gets sent over the network. As soon as the job is on the remote machine it is listed in the remote queue entry of the *lpstat* display.

If *lpstat* hangs while checking a remote queue, then you probably have problems with the name server, routing or the setup of the remote *lpd* daemon.

10.7 Some printing hints

10.7.1 Saving trees

There are several tools on AIX that can be used to preview printer output. I suggest using them for quick checks as it is faster and more sensible than wasting paper on test prints. On AIX 3 you can use the /usr/lpp/DPS/showps/showps utility to view PostScript documents on X servers that support Display PostScript. As Display

PostScript is a separate option on AIX 4 that has to be paid for, most people will no longer have *showps* by default.

For documents generated with *troff*, *xpreview* is also an option. In this case it is necessary to use *-TX100* as the output device specification. You can then use *xpreview* to view the file when running X. If Display PostScript is installed, *xpreview* will also display PostScript documents.

If you are working with AIX 4 and do not want to spend money on the DPS support or you need to display PostScript on an X terminal that does not support DPS at all, you can always resort to GhostScript and GhostView from the Free Software Foundation. They can be found on well-stocked FTP servers on the Internet (see page 438), and most user groups will also be able to get you a copy.

10.7.2 PostScript tools

AIX comes with the Adobe transcript utilities to convert ASCII files to PostScript. The command to do this is *enscript*, which is included in the *bos.txt.ts* file set on AIX 4 and *txtfmt.ts.obj* on AIX 3. The same file set also includes the PostScript version of *troff*, called *psroff*.

If you are using *enscript* on non-US paper sizes and you are getting tired of specifying the paper size each time you use it, set the environment variable *ENSCRIPT*, which can be set with all the command line arguments that *enscript* understands. Mine is usually set to *-dnetps -MA4,* which sets not only the paper size but also the printer queue.

10.7.3 Using *troff* with non-US paper sizes

The *troff* formatter on AIX 4 at last supports A4 paper sizes, which was not the case on AIX 3. Use the *-MA4* flag to set the paper size to A4. As *psroff* uses *troff* under the hood, the flag can be used there as well. Setting the paper size to A4, however, will not affect the printed area on the page as this is handled by *troff* formatting commands.

11

AIXwindows

AIXwindows is IBM's packaging of the X Window system, OSF/Motif, and various other enhancements. On AIX 3 it comes standard with Display PostScript and on AIX 4 it contains the common desktop environment (CDE) from the common open software environment (COSE). There are two parts of AIXwindows: the 2D package, which will be discussed here, and the 3D package, which includes the more advanced graphics libraries OpenGL, graPHIGS and PEX. The 3D package needs the 2D package as a prerequisite as all graphics capabilities on the machine interact with X in one way or another. X is in full control of the display. To achieve good performance with the 3D libraries, windows can be assigned to them where they interact directly with the graphics hardware without going through X calls. All input (keyboard, mouse, tablet), however, is still handled through X.

11.1 Some X basics

The X window system is an extremely modular windowing system for any kind of task. In contrast to other systems, such as the Presentation Manager or MS-Windows, it is not one integral piece of software but a collection of several components (Figure 11.1).

First there is the X server, the program that displays the output and gets the input events (mouse, keyboard, tablet) from the user. It also supplies the fonts for the application. Then there is the X library, Xlib, which contains the interfaces to the X server. It is linked to the client program and uses the X protocol to talk to the server. This separation allows X programs to run on a totally different machine from the server. Xlib takes care of the communication and the X client program does not need to deal with the details. In addition to Xlib there are other libraries that simplify the creation of X programs (libXt.a) and supply a common look and feel (libXm.a for Motif).

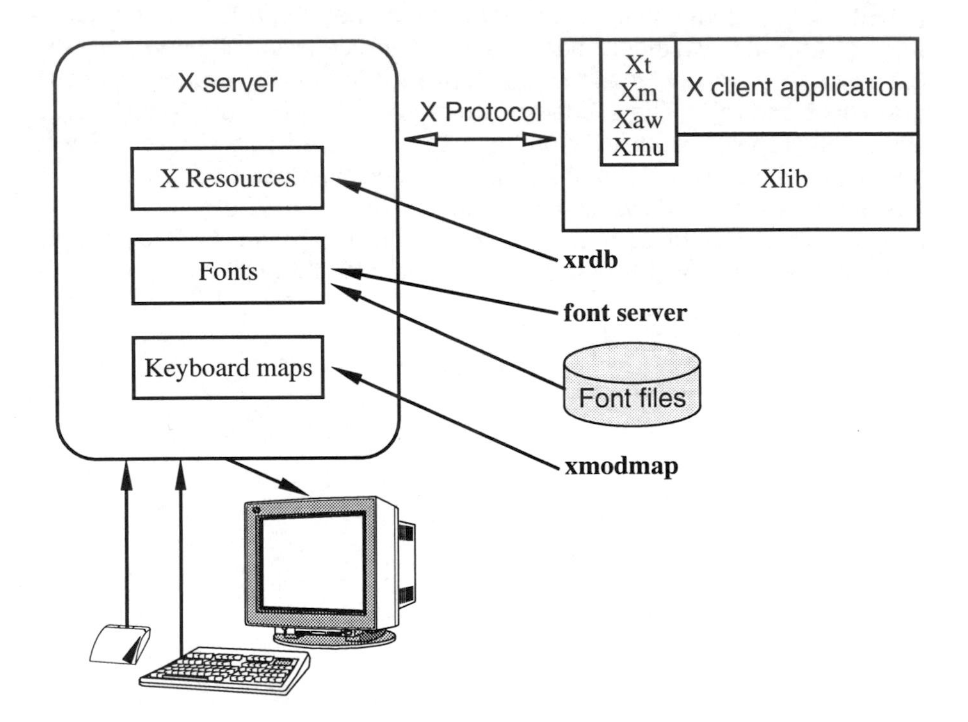

Figure 11.1 Clients and the X server.

A very special client program is the window manager. It is usually possible to run many instances of a client on one X server, but one can only run one window manger per server. The window manger controls the interaction between the clients and is used to communicate user control activities, for example moving a window, to the application and the server. The default window manager for AIXwindows is the Motif window manager (*mwm*) on AIX 3 or the CDE desktop manager (*dtwm*) on AIX 4. They are responsible for the pseudo-3D frames around the windows and the menus that pop up when you press the mouse buttons on the root window. You can also use other window managers, for example *twm*, which is shipped as sample code with AIX.

X applications use the contents of the *DISPLAY* environment variable to find out how to contact the server. It is usually set to something like *:0.0* for local servers or *machine.name:0.0* for remote servers. The part before the colon specifies the location of the server and the part after it specifies the server number and the display number. Unless you run multiple servers on a machine or have multiple displays controlled by one server they are set to zero.

Fonts are stored in /usr/lib/X11/fonts and several subdirectories of it. The local X server knows those locations automatically; other X servers may need to use the font server to access all fonts that are available on the machine.

X resources can be set for applications external to the server or they can be loaded into the X server with the *xrdb* command. How to handle X resources depends on your environment. This is discussed further in Section 11.2.5.

Depending on the type of keyboard you have, you need to load a keyboard map file that tells the server which keyboard events correspond to which character or key symbol.

The following pages will tell you how to set up the server and some basic clients. Some hints on how to configure your X environment for special circumstances are also given.

11.2 Configuration

Although AIX 4 will install itself with the basic AIXwindows runtime system and the COSE desktop (or CDE), if there is a graphics card in the system at install time, AIX 3 needs manual installation of AIXwindows. When you install AIXwindows you can choose a minimum runtime system, some added extension or the complete development system. There is also a wide variety of fonts that can be installed. If you are not limited by disk space I suggest that you install all parts of the X system and all X fonts apart from those fonts that support code sets that you do not need.

AIX 3 contains a collection of tools in the X extensions that you might want to install. They are the X.desktop, Display PostScript, the Motif version of SMIT and the X customization utility *custom*. AIX 4 contains various tools in unbundled form. The X.deskop has been replaced by the CDE and Display PostScript is no longer shipped with AIXwindows but is an option that has to be ordered explicitly at an extra charge.

On both AIX releases you should install the development tools and sources as they contain many useful utilities and some additional standard X libraries.

If you need to know the MIT X release that your current X server is running, check the output of *xdpyinfo*. The vendor release number is usually the X11 version number. Unless you are working with a very odd application, all applications written for a lower release number should work with newer servers.

The following sections discuss AIXwindows without CDE. CDE uses many of the mechanisms discussed here but has some major additions to the standard X environment. The relevant information for CDE, which is the default user interface on AIX 4, is to be found in Section 11.3.

11.2.1 Starting X via *xinit*

If you are already logged in, then *xinit* is the program to start the X window system. It will use either ~/.xserverrc or /usr/lpp/X11/defaults/xserverrc to configure the X server. After the X server has been started, the commands in ~/.xinitrc or /usr/lpp/X11/defaults/xinitrc will be executed. You can also use the *startx* script instead of *xinit* to start the X environment. It will automatically figure out which resources to load as there are several different conventions now for X configuration files.

The default xserverrc file will try to load the extensions for Display PostScript (and the PC simulator on AIX 3) when they are present. If you want to add your own options you should copy /usr/lpp/X11/defaults/xserverrc to ~/.xserverrc and adapt it to your needs. Simply remove all the checks for extensions that you do not want to load and add your own options to the initial setting of *$EXTENSIONS*. The options I set usually look like this:

```
EXTENSIONS="-T -s 0 -bs"
```

-T Disables the <CTRL><ALT><BACKSPACE> key combination that terminates the server.

-s 0 Disables the screen saver.

-bs Activates the backing store capability of the server.

The *-bs* option will cost you some memory, which is traded for a better visual performance of the X server. The smaller models particularly will feel more responsive when backing store is used as the X server does all work of saving and restoring the contents of obscured windows. Only in a memory-constrained environment or when most windows are updated continuously is the default disabled backing store to be preferred.

The second startup file is ~/.xinitrc. The .xinitrc file shown here depends on some other configuration files shown later in the chapter. The correct placement of icons and other window manager properties depends on them. It is based on the file shipped with AIX 3. The one that comes with AIX 4 uses slightly different values for the keyboard setup. The following sample can be used on both releases.

```
#!/usr/bin/ksh
# $HOME/.xinitrc
# X client startup script
```

```
# afx 1/93

# Make sure we have at least one active connection to the server
xclock -geometry 70x70-0-0 -update 1 -padding 0 -fg AntiqueWhite1 \
-bg black -hd CadetBlue -hl AntiqueWhite1 &

# Now let's take care of the keyboard mapping
# Unless we are on an Xstation we will map the keyboard for the locale
if [ -z "$XSTATION" ]
then
    KBD=""
    XDIR=/usr/lpp/X11/defaults/xmodmap

    if [ -r $HOME/.Xkeyboard ]
    then
        KBD=$HOME/.Xkeyboard
    else
        KBD_LANG=`/usr/lpp/X11/bin/querykbd`

        if [ "$KBD_LANG" = "NULL" ]
        then
         dspmsg $MSG/xinit.cat 26 '1356-825 xinit: Failed to query odm \
for keyboard id\n'
        else
            if [ "$KBD_LANG" != "C.hft" ]
            then
                if [ -r $IMKEYMAPPATH/$KBD_LANG/keyboard ]
                then
                     KBD=$IMKEYMAPPATH/$KBD_LANG/keyboard
                else
                    if [ "$IMKEYMAPPATH" = "/usr/lib/nls/im.alt"      \
                        -a -r $XDIR/$KBD_LANG/keyboard.alt ]
                    then
                        KBD=$XDIR/$KBD_LANG/keyboard.alt
                    else
                        if [ -r $XDIR/$KBD_LANG/keyboard ]
                        then
                            KBD=$XDIR/$KBD_LANG/keyboard
                        fi
                    fi
                fi
            fi
        fi
    fi
    if [ "$KBD" != "" ]
    then
        xmodmap $KBD
    else
        if [ "$IMKEYMAPPATH" = "/usr/lib/nls/im.alt"    \
                    -a -r $XDIR/$LANG/keyboard.alt ]
        then
            xmodmap $XDIR/$LANG/keyboard.alt
        else
            if [ -r $XDIR/$LANG/keyboard ]
```

```
                then
                    xmodmap $XDIR/$LANG/keyboard
                fi
            fi
        fi
fi

# now we are ready to start other X clients

# Make sure we have a flicker free background by choosing a dark color
xsetroot -solid black

# Let's have a mail check icon
xbiff -geometry -80-0 -fg yellow -bg black&

# I like InfoExplorer to be always ready
info -n cl -q -iconic &

# start the initial terminal window
aixterm -geometry 80x25+0+0 &

# exec mwm last to make it the father of all processes run under X
# this ensures that terminating the window manager will terminate X
exec mwm
```

The X server has a habit of resetting itself after the last client has closed the connection to the server, therefore we need to establish one connection before we do anything with the server that does not keep the connection, such as loading the right keyboard mapping. Here we start a clock. I like to have a visual indication that the X server is active, so I set the update interval to 1 second, which will give me a small moving tick for the seconds. If your system is highly loaded then you might want to skip the ticking seconds as they use up some CPU capacity. You can start whatever you like here as long as it keeps a permanent connection to the X server until your window manager is loaded.

The second important action is to load the appropriate keyboard map. This section is copied directly from the IBM-supplied xinitrc script. It determines the correct keyboard map and loads it into the server. Unless you need some alternate map you do not need to do anything special here. If you want an alternate map you should create a symbolic link from the correct file in /usr/lpp/X11/defaults/xmodmap to $HOME/.Xkeyboard. Instead of using the whole logic for selecting the correct keyboard, a simple call to *xmodmap* with the right keyboard map parameter might be preferred.

I do notice flicker even on ISO-compliant monitors so I keep a black root window: the default gray pattern puts too much strain on my eyes.

As I use InfoExplorer quite often I start it right away, but make it an icon initially. The *-q* flag inhibits startup messages and the *-n cl* sets the initial navigation page to the commands list.

The next client is an *aixterm*, after which the window manager is finally started. All clients usually need to be started in the background. Note the window manager. It will be started via *exec*, which ensures that it inherits the father process id of all started processes under X. Thus, you can quit X by terminating the window manager.

On AIX 3 you can start X with **open xinit** instead of just running **xinit**. This will allow you to toggle between X and an ASCII session in case of problems. As AIX 4 no longer supports multiple virtual terminals, this functionality is lost. A workaround for most ordinary uses is the use of virtual desktops with CDE; this is discussed later.

11.2.2 Starting X via *xdm*

This is the preferred method of logging in on a workstation or Xstation. Instead of logging in and then starting the X environment, the user logs directly into X. Running under control of *xdm* has some more advantages: access to the X server is controlled on a per user basis via the XDMCP protocol and the MIT Magic Cookie instead of on a host basis via the *xhost* command. There is no difference when logging into the workstation or an Xstation. And by using the *chooser* one can log into other machines on the network directly without the need for logging into an intermediate host. The configuration files shown here will work on AIX 3 and 4.

To activate *xdm* you have to set up some configuration files in /usr/lib/X11/xdm. First you need to configure Xservers, which tells *xdm* about local servers or servers that do not speak the XDMCP protocol. Xstations usually speak XDMCP so you don't need to configure them here. The following entry can be used to configure the local server on the workstation:

```
:0 local /usr/bin/X11/X -force -T -s 0 -bs -x dps
```

:0 The name of the display. Older versions used *unix:0* here.

local We deal with a local server here.

/usr/bin/X11/X The full pathname of the X server.

-force This forces the X server to start even if the controlling tty is not the console. This is the only flag in the above line that is absolutely necessary to make *xdm* work.

-T This disables the <CTRL><ALT><BACKSPACE> key combination for killing the server.

-s 0 This disables the screen saver.

-bs Enables backing store. For machines that have only 32MB or less memory the backing store option might not be optimal.

-x dps Loads the Display PostScript extension. If you do not need Display PostScript then do not include this flag as this will save a few megabytes of memory. When running a system with multiple users that can log in through XDM on the console, loading the Display PostScript extension opens up a security hole and should be avoided. This applies only to the local console. If you want to use the PC simulator on AIX 3 then include the *-x pc-sim* option.

The key configuration file is xdm-config. Here you can set the names of the other configuration files. In a diskless environment it might be useful to keep the configuration files in /etc/xdm for example. Only the xdm-config file is needed in the shared /usr/lib/X11/xdm directory: all local configuration files can be kept in a local directory. You should always configure the xdm-errors file in some other directory, such as /var/log, so that it will not cause problems in the /usr file system should it grow too quickly. The xdm-errors file will store all output from *xdm* and the setup scripts until a user has logged in. Some of the resources can be set for all servers or for specific servers. When setting them for all servers the notation

```
DisplayManager*session:          sessionfile
```

is used. When setting the resource for a specific server, then the notation

```
DisplayManager._0.session:       sessionfile
```

is used. The above resource is set only for the *:0* server. As the ':' has already a reserved meaning for X resource files the '_' is used instead. If you want to configure files specifically for an Xstation named *xst1* then you would use DisplayManager.*xst1_0*.session for the resource name.

You should not need to change any of the files for a first try, but there are some things that might improve usability. Later in this section you will find some sample files. Here are the more important resources that point to files:

setup The file to be executed before the *xdm* login window appears. This is the right place to set up the keyboard mapping and perhaps an attractive screen background.

startup Executed with root permission after the user has logged in. Here you can, for example, assign the console to the user. This should only be done when logging in via the console screen, as it makes little sense when serving several X terminals.

reset The reverse of startup. It is run after the session ends. If you have assigned the console in startup you now need to change the ownership back to root.

resources Sets the initial X resources for the login program. You can set your own greeting in the file specified by this resource.

session This script is run after the user has logged in with the id of the user. Here you can set up initial environment variables, make sure that the user's profile is read and do whatever else is needed. The default Xsession script will then execute the *startx* script for the user which figures out which X profiles are needed.

authorize If you want to use XDMCP authentication you have to set this to true.

After adapting these files, you then need to run *xdmconf*, which can also be found in this directory. It will configure the system to run *xdm* after the next boot. You can also start *xdm* directly after running **xdmconf** via **startsrc -s xdm**. This will start an X server, which will display a login window.

Here is my Xsetup file:

```
#!/usr/bin/ksh
# Xsetup
# X Setup file for xdm
# This file is run with root permission before the xdm login window
# is displayed.
# Set up any keyboard mapping in here.
# afx 2/93

# Make sure the base environment variables are available
set -a
. /etc/environment
set +a

# set a nice background for the login window
/usr/bin/X11/xsetroot -solid grey60

# Set up the keyboard for the server
# If the display is unix:0 or :0 then query the ODM.
# If it is any other screen then query the xstation configuration file.
# If none of the above results in a valid keyboard configuration file
# then emit an error message and load the default keymap,
# else load the right keyboard map.

DefaultKBD=en_US
XDIR=/usr/lpp/X11/defaults/xmodmap
KBD=""

# are we on a native screen?

D=`echo $DISPLAY|cut -f1 -d\:`

if [ -z "$D" -o "$D" = "unix" ]
then
	# we are on a native display.
	# check the ODM for the local configuration

	KBD_LANG=`/usr/lpp/X11/bin/querykbd`
	if [ "$KBD_LANG" = "NULL" ]
	then
		echo "xdm: Failed to query odm for keyboard id"
		KBD_LANG=DefaultKBD
	fi
	KBD="$XDIR/$KBD_LANG/keyboard"
else
```

```
        # Doesn't look like a local display.
        # Either remote access or Xstation.
        xstcf=/etc/x_st_mgr/x_st_mgrd.cf
        KBD='awk "
        BEGIN           { found=0 }
        /^$D/           { found=1;
                          next }
        /-p /           { if (found==1) l=\\$2;
                          next }
        /-l /           { if (found==1) k=\\$2;
                          exit }
        END             {
                          printf(\"%s/%s\\n\",l,k);
                        }
        " $xstcf'

        if [ $? != 0 ]
        then
                echo "xdm: cannot find keyboard for the xstation $D"
                KBD="$XDIR/$DefaultKBD/keyboard"
        fi
fi

if [[ "$KBD" != "" ]] ; then
    xmodmap $KBD
else
   echo "xdm: Don't know how to find the right keyboard for $DISPLAY\n"
fi
```

The Xsetup file attempts to determine which keyboard is configured in the ODM for workstations or in the Xstation configuration files, and if it finds one it loads it. Otherwise it loads a default keyboard map. Most people will not need the check for different keyboard maps like the one above as they probably run only one type of keyboard and can hardcode the loading of the keyboard map for this one keyboard type. However, I know of several development and support sites where people use different keyboards because of personal preferences. This script does it all automatically.

The next important script is Xsession, which sets up the basic user environment. The one I present here is very Korn shell oriented. Other shells will require some reworking to read the user profiles so that the user's environment variables are set up correctly.

```
#!/usr/bin/ksh
# Xsession
# xdm session file
# afx 2/93
#
# create a stdout and stderror file for this session
exec > $HOME/.xsession-errors 2>&1

# load the global user environment
set -a
```

```
LOGNAME=$USER
. /etc/environment
set +a
. /etc/profile

# load the user's profile to set up all personal environment variables
. $HOME/.profile

# see if the failsafe button was pressed
case $# in
1)
        case $1 in
        failsafe)
                (mwm &)
                exec aixterm -geometry 80x35+0-0 -ls
                ;;
        esac
esac

startup=$HOME/.xsession
resources=$HOME/.Xresources

if [ -f /usr/bin/X11/startx ]; then
        exec /usr/bin/X11/startx -t -wait
elif [ -f $startup ]; then
        exec $startup
else
        if [ -f $resources ]; then
                xrdb -retain $resources
        fi

        if [ -f "/usr/lib/X11/$LANG/xinitrc" ]; then
                /bin/ksh /usr/lib/X11/$LANG/xinitrc
        elif [ -f "/usr/lpp/X11/defaults/$LANG/xinitrc" ]; then
                /bin/ksh /usr/lpp/X11/defaults/$LANG/xinitrc
        elif [ -f "/usr/lpp/X11/defaults/xinitrc" ]; then
                /bin/ksh /usr/lpp/X11/defaults/xinitrc
        else
                (mwm &)
                exec aixterm -geometry 80x35+0-0 -ls
        fi
fi
```

First Xsession sets up an error log file that acts as *stdout* and *stderror* for all X programs that are started via the startup scripts or the window manager. If you have problems with X clients you may find error messages in this file.

The script then initializes the user's environment by sourcing several profiles. By using the *-a* option an explicit export of the variables is not needed. If the user has pressed the *failsafe* button on the XDM login window then only a minimum environment is started. This option is quite useful when you have errors in your .xinitrc file or window manager configuration that terminate your session before you even have a terminal window to work with. In normal operation the script tries to find out how to start your X session. Usually it will find the *startx* command which in turn will then load your X resources and run your personal X startup file.

When using *xdm* I suggest a slightly different .xinitrc file:

```
#!/usr/bin/ksh

# X client startup script for running under XDM
# afx 1/93

xclock -geometry 70x70-0-0 -update 1 -padding 0 -fg AntiqueWhite1 \
-bg black -hd CadetBlue -hl AntiqueWhite1 &

# set RDISPLAY to have our display name ready for remote connections
export RDISPLAY="`hostname``echo $DISPLAY | sed 's/unix//'`"

# Make sure we have a flicker free background by choosing a dark color
xsetroot -solid black

# Lets have a mail check icon
xbiff -geometry -80-0 -fg yellow -bg black&

# I like InfoExplorer to be always ready
info -n cl -q -iconic &

# start the initial terminal window
aixterm -geometry 80x25+0+0 -ls &

# exec mwm last so that to make it father of all processes run under X
# this ensures that terminating the window manager will terminate X
exec mwm
```

The major difference to the .xinitrc script for *xinit* is the missing keyboard adaptation. This is the task of the setup file from *xdm*. The second change is the *-ls* option for *aixterm*, which will make this shell a login shell. This, in turn, will run the .profile explicitly in this window, so that messages that are triggered by .profile are not lost. When running under the control of *xdm* it is no longer necessary to start a client to keep the connection open at all times as *xdm* does that for you. I still like to keep the clock however. The environment variable *RDISPLAY* will be used later to grant access to remote ids.

When you run X under *xdm* then you will occasionally run into permission problems either because you have old clients that were compiled with X11R3 libraries that do not know about the new authentication mechanism or because you work with different ids and need to grant access to other ids. The only way to grant access to the old clients is via the *xhost* command. To enable the old client to connect to your server you need to run **xhost +clienthost** even if the client host is your local machine. This disables the new authentication mechanism for this host.

Newer clients can get access with the help of *xauth*. This program is used to manipulate and extract authentication information from your session. Unless configured otherwise, *xdm* will store a key string in your $HOME/.Xauthority file when you log in via *xdm*. The default method with which this key is generated is called

MIT-MAGIC-COOKIE-1. It consists of the display name and a unique string. Other methods are available for some systems, but not currently for AIX. The key is generated by *xdm* and passed to the server it controls. Any client who wants to access the X server will now need this authentication information to connect to the server. The local X library with which your client program is linked will extract the information automatically when contacting the server.

If you are logged in on a remote machine and want to start a program that uses your local X server, you need to tell the remote X library the authentication string that is needed to connect to your local server otherwise the connection is refused. The easiest way to do this is to copy the information from the local .Xauthority file to the remote .Xauthority file with *xauth* and *rsh*. You can pipe the output via a remote shell to the other id, where *xauth* is used to merge the authentication for your display into the authentication database. Assuming that you have the correct entry in $HOME/.rhosts on the other client machine the following will allow the user *friend* on the machine *remote* to connect to your server:

```
xauth extract - $RDISPLAY | rsh remote -l friend 'xauth -f
$HOME/.Xauthority merge -'
```

The variable *RDISPLAY* that was set in .*xinitrc* is the right *$DISPLAY* value for remote systems that want to connect to the local host. If you need that feature often, you might want to put the following function in your .kshrc file:

```
remotex () {
if  [ -z "$2" ]
then
 xauth extract - $RDISPLAY | rsh $1 'xauth -f $HOME/.Xauthority merge -'
else
 xauth extract - $RDISPLAY | rsh $1 -l $2 'xauth -f $HOME/.Xauthority
 merge -'
fi
}
```

This function takes the remote host name and, if necessary also the remote id as parameters and transfers the authentication information to the other machine.

If you run into trouble with *xdm* then there are various places that can be checked for clues. First, try the file that is specified with the *errorFile* resource in xdm-config. All errors that *xdm* encounters are logged here. If you cannot get *xdm* to run and have nothing in the error file then you might want to set the *debugLevel* resource to 99. This will give you a great deal of debugging output on the console screen at the next start of *xdm*. If you encounter log in problems or problems with the user profiles there are two more files that can be checked. The Xsession script writes its output to $HOME/.xsession-errors. As soon as it has passed control to *startx* another error file is used, $HOME/.xerrors. Both offer the standard output of the scripts as they do not have a terminal to send the output to. In .xerrors you will also find error messages from programs started via *mwm* as all the programs started under the control of *startx* inherit this output file.

11.2.3 Using the *chooser*

The *chooser* is an addition to *xdm* that allows you to choose a host to log in from a list of available hosts. It is very useful if in your network of servers and Xstations users need to access different machines from different terminals, for example, in a student lab in a university.

Configuring the chooser is simple. All that is required is to set the chooser resource in xdm-config so that *xdm* will know where to find the *chooser* program and to set up the *chooser* configuration file Xaccess. In xdm-config you need to include the following lines:

```
DisplayManager*chooser:         /usr/lib/X11/xdm/chooser
DisplayManager.accessFile:      /usr/lib/X11/xdm/Xaccess
```

To enable global access to the chooser only one line in Xaccess is needed:

```
*
```

However, you may want to use this configuration to enable automatic detection of hosts that are willing to allow XDM log in:

```
*         CHOOSER BROADCAST
```

You need to set this up on each host that is willing to accept XDM log ins via the *chooser.*

Instead of getting an XDM login window you will now get a chooser window where you can select the login host, which will then present the XDM login window.

11.2.4 X server options

The local X server can be adapted to specific needs with various options depending on the underlying graphics card. Some cards support multiple visuals such as pseudocolor and truecolor. Options to the X server are set on the *xinit* / *startx* command line or in one of the ~.xserverrc, /usr/lpp/X11/xserverrc, /usr/dt/config/Xservers, /etc/dt/config/Xservers or /usr/lib/X11/xdm/Xservers files. When using the *xinit* command be sure to prefix X server options with two minus characters, as in **xinit -- -bs**. Some of the interesting options have been discussed elsewhere in this chapter, so only a brief overview of the most important ones is given here.

-P This option is discussed in Section 11.2.8.

-auth file Specifies the authentication file for X server access. It defaults to ~/.Xauthority.

-bc Turns off a bug workaround that makes the server compatible with older X clients. I have not yet found a reason to use it.

-bs This enables backing store, which is off by default. When using remote connections to X clients this might improve the perceived performance. It uses more X server memory but saves some CPU / communications time on the client side.

-cc visualnumber[:display]
Specifies the visual type. This is dependent on your graphics card. Use **xdpyinfo** to find out what visuals are supported by your card.

0 StaticGrayGrayscale only with a static color map.
1 GrayScaleGrayscale only with a modifiable color map.
2 StaticColorColor with a static color map.
3 PseudoColorPixel values index a color map that is user changeable. This is the default for X.
4 TrueColorPixel values are a composition of indices that point into different fixed maps for red, green, and blue.
5 DirectColorPixel values are a composition of indices that point into different user-definable maps for red, green, and blue.

The optional display part allows you to specify different visuals for multiheaded servers. When using CAD or other graphics applications you may want to set a different visual from the default *PseudoColor* visual that is used by X.

-d depth[:display] Sets the pixel depth of the display. With this parameter you can restrict the number of bits per pixels that is available for X. The optional display part allows you to specify different depths for multiheaded servers.

-D file Allows you to specify a different color database from the default /usr/lib/X11/rgb.(dir | pag). Use the *rgb* command to create the database files from a rgb.txt file.

-fp path Sets the default font path. This can be used to tell the X server to use a font server instead of the default font path, for example *tcp/fonserver:7500.*

-s seconds Sets the screen saver timeout. Use zero to disable it.

-T Disables the termination of the server by the <CTRL><ALT><BS> key sequence.

-wm Forces backing store on all mapped windows. Use it together with *-bs*, but check if it is really better than running without it. This greatly depends on the hardware and the client programs.

11.2.5 Setting X resources

X applications usually are composed of a complex widget hierarchy. With the proper syntax one can specify resources for the whole application, complete subtrees of widgets or individual widgets. The names of these individual components represent the hierarchy of the components of which the application is composed. Each application usually belongs to a class that can be used to set resources. An application class is usually the name of the application with its first letter capitalized. Many programs whose names start with X have the first two letters capitalized, as in XTerm. Consider, for example, a highly customizable program to play audio CDs with the CD player of the RS/6000, which I will call *xcd*. Its class name is XCd. Its individual components are all configurable to the extent that you can have totally different invocations of the same program. Resources set with *XCd.resourcename* are set for all invocations of *xcd*, whereas resources set with *xcd.resourcename* are set only for the specific instance of the application that was started with the name *xcd*.

When using dots '.' to separate the application name from the resource it is necessary to specify the exact resource. One can also use an asterisk '*' to specify resources. When using this method the resource will be set anywhere in the part of the application before the asterisk, for example, *xcd*geometry* would set the geometry for all windows of the *xcd* program, whereas *xcd.tracks.geometry* would set the geometry for the tracks component of *xcd* only. This is usually the desired method as real applications have windows of different sizes that need to be configured individually. In fact, for this sample program *xcd.tracks.geometry* is wrong because the tracks object is connected to the main program not directly, but via another component that is not accessed in the configuration. This happens quite often and glue widgets are required in applications to join all the parts together. To skip over this unspecified component (which is a FormWidget in this case) one can use an asterisk again, as in *xcd*tracks.geometry*. This is sufficiently specific if there is only one *tracks* component in *xcd*, but of course *tracks* can have other subcomponents with individual configurations, as in *xcd*tracks.t1.geometry* for the geometry of a pushbutton for track 1.

The example above used specific names for all sub resources. Of course, these can be class names as well. These class names are the names of the widget types used to construct the application, for example *Xcd.FormWidget.FormWidget.PushButtonWidget.geometry* would be the exact class specification for *xcd*tracks.t1.geometry*, but it would apply to all pushbuttons that are exactly within two FormWidgets in the application. Depending on what you need to configure, a resource specification might contain a mix of resource names and classes.

The exact specification of a component in an X application has to be looked up in its documentation. Usually, not all components are configurable externally and not all of them are published. Search for the application name and the word resources in InfoExplorer to find the resources for applications shipped with AIX. Check the application defaults directory /usr/lib/X11/app-defaults for examples.

11.2.6 Resource file configuration

There are numerous places where X applications can be configured. To make matters more confusing there is no standard for all types of files and one can have language-specific files as well. Usually applications search for resources in the following sequence:

- Command line;
- A resource file that is specified via *$XENVIRONMENT*;
- $HOME/.Xdefaults-<hostname>;
- Resource manager properties in the X server, which are the resources that you load via the *xrdb* command;
- $HOME/.Xdefaults;
- $XAPPLRESDIR/<xlass>;
- $HOME/$LANG/<class>;
- $HOME/<class>;
- /usr/lib/X11/$LANG/app-defaults/<class>;
- /usr/lib/X11/app-defaults/<class>;
- Predefined resources in the application.

The sequence above is still not complete. There are just too many variations to this theme. Fortunately, 98% of all X application resources can be found somewhere in this path. The notation *<class>* in the above list stands for X resource classes. They are usually the application name with the first letter capitalized, as in Mwm. As soon as a resource is found in the above search path the search is stopped. This explains why changes to .Xdefaults are sometimes not picked up. If the resource is already specified in the X server's database then the value of the resource in .Xdefaults will no longer be checked. Thus, once you use *xrdb* to load this database you have to continue to do so otherwise your new resources will not be picked up. Note that CDE uses *xrdb* for loading resources.

System-wide defaults should be set in the /usr/lib/X11/app-defaults directory for the class of the application. Each user can then override it with personal preferences in .Xdefaults. Here is my minimal .Xdefaults file:

```
! global defaults
! those work for all clients that do not have their own resources
*font:              -ibm--medium-r-medium--20-140-100-100-c-90-*-*
*fontList:          -ibm--medium-r-medium--20-140-100-100-c-90-*-*

! Window manager defaults
! Pointer to the button stanza in .mwmrc
Mwm*buttonBindings:       DefaultButtonBindings
! the keyboard focus is where the pointer is. If you want a more
! PM / MS-Windows like behavior then use explicit instead of pointer.
Mwm*keyboardFocusPolicy: pointer
```

```
! Do use save unders for performance
Mwm*saveUnder:            true
! Pointer to default window menu in .mwmrc
Mwm*windowMenu:           DefaultWindowMenu
! I want my icons to line up on the right side, starting at the top
Mwm*iconPlacement:        top right
! Icons should be automatically placed by mwm
Mwm*iconAutoPlace:        true
! I want to place windows myself
Mwm*interactivePlacement: true
! I do not want windows to raise automatically
Mwm*focusAutoRaise:       false
! If a client has it's own icon picture it should be used
Mwm*useClientIcon:        true
! A Border of 6 pixels around windows is enough
Mwm*resizeBorderWidth:    6
! Default font for mwm
Mwm*fontList: -adobe-helvetica-bold-r-normal--14-100-100-100-p-82-*-*
Mwm*title*fontList: -schumacher-clean-bold-r-normal--13-130-75-75-c-
80-*-*
Mwm*menu*fontList: -adobe-helvetica-bold-r-normal--17-120-100-100-p-
*-*-*
! Icons should have a picture, a label and a full label when in focus
Mwm*iconDecoration:       image label activelabel
! Choose some colors that suit you, the following are the default colors
Mwm*iconImageBackground:        AntiqueWhite1
Mwm*activeForeground:           AntiqueWhite1
Mwm*activeBackground:           grey60
Mwm*menu*foreground:            AntiqueWhite1
Mwm*menu*background:            grey60
Mwm*foreground:                 AntiqueWhite1
Mwm*background:                 grey40

! Mwm client defaults

! xbiff
! The small mailbox icon looks a lot better without any decoration
Mwm*XBiff*clientDecoration:     -all
! Do not put an icon in the iconbox for biff
Mwm*xbiff*clientFunctions:      -minimize

! xclock
! The clock looks a lot better without any frames and buttons
Mwm*xclock*clientDecoration:    -all
! Do not put an icon in the iconbox for xclock
Mwm*xclock*clientFunctions:     -minimize

! aixterm
! be sure to specify the right code page else NLS will not work
aixterm.font:      -ibm--medium-r-medium--20-14-100-100-c-90-iso8859-*
! I prefer a dark background with light foreground
aixterm.background:       midnightblue
aixterm.foreground:       wheat
! Make sure the cursor is easy to find
```

```
aixterm.cursor:            red
aixterm.fullCursor:        true
aixterm.pointerColor:      green
! The mouse cursor should jump into the window when deiconifying
aixterm.deiconifyWarp:     true
! No border needed
aixterm.internalBorder:    0
! Use fast scrolling
aixterm.jumpScroll:        true

! xterm
! Basically the same resources as for aixterm
xterm*font:          -ibm--medium-r-medium--20-14-100-100-c-90-iso8859-1
xterm*background:          midnightblue
xterm*cursorColor:         red
xterm*pointerColor:        green
xterm*fullCursor:          true
xterm*deiconifyWarp:       true
xterm*foreground:          wheat
xterm*internalBorder:      0
xterm*jumpScroll:          true
! Make sure xterm handles NLS input
xterm*eightBitInput:       true
! Make sure backspace works as labeled
xterm*stty:                erase ^H
```

The resources listed above are only a small sample. In my experience most questions about resources concern the window manager resources, which I present here in the hope that you will find it easy to adapt the window manager to your needs.

All the resources of standard AIX applications can be found in InfoExplorer. Simply search for the application name or the application name and the word resources. You can spend days trying to find out what colors are attractive and which fonts are the most pleasing. I suggest avoiding fancy candy colors and elaborate fonts: the simpler the better. Use colors sparingly to focus the eye's attention on key areas on the screen. The more elaborate your color setup the quicker your eyes tire. The *custom* utility that comes with AIXwindows since AIX 3.2.3 is also quite helpful for adapting the resources of the IBM-supplied X programs.

11.2.7 Configuring the Motif window manager

The Motif window manager is configured either with ~/.mwmrc for individual users or system wide with /usr/lib/X11/system.mwmrc. It controls the menus as well as mouse and keyboard behavior of the window manager. The menus and keyboard commands that are used by *mwm* are activated by setting the *Mwm*buttonBindings* resource in either the application defaults file or .Xdefaults. If it is not set explicitly then *DefaultButtonBindings* is used. The entry for *DefaultButtonBindings* in the sample configuration file below sets up different menus for the mouse buttons on the root menu as well as the reaction to mouse clicks in various parts of windows. The general format is

```
Butttondefinition         where on the screen       action
```

or

```
<Btn1Down>                root                      f.menu RootMenu
```

The *DefaultWindowMenu* has a similar function except for the system menu, which is activated with the button at the upper left corner of the window. Its entries look as follows:

```
Label         Shortcut    Key alternative           action
```

or

```
"Restore"     _R          Alt<Key>F5                f.normalize
```

Characters preceded by an underscore are shortcuts that can be used when the menu is active. The key definitions can be used to activate the functions directly without going through the menu. Unfortunately, this removes these keys from applications. Use the PassKeys option in this menu to toggle the interception of those keys by the window manger. When the window manager works with explicit keyboard focus then one can also use the keyboard commands described with the *DefaultKeyBindings* entry. Their format is as follows:

```
Key                       where                     action
```

or

```
Shift<Key>Escape          icon|window               f.post_wmenu
```

The actions that are available as well as the keys are documented in InfoExplorer. It is very easy to set up menus and alternate keyboard behavior with this configuration file. If you wanted to set up a print screen key for windows, for example, you could use the following in the *DefaultWindowMenu* definition:

```
"Dump Screen"  _D  Alt<Key>F12  ! "(xwd |xpr -device ps | lp -dpp)"
```

Using <ALT-F12> you now can start a screen dump to the PostScript printer *pp*. Unfortunately, you still need to click in the window to be printed with the mouse (the cursor changes to a small cross) to select the window to be printed.

In the following sample, the behavior of the mouse buttons (in *DefaultButtonBindings*) is specified slightly different from the system-supplied default.

```
#
# menu pane descriptions
#

Menu RootMenu
{
    "Main Menu"      f.title
    "AIXterm"        ! "aixterm -ut -T `hostname -s`"
    "SmallTerm"      ! "aixterm -fn Rom10.iso1 -ut -T `hostname -s`"
```

```
    "XTERM"         ! "xterm -ut -T `hostname -s`"
    no-label        f.separator
    "Root"          ! "aixterm -fg yellow -T ROOT -e su - root"
    no-label        f.separator
    "Utilities"     f.menu UtilMenu
    "Config"        f.menu ConfigMenu
    no-label        f.separator
    "Terminate X"   f.quit_mwm
}

Menu UtilMenu
{
    "Utilities"     f.title
    "InfoExplorer" ! "/usr/lpp/info/bin/info_gr"
    "SMIT"          ! "msmit"
    "Customize"     ! "custom"
    "X-Calc"        ! "xcalc"
    "XBiff"         ! "xbiff"
    "Xmh"           ! "xmh -fg yellow -bg blue"
    "Xman"          ! "xman"
    "xload"         ! "xload"
    no-label        f.separator
    "Print Bitmap" ! "(xwd -bitmap | xpr -device ps| lp -dps0)"
    no-label        f.separator
    "Xlock Remote" ! "xlock -remote -mode blank"
    "Xlock Blank"  ! "xlock -mode blank"
    "Xlock Life"   ! "xlock -mode life"
    "Xlock Swarm"  ! "xlock -mode swarm"
    "Xlock Quix"   ! "xlock -mode qix"
}

Menu ConfigMenu
{
    "Configure X"         f.title
    "Black Root"          ! "xsetroot -solid black"
    "Darkblue Root"       ! "xsetroot -solid midnightblue"
    "Gray Root"           ! "xsetroot -solid gray60"
    no label              f.separator
    "Screen Save On"      ! "xset s 200"
    "Screen Save Off"     ! "xset s off"
    no-label              f.separator
    "Shuffle Up"          f.circle_up
    "Shuffle Down"        f.circle_down
    "Refresh"             f.refresh
    no-label              f.separator
    "Reload Xdefaults"    ! "xrdb -load ~/.Xdefaults"
    "Remerge Xdefaults"   ! "xrdb -merge ~/.Xdefaults"
    "Restart MWM"         f.restart
    no-label              f.separator
    "Terminate X"         f.quit_mwm
}

# button binding descriptions
```

```
Buttons DefaultButtonBindings
{
  <Btn1Down>       root          f.menu RootMenu
  <Btn2Down>       root          f.menu ConfigMenu
  <Btn3Down>       root          f.menu UtilMenu
  <Btn1Down>       frame         f.raise
  <Btn2Down>       frame         f.lower
  <Btn3Down>       frame|icon    f.post_wmenu
  Meta<Btn1Down>   window        f.minimize
  Meta<Btn2Down>   window        f.resize
  Meta<Btn3Down>   icon|window   f.move
}

Menu DefaultWindowMenu MwmWindowMenu
{
  "Restore"        _R    Alt<Key>F5   f.normalize
  "Move"           _M    Alt<Key>F7   f.move
  "Size"           _S    Alt<Key>F8   f.resize
  "Minimize"       _n    Alt<Key>F9   f.minimize
  "Maximize"       _x    Alt<Key>F10  f.maximize
  "Lower"          _L    Alt<Key>F3   f.lower
  "PassKeys"       _P    Alt<Key>F6   f.pass_keys
  no-label                            f.separator
  "Kill Window"    _K    Alt<Key>F4   f.kill
}

Menu NoAccWindowMenu MwmWindowMenu
{
  "Restore"        _R    f.normalize
  "Move"           _M    f.move
  "Size"           _S    f.resize
  "Minimize"       _n    f.minimize
  "Maximize"       _x    f.maximize
  "Lower"          _L    f.lower
  "PassKeys"       _P    f.pass_keys
  no-label               f.separator
  "Kill Window"    _K    f.kill
}

# key binding descriptions

Keys DefaultKeyBindings
{
  Shift<Key>Escape             icon|window          f.post_wmenu
  Meta<Key>space               icon|window          f.post_wmenu
  Meta<Key>Tab                 root|icon|window     f.next_key
  Meta Shift<Key>Tab           root|icon|window     f.prev_key
  Meta<Key>Escape              root|icon|window     f.next_key
  Meta Shift<Key>Escape        root|icon|window     f.prev_key
  Meta Ctrl Shift<Key>exclam   root|icon|window     f.set_behavior
  Meta<Key>F6                  window               f.next_key transient
}
```

11.2.8 Running a multiheaded server

Running a multiheaded server requires a modified ~.xinitrc and a modified ~.xserverrc or /usr/lib/X11/xdm/Xservers file; the rest of the configuration does not need to be changed. In the server configuration file you need to specify which graphics card should be configured where, and in the ~.xinitrc file you have to start clients with the appropriate *$DISPLAY* and a window manager that knows about multiple displays.

You tell the X server where each display is via the *-P* option. You include one for each screen with the position of the screen in a 4 by 4 matrix. To configure two displays next to each other you would use *-P11 1 -P12 2* on AIX 3, which would tell the X server that display 1 (the number comes from the *lsdisp* command, on AIX 4 it is the device name of the adapter) is the left display and that the screen attached to the second graphics card is the right display. If you modify the standard ~.xserverrc file on AIX 4 then you should set the variable *EXTENSIONS* for multiscreen support as:

```
EXTENSIONS="-P11 nep0 -P12 nep1"
```

The first adapter listed here will become display *:0.0* and the second *:0.1*. A typical entry for the Xservers file when using *xdm* on AIX 3 would be:

```
:0 local /usr/bin/X11/X -force -P11 1 -P12 2 -T -s 0 -x dps
```

The ~.xinitrc file needs a little more tweaking to work correctly. The following sample will work on anything from one up to four screens. Note that most hardware combinations usually only support two screens. NLS keyboard setup is omitted for brevity in this example and if you use *xdm* for log in, then you will not need to do it here anyway.

```
# Initial actions that are needed before the screen specific things
# we need one connection allways open so execute the clock first
xclock -geometry 70x70-0-0 -update 1 -padding 0 -fg AntiqueWhite1 \
-bg black -hd CadetBlue -hl AntiqueWhite1 &

# If one does not use XDM for log in then the keyboard should
# be loaded here, right after the first client

# check for multiple servers:
let sn=`xdpyinfo|awk '/number of screens\:/ {print $4}'`-1
# check for display name
DSP=`echo $DISPLAY|cut -f1 -d\.`

# On multiscreen servers this will be executed for each screen
common () {
xsetroot -solid black
}

# For each of the additional screens we have one function
xinitrc1 () {
export DISPLAY=$DSP.1
```

```
common
info -n cl -q -iconic &
aixterm  -geometry 80x25+0+0 &
}

xinitrc2 () {
export DISPLAY=$DSP.2
common
aixterm  -geometry 80x25+0+0 &
}

xinitrc3 () {
export DISPLAY=$DSP.3
common
aixterm  -geometry 80x25+0+0 &
}

# now the things for the default screen which is always present

export DISPLAY=$DSP.0
common
export RDISPLAY="`hostname``echo $DISPLAY|sed 's/unix//'`"
xbiff -geometry -70-0 -fg yellow -bg black&
aixterm -ls -geometry 80x25+0+0 &

# now start all xinitrcs for the additional screens
if [ $sn -ge 3 ]
then xinitrc3
fi
if [ $sn -ge 2 ]
then xinitrc2
fi
if [ $sn -ge 1 ]
then xinitrc1
fi

# mwm needs to be exece'd last
# If we have more than one screen, start it with the multiscreen flag
if [ "$sn" = -1 ]
then
      exec mwm
else
      exec mwm -multiscreen
fi
```

Even though the window manager now controls all the screens you can have individual window manager resources for each screen by using the *-screens* option on the window manager command line. If you have two screens then *:0.0* is the screen that gets the first name and *:0.1* is the one that gets the second name specified with the screen resource line in *-screens disp0 disp1*. You can now use these resources to specify a different behavior of *mwm* for each of the screens:

```
Mwm*disp0*useIconBox:     true
Mwm*disp1*useIconBox:     false
```

The above lines in your .Xdefaults file would tell the window manager to use an icon box on one screen and not on the other.

11.2.9 The font server

The font server that was introduced with X11 release 5 is a great improvement for managing heterogeneous X environments. It allows any X11R5 X server on the network access to its fonts without any portability problems as the fonts are now stored in portable binary format. Since only the font server needs to store the fonts, diskspace is not wasted on all other machines. On a RISC System /6000 this might save more than 18MB of disk space! To use the font server you need to configure a machine as font server and tell the clients where the font server is.

The configuration for the font server is in /usr/lib/X11/fs/config. You will need to modify it for your environment. The font catalog entry in the following file is on one line. It has been spread out for printing here.

```
# sample font server configuration file
use-syslog = off
catalogue = /usr/lib/X11/fonts/,/usr/lib/X11/fonts/misc/,
/usr/lib/X11/fonts/75dpi/,/usr/lib/X11/fonts/100dpi/,
/usr/lib/X11/fonts/Type1/,/usr/lib/X11/fonts/Speedo/,
/usr/lib/X11/fonts/i18n/,/usr/lib/X11/fonts/oldx11/,
/usr/lib/X11/fonts/oldx10/,/usr/lib/X11/fonts/bmug/,
/usr/lib/X11/fonts/info-mac/
error-file = /var/log/fs-errors
# in decipoints
default-point-size = 120
default-resolutions = 75,75,100,100
# This should be 7000 to match the rest of the world,
# but 7000 is already being used by the X-Station people.
# (Pre AIX 3.2.4) :-(
port = 7500
```

If you use *syslog* for error logging then set *use-syslog* to on. All font directories that the font server should make available to others are listed in the *catalogue* line. In the above example I omitted the Japanese fonts (they are included in the AIX 3 default) as I do not have them installed. If you list a font directory here that is not accessible, the font server will abort. You will then find an error message in the file that is specified with the *error-file* keyword or in the *syslog* output. With *default-point-size* and *default-resolutions* you specify which font sizes and resolutions the font server should supply if none of them is specified. A standard font server usually listens on port 7000. This was, unfortunately, used by older versions of the Xstation manager and might still be used by NIS. Thus, the IBM-supplied font server uses port 7500 by default. If you run in a heterogeneous environment you need to tell all the clients of this font server to use the number specified here. To activate the font server run **fsconf**. It will add the font server startup to /etc/rc.tcpip and make the font server a daemon that can be started via *startsrc*.

How do you tell a client to use the font server? If it is an IBM Xstation you can do so in the Xstation configuration menus in SMIT. Other X terminals will have other means. The generic method that works everywhere is the *xset* command. By using **xset fp+ tcp/fontserver.domain.name:7500** the client will use the font server if the other font path entries did not contain the requested font. The *xset* command appends the font server to the current font path and expects the font server to listen on port 7500. You can also use the font server for a workstation. Simply start the X server with the option *-fn tcp/YourFontServer:7500* and it will use the font server.

For diskless machines or */usr* clients it makes particular sense to use the font server as it is much more efficient than loading fonts via NFS, which has much more overhead than the font server protocol.

11.3 Using CDE

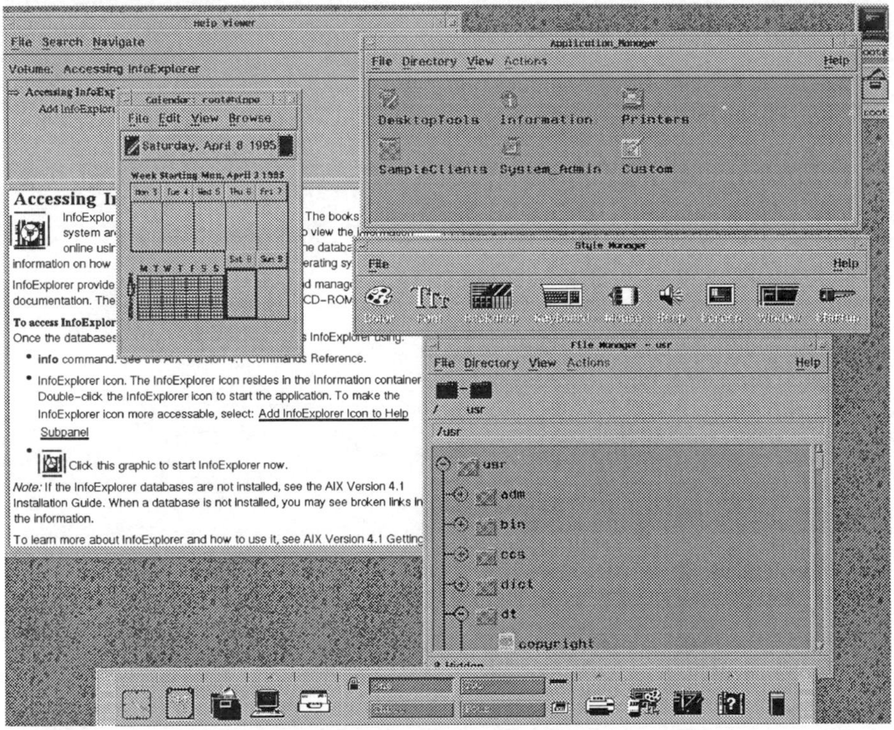

Figure 11.2 The COSE desktop environment.

The CDE comes as standard with AIX 4 (Figure 11.2). It is an integrated collection of graphical tools that make using the system easier. It replaces the *xdm* log in with the *dtlogin* program and the Motif window manger with the desktop window manger (*dtwm*) and has tools for file management, e-mail, a calendar, and its own integrated help system. Its biggest advantage over previous attempts to put a desktop environment on top of X is support by a large number of vendors. The end user gets a more attractive interface to some tasks at the cost of a high resource demand compared with a normal X environment. On AIX 4 the memory-hungry HFT subsystem for the console was removed but virtual terminals are now supported by CDE, which also needs plenty of memory. An AIX machine with AIXwindows can be used with 32 MB main memory, whereas the COSE desktop requires at least 48 MB. In addition, it is color hungry, which makes using graphics adapters with only one color map painful when working with applications that need many colors.

Not only is CDE resource hungry, it also opens up a whole new world. To describe its facilities fully I would need to at least double the size of this book. There is a redbook on the CDE, check out (*AIXwindows Desktop Handbook*, 17).

11.3.1 Configuring the login manager

When installing AIX 4 on a machine with a graphics adapter, X will be automatically installed, and with it the CDE. The standard ASCII log in mechanism is replaced by the *dtlogin* program, which will be started out of /etc/inittab with **startsrc -s dtsrc**. As *dtlogin* is based on *xdm*, its configuration is similar and in most cases it is only the file and directory names that are different. The shipped default configuration of CDE can be found in /usr/dt/config, but one should not modify those files. System-specific adaptations should take place in /etc/dt/config, which can hold the same files as /usr/dt/config but will not be overwritten when one updates the software.

In addition to *xdm*'s functionality, *dtlogin* allows better control of the login process. The *dtlogin* program spawns a child for each display that is controlled through *dtlogin*. For each of these displays a server is started, together with the login program *dtgreet*. *Dtgreet* allows one to switch back to an ASCII-based login on the console, change the language or get a simplified login without running the user's profiles. After successful authentication the *dthello* program is run to display a welcome message while the rest of the desktop is initializing.

The main configuration file for the CDE log in is /etc/dt/config/Xconfig. Like the other configuration files in /etc/dt it might not be present initially. Simply copy it from /usr/dt. Here is a simple version to start with:

```
Dtlogin.errorLogFile:          /var/dt/Xerrors
Dtlogin.pidFile:               /var/dt/Xpid
Dtlogin.accessFile:            /etc/dt/config/Xaccess
Dtlogin.servers:               /etc/dt/config/Xservers
Dtlogin*resources:             /etc/dt/config/%L/Xresources.xstation
Dtlogin*_0*resources:          /etc/dt/config/%L/Xresources.console
Dtlogin*startup:               /etc/dt/config/Xstartup
Dtlogin*reset:                 /etc/dt/config/Xreset
Dtlogin*_0*setup:              /etc/dt/config/Xsetup.console
Dtlogin.*.setup:               /etc/dt/config/Xsetup.xstation
```

```
Dtlogin*failsafeClient:         /usr/dt/config/Xfailsafe
Dtlogin.exportList:             ODMDIR NLSPATH TZ MANPATH
Dtlogin*authorize:              True
```

The above file sets up configuration files similar to the *xdm* configuration. There are several additions, however, which are not needed in most cases, for example the *exportList* resource to configure environment variables to be given to the client. On AIX this is not needed as the login process that is integrated in *dtlogin* will in any case export the usual variables specified in /etc/environment. Many more options can be set in this file for specific needs – check the man page of *dtlogin* for more information.

The /etc/dt/config/Xservers file is again similar to the XDM Xservers file:

```
:0   Local local@console /usr/bin/X11/X -T -force :0
```

The *local@console* entry is the only new item. It tells *dtlogin* that this server needs to be started locally, and the /dev/console device should be used if the user wants a regular command line login. The other files listed perform the same functions as their *xdm* equivalents.

The *Xresources* files are loaded according to the setting of $LANG. Of course, it is possible to skip this and specify a full path directly. Use the X resources in this file to change the greeting message, colors, bitmap and whatever needs to be adapted to your needs.

An interesting addition of the desktop login is the *dthello* program. Its message can be configured by modifying either the appropriate X resource or the /usr/dt/bin/Xsession script. The script approach allows for more flexibility. First copy the Xsession script to /etc/dt/Xsession and then edit this file. Do not forget to inform the *dtlogin* about the new Xsession file by using

```
Dtlogin*session:           /etc/dt/Xsession
```

in the Xconfig file. To change the greeting message use the DTHELLO_ARGS environment variable in the Xsession file.

```
DTHELLO_ARGS="-fnt rom14.iso1 -file /etc/motd"
```

It is then necessary to get rid of the default string by setting it to null. You also might want to add a delay so that users can read the displayed message. This can be done a few lines down in the script where *dthello* is called. It then looks like

```
$DTHELLO $DTHELLO_ARGS -string "" &
sleep 10
```

If you need to display more than one file the *-file* parameter can be repeated.

11.3.2 Using the session manager

When logging in through the *dtlogin* program, one usually starts a CDE session that is controlled by the session manager *dtsession*. The session manager loads the configured resources, starts the clients that make up the saved environment from the previous session, and then runs the *dtwm* window manger. The session configuration files are stored in ~/.dt/sessions/current. One can also have a home session that will always be used at startup; this would be ~/.dt/sessions/home. The session manager modifies these files at will, so fiddling with them manually might not be very useful as the changes are easily overwritten by the session manager.

The user environment of the CDE is quite different from the standard X environment. When logging into CDE it tries to launch again all applications that were active during the previous session. This is quite convenient for most users but presents some problems for more elaborate setups.

With CDE there is normally no ~/.xinitrc file. The correct place to start your own applications under CDE is a running *aixterm* or the file and application managers. The session manger will remember to restart them for you so there is no need to modify any startup files. However, the session manger cannot remember commands that change something in the environment and then exit, such as *xsetroot*. They can be run from ~/.dt/sessions/sessionetc, but you should not start normal X applications there. Typical things to be done here are setting a different mouse cursor bitmaps or changing the keyboard mapping. The sessionetc file needs to be executable like any other shell script.

The CDE session manager will execute ~/.dtprofile at startup, but this file is not a good place to start your own applications. Its only use is to tell CDE that you want your standard profile executed. This is done by setting the environment variable **DTSOURCEPROFILE=true**. Your .profile should not execute anything that needs a controlling tty when run from *dtsession*. You can use the variable *$DT* to check in your .profile whether it is executed from the desktop or a normal login process, for example

```
if [ -z $DT ] ; then
        # any commands that need a tty come here
fi
```

If you do not want to use the CDE window manager (*dtwm*) you can tell CDE so by modifying ~/.dt/sessions/current/dt.resources. If you want to use *mwm* then the entry would be

```
dtsession.wmStartupCommand:      /usr/bin/X11/mwm
```

This causes some problems however. Usually terminating the window manager terminates the whole session, but when setting up *mwm* as the window manager for a CDE session this will not work and you need to kill the *dtsession* process instead. Killing the session manager will not save your current environment and you will always get the environment that was active before you switched to *mwm*. CDE is not very cooperative when it comes to custom environments that do not fit into the CDE scheme of things.

Another problem area is the X resources of applications. The resources of files in application defaults directories are still used, but the user's ~/.Xdefaults file is completely ignored. Instead, the resources in ~/.dt/sessions/currrent/dt.resources are loaded into the X server. The politically correct way to modify them is via the *EditResources* application in the administrator part of the applications toolbox of

CDE (this is really just an editor) or the custom utility that comes with AIX. If you still want to use your ~/.Xdefaults file you can load it with **xrdb -merge ~/.Xdefaults** in the sessionetc script. If you only want to load the file once and you never change it afterwards, you do not even need to load it each time. Using **xrdb -merge ~/.Xdefaults** once will load it into the X server and the session manager will dump the X server's configuration database to the dt.resources file at logout so that your resources are included from now on. However, it is important to remember that your ~/.Xdefaults file is never again read by applications once resources are loaded into the X server, so you have to use *xrdb* every time you change it.

11.3.3 Adding applications to CDE

The CDE front panel as well as the application manager can easily be extended with your own applications, although the programs that control them are separate entities. The front panel is a function of the CDE window manager *dtwm*, whereas the application manager is a special instance of the file manager.

Whichever you want to use, you must first define an action that can be used by the desktop. This can be done with the *CreateAction* utility in the application manager of the front panel (the application manager is the icon with the calculator and the pens on the right side of the front panel). After selecting the application manager, select the desktop tools. Simply give *CreateAction* a name for your action, choose an icon and set the commandline. If it is not an X application you will also need to specify that. When you save it, two files will be created: one in your home directory that has the application name and another as ~/.dt/types/applicationname.dt. The file in your home directory is just a placeholder, so move it to some directory in your *$PATH*, such as ~/bin. The file in the ~/.dt/types directory is the one that specifies the action.

If you then use the file manager and drag the icon of your new application onto one of the Install Icon fields of the subpanels of the front panels (use the middle mouse button) the action will be available from the front panel. Under the hood, a new control that contains the necessary references will be installed in the directory ~/.dt/type/fp_dynamic.

If you want to make your new tool available through the application manager, simply use the file manger to copy the application to ~/.dt/appmanager and then select *ReloadApps* from the *DesktopTools* in the application manager. This will integrate your new tool in the application manager. What happens is that the application manager will transfer links to its default configuration to /var/dt/appconfig/appmanager/user-host-display and add a link to the action in your home directory.

Should you need to remove things from the front panel, then copy the front panel definition from /usr/dt/appconfig/types/C/dtwm.fp to your ~/.dt/types directory and edit it. Do not remove definitions, but add the line

```
DELETE true
```

to each of the items that you want to delete.

As with other CDE configuration items, use /etc/dt as a base directory for system-wide configuration when needed and copy the files from /usr/dt instead of editing those.

11.3.4 The desktop Korn shell

You may have already guessed that I am not a big fan of CDE, but a hidden gem is the desktop Korn shell or *dtksh*. This is a ksh-93 with X and Motif support. With it you can write Korn shell scripts with graphical user interfaces. To make this task easier, AIXwindows includes *dtscript*, a version of AIC, the AIXwindows Interface Composer (or really UIM/X), which allows you to build X/Motif-based shell scripts with an interactive design tool.

To describe these fully is beyond the scope of this book, but *dtscript* is relatively easy to learn by experimenting. Simply grab a window in the *dtscript* editor, add some buttons and set their properties (right mouse button). Use any shell commands in the callback fields of the buttons. There is no need to dig deep into X programming, this is one of those 'just do it' things that can be learned easily by exploring.

11.3.5 CDE login without CDE window management

Although the CDE login has more features than the *xdm* login (better authentication method support, support of AIX password rules, escape to command line login), one does not neccessarily want to run with the complete resource consuming desktop simply to obtain the new login features. Each user can configure the environment variable *SESSIONTYPE* in the ~.dtprofile script and set it to *xdm*. This will run the user's .xsession script instead of starting up the whole desktop. All the normal X configuration methods that have been discussed previously will work without any interference from CDE.

11.4 Differences from the X Consortium distribution

Those who are familiar with the MIT X distribution (or X Consortium nowadays) will sometimes miss libraries and commands on AIX because they are stored in different places. Usually all X libraries are in /usr/lpp/X11/lib and the entries in /usr/lib are symbolic links to them, but not all MIT libraries are there by default. The missing libraries as well as the commands you might be missing are shipped partly as source code examples and need to be compiled first. See /usr/lpp/X11/Xamples/README for details.

In addition to the X Consortium code in the Xamples directory, AIXwindows has a huge number of source code examples. There are examples to explain how to extend the X server or how to accomplish specific tasks that are considered too esoteric for the normal AIXwindows shipment. The *X11.samples.** (or *X11dev.src* on AIX 3) components of the AIXwindows package contains all the missing goodies that you might need. The advantage of the sample shipment is easy access to the source. The disadvantage is that there is no formal support for these utilities.

If you develop X programs you should browse the /usr/lpp/X11/Xamples directory tree. Even if you are not a developer you will still find many useful programs there. Most of them are already compiled and it is only necessary to include /usr/lpp/X11/Xamples/bin in your path to access them. To make full use of all of the utilities you should follow the instructions in the /usr/lpp/X11/Xamples/README file on how to compile and install them all including the supplied manual pages.

For those who are not yet experienced in the X world here is a brief list of the most important utilities you can find there and their use.

xclipboard A program that can be used as a clipboard for the X cut and paste buffer.

xdpyinfo Lists information about the running X server, such as the X version number, the extensions that are loaded, the available visuals, and so on.

xwininfo Gives you information about the properties of one specific window, for example its title, id, size, etc.

xprop This utility lets you find out about the window manager properties of a specific X client.

xscope This is a tracer. It can be used to trace the communication between an X application and the server. If you start playing with it you should log its output to a file via *tee*; usually there is a lot of it.

xwud This is the opposite of the *xwd* program. It lets you display windows on the screen that were previously dumped via *xwd* (*xwd* comes with the supported standard clients). On AIX 4 this command is also part of the standard clients.

appres You can use *appres* to list currently available resources for clients. It is very useful to confirm what you think is set for a client.

twm The standard MIT window manager. It uses fewer resources than the standard Motif window manager (*mwm*) used by AIXwindows. If you run on monochrome screens or displays with limited colors it is usually easier to get *twm* up and running than to configure useful color resources for *mwm*.

xfd Use this to display the individual characters of a font and their hexadecimal values.

xfontsel This utility allows you to construct a logical font name by selecting its properties, such as foundry, width or encoding. Use it to select fonts for your windows.

xlsfonts Lists all fonts that are currently available for the server.

xcalc If you do not have a pocket calculator next to the terminal use this one.

xload Displays an approximation of the machine load.

There are more useful utilities in there, so go and explore the Xamples yourself.

11.5 Xstations

Xstations or X terminals are terminals that have their own processor to display graphical information. They are quite cost efficient compared with diskless workstations because the investment in hardware and software required is much less and daily maintenance of the system is much less onerous as it is only necessary to maintain their server. Numerous vendors offer Xstations. They all should work together with AIX as long as they have no dependency on vendor-specific programs on the server host. Most of them are controlled via *xdm* and support the font server. These are usually the only components on AIX that need to be set up.

Although older IBM Xstations work only with the Xstation manager from IBM, the newer ones can use it but do not depend on it. Configuring an Xstation 140, 150 or 160 is very much like the configuration of non-IBM Xstations.

11.5.1 Configuring an Xstation 130

Older IBM Xstations usually communicate with their boot server through several protocols. First they request a network address from the boot server via the bootp daemon (*bootpd*). Then the boot image (the X server code) is fetched from the boot server via the *tftp* protocol (if needed). They then get their configuration options from the Xstation manager daemon (*x_st_mgrd*). The Xstation manager will configure the keyboard and start a login window on the Xstation unless you use the X display manager *xdm*, which is the better choice in my opinion. When using *xdm* the Xstation will then try to contact an *xdm* server via the XDMCP protocol. The *xdm* then takes control of the terminal window and starts either a login window or the *chooser* client that lets the user select a login host. The Xstation manger uses a user-configurable port number over which it communicates with the X terminals. Older IBM Xstations have a default port number of 7000. This conflicts with NIS and the font server. Newer versions of the Xstation manager daemon use port 9000 by default. You can use whatever port you want as long as it is the same everywhere. The Xstation manager daemon gets its port number out of /etc/services. If you change this file use **inetimp** (on AIX 3 only) and then **refresh -s inetd** to update the *inetd* super server.

You could also configure the Xstation to boot directly off the built-in hard disk. This is not much faster than booting over the network, but it greatly reduces the network traffic. When booting off the hard disk the *bootp* and *tftp* steps are not used.

IBM Xstations can be configured easily via SMIT. First define an Xstation type that is a collection of configuration options that applies to several Xstations and then configure an Xstation, its font path setup and optionally the *xdm* program. The Xstation configuration in SMIT is hidden in the devices section; use **smit x_config** for the fastpath.

The name of an Xstation type must be in the form x_st_mgr.*xxxx,* where the x is user definable (four characters). Use something like *130e* for an Xstation type that configures Xstations model 130 on Ethernet. The Xstation type specifies the network hardware (Ethernet or Token-Ring), the port number of the Xstation manager program, the directory where the configuration information is stored, and a boot file which is different for each type of Xstation and X release. In addition, you need to specify a name server, default gateway, and subnet mask if needed.

When defining an Xstation type you create a file in /etc/x_st_mgr which is named 130e.cf, for example, when creating an Xstation type named *x_st_mgr.130e.* It contains the location of keymap files, NLS messages, the server code, fonts, and RGB color name files for the server. In addition, an entry in /etc/bootptab is made for this Xstation type, which will contain defaults for the *bootp* daemon.

```
* Xstation NAME                          [baboon.your.domain]
* Xstation Network TYPE Name             [x_st_mgr.130e]             +
* Hardware ADDRESS                       [08005a810007]
* Make this host PRIMARY BOOTSERVER?     [y]
* Secondary Server DELAY Time            [0]                        +#
* INPUT device                           [mouse]                     +
* Tablet PORT                             com1                       +
* Fixed DISK?                            [y]
* Page PIXMAPS to fixed disk?            [y]
* FONTS file access method               [Try disk first, try ne>    +
* BOOTFILE access method                 [Try disk first, try ne>    +
* Hardware pan SHAPE                     [none]                      +
* XDMCP mode                             [indirect]                  +
* xdmcp HOST                             [xdmhost.your.domain]
* LANGUAGE                               [English    (United Sta>    +
* KEYBOARD                               [English (United States>    +
* Keyboard FILE                          [keyboard]
* FONT for login window                  [Rom14]                     +
* LOCATION for login window              [Upper left]                +
* LPF key port                           [none]                      +
```

Figure 11.3 Configuring an Xstation 130.

Once you have configured an Xstation type you can configure the Xstation itself. The Xstation name must be known to the system by either */etc/hosts* or the name server before it can be configured. The SMIT screen in Figure 11.3 is for an Xstation 130. The configurations for other models will be similar. The Xstation name entered here must be the network host name of the Xstation. Use an Xstation type that you defined previously and set the hardware address. (The hardware address of an Xstation is typically displayed on its screen when it boots.) This should be the minimum to make it work. If you have multiple boot servers to ensure a backup is available then configure a delay on the backup server so that the primary server has enough time to respond to the boot requests. If you have a fixed disk in the Xstation then configure the system to use it for paging pixmaps to disk. You should also tell the system to try the disk first and then the network for font and boot file access. This will greatly reduce the network load when you have larger numbers of Xstations. In terms of performance it is not a gain for the Xstation, at least not on lightly loaded networks, as the hard disk is not faster than the network. If you prefer to have a large virtual screen then configure the pan shape to your liking. This will allow you to use all of the video memory in the Xstation and get an X server that is larger than the display.

I strongly suggest using *xdm* and XDMCP for managing Xstation logins. Set the XDMCP mode to one that fits your environment. If you use indirect and then set the XDMCP host to a machine that has the *chooser* configured you can select the login host on the Xstation. The other options are only relevant if you do not use *xdm*. The *xdm* configuration itself is discussed in Section 11.2.2. When you press <ENTER> after having filled in all the fields, an entry like the following will be created in /etc/x_st_mgr/x_st_mgrd.cf.

```
baboon.your.domain DISPLAY=baboon.your.domain:0; export DISPLAY;\
      XSTATION=baboon.your.domain; export XSTATION; \
      LANG=En_US; export LANG; \
      /usr/lpp/x_st_mgr/bin/pclient \
      -p /usr/lpp/X11/defaults/xmodmap/En_US \
      -l keyboard \
      -s 5 \
      -m /usr/lpp/X11/bin/xmodmap \
      -a "/usr/lpp/X11/bin/aixterm -fn Rom14 -geometry 80x25+0+0 \
       W -e /usr/lpp/x_st_mgr/bin/login"
```

The *pclient* program does the keyboard setup and will start a login window with the *login* script of the Xstation manager. If the settings that are available via SMIT are not enough, you can also modify this file manually. At the time of this writing it is not possible to configure ISO code pages for example. One needs to change En_US to en_US manually in the file. This, unfortunately, has the side effect of breaking scripts that are used by SMIT to change the configuration. You need to change it back to En_US so that those scripts work again when modifying this entry via SMIT. The above entry is used only when you do not run the Xstation under XDMCP control.

After having configured the Xstation you need only add the right font configuration and you are ready. The default font path for the Xstation uses only a small number of fonts in /usr/lib/X11fonts and not its subdirectories. Numerous applications need a more complete font set. Font paths are defined for Xstation types via

smit x_fpe. You can either use the Xstation manager, NFS, TFTP, or the font server for accessing fonts. I strongly suggest using the font server as it is the most efficient method. The font access you specify will be added in the configuration files in /etc/x_st_mgr, for example 130e.cf if the Xstation type is 130e. You can also modify these files manually without using SMIT, but you must make sure that all the font path entries are on one line.

Xstation trouble shooting

There are a few things that can go wrong when trying to boot Xstations. Check the following items if you have problems.

- Are the cables connected properly and are you using the right ring speed on Token-Ring?
- Are the Xstation and the Xstation manager using the same port number? Compare the decimal entry in /etc/services with the hexadecimal entry under the T170 flag in /etc/bootptab. Does this port number conflict with any other service on the network such as NIS or a traditional font server configuration? Port 7000 would be $1B58_H$ and port 9000 is 2328_H.
- Use *iptrace* and *ipreport* or *tcpdump* to see if the Xstation and the boot host can communicate. If there are *tftp* problems you might even see the *tftp* error message in clear text in the trace.
- Check whether there are any errors in the *xdm* and font server error files if you use those services.

11.5.2 Configuring other X terminals

Non-IBM X terminals usually come with their own installation methods, but most of them adhere to the following model, which also works for the Xstations 140, 150 and 160, which are sold by IBM.

One configures an IP address, a router, and a name server on the Xstation. Then the way one logs in is configured. Usually this is an XDMCP broadcast. Font access is configured and should be done via the font server, or if not available by setting up *tftp* or NFS font access. When using *tftp* be sure to set up the /etc/tftpaccess.ctl file on AIX to control which directories are accessed by *tftp*. If working in a non-US environment the keyboard may also need to be configured, but this is usually done by loading a keyboard map in the Xsetup file of *xdm* or CDE.

This is basically all one needs to do, the exact method to be followed depends on the manufacturer.

11.6 More X hints

It does not need an X guru to configure a usable X environment. Many simple tricks that can make life easier under X. Here are a few.

11.6.1 How to get rid of the <CAPS LOCK> key

Some people think that the <CAPS LOCK> key is absolutely useless and that a <CTRL> key should be in this position. Under X it is relatively easy to remap the keyboard to work this way. The following example is for my German keyboard. On a US keyboard the key is called *Caps_Lock* and not *Shift_Lock*. Include the *xmodmap* line in your ~/.xinitrc file if you want to get rid of the caps lock behavior.

```
# remap CapsLock to CTRL. On non-US keyboards this is called Shift_Lock,
# on US keyboards it is Caps_Lock
xmodmap -e "remove Lock = Shift_Lock" -e "keysym Shift_Lock = Control_L"
-e "add Control = Control_L"
```

11.6.2 Remapping keys for *aixterm*

You may sometimes want to remap keys on the keyboard for specific programs. Not all X programs support the following mechanism, but many do. If you want to start up *aixterm* with function keys that execute commands for you, you could include the following in your ~/.Xdefaults file:

```
aixterm.Translations: #override \
      <Key>F1: string("vi ~/.Xdefaults\^M") \n\
      <Key>F2: string("/usr/bin/smitty\^M") \n
```

The above lines would modify the <F1> key to run *vi* on your ~.Xdefaults file and <F2> to run the ASCII version of SMIT. Note that the *^M* is a real control-M character. Use <CTRL-V><CTRL-M> to enter this character in *vi*. There should be no further spaces or tabs after the final backslash on the lines. You can get the names of the keys out of the include file: /usr/include/X11/keysymdef.h.

11.6.3 Using applications that require older X libraries

AIX uses shared libraries not only for the standard C library but also for most of the X libraries, such as libX11.a or libXm.a. Depending on your AIXwindows release and installation, the shared libraries will include the objects for several X releases from X11R3 up to X11R5. Different releases of Motif are also available. The included compatibility objects in some cases will not work with older applications, for example on AIX 3.2.5 X11R5 with Motif 1.2 is the default but some applications need to run explicitly with the X11R4 libraries. This can be accomplished by specifying a $LIBPATH that points to the older libraries first. To run the old application you could use the command

```
LIBPATH=/usr/lpp/X11/lib:/usr/lib youroldapp
```

to run the application with the old libraries. Check out the README files in /usr/lpp/X11 for details on the current release. If you are using AIX 4 you will need to install the compatibility libraries explicitly since they are not installed automatically. They will have a name like X11.comapt.lib.X11R3.

Note that you cannot set $LIBPATH and then run an *aixterm*. Like all SUID programs, *aixterm* will clear the $LIBPATH environment variable for security reasons. You must reset it within *aixterm* if it is needed for other applications.

11.6.4 Application-specific terminal windows.

For some applications that one wants to run in *aixterms*, a set of resources other than the ones one usually uses would be helpful. For example, suppose you have an editor called *e3* that you want to run with different colors and a different default window size. To do so you start your *aixterm* from the window manger via the following entry in .mwmrc:

```
"Editor"      ! "aixterm -name e3 -e e3"
```

Specify any editor window-specific resources in your .Xdefaults file as in

```
e3.foreground:      white
e3.background:      blue
e3.geometry:        80x33
```

Any resources that you have set for *aixterm* are still valid for the renamed *aixterm* unless they are overridden by the *e3* resource specification. Together with the keyboard override mechanism (see Section 11.6.2) you can remap the keyboard for specific terminal windows.

11.6.5 Getting fonts for other machines

Often, when using OEM terminals or PCs with an X server, you do not have the fonts that come with AIXwindows. However, there are two ways of accessing these fonts: when using AIXwindows up to version 1.2.2, which contains X11 release 4, get an SNF to BDF converter from some Internet FTP server and convert the IBM-supplied SNF fonts to BDF fonts and then use *bdftosnf* on the target machine to create the SNF fonts for this machine. With X11 release 5, which is sold by IBM as AIXwindows 1.2.3 (or comes with AIX 4), the font server is supplied. If your OEM X server is also at least an X11R5 server you should be able to obtain the fonts from the IBM font server daemon over the network without much hassle. See Section 11.2.9. If your server is not up to X11R5 yet or has no font server support, you can convert the IBM-supplied PCF fonts to BDF fonts with the *pcftobdf* program that comes with AIXwindows, but only on AIX 3.2.5 since this tool is no longer distributed with AIX 4.

11.6.6 Adding fonts

If you add or modify fonts on a system you need to set up the font name mapping for the X server, for example by having an application that has additional fonts in /usr/lib/myapp/fonts. Each font directory must have a file fonts.dir that maps the file names to X font names. It can be created by running the command **mkfontdir /usr/lib/myapp/fonts**. The first line of the generated fonts.dir file will be the number of the fonts in the file; the other lines map font file names to X font names. Should you need to access any given font through a different name you can do so by using the file fonts.aliases in the font directory. Like fonts.dir, it maps font names to X font names; the only difference is that it does not have the number of mappings in the first line.

Although shipped fonts on AIX are in compressed format (.Z ending), it is not necessary to uncompress them as the X server does it automatically. If you have an application with many uncompressed fonts I suggest running *compress* on them and then updating fonts.dir and fonts.aliases to save disk space.

After having created the new font directory and the fonts files, run **xset fp+ /usr/lib/myapp/fonts** to tell the running X server about the new fonts or update the font server configuration file.

11.6.7 Printing windows

Printing windows is relatively easy. Simply run **xwd | xpr -device ps | lp -dps0** to print a window on the PostScript printer ps0. Several options of *xwd* and *xpr* allow you to influence the way a window looks when printed. You can also use them to produce encapsulated PostScript files. The *xwd/xpr* combination has one major drawback however: color windows do not print particularly well on black and white printers. If you need high-quality screen dumps you should explore *pbmplus* or *Imagemagick*, which are part of the X11 source distribution tape. Other useful tools that are available on the Internet for this purpose are *xgrabsc* and *xv*. They all allow you to obtain better images off the screen than the standard *xwd/xpr* combination.

11.6.8 X speed up and resource conservation hints

Using the right $DISPLAY

The setting of the *DISPLAY* environment variable has a major impact on the performance of local X servers. If wrongly specified, then the data that is passed back and forth between the X server and the client application takes a longer path than necessary. Here is a list of possible values for a local client on the machine *blackice*:

:0 This tells the client to connect to the X server with the fastest possible method. On AIX this is via shared memory transport (SMT). This avoids using sockets altogether and the server communicates with the Xlib via a shared memory segment. (This has nothing to do with the X11R5 shared memory extensions, which affect only bitmap copies.)

unix:0 The classic specification for local connection uses local UNIX sockets without going through any IP sockets.

localhost:0 When specifying the display in this way, much time is lost in the IP code as real IP sockets are used.

blackice:0 This is the worst possible method. All traffic passes down to the network layer, which adds even more overhead then using only IP sockets.

Font access

If you have many fonts configured for your X server, and you are using font resources in .Xdefaults to tell *aixterm* (this works with other clients as well) the font it should use, then *aixterm* will take longer to start up as it would were the font name specified on the command line.

Another thing you should consider is the number of fonts that you use. If you only use a small number of fonts then the X server will not need to reaccess the font database every time. You could also restrict your font use to only one font directory and copy all the fonts you need into it, run *mkfontdir* in there and then use *xset* to limit the font path of the server to this directory. Yet another method of reducing the overhead for font information is the use of a font server, see Section 11.2.9.

Desktop gadgets

There are plenty of programs that run under X that produce an attractive desktop display but if every user on a machine serving Xterminals runs a number of them performance may suffer with no benefit other than a cosmetic one for the users. For example, I like to run my *xclock* with a ticking second display so that I know if the X server is still alive in an unstable environment. The ticking second means that *xclock* uses much more CPU time than it would just advancing the minute hand every 60 seconds. I also have a CD player utility and a calendar. Most gadgets are harmless on a single-user workstation, but with several users with Xstations on one CPU they suddenly become an issue. Check for the CPU use of those little gimmicks with *pstop* (see Section 23.4.3) if you think you are affected by them. In addition to CPU use, the network may also be affected in an Xstation environment.

Fancy screen backgrounds

When people first discover X they usually load attractive bitmaps or color pictures into the root window via *xsetroot* or *xv*. A simpler version of that theme is the CDE backdrop, which is also a way of loading images into the root window. If you are running in a memory-constrained environment this an absolute no-no. It takes more than a megabyte to store a color picture in the root window of the X server, and the X server has more work to restore the screen after a window that obscured the root window has been removed. An additional drawback of color background pictures is their use of colormap resources. You could easily run out of colors for your applications when loading complex colored backgrounds.

Faster processing of .xinitrc

If you work on a heavily loaded system and your ~/.xinitrc starts many clients, a *sleep 2* after the start of each one might speed up the processing of the ~/.xinitrc file as there are fewer programs trying to do the same thing at the same time. All clients perform a great deal of setup work when they initially connect to the server, therefore they spend less time fighting for the same resources when not started in parallel.

Resource loading

If you have a very large .Xdefaults file that is processed by every application at startup you might want to load the resource file into the X server instead via **xrdb -load /.Xdefaults**. Unfortunately, this costs resources in the X server. Another way to load resources is via *$XUSERFILESEARCHPATH*. Set this environment variable to a directory that contains application-specific configuration files similar to those in /usr/lib/X11/app-defaults and do not specify resources for those applications in .Xdefaults. This again costs resources in the file system. Depending on your constraints you need to experiment with these mechanisms until you find the one that suits you best. In addition, for some applications that do not accept resources in any other place but the server or .Xdefaults, this does not work.

12

Managing serial lines and terminals

Serial lines are still the most common method of connecting terminals and printers to UNIX systems, but they do cause some problems even for experienced system administrators. Although configuration via SMIT makes it easy under AIX, there are still many things to be aware of when working with serial lines. This chapter guides you through the essentials.

For a UNIX system a serial line or tty (teletype terminal in ancient times) is characterized by its hardware parameters, its line disciplines and optionally a controlling program such as *getty*. Controlling the hardware parameters is usually easy, since it all depends on the connected device. One selects the fastest available speed for both sides, 8 data bits, no parity and 1 stop bit if possible.

The hard part is managing the line discipline, which controls the handshake, optional character translation, reaction to inaccessible devices and more. To ensure that no characters are lost during transmission one needs to introduce some form of handshaking. You should always aim for hardware handshake, such as RTS/CTS or DTR/DSR, and avoid software handshake via XON/XOFF whenever possible. Software handshake has a higher latency as often there are characters already in a buffer that must be processed when the control character arrives. Hardware handshake, in contrast, will work immediately. Using software handshake removes two characters from the transmissible character set and may cause problems when transmitting binary data, whereas hardware handshake uses additional signal lines. You will find that all modems support RTS/CTS and most printers will support DTR/DSR and XON/XOFF. Terminals usually support RTS/CTS as well as XON/XOFF.

To avoid hard-coded dependencies on terminal capabilities, the termcap and terminfo databases were introduced. These databases store terminal capabilities and make it possible for an application to clear the screen or move the cursor on any terminal without exact knowledge of how this is done. AIX supports only the terminfo database, although a mini termcap database is also there for compatibility.

AIX 3 supported a very old version of curses and the terminfo database. AIX 4 has a newer version of curses and terminfo. If you want to run old AIX 3 applications on AIX you might need to install the compatibility libraries (*bos.compat.termcap**).

12.1 Configuring terminal ports

The standard configuration of a terminal port on AIX is pretty straightforward. Run **smit tty** and select “Add a TTY”. You will be prompted for the type of interface, RS232 or RS422, and the port where the tty should be defined and you will then find yourself in a menu where you can specify the basic attributes for the tty.

If you are configuring a terminal on the tty you should set the correct terminal type. If you do not know the exact name under which your terminal is known, browse the files in /usr/share/lib/terminfo for known terminals (on AIX 4 you might need to install additional terminal files for non-IBM terminals). The “Enable LOGIN” field should be set to *enable* for normal terminals and *disable* for output-only devices. The *share* and *delay* options are used when configuring the tty for modems, UUCP or Kermit where the port is used for dialing out as well as incoming connections.

If you are configuring the console tty, then you should include the *clocal* STTY attribute in both the RUN TIME and LOGIN fields. This will ensure that output to the tty is not blocked even when the tty is turned off. There are still some badly behaved programs that try to write to the console in case of errors instead of using more sensible means such as the error log or *syslogd*. However, using *clocal* has one dangerous side-effect. A session on that terminal will not be terminated when the terminal is turned off. One needs to log out explicitly. As the default console speed is 9600bps before *getty* starts you will not see any output from the boot sequence if you configure the console tty for higher speeds. Only after *getty* is active is the speed you configure here set.

The default program that is run on the tty is *getty*, which will monitor the tty line and allow you to log into the system. *Getty* is started out of /etc/inittab with the *respawn* option. While you are logged in *getty* is replaced by the shell you are using, which inherits the process id of *getty* so that *init* thinks *getty* is still running. As soon as you log out and terminate your shell, *init* starts a new *getty* because of the *respawn* option. If there is much noise on a unconnected tty line then there may be many *getty*s respawning. *Init* will notice this and stop respawning *gettys*. If this happens on your system you will see *ttyhog* errors in the error report. If you do not use a serial connection you should remove the tty definition or at least deactivate it with **rmdev -l ttyn** so that line noise doesn't start to trigger the *getty* program. On AIX *getty* and *login* are one and the same executable and are also available as *tsm* or terminal state manager, which controls all aspects of a terminal when used for normal log in.

12.1.1 Character mapping for terminals

When using terminals in a non-US environment you may need to adapt the character set mapping of the terminal. The entry for "CODESET map file" should be set according to your terminal. If your terminal uses the same code page as the rest of the system then the default of *sbcs* (single byte character set) is usually sufficient unless you work with one of the Asian languages that need more than one byte per character. The CODESET map files specify the width of characters only. In addition, you can select input and output map files for specific terminals such as the VT220 in 7bit mode. This can also be used to integrate your own special mappings by specifying a user-defined file here. This should only be necessary for very old terminals as all current models support the same ISO code pages as AIX. You may sometimes need several different maps that are changed at runtime when dealing with very old applications that still work with 7bit NLS code. However, a non-privileged user cannot load terminal maps into the tty driver. The solution is to use the *setmaps* command in rc.local, for example, to load but not activate the map. As soon as the map is loaded any user can activate or deactivate it. To preload the map you could use

```
setmaps -o vt220.out < /dev/ttyX
setmaps -i vt220.in < /dev/ttyX
setmaps -t NOMAP < /dev/ttyX
```

at boot time. After a map is loaded the user can switch to the map via **setmaps -t vt220** and back to no map via **setmaps -t NOMAP**. Note that when you try to set a map on one pty it is available for all ptys.

12.1.2 Some *terminfo* hints

On AIX 3 some of the terminals available in the /usr/share/lib/terminfo/*.ti files are not yet available because the file has not yet been compiled, for example virtual.ti, which contains the entry for the ANSI terminal. Some entries are even commented out. So check those entries and if necessary compile the file with the *tic* command, as in **tic dec.ti**. You may not even have the source files for the terminfo entries since installation is optional to save disk space. On AIX 3 they can be found in the *bos.data* install image.

On AIX 4 there are even fewer terminfo files on the system by default. Only IBM and DEC terminal definitions are loaded initially. All others need to be installed manually from the *bos.terminfo.** file sets.

There are three IBM terminals commonly available: the 3151, 3152 and the 3153. The 3152 is a newer, more ergonomic terminal that can work as either a 3151 or a VT320. The 3153, which is the newest member of the 315x family, has a 3151 emulation in its latest revision, whereas initially it was shipped only with WYSE and VT emulations. The terminfo entry for the IBM 3151 terminal that is shipped with AIX 3 still assumes the old 3151 keyboard, which has a cursor block that is modeled after a 3270 terminal. However, most users today order the 3151, 3152 or the 3153 with a PC-type keyboard. You can add the following to the ibm.ti file to get the <Home>, <Page Up> and <Page Down> keys working:

```
ibm3151-pc|IBM 3151 or 3152 with PC or PS/2 type keyboard,
        el@, kel@, kclr@, kbtab@,
        knp=\EI, kpp=\EL\r, kend\E2,
        lines#25,
        use=ibm3151,
```

The lines entry will give you support for the 25-line configuration of the terminal. Omit it if you have your terminal set to 24 lines. Instead of setting the terminal type to *ibm3151* you now can set it to *ibm3151-pc* and the cursor pad keys work as labeled. You have to run **tic ibm.ti** first to get the new entry into the terminfo database. When running *tic* you will compile all entries in the file. Should you have a restrictive umask set for root remember to use *chmod* afterwards to make the terminal database readable for the users.

On AIX 4 the above entry is already shipped as *ibm3151-51* with one minor difference. Although there is an *ibm3151-25* entry for 25 lines and an *IBM3152-PS2* entry for the PC-type cursor pad, there is no entry for the PC-type keyboard with 25 lines. You have to modify the *ibm3151-51* entry yourself.

12.2 Setting up UUCP

Even in our modern WAN times the old UNIX-to-UNIX Copy Program (UUCP) has its place. It is still one of the most cost-effective means of connecting machines that are far apart when a permanent connection is not needed. UUCP is ideal for mail exchange and low-volume file transfer, for example obtaining nightly reports from remote branches.

The UUCP that comes with AIX is the more modern Basic Networking Utilities (BNU) version. When searching in InfoExplorer for an introduction you should search for BNU not UUCP. All UUCP configuration files can be found in /etc/uucp and the commands are either in /usr/bin or /usr/sbin/uucp. If your version of AIX still does not allow RTS/CTS configuration via SMIT, obtain the necessary workaround from the support center as you need to configure modems with this type of hardware handshake for reliable connection.

UUCP is usually run between two sites that are connected via modems. The following example will connect the machines rhino and hippo via two modems. The connection will allow full access for both machines in both directions.

(1) Set up the ttys that are used to connect the modems to rhino and hippo for the fastest speed the modems can accept. Use 8 bits, no parity 1 stop bit. Use RTS/CTS flow control. Deactivate XON/XOFF flow control. Make sure that *clocal* is not set and that *hupcl* is set in the run and log modes of the tty. *Clocal* would ignore a disconnect from the modem and *hupcl* is needed so that the connection is closed on the AIX side when it receives a close signal from the modem.

(2) The modems need to be configured accordingly. They should be configured to do a soft reset on loss of DTR. The speed between DTE and DCE (computer and modem) should be locked to the highest common speed that is supported by the modem and the RS/6000. Carrier detect should follow the true carrier signal. The modem should use RTS/CTS. The modem should be configured for short textual return messages. You might want to set it to no messages once you have tested the setup to avoid confusing the *getty* program with CONNECT messages.

(3) Set the login for the ttys to *delay*. With this setting *getty* will not lock the port so that it can be used outgoing as well. As soon as no other program is active on the port but characters are coming in, *getty* will take over the port to allow log in.

(4) Configure the *uucp* user id. As shipped AIX 3 already has a *uucp* user id, but its configuration is not complete. Edit /etc/passwd and set the login program for the *uucp* user to /usr/sbin/uucp/uucico and the home directory to /var/spool/uucppublic. Include /usr/sbin/uucp/uucico in the shells stanza in /etc/security/login.cfg. Set a password for *uucp* on each machine and then delete the ADMCHG flag from the *flags* entry for *uucp* in /etc/security/passwd. Automatic UUCP logins are not capable of changing

the password so this mechanism is useless here. On AIX 4 there are already two UUCP user ids: the *uucp* id for UUCP maintenance work and *nuucp* for automatic transfers via *uucico*.

(5) If you are not using TCP/IP set the host name manually in rc.local, for example via **uname -S rhino**.

(6) Configure /etc/uucp/Systems. On rhino:

```
hippo Any ACU 19200 HipposPhoneNumber "" \r\d\d\d\r\d\r\d\r in:--
in: uucp word:--word: SecretPassword
```

The entry should be one line. Do the same on hippo with reversed host name, telephone number and password. This entry defines a chat script that is executed for the log in at the remote system. Hippo can be called at any time via an automatic calling unit (today every modem has one) which is connected with 19200 bps. The unit should dial the telephone number listed here and then send a few carriage returns intermixed with delays. As soon as the string "in:" appears from the modem the string "uucp" should be sent. Then when the string "word:" comes from the remote system the password is sent.

(7) Configure /etc/uucp/Dialers. On both machines:

```
tbfast =,-, "" \dAT\r OK \dATS50=255\r OK \dATDT\T\r\d\d\d\d\d\d
CONNECT
```

This line is extremely modem specific. You will need to know exactly how your modem works before you can construct the Dialers entry. It defines the strings that are sent to the modem (nickname tbfast) for dialing a number. The '=,-,' entry tells UUCP to wait for a dial tone and then pause a bit. We do not wait for anything after that '""' but continue with the dial string. First the modem is sent an attention command and it should respond with OK. Then the register 50 on the modem is changed to 255 so that the modem starts in high-speed mode. If this is acknowledged by the modem with another OK the number is dialed and the script expects a CONNECT message from the modem.

(8) Configure /etc/uucp/Devices. On both machines:

```
ACU tty0 - 19200 tbfast
Direct tty0 - 19200 direct
```

The first entry defines tbfast as an autodialing unit that is connected via tty0 and should be accessed with 19200 bps. The second allows direct access to the modem. This can be useful if you want to log in to the modem to change register settings. You can do this via **cu -ml /dev/tty0**.

(9) Configure /etc/uucp/Permissions. On rhino:

```
LOGNAME=uucp VALIDATE=hippo REQUEST=yes SENDFILES=yes
MACHINE=hippo COMMANDS=rmail:uucp:uux READ=/ WRITE=/
```

Hippo should be configured in the same way with the host name exchanged. When a user *uucp* logs in from hippo it may request or send files regardless of which system queued the transfer request, has read/write access to the whole file system and can execute the *uucp*, *rmail* and *uux* commands. This entry is, of course, quite insecure. Set READ, WRITE and COMMANDS to whatever suits you without giving too much access. The entries in this file can be very system specific. The above is only a small example. You should look up the Permissions file in infoExplorer for a full description of what you can do.

(10) If your goal is automated file transmission then you should run the UUCP I/O daemon from *cron* at some convenient time. To do this you need to modify the crontab entry for the *uucp* user. Use **su uucp** and then **crontab -e** to do this or edit /var/spool/cron/crontabs/uucp and then kill the *cron* daemon. Do not try to use **su - uucp** as this would present you with the *uucico* program as your current shell. Your crontab entry on rhino might look as follows:

```
33 21 * * 1-5 /usr/sbin/uucp/uucico -r1 -s hippo
```

This would start the communication with hippo every weekday night at 21:33. Use *info* to see how cron table entries are defined (search for *crontab*). If you have heavy UUCP requirements, then using the predefined entries in *uucp*'s crontab may be interesting. They use additional configuration files for periodic tasks.

With the above definitions it is now easy to transfer files between the systems via the *uucp* command: **uucp hippo!/etc/hosts rhino!/etc/hosts.from.hippo** would transfer the file /etc/hosts from hippo to rhino no matter where it was executed. If one machine is left out of the command then the local machine is assumed.

Usually one needs a more restrictive setup. Assuming that rhino is the central site from which hippo is maintained the Permissions files would be quite different.

On rhino:

```
LOGNAME=uucp VALIDATE=hippo REQUEST=no SENDFILES=no MACHINE=hippo \
COMMANDS=rmail READ=/var/spool/uucppublic WRITE=/var/spool/uucppublic
```

On hippo:

```
LOGNAME=uucp VALIDATE=rhino REQUEST=yes SENDFILES=yes MACHINE=rhino \
COMMANDS=rmail:uucp:uux READ=/ WRITE=/
```

This setup allows rhino to request files from hippo and even execute commands there, whereas hippo can only queue mail for rhino.

All the above samples use *uucp* as login name. As soon as you have more than one connection you should use different login names so that you can specify different access permissions for the systems.

A very good book on UUCP is published by O'Reilly and Associates: (*Managing UUCP and Usenet*, 35). If you need UUCP for your daily business you should read it since it covers all the nitty gritty details of working with UUCP.

12.2.1 Debugging UUCP

UUCP can be a bit tricky to set up, but there are tools to help you. First you should check your UUCP setup via **/usr/sbin/uucp/uucheck -v**. This will tell you how UUCP interprets what you configured into the Permissions file.

If everything looks fine here you should try to connect to a remote system manually via the *cu* command. Use **cu -d remote** to connect to the remote system. You will see how UUCP tries to establish the connection. Should this be successful then the modem and the lines are usually fine.

The next step is to queue a file transfer via the *uucp* command and then execute **/usr/sbin/uucp/uutry remote**. It will display its progress while trying to connect to the remote system. A typical error that can be found is a wrong NLS configuration. If you configure a system to display a German log in message then a chat script that waits for "password" will fail as the German word is "Passwort" (another reason to set LANG=C in /etc/environment).

Apart from this typical NLS error you might see that a modem generates more than the expected messages and thus confuses the chat script. Most modems can be configured to return no messages at all.

13

Backup

One of the most neglected system administration tasks is backup. Although good backups are the only safeguard against many problems resulting from disk crashes, stupidity, or vicious intruders, they are rarely generated. Most backup tasks can, however, be automated, with either some home-grown scripts or commercial archiving software such as ADSM/6000. AIX comes with the basic means for backup that can be used for anything from small routine backups to full-scale system cloning.

13.1 System backup

AIX provides a way of generating bootable backup images of the system. On AIX 3 this is limited to the root volume group, but AIX 4 includes additional commands with the same functionality for other volume groups. One should always have a current system backup to ensure fast recovery after disaster strikes. It is much easier to get the base system back from such a backup than to install from scratch. System backups can easily be used to clone existing systems, a feature that makes bulk installations of specific configurations much easier.

The following sections discuss custom clone tapes, but if you omit the custom part you have a plain system backup that can be used for disaster recovery. You should generate a system backup before and after every time you apply major updates or configuration changes to the system.

13.1.1 Cloning AIX 3.2 systems

By using **mkszfile && mksysb -f /dev/rmt0** you can create clone images of the current root volume group. Alternatively, you can also run **smit mksysb**. These images can then be installed on different machines. Unless the target machine requires a driver that is not present on the original machine this mechanism works quite well.

In addition to device information, other system configuration parameters need to be adapted to the new system, for example network addresses. You should therefore configure only as much as is common on all your systems when preparing a clone master. Machine-specific features should not be configured on the master to avoid conflicts in a networked environment. The individual adaptation of the clone can be done when it boots the first time with a simple script that is executed only once at the first boot. The script is conveniently called /etc/firstboot. If it exists it will be executed by the cloned machine immediately after /etc/rc. It will be executed only once and then renamed to /etc/fb_hh_mm_MM_DD according to the current date. This is handled by the *fbcheck* entry in /etc/inittab.

The cloned system will contain all the file systems in the root volume group of the master that were mounted at the time the clone image was created. The list of file systems to be created is generated by the *mkszfile* command. It creates /.fs.size, which stores the sizes of the file systems for the clone in a form similar to that in Figure 13.1.

```
imageinstall
rootvg 4 hd4 / 2 8 jfs
rootvg 4 hd1 /home 21 84 jfs
rootvg 4 hd3 /tmp 3 12 jfs
rootvg 4 hd2 /usr 178 712 jfs
rootvg 4 hd9var /var 3 12 jfs
```

Figure 13.1 /.fs.size on AIX 3.2.

Each record contains the volume group, the logical partition size, the name of the logical volume, the name of the file system, the size in physical partitions, the size in megabytes and the type of the file system. Make sure that /usr and /tmp have at least 8 MB free before creating the tape to avoid problems with the installation of the new image.

Unfortunately, there is no way of influencing paging or dump space sizes when installing from these tapes. They will be created according to the internal logic of the installation commands. The placement of the file systems on the disk will be handled by the installation routines and is not controllable by the user.

13.1.2 Restoring files from an AIX 3.2 system backup

AIX 3.2 stores the image in tar format. The image is the third file on the tape. To get a file off the tape you need to position the tape to the right tape file and then restore the file using a non-rewinding tape device. Assuming that a system backup tape is in the tape drive and is accessible as /dev/rmt0 and that the file to restore is the *vi* editor (/usr/bin/vi) that was accidentally deleted one would use the following commands:

```
cd /
tctl -f /dev/rmt0 rewind
tctl -f /dev/rmt0.1 fsf 3
tar -xvf /dev/rmt0.1 ./usr/bin/vi
```

All files are stored relative to root and therefore we need to *cd* to / first. It is then necessary to ensure that the tape is in the right starting position and to advance to the third image on the tape. There we read the file back; note that the file name is specified relative to root exactly as it was stored.

13.1.3 Cloning AIX 4 systems

AIX 4 has more functionality for system backups. File system sizes and placement can be controlled through configuration files and different installation methods and options can be specified. On AIX 4 *mkszfile* no longer generates /.fs.size but /image.data instead, which is much more elaborate then its predecessor. Further customization possibilities are given through the /bosinst.data file that is created by the *mksysb* command unless there is already a user-generated one. The default for /bosinst.data can be found in /usr/lpp/bosinst/bosinst.template.

To generate a system backup use **smit mksysb** or **mksysb -i /dev/rmt0**. The new *-i* option of *mksysb* will call *mkszfile* automatically. If you specify *-m* then *mkszfile* will generate logical volume maps that will be included in the image. With these the exact physical placement of the file systems can be cloned. The new *-e* parameter will tell *mksysb* to exclude the files listed in /etc/exclude.rootvg from the backup.

When creating the /bosinst.data and /image.data files manually with *mkszfile* you can modify the boot images characteristics. The bosinst.data file (Figure 13.2) controls how a *mksysb* image is installed, whereas the image.data file defines the characteristics of the root volume group and the file systems within it.

```
control_flow:
    CONSOLE =
    INSTALL_METHOD = overwrite
    PROMPT = yes
    EXISTING_SYSTEM_OVERWRITE = yes
    INSTALL_X_IF_ADAPTER = yes
    RUN_STARTUP = yes
    RM_INST_ROOTS = no
    ERROR_EXIT =
    CUSTOMIZATION_FILE =
    TCB = yes
    INSTALL_TYPE = full
    BUNDLES =

target_disk_data:
    LOCATION = 00-00-0S-0,0
    SIZE_MB = 1307
    HDISKNAME = hdisk0

locale:
    BOSINST_LANG = en_US
    CULTURAL_CONVENTION = C
    MESSAGES = C
    KEYBOARD = de_DE
```

Figure 13.2 The bosinst.data file.

The bosinst.data file sets initial options for system installation. To clone systems you may want to adapt this file to your needs. Not all of the following parameters need to be adapted.

CONSOLE Defines the console device. You must set this if you set prompt to no so that the system knows which device to use for the console. You could use /dev/lft0 or /dev/tty0 for example.

INSTALL_METHOD Sets the installation method, which for clone tapes is usually overwrite. The preserve and migrate options are available for updating systems but not for cloning.

PROMPT Set this to no for an automated install. If it is set to no be sure to specify all the parameters needed in the other entries.

EXISTING_SYSTEM_OVERWRITE
You need to set this to yes for automated overwrite installs on systems that already have AIX installed.

INSTALL_X_IF_ADAPTER
This is not used when cloning systems; otherwise it would specify whether or not AIXwindows will be installed if a graphics adapter is found.

RUN_STARTUP Set this to yes if you want the system to run the install assistant after the first boot.

RM_INST_ROOTS If set to yes, the /usr/lpp/*/inst_roots directories will be cleaned up after installation. Unless you want to run a server system for diskless machines this should be set to yes.

ERROR_EXIT That option can be used to run your own programs should the installation fail. You have to specify the complete pathname here.

CUSTOMIZATION_FILE
If you specify a file name here, then this program will be executed immediately after the installation program.

TCB Set this to yes if you want to have the TCB active on the new system. You cannot activate the TCB at a later stage.

INSTALL_TYPE On a *mksysb* installation this is always a full installation.

BUNDLES On a *mksysb* installation this is meaningless, Otherwise it specifies which software bundles need to be installed initially.

LOCATION This is the location code for the installation disk. If it is not set the installation routine will try to find a suitable disk automatically. A location of 00-00-0S-0,0 would specify the disk with SCSI address 0 on the integrated SCSI adapter. See **lsdev -C** for more location codes.

SIZE_MB You could specify a disk size in megabytes here, but it is not necessary. By specifying the keyword largest and no location code, the system will try to use the largest disk for installation.

HDISKNAME You could specify a disk name here, for example *hdisk0*.

BOSINST_LANG Here you set the language that is used during the installation.

CULTURAL_CONVENTION
The locale used for the installed system is specified here. You can leave it blank for a *mksysb* tape.

MESSAGES Specifies the language for system messages. You can leave it blank for a *mksysb* tape.

KEYBOARD This specifies the keyboard map to install. You can leave it blank for a *mksysb* tape.

The /image.data file contains several stanzas that describe the root volume group and the logical volumes it contains. If one sets EXACT_FIT to yes in the *logical_volume_policy* then the disk that is used to install the system must exactly fit the description in this file. The SHRINK parameter defines whether or not the logical volumes should be shrunk to their minimal size at install time.

The *vg_data* stanza describes parameters of the volume group. Use the PPSIZE parameter to set different default physical partitions sizes; the default is 4MB.

There is one *lv_data* stanza for each logical volume. All the characteristics of the logical volume can be adapted here. They are particularly useful when cloning systems to define the disk location and maximum size parameters.

Finally, the *fs_data* stanza that exists for each of the file systems can be used to modify the file system block size and activate compression for the file system.

Like AIX 3, AIX 4 will execute /etc/firstboot if it exists when the system boots for the first time after installation. This is triggered by the *fbcheck* entry in /etc/inittab.

13.1.4 Restoring files from a AIX 4 system backup

The procedure is similar to the one used for AIX 3.2. Simply use the *restore* command instead of *tar* (AIX 4 uses the backup by file format for system images). When using *restore* on a non-rewind tape you need to specify the *-s* flag to tell *restore* about it. The image backup is still in the third position on the tape. To restore /usr/bin/vi one would use the following commands:

```
cd /
tctl -f /dev/rmt0 rewind
tctl -f /dev/rmt0.1 fsf 3
restore -xqf /dev/rmt0.1 -s 1 ./usr/bin/vi
```

13.1.5 Using *savevg/restvg* on AIX 4

AIX allows the archival of volume groups other than the root volume group with the *savevg* and *restvg* commands. To save the volume group *homevg* you could use either **smit savevg** or the command

```
savevg -i -f/dev/rmt0 homevg
```

where the *-i* option would create a /tmp/vgdata/homevg/homevg.data file. This file is like the /image.data file created by the *mkszfile* command, but in this case it is created by the *mkvgdata* command, which is really just a link to the *mkszfile* command. As with *mksysb* there is also a *-m* flag to create map files. If there are files you want to exclude from the backup of the *homevg*, use the *-e* flag to tell *savevg* to exclude the files listed in /etc/exclude.homevg. The backup will include the /tmp/vgdata/homevg/homevg.data and /tmp/vgdata/homevg/filesystems files for reference by the *restvg* command. The filesystems file is a complete copy of the /etc/filesystems file.

To restore a backup created by the savevg command use *restvg*, as in

```
restvg -qf /dev/rmt0 -s
```

This would not only restore the *homevg* volume group on the physical volumes it has been residing on previously, it would also shrink the restored file systems to their minimum size. If you try to restore a volume group and the disks the volume group was on are assigned to a volume group at restore time, then the command will abort. The disk for the volume group needs to be unallocated for *restvg* to work.

If you want to restore the volume group to different hard disks, make sure they are already known to the system (available state) and do not currently belong to a volume group. Then execute

```
restvg  -qf /dev/rmt0 hdiskN
```

to restore the backup onto a different hard disk. Should you need to restore individual files from this backup, use the standard *restore* command, for example:

```
cd/
restore -xqf /dev/rmt0 ./home/afx/.profile
```

Use the *-T* flag to list the contents of the tape if needed.

If you did not use the *-i* option on *savevg* but created the homevg.data file manually by running **mkvgdata homevg**, you can change the characteristics of the volume group and its file systems by editing the homevg.data file. You can adapt characteristics such as the physical partition size or the block size and compression algorithm of the file systems in the volume group.

The *savevg* command saves only three additional files at the beginning of the archive, apart from which it simply generates a normal backup file. Before the two files mentioned above, another file is saved that describes the location of the file system and volume group data files.

13.2 Archiving commands

There are many commands available on AIX that can be used for backups. Each has different features and limitations. Table 13.1 attempts a basic comparison. The values in parentheses in the table point to behavior that depends on the options used. The backup command, for example, reacts differently when used for file system dumps than when used for backup by file.

Table 13.1 A comparison of archiving commands.

	backup/ restore	*rdump/ rrestore*	*tar*	*cpio*	*pax*
Raw devices	(Y)	(Y)	N	N	N
Files	Y	N	Y	Y	Y
File systems	Y	Y	N	N	N
Special files	Y	Y	Y	Y	Y
Sub-directories	N	Y	Y	N	Y
Default archive	/dev/rfd0	N/A	/dev/rmt0, $TAPE	*stdin/ stdout*	*stdin/ stdout*
Selective restore	Y	Y	Y	*ksh regex*	*regex*
Rename on restore	N	N	N	Y	Y
Compression	(Y)	N	N	N	N
Verification	N	N	N	N	N
Error recovery	(Y)	N	N	Y	Y
Preserve modification time	Y	Y	Y	Y	Y
Multiple volumes	Y	Y	Y	N	Y
File format	*backup, dump*	*dump*	*tar*	*cpio*	*tar, cpio*
Incremental backup	Y	Y	N	N	N
Bytesex sensitive	(N)	N	N	Y	(N)
U/Gid > 65535	Y	Y	(Y)	N	N
ACL support	Y	N	N	N	N
AIX only	(Y)	N	N	N	N

13.2.1 *backup/restore*

These are the native AIX commands for backups. Only they can save and restore ACLs, so if you need ACLs you have no other choice. *Backup/restore* support two types of backups, either by file or by i-node. Using i-node is another way of saying file system dump. The *mksysb* command on AIX 4 uses the file method. The dump method has support for incremental backups, which reduces the amount of time and tape needed for backups. This method is compatible with the BSD *dump* command and the AIX *rdump/rrestore* commands.

Backup and *restore* use /dev/rfd0 as their default device. Both are verbose commands that tell you what they are doing, and unless you specify the *-q* flag you are even prompted to press enter when the archiving device is ready.

Backup by file

Apart from the rare cases of data interchange with AIX PS/2 or AIX on the RT, there is no need to worry about data format compatibility. In these cases you need to specify *-o* when using backup on AIX on a RS/6000 to make the backup readable on the other systems. Non-AIX systems cannot read backups created with backup in file mode. You have to use one of the other commands for interoperability.

Typically one would pipe the output of *find* into *backup* to generate a backup, as in

```
cd /
find ./home -print | backup -iqf /dev/rmt0
```

The above commands create a relative backup of the /home directory and its subdirectories using the tape in drive 0 to archive the files. The backup is done relative to root so that one can easily restore the /home tree elsewhere. To restore from this tape the commands

```
cd /
restore -xqf /dev/rmt0
```

would be used.

If you only want to list the table of contents use the *-T* flag instead of *-x*. To restore only specific files place their names on the commandline exactly as they were stored; use *-T* to check it if you have doubts.

The *backup* command supports a simple form of compression and it uses the same algorithm as the *pack* command. It is triggered by the *-p* flag. As this method is not reliable for files larger than 24MB, large files are not compressed. Since *pack* is not a very good compression anyway, I suggest piping the output of *backup* through the *compress* command instead.

Backup by i-node

If you come from a BSD environment you will be familiar with the *dump* command, which is similar to backup by i-node. Backup by i-node has the advantage of making incremental backups. To use incremental backups the file /etc/dumpdates must exist. If it is missing on your system create it with **touch /etc/dumpdates**. To generate a full backup of /home use

```
backup -0uf /dev/rmt0.4 /home
```

This will place a level 0 dump on the tape. In /etc/dumpdates you will get an entry like:

```
/dev/rhd1 0 Thu Aug 25 16:23:53 1994
```

Instead of using /home for the command you could also use /dev/rhd1. The next backup that only stores the incremental changes would be initiated with

```
backup -1uf /dev/rmt0.4 /home
```

The /etc/dumpdates file now also contains an entry for the level 1 dump.

```
/dev/rhd1 0 Thu Aug 25 16:23:53 1994
/dev/rhd1 1 Thu Aug 25 16:39:33 1994
```

In the case of loss this file system can be restored by creating a completely new and empty /home file system. Make the new file system your current directory and restore the data from the tapes. First insert the level 0 tape and run

```
restore  -qrf /dev/rm0
```

Then insert the level 1 tape and run the command again.

```
restore  -qrf /dev/rm0
```

You should now have all your files back. You can also restore individual files. Go to the directory that represents the file system that was backed up and enter the command:

```
restore -qxf /dev/rmt0.4  ./Yourfile
```

Note that you need to enter a relative pathname here. File system backups can also be restored interactively with the *-i* flag instead of *-x* or *-r*. You can get the listing of a dump tape with the *-t* flag.

This form of backup can be used if you run a level 0 full backup every Friday (or the weekend) and generate a delta every day, where level 1 maps to Monday, level 2 to Tuesday and so on. This type of backup also can be done remotely with *rdump,* which is discussed next.

13.2.2 *rdump/rrestore*

These commands are the remote versions of *backup* in file system mode. They are compatible with their BSD versions. Their major difference from *backup* and *restore* is the destination of the backup, which is always a remote tape. The target machine needs a proper /.rhosts file to make it work, which might preclude the use of these commands at your site if you have high security demands. On AIX 4 you may need to add a symbolic link in /etc if you have not installed the compatibility links. Use **ln -s /usr/sbin/mnt /etc** to create it. As with backup you need the file /etc/dumpdates. To backup /home to the remote system server the command looks like

```
rdump -0uf server:/dev/rmt0.4 /home
```

Rdump needs a few more parameters so that it knows about the tape length. For an 8 mm 2.3 GB drive the parameters are *-d6250 -s33000*. Using a 5 GB tape drive in compressed mode the *-s* parameter value is 80000. Restoring from a remote tape is like restoring from the local tape:

```
rrestore  -rf server:/dev/rm0
```

Most other flags from *restore* work on *rrestore* as well.

13.2.3 *cpio*

Cpio (for CoPy In/Out) is the old-timer among the UNIX backup commands. As it has problems with byte ordering it is not necessarily a good option when exchanging files between different systems. Its main advantage over the other UNIX classic, *tar*, is that it recovers better from tape errors. To backup /home one could use:

```
cd /
find ./home -print | cpio -o > /dev/rmt0
```

For the above command there is actually a short-cut built into *find*:

```
find ./home -cpio /dev/rmt0
```

To restore this archive the reverse command would be

```
cd /
cpio -i < /dev/rmt0
```

Listing the contents of an archive is done with **cpio -it < /dev/rmt0**.

If you need to read a *cpio* tape from a system with a different byte order (for example an Intel-based system), you can use the *-s* option to swap bytes. Even then it might not work if the archive has a binary header. To get an ASCII header use the *-c* flag when creating an archive.

13.2.4 *tar*

Tar (for Tape ARchive) is the most widely used command for file exchange between UNIX systems. It is available on every UNIX system as well as on many other operating systems and it does not have any problems with byte ordering. Its only drawbacks are lack of ACL support on AIX and no error recovery on tape errors. When you are using long user or group ids (>2 bytes) it might be problematic to exchange archives with non-AIX systems as not all UNIX systems support long ids. Backing up with *tar* is easy enough:

```
cd /
tar -cf /dev/rmt0 ./home
```

As in the other examples this would create a relative backup of /home. To restore use:

```
cd /
tar -xf /dev/rmt0
```

Listing of a *tar* archive is done with the *-t* and optionally the *-v* flags. When using *tar* in pipes you should use the *-B* flag for blocking, as in

```
tar -cBf - /home | compress | dd of=/dev/rmt0
```

To restore such an archive you would use:

```
dd if=/dev/rmt0 | uncompress | tar -xBf -
```

When using *tar* directly to a tape you do not even need to specify *-f/dev/rmt0* as this is the default. You can set another default tape device with the environment variable TAPE.

13.2.5 *pax*

Although *pax* stands for Posix Archiver eXtracter it is rumored that the Latin word for peace was the true origin to join the *cpio* and *tar* fans. *Pax* can handle both formats; it defaults to *tar* format but with the added error recovery of *cpio*. Archiving /home with *pax* is done with

```
pax -wf /dev/rmt0 /home
```

To restore it use

```
pax -r -pe -f /dev/rmt0
```

and to list it just

```
pax -f /dev/rmt0
```

The *-pe* option in the restore command is used to preserve not only the modification time but also the ownership of the files. When using *pax* it is not necessary to use relative pathnames. They can be changed when restoring file, regardless of whether the archive was created with *pax*, *tar* or *cpio*.

```
pax -rpe -f /dev/rmt0 -s:^/home:/tmp/test:g
```

The above command would restore the files from /home in /tmp/test. When reading archives *pax* will automatically use the correct format. To write explicitly in *cpio* or *tar* format use the *-x* option for specifying the format.

13.3 Remote backup

Should you want to use commands apart from *rdump*/*rrestore* for remote backups you can do so easily with the remote shell. I routinely use *tar* to back up to remote tapes or directories. Here is a commandline to do a remote backup for /home:

```
cd /home
tar -c -B -f - . | rsh server "dd ibs=512 of=/dev/rmt0 obs=16k"
```

The *-B* flag for *tar* tells it to perform blocking with 512-byte blocks, which is necessary on pipes. With the *-f -* option the output of *tar* is sent to *stdout*. The remote shell sends the data to *dd*, which writes to the tape. Using an output block size of 16 KB speeds up the process quite a bit on my QIC525 drive; experiment with your drive to see which block size gives the best throughput. To restore from a remote tape you then can use

```
cd /home
rsh server "dd if=/dev/rmt0 ibs=16k obs=512" | tar -xf -
```

If you are short of tape space you will want to compress the data. For compression you need a slightly different pipeline:

```
tar -cBf- . | rsh server "compress | dd of=/dev/rmt0 obs=16k conv=sync"
```

and to restore it use

```
rsh server "dd if=/dev/rmt0 bs=16k" | uncompress | tar  xf
```

Another typical use would be to create a remote copy of a directory, as in

```
tar -cBf - . | rsh server "(cd /target; tar -xf -)"
```

For all the above commands a properly configured /.rhosts file is assumed.

13.4 Restoring absolute backups to different directories

Of all the backup commands only *cpio* and *pax* allow you to change the pathnames of files when restoring from absolute backups. As *pax* can handle *tar* format, you can restore absolute *tar* archives with it as well. But what about *backup*? There is an easy trick that works for all commands. First list the tape's contents to see the absolute pathnames. Then mount the target directory that you really want on to a mount point that reflects the absolute name. For example, if you have an absolute backup of the home directory of *artur* and you want to restore the file /home/artur/somefile. But you do not want to overwrite the existing somefile in *artur*'s home directory. Create a directory /tmp/artur and mount it over /home/artur. Now you can run the restore.

```
mkdir /tmp/artur
mount /tmp/artur /home/artur
restore -xqf /tmp/artur.backup /home/artur/somefile
umount /home/artur
```

Now you have the file in /tmp/artur/somefile.

13.5 Tape device names

The tape device names on AIX trigger different behaviors and densities. Each tape device can have two different densities and it can be set to rewind or not on close, and retention on open is also available.

Table 13.2 The functions of tape device names.

Device name	Rewind on close	Retention on open	Density setting
/dev/rmtX	Y	N	1
/dev/rmtX.1	N	N	1
/dev/rmtX.2	Y	Y	1
/dev/rmtX.3	N	Y	1
/dev/rmtX.4	Y	N	2
/dev/rmtX.5	N	N	2
/dev/rmtX.6	Y	Y	2
/dev/rmtX.7	N	Y	2

Use the InfoExplorer article 'Tape Drive Attributes' to determine which density settings correspond to the capabilities of a specific drive. Some tape drives that have more than two different density settings need to be configured via **smit chgtpe** or *chdev* so that the density settings of the tape device names match your needs.

13.6 Some thoughts on tapes and drives

AIX supports a wide variety of tape drives from simple quarter-inch cartridges to classic nine-track tapes. As shipped, the block sizes of the tape devices that AIX uses are not always optimal, for example the 8-mm drive works best with a physical block size of 1 KB or multiples of it but has a default block size of 512 bytes on AIX 3. The block size of a tape is changed with **chdev -l rmt0 -ablock_size=1024** for example.

Should you have problems reading foreign tapes it sometimes helps to use a block size of zero. Using *pax* instead of *tar* when reading tapes with errors often allows you to skip over the error and access at least the rest of the data.

If you have no clue at all what the tape format is, try reading the data with the *dd* command and then analyze it with *od -c*, *file* and the various archiving commands. If you cannot even read it with *dd*, then the tape is probably defective or written using a totally obscure method.

When using quarter inch cartridge (QIC) tapes, it pays to retention them with *tctl* after inserting them into the drive. After retentioning the tape will be perfect on the spool, and by the time this activity has finished the tape will have the right temperature. Data losses on QIC tapes are usually caused by using tapes that are too cold.

Electronically controlled doors on tape units can usually be opened with **tctl offline**. This is very helpful for unattended backups as no one will be able accidentally to overwrite a tape that has been left in the drive.

There are still people who believe that buying video tapes for the 8mm drive or DATs for the 4-mm drive is a good way of saving money. I think this is a good way of losing money. Data-grade tapes are inspected much more thoroughly by the manufacturers than the consumer video and audio tapes. It does not make sense to save a few nickels on tapes when the data on the tape is crucial for your business.

Another thing to consider is the storage location for your backups. Having short-term work backups next to the machine is usually OK, but you should occasionally (somewhere between once a week and once per quarter) store complete backups in a different building. This will prevent a total loss in case of fire or theft.

Labeling of tapes is also critical. Make a habit of writing the following information on the label: who created the tape when and with which command. What tape unit was used (8-mm compressed or the old 2.3-GB unit)? and from which machine was the backup taken? Noting the AIX release level also would not hurt, at least for root volume group backups. For volume group backups a printed copy of the /image.data (or vgname.data) file might be helpful.

13.7 Backup strategies

One should always have a current system backup of the root volume group. Not only is it needed to recover from catastrophic crashes, it also allows you to restore individual files and it will be needed to access maintenance mode.

Current, in this sense, is after (and probably before as well) each update to the system that changes the boot image. Major configuration changes that are time-consuming to reproduce also make a full system backup very useful.

Unless you have only one disk or have to make do with limited resources, the root volume group, the basic AIX installation, should be separate from other applications and your data, which should be in their own volume group. On AIX 3 there is no default mechanism to back up the non-root volume groups, so it is necessary to resort to the backup commands shown previously to do this. AIX 4 adds the *savevg* command for saving complete volume groups.

One of the problems with backups is how to find the data in case a restore is needed. This is usually easy with full system backups, but how do you know which of your daily delta tapes contains the one file that was accidentally erased? The answer to this question can be obtained by wrapping the archiving command in a shell script that saves a table of contents after archiving. The following is a crude approximation:

```
#!/usr/bin/ksh
# sample script that creates a backup of /home
# The contents of the tape will be listed in
# /var/log/Programname.MMDDYY.Z
#
# afx 8/94

SOURCE=/home
TAPE=/dev/rmt0
LOGDIR=/var/log
LOGFILE=`basename $0`.`date +"%y%m%d"`
LOG=$LOGDIR/$LOGFILE
TMP1=/tmp/$LOGFILE.1.$$
TMP2=/tmp/$LOGFILE.2.$$
DIFF=/tmp/$LOGFILE.diff.$$

cd $SOURCE

tar -cvf $TAPE . | cut -f2 -d\  > $TMP1
tar -tvf $TAPE > $LOG

cut -c 45-1024 $LOG | cut -f2 -d\  > $TMP2
diff $TMP1 $TMP2 > $DIFF

if [ -s $DIFF ]
then
        mail -s "Problems backing up $SOURCE" root < $DIFF
else
        rm -f $TMP1 $TMP2 $DIFF
        compress $LOG
fi
```

The data is archived with the *tar* command. The list of files that is processed by the *tar* command is saved. To make comparisons easier, the archive indicator is stripped with *cut*. Then the table of contents is read back into the log file. The list of files is extracted from the log file and compared with the list of files that was archived. If the comparison shows any differences, *root* is notified via mail. Should the list be identical we clean up and compress the log file.

Although the above sample uses *tar*, similar functionality can be achieved with any of the backup commands. Commercial system such as ADSM/6000 are provided with functions for the proper cataloging of tapes.

14

Network installation

Since version 3.2, AIX has had a network install utility, although it was really only an installer for system backup images. The AIX 4 network install manager (NIM) concept goes further in offering not only network installation, but also pull and push updates. The diskless workstation concept that was supported in AIX has been redesigned to fit into the NIM scheme. This chapter discusses network installation of stand-alone systems on AIX 3.2 and 4.1.

14.1 Network installation on AIX 3.2

Network installation on AIX 3.2 allows you to install custom images over the network. You create the images, power on the client and make it boot over the network. Select the right boot host and then one of the images it offers.

To get a system to boot via the network requires the right boot code on the system. On newer RS/6000 models the network boot is usually triggered by booting with the key in secure mode. When the LEDs display a steady 200, turn the key to maintenance and then press the reset button. If you have a very old system then this will not work. Nor will it work for PowerPC-PCs, which only support AIX 4.

Once the system displays the network boot screen you can set the necessary parameters to connect to the install server. You will need to set the network address of the client, the server and optionally a gateway. Once the system has contacted the install server you will be able to select an install image for this system, after which installation is as usual.

14.1.1 Creating a network install image

A network install server must have TCP/IP and NFS up and running. The following steps will guide you through the setup of an install server. First you need to set up the server and the network install id.

(1) The user id *netinst* must exist. Create it with **smit mkuser** and set the attributes *login*, *rlogin* and *su* to false.

(2) Copy the necessary installation files to the home directory of *netinst*:

```
cd /usr/lpp/bosinst
cp -r bin db scripts ~netinst
```

(3) Make sure that no one can tamper with them and change the ownership of the copied files to netinst:

```
chmod -R go-rwx ~netinst
chown -R netinst.staff ~netinst/*
```

(4) Make sure *inetd* knows about the network install daemon. This daemon is usually inactive: uncomment its entry in /etc/inetd.conf:

```
instsrv stream tcp nowait netinst /u/netinst/bin/instsrv
instsrv -r /tmp/netinstalllog /u/netinst/scripts
```

The above entry is one line. The *instsrv* service also needs a port number. Add the following entry to /etc/services if it does not already exist:

```
instsrv        1234/tcp        # network install service
```

Now you need to tell *inetd* about it. Run **inetimp && refresh -s inetd**.

(5) Run **/usr/lpp/bosinst/ninst $(hostname) curdate**. If this returns the current date in MMDDhhmm.ssYY format, then the setup is OK so far.

Now you can prepare the data that is to be served. Set up a file system to hold the installation and LPP images that you want to serve. The size depends on the number of images and installations you want to serve, but 100MB is probably not too large initially. The following steps assume a directory named /inst.images in which all the installation images will be stored. If you intend to serve a large number of different images you should set up a directory structure in this file system to organize the data. I will assume a flat structure in the following examples.

You can serve system backup images as well as images that were taken from original install tapes. Copy the image to the image directory and then update the install menus so that the images can be selected at the client.

To copy an image from a tape that was generated with *mksysb* use the *dd* command, as in

```
dd if=/dev/rmt0 of=/inst.images/bos.obj.mksysb.info conv=sync fskip=3
ibs=32k obs=512
```

where *info* is some form of identification for that image so that you can identify the image later on if you have more than one. The *bos.obj* at the beginning of the image name is mandatory. The *fskip* parameter tells *dd* to use the third image on the tape. You might need to set the block size of the tape to 512 with **chdev -l rmt0 -ablock_size=512** first as install images are written with small blocks.

To copy a boot image from an original install tape use the same procedure. Again, the *bos.obj.** name is mandatory.

You can also put LPP install images on the server. Use **smit bffcreate** or the *bffcreate* command to copy the install images you want to the installation file system. If you want to use individual install images to install a system be sure to include all the images needed (*bos*, *bosnet*, *bsl*, *bsm* and any optional driver LPPs for the hardware you want to support).

After having copied all the images you want to serve you should make sure that no one can tamper with the files. They have to be readable by the *netinst* id.

```
find /inst.images -type d -print | xargs chmod 755
find /inst.images -type f -print | xargs chmod 644
```

Now you need to make the images available. This is done by editing the ~netinst/db/choices file. The images that you created can be made available simply by putting the line

```
/inst.images/*
```

in the choices file. This will make all images available. Now you can set up a description of the images that the server offers. Classes allow you to group images together into one menu point. They are not that useful for *mksysb* images alone, but if you have a server that offers many LPPs then the class file can be used to group images into specific offerings. See the class.sample file in ~netinst. To use classes, set up files with names such as ~netinst/cl.YourClassName. Since class description files are processed by the C preprocessor, you can use all the preprocessor defines to make the setup easier.

Having set up all the data you need to export the file system with NFS. Make sure that it is exported as read only.

14.1.2 Installing via a remote tape

AIX 3 has no means of offering network installation via a remote tape drive. A little trick can get around this.

(1) Use the steps outlined in the previous chapter to set up a network install server.

(2) Create a directory called /var/netinst.

(3) Add /var/netinst/* to the choices file.

(4) Edit ~netinst/scripts/getdb. Search for the string 'xargs ls -Lld' and remove the *L* flag, which would prevent the script from finding devices.

(5) Link the tape device into the directory:
```
ln -s /dev/rmt0 /var/netinst/bos.obj.rmt
```

(6) Now the client can select the tape in the installation menu. Of course, you have to be sure that the tape is in the drive when you install.

14.2 Using NIM on AIX 4

The NIM on AIX provides all of the functionality that was available on AIX 3. In addition, it can generate network boot diskettes for the older systems so that these can also be installed via the network. It also allows updates of clients and installation and updating of clients started by the server. Unfortunately, the PowerPC-PC models do not work with network boot mechanisms.

If you want to set up a NIM master you need to install the *bos.sysmgt.nim* file sets. Before you do so I strongly suggest creating the file systems /tftpboot and /export, as otherwise the installation of NIM itself will create those directories in the root file system. Their contents can become quite large when working with NIM.

In a NIM environment there is always one and only one master system that controls the environment. All other systems are clients. NIM clients can also be servers, but they do not control the environment. Although NIM also supports disk and dataless systems, I will focus on stand-alone systems.

In the NIM environment there are three object classes that are commonly referenced: machines, resources and networks. They are managed in ODM classes (*nim_object*, *nim_attr* and *nim_pdattr*). Machines comprises the different types of systems that NIM supports, whereas the networks class consists of the different physical networks. The resources class is made up out of the resources that are needed to install or update a system. Resources can be offered not only from the master but also from other clients, which then become servers.

All NIM resources are made available to the clients via NFS. They are not permanently available but are only allocated when needed. This can be quite confusing as all install or update operations will automatically deallocate a resource after use and it is then necessary to allocate it again for the next operation. Because of this constant allocation/deallocation one should be careful not to edit the /etc/exports file manually while working with NIM. It will modify the file to make resources (un)available.

The major resource that NIM manages is the shared product option tree (SPOT). It contains all the images for installing via the network. It is usually located in /export/exec. Each SPOT has one or more network boot images in /tftpboot, depending on the networks supported. As AIX 4 does not include all drivers for all devices automatically, network type-specific boot images are used.

All of the following NIM activities can be performed by SMIT with the menus under **smit nim**. Figure 14.1 shows the sample NIM environment.

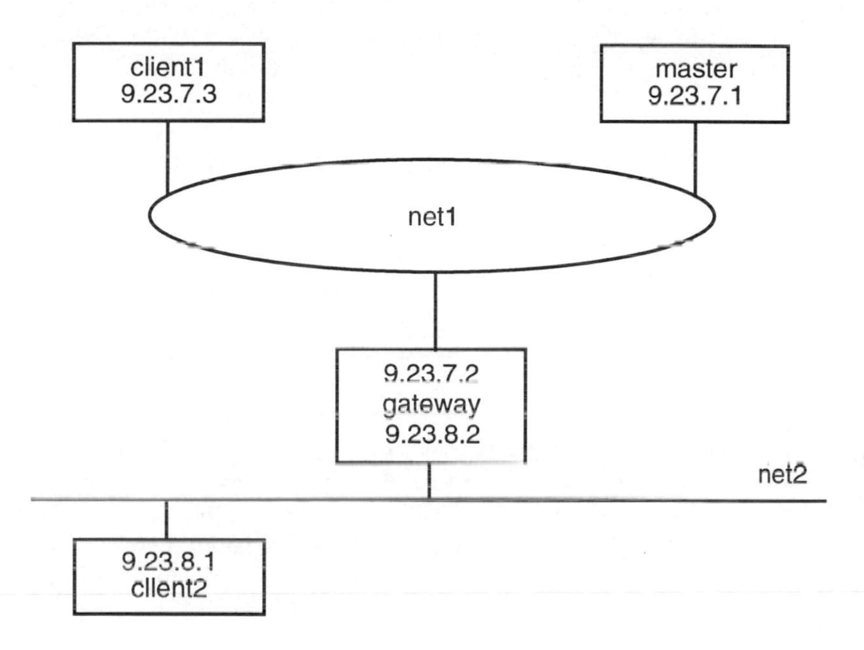

Figure 14.1 A sample NIM environment.

14.2.1 Setting up a NIM environment

First create the file systems /tftpboot and /export, otherwise NIM will fill your root file system with them. Then install the *bos.sysmgt.nim* file sets. If you have already installed the NIM file sets before you created the file systems, be sure to create the directory /export/nim/scripts after creating the file systems, as the *nim* command assumes that it is already present. Now you can run the *nimconfig* command (or **smit nimconfig**) for the initial setup. You need to specify the primary network for the NIM master, a network name for it and a port number that the clients can use to communicate with the master. When working with a Token-Ring network you also need to specify the ring speed, and on Ethernet you must set the cable type even if you have an integrated adapter that does not have a software-selectable cable type. There is no fixed port number for NIM. Check in /etc/services whether the port you want to us is already taken. If not, I suggest adding the port number you are using to /etc/services. The IBM examples use 1058.

```
nimconfig -a pif_name=tr0 -a netname=net1 -a master_port=1058 -a
ring_speed=16
```

This will define a network object and start the NIM communications daemon *nimesis*, which listens on the specified port number. It will also create the configuration file /etc/niminfo. Running *nimconfig* will define this system as the master of the NIM environment. From now on the *nim* command is used to configure NIM.

If you need to support more network types, you now can run the *nim* command to define them, for example

```
nim -o define -t ent -a net_addr=9.23.8.0 -a snm=255.255.255.0 net2
```

This will register the Ethernet network as net2. If you need routing as in Figure 14.1, then the *nim* command can be used to set it up, as in

```
nim -o change -a routing1='net2 9.23.7.2 9.23.8.2' net1
```

This would tell NIM to route packets to the net 9.23.8 via the address 9.23.7.2, which is reached via its own network interface on net1. The command has enough information to allow NIM to construct the reverse routing for the clients from it (from net2 to net1 via 9.23.8.2). Note that the name of the routing attribute is *routing1*. If several instances of an attribute can be specifed then the atribute name needs to have a sequnce number appended. If you forget it, *nim* will remind you.

To list the NIM definitions made so far, the *lsnim* command can be used. To see a list of all resources simply run *lsnim* without parameters. Individual resources then can be listed with **lsnim -l resourcename**, for example **lsnim -l net2**:

```
net2:
   class       = networks
   type        = ent
   net_addr    = 9.23.8.0
   snm         = 255.255.255.0
   Nstate      = ready for use
   prev_state  = information is missing from this object's definition
   routing1    = net1 9.23.8.2
```

As you can see, the routing information has been automatically defined from the previous route change on net1. As the net2 resource has not yet been used its *prev_state* is undefined ("information is missing from this object's definition").

The definition of NIM clients is done with the *nim* command as well. To set up a stand-alone client system run

```
nim -o define -t standalone -a if1='net1 rhino 08005acd0706'
-aring_speed=16 -aplatform rs6k client1
```

The above command defines a stand-alone client system that has the host name rhino on the network net1 with the hardware address 10005A4F9798. Its ring speed is 16 Mbit. The hardware architecture of the client is the classic RS/6000 architecture. Other platforms available are *rs6ksmp* for the SMP systems and *rspc* for PowerPC-PC systems. The name it is known under in NIM is client1. Note that the if1 attribute above is space sensitive. Do not use more than one space between the individual parts. If the client system were on a non attached network (as on net2, which was defined above), NIM would already know how to route to it because of the routing1 object that was defined previously. So setting up a client called lion on net2 would be done with a command such as

```
nim -o define -t standalone -a if1='net2 lion 01005ac73277'
-aplatform=rs6k -acable_type1=dix client2
```

Starting with AIX 4.1.3, the hardware address is no longer needed in this command.

I used NIM client names that are different from the host name in the above example. In a production environment they would be probably the same. The major difference between them is that there is only one client name per client, but a client can have several network interfaces with differing host names.

When setting up a server for installation images, one needs yet another file system, for example /inst.images, to hold complete installation images. It saves quite a bit of space when you create this file system with compression enabled and a block size of 512. Populate it with the install images from tape with

```
nim -o define -t lpp_source -a location=/inst.images -a server=master
-a source=/dev/rmt0 images1
```

This command defines a new NIM object, images1, of the type *lpp_source*. It is created from the files on /dev/rmt0 in the directory /inst.images on the server master. The *lpp_source* type is used for any type of LPP image that is stored on a server. Everything that can be installed via the *installp* command is of this type. If the images in this resource can be used to install a system, then NIM sets the *simages* attribute of the images1 object. This is a flag that NIM uses to distinguish between simple LPP collections and installable image collections that include all the images for an initial installation.

The above command specified a source for the resource. This will tell NIM not only to define the resource, but also to copy the data from the device specified with the source attribute to the directory specified with the location attribute. If source is not specified, then NIM assumes that the images are already in the directory specified by the location attribute. To make the directory usable for installation, a .toc file is needed. This will be automatically created by the *nim* command.

The above command will load only a minimal set of install images on to the disk. I suggest using the *bffcreate* command or **smit bffcreate** to load everything else you need into this directory. After that you need to run **nim -o check images1** to update the NIM information about this resource and update the *simages* attribute and the .toc file.

Even though we loaded all the images into this directory, NIM will still only install the minimum subset that it thinks is necessary. To tell NIM about the other file sets, you can use bundles. Bundles are just lists of install images or file set names. Create a list of the files in the directory and make it available to NIM.

```
mkdir /export/nim/bundles
cd /inst.images
ls | sed 's/\.4\.1\..*$//' > /export/nim/bundles/bundle1
```

The *sed* step above removes the version number of the AIX 4 installation images. Edit the bundle1 file to exclude what you do not want in this bundle. Then define it for NIM:

```
nim -o define -t installp_bundle -aserver=master -a
location=/export/nim/bundles/bundle1 bundle1
```

The bundle1 object will be used later on when installing the client to obtain all the additional software that is needed in one step.

Having loaded all necessary images, set up a SPOT to make the images available. If the images correspond to the system on which the NIM master is running or you are only dealing with stand-alone systems, then you can do so with a /usr SPOT. Otherwise you should set up a different SPOT.

```
nim -o define -t spot -a location=/usr -a server=master -a
source=images1 spot1 2>&1 | tee /tmp/nimlog
```

This command will set up the network boot images in /tftpboot, and the directory /usr/lpp/bos/inst_root is set up with the required prototype files from the *lpp_source* object, in this case images1. It can take quite a while for this command to finish, especially if the server has the TCB installed.

The network boot images in this example are created in the directory /tftpboot under names such as spot1.rs6k.ent. There is one image for each hardware architecture and each network type that is supported by it.

Now that we have a boot image we are nearly ready for the first installation, but one thing is missing: the initial setup of the client. You can have prototype files for client setup and scripts that will be executed automatically after the client has installed the images. The client prototype file resides in /export/nim/files. Create this directory and copy the file /var/adm/ras/bosinst.data into it under the name bosinst.custom. Edit bosinst.custom to suit your needs.

The sample file in Figure 14.2 sets the defaults for the installation so that the user does not need to interact with the system to set up the installation. Adapt it to your needs. The example in Figure 14.3 reflects my preference for a German keyboard with classic UNIX messages. The fields of this file are discussed in Section 13.1.3.

```
control_flow:
    CONSOLE = /dev/lft0
    INSTALL_METHOD = overwrite
    PROMPT = no
    EXISTING_SYSTEM_OVERWRITE = yes
    INSTALL_X_IF_ADAPTER = yes
    RUN_STARTUP = yes
    RM_INST_ROOTS = no
    ERROR_EXIT =
    CUSTOMIZATION_FILE =
    TCB = yes
    INSTALL_TYPE = full
    BUNDLES =

target_disk_data:
    LOCATION =
    SIZE_MB = largest
    HDISKNAME =

locale:
    BOSINST_LANG = en_US
    CULTURAL_CONVENTION = C
    MESSAGES = C
    KEYBOARD = de_DE
```

Figure 14.2 bosinst.custom for automated installation.

The other file to set up is client1.script. It is executed after the images are installed. This script executes client specific actions and resides in /export/nim/files (Figure 14.3).

```
#!/usr/bin/ksh
nimclient -p
chdev -l sys0 -amaxuproc=80 -aautorestart=true -P
sysdumpdev -D /var/adm/ras
chfs -asize=16000 /
chfs -asize=32000 /var
chfs -asize=32000 /tmp
chdev -l tr0 -a mtu=4096
mkdir /var/log
touch /var/log/debug
echo "*.debug\t\t /var/log/debug" >> /etc/syslog.conf
echo "*.debug\t\t @loghost.your.domain" >> /etc/syslog.conf
echo "hosts=local,bind" > /etc/netsvc.conf
echo "domain your.domain\nnameserver 9.23.7.1" > /etc/resolv.conf
```

Figure 14.3 A sample client setup script.

The script can do anything you need to do initially to set up the system; the commands in Figure 14.3 are only a small sample. It will be run before the system creates the new boot image on the client. Standard daemons are not active at this stage. You still need to tell NIM about the bosinst.custom and the client1.script file:

```
nim -o define -t bosinst_data -a server=master -a
location=/export/nim/files/bosinst.custom bosinst1
nim -o define -t script -a server=master -a
location=/export/nim/files/client1.script script1
```

Now that everything is in place, the master needs to allocate the defined resources for the client.

```
nim -o allocate -alpp_source=images1 -aspot=spot1 -ascript=script1
-abosinst_data=bosinst1 -ainstallp_bundle=bundle1 client1
```

Having allocated all the resources required for the client you can initiate the install process. First tell the master to start the install process:

```
nim -o bos_inst -asource=rte client1
```

The source attribute for the *bos_inst* operation can be either *spot*, which will then use the /usr file system of the server for installation, *rte*, which will use the *lpp_source* resource allocated previously, or *mksysb*, which would then use a *mksysb* image.

This command will create a file in /tftpboot with the name rhino.info. It contains NIM-variable assignments for the client that are used during the network boot. It will end up under the name /etc/niminfo on the client during the NIM initialization.

If the client is already under NIM control, then it will be automatically booted and installed. Systems that are not yet under NIM control need to be kickstarted manually. To initiate the network boot on the client, boot the system with the key in secure mode. When the LEDs display a steady 200, turn the key to maintenance and then press the reset button. PowerPC-PCs will use a different method to start a network boot; check your documentation on how to do this if they support it at all. Very old RS/6000s will not have network boot support built in. In this case you can create a network boot diskette and then start the system in service mode from the diskette. The diskette is created on the master with the following command:

```
bosboot -r /usr/lpp/bos.sysmgt/nim/methods/IPLROM.emulation -d /dev/fd0
```

You could also create a boot tape if the target system does not have a diskette drive.

While the boot/installation process is running, you can use **lsnim -l client1** to monitor progress. If you initiate the boot request manually from the client's boot screens, then the above *bos_inst* operation will fail with a timeout, but it still allocates the resources for the client and the installation will start as soon as the master receives the boot requests from the client.

A successful installation will deallocate the resources that have been previously allocated to the client. Should the installation hang and you can no longer access the client object, use **nim -o reset -F client** to get the client into a state where its NIM resources can again be controlled by the NIM master.

14.2.2 Installing additional software

Installing additional software on the client can be done from the server if the client allows it (run **nimclient -p** on the client to enable push installation from the server). Either use **smit bffcreate** or use the *source* attribute on the *nim* command as shown below to get the images onto disk. For example, to get the C compiler images from tape into the /lpp.images directory and define it to NIM you could use **smit nim_mkres** or thc following command:

```
nim -o define -t lpp_source -a location=/lpp.images -a server=master
-asource=/dev/rmt0 -a packages="xlC.msg.en_US xlC.rte xlC.C xlC.cpp"
xlcimages
```

Without thc *source* attributc thc *nim* commad would assume that the files are already in the directory specified. Now that you have thc C compiler under NIM control in the *xlcimages* resource you need only two commands to install it. First allocate the resource for the client:

```
nim -o allocate -a lpp_source=xlcimages client1
```

This will put the directory associated with the *xlcimages* resource into /etc/exports to make it available for the client. To install these file sets from the server run

```
nim -o cust -afilesets="xlC" client1
```

If you want to trigger the installation from the client then the following command can bc uscd:

```
nimclient -o cust -afilesets="xlC"
```

You might want to pipe the above command through *tee* as it will emit thc usual status messages of *installp*. If you do not specify any file sets, then all the file sets in the *lpp_source* that is allocated to the client will be installed. As with thc basic installation you can execute a script on the client. Simply allocate a script to the client before performing the *cust* operation.

14.2.3 Integrating stand-alone systems into NIM

You can integrate any AIX 4 system that is already running into NIM by installing the *bos.sysmgt.nim.client* file set. Then, simply by running *nimint*, the client can be controlled via NIM from the master. To get the client1 system in Figure 14.1 into the NIM environment you would use the following command:

```
niminit -aname=client1 -apif_name=tr0 -amaster=master1 -aring_speed=16
-amaster_port=1058 -aplatform=rs6k
```

From now on this system can be controlled via NIM.

14.2.4 Setting up mksysb images for NIM

Installing a *mksysb* image is much faster than using the standard NIM installation, which will install components individually (see page 233 for details on *mksysb* images). However, it also has the drawback that the image needs to include all the necessary drivers for the target system. If it does not include the necessary drivers, the system will probably not come up.

Copy the *mksysb* image to disk with

```
dd if=/dev/rmt0 of=/inst.images/mksysb.image conv=sync fskip=3 ibs=32k
obs=512
```

Then define it for NIM use:

```
nim -o define -t mksysb -a location=/inst.images/mksysb.image
-aserver=master mksysb1
```

It can then be allocated and installed:

```
nim -o allocate -amksysb=mksysb1 -abosinst_data=bosinst1 -aspot=spot1
-a lpp_source=images1 client1
nim -o bos_inst -asource=mksysb client1
```

The above allocation of the *bosinst_data* resource is needed for automatic installation. The standard installation from a *mksysb* image would request user input on the console of the client. Although the image should have all the data needed, the *spot* and the *lpp_source* resources are also required for the initial boot.

14.2.5 More customization

There are many customized files that one might want to add to a NIM client right away. One way to do this is to export a file system that contains these files and then use the NIM script object to copy these files onto the client. Assuming that the files .profile, .kshrc, hosts and rescolv.conf are in the /export/nim/custom directory, one can copy these files to the client with the following entries in the script that was defined above (Figure 14.3).

```
C=/tmp/custom.$$
mkdir $C
mount master.your.domain:/export/nim/custom $C
cd $C
cp .profile .kshrc /
cp hosts resolv.conf /etc
cd /
umount $C
rmdir $C
```

Note that the NFS mount will work only if name resolution works. The client setup script needs to install either a resolv.conf file or a hosts file that has all relevant entries before the NFS mount can be made, but first you need to export the directory /export/nim/custom on the master with **mknfsexp -d /export/nim/custom -t ro -B**.

14.2.6 NIM commands on the client

Many of the master commands are available on the client as well via the *nimclient* command, for example *nimclient -l* is equivalent to *lsnim* on the master. The other options of *nimclient* work like the *nim* options on the master. For example, you can allocate resources to the client with **nimclient -o allocate -a spot=spot1 -alpp_source=images1** and then boot from the client with **nimclient -o bos_inst -a source=rte**. As you are already on the destination client the client specification is not needed for these commands.

14.2.7 NIM troubleshooting

When working with NIM there are several places where one can obtain information about problems. First of all there is *syslogd* (see page 129). Configure the *bootpd* daemon and the *tftpd* daemon in /etc/inetd.conf to log all interesting events there by adding *-d -d -d* to the *bootpd* entry and *-iv* to the *tftpd* entry. Then run **refresh -s inetd** to update *inetd*. NIM itself also logs some information in /var/adm/ras. The file nim.installp logs all *installp* actions performed by NIM. Other files in this directory on the client will give you information about the boot process.

Should you get stuck during an installation or need to deallocate resources, then use **nim -o reset -F clientname**. This will make the resources accessible again.

Booting trouble can be caused by a client that does not support network boot (for example the 40P) or by a misconfiguration of the server (*bootpd* or *tftpd* not active, interfaces or resources wrongly configured). Typically you will see the boot error messages in *syslog* output. The *tftp* step also will have information in *syslog* in case of problems. In addition, running an *iptrace* during the *tftp* step will reveal more about the *tftp* operation. Should the client be stuck at booting with a LED code then check InfoExplorer for the 6xx codes. The odd ones usually refer to problems whereas the even ones are status indicators.

Sometimes even this information is not enough. In this case turn to the kernel debugger. Enable it in the boot image by running a check operation on the SPOT and setting the debug attribute as in **nim -o check -a debug=yes spot1**. If you now boot and have a terminal connected to the serial port 1 of the client system you can control the boot process from there. The system will boot over the network and the kernel debugger will wait for your commands at the tty. Use **lsnim -l spot1** to get the debug entry points from the master (*enter_dbg_up* and *enter_dbg_mp*). Use the one that is appropriate for your client. Set the value of this address to 1 in the kernel debugger by using the command **st address 1**. Now use the **g** command to start the debug process. The kernel debugger will display all commands executed during the boot process on the tty. Interrupts will halt the system when the debugger is running. Use the **g** command again to continue.

14.2.8 NIM security considerations

Using NIM to control other systems opens up potential security holes. If the client allows the master to control it remotely with **nimclient -p** an /.rhosts entry for the root account on the master will be created. In environments where the security requirements are strict, I suggest using NIM only for initial installation but never for push operations from the server.

When using a master that controls other servers, the master can control any file system exports on the servers. This might be undesirable in some environments.

As NIM uses *tftp* to transfer boot images to the clients, the *tftpd* daemon needs to be enabled on the server. By default the *tftpd* daemon is enabled with write access to the server and no access control at all. I suggest removing the *-n* flag from the *tftp* line in /etc/inetd.conf and refreshing *inetd* to remove write access. In addition, the file /etc/tftpaccess.ctl should be set up to only allow *tftp* access to the directories needed. The entry *allow:/tftpboot* will only allow access to the /tftpboot directory.

Of course, tampering with the installation images on the server is also a potential problem, so make sure that the images are only writable by root.

15

Operating system updates

Although everyone wants bug-free software, this is unfortunately rarely achieved. Updates and bug fixes for applications and operating systems are therefore common. AIX has its fair share of these, not least because IBM tries to be very responsive to customer problems caused by even minor bugs. However, the way in which AIX updates are handled is not necessarily an easy one. On AIX 3.1 cumulative updates were issued every few months. This made it easy to specify exact AIX release levels, which is required by both software vendors and support engineers. However, this resulted in huge updates that contained much more than one wanted to fix, therefore AIX 3.2 introduced individual fixes. However, these fixes had prerequisites and the process got out of hand. Suddenly a simple shell fix was more than 150MB in size because of all prerequisite fixes. With AIX 3.2.4 an attempt was made to contain this accumulation of fixes by structuring them into subsystems. Still the prerequisites where monstrous, but at least now there were defined levels to check against. AIX 4 offers a different strategy again with greatly reduced prerequisite chains and a very fine granularity of interdependencies of installable file sets. No matter what release you are on, do not install updates unless you need to or, in other words, do not touch a running system.

Updates in IBM language are called program temporary fixes (PTF). They are used to enhance products or are the result of authorized problem analysis reports (APARs), IBM speak for accepted bug report. Fixes are identified by numbers such as U491103 in AIX 3 or a more meaningful file set/release number combination in AIX 4 such as *bos.rte.security:4.1.2.1*, whereas APARs have numbers such as IX40748. Any given PTF can fix a number of APARs. An APAR can be fixed by more than one PTF as sometimes the original bug fixes are not good enough or more APARs are fixed in the same area and a newer PTF is introduced so that the old PTF is superseded.

Regardless of what is in the PTF, make sure you have a system backup before you install it. Then make a second one that reflects the changes after installation of the PTF. It is quite difficult to ensure that a PTF does not break other things as soon as one tries to fix more than just a few trivial bugs, therefore the first system backup is needed for easy recovery in the case of trouble. This sounds a bit frightening, but although I have heard of cases of PTFs breaking things that worked before, I have never experienced this myself.

There are two reasons for updates: support for new features or hardware and fixes to real problems. Apart from this, you should never put any updates on a system; in other words, if it ain't broke don't fix it.

Checking for installed PTFs is quite different between AIX 3 and 4. On AIX 3 use *lslpp* for all operations. If you want to know which fixes are installed on your system, use **lslpp -A**, which will list the PTFs, the APARS fixed by them and the APAR text, but usually not what was changed to fix the problem. To list the installed PTFs and LPPs use **lslpp -al**. If you want to know only the maintenance levels that are installed, use **lslpp -m**. Using **lslpp -L** will list not only the maintenance levels but also the sub-system fixes on top of it. Since AIX 3.2.4 there is a new command, **oslevel**, which will tell you about the installed operating system level as well as the subsystems that are below (*-l*) or above (*-g*) this level.

On AIX 4 the *instfix* command is used to show PTF information. Run **instfix -i** to see which PTFs are installed. A more detailed list of the installed file sets can be obtained by running **instfix -ic**. To check whether fixes for a specific APAR are installed, use **instfix -ick IXnnnn**. When you are looking for more information on fixes, use the *-a* option together with either *-i* for the installed fixes or *-d file/device* for the fixes on a file or distribution medium. Simply to list fixes on a PTF tape, file or directory, use *-Td file/device*.

15.1 Updates on AIX 3.2.5

Since AIX 3.2.4 there are two types of updates: fixes that you explicitly request and complete collections of PTFs that will bring you to a new enhancement level of AIX. Those tapes that will bring you up to a new level are called preventive maintenance packages (PMPs), and contain fixes and enhancements to support new hardware or software features. The code on the PMP tape will bring all the subsystems that are covered by this tape up to a new maintenance level (3.2.5 for the OS for example). When requesting an individual fix for a subsystem you will get a cumulative update that includes all the fixes for this subsystem. Once a product, more explicitly a sub-system, is at a certain maintenance level then subsequent dependent fixes assume that maintenance level as a base. This reduces the need to have everything covered in a PTF tape and in theory should drastically reduce the size of a PTF. Unfortunately, because of interdependencies with other subsystems the size of a PTF tape can still be enormous.

To install individual fixes (whether you received the full PMP tape or an explicit fix) you should use SMIT as this will make the selection of the fix to install easier. All of this can be done directly on the command line, but I find it too cumbersome to use for most cases. Using SMIT has the advantage that it filters the selectable items in such a way that it is easy to identify specific fixes, enhancements or just the latest and greatest code.

Run **smit install_selectable** and then select subsystems to install specific fixes. You can then select a specific fix to install. Normally you will also want to install prerequisite fixes automatically.

In some cases, however, it is more convenient to install not at a fix level. The other items in the *install_selectable* menu allow you to install enhancements that are new features of the system, maintenance levels which will bring your system to a given AIX level, or you can install any product at the latest available level that is on the medium.

If you are not at the latest AIX level yet, the fix tape will probably include a new version of *installp*. On very old AIX releases it will first be necessary to install the latest *installp* manually and SMIT installation menus via a specific PTF. On newer AIX 3.2 releases (starting with 3.2.4) this should be done automatically when the *installp* command detects a newer version of itself on the tape. It then will automatically install the new version and then whatever you have selected.

When updating a system, try not to commit the software, use only the apply method (unless you are very tight on disk space). Using apply only will save the current files and you can then reject the applied fixes to get back to the original level. As soon as the fixes are committed, it becomes much more troublesome to get rid of them. Applied fixes can be removed with **smit install_reject** or **installp -rB -X lppname**. If you are sure that you want to keep them, you can use **smit install_commit** or **installp -c -g -X all**, where *all* should be replaced by specific LPP names if you do not want to commit all of them.

Whereas I opt to install and update only specific pieces to avoid changing things unnecessarily, some of my colleagues argue that installing everything will cause less trouble because then you can be sure that all the pieces fit together. Both points are valid, as both procedures have failed occasionally. Although most people do not have much trouble with updates apart from the time it takes to install them, there are numerous examples of updates causing problems. The best protection against these is a full system backup before the update.

Updates on AIX 3 leave many probably unnecessary items in the file system. Unless you run a /usr server for which those files are needed you can recover some of the space with the *ptfdir_clean* command. It will remove superfluous files from committed updates.

15.2 The AIX 4 update mechanism

As AIX 4 uses a different packaging from AIX 3, the update method is also different. Updates now usually operate on a file set level. Instead of having only a nondescript Uxxxxx number, one can identify update file sets with names that follow the form *fileset:version.release.modification.fixlevel*. The apply/commit concept of AIX is no longer valid for file sets, but it still works for PTFs, if one saves the overwritten files at PTF install time.

Use **smit install_fileset** to install specific PTFs or **smit install_maintenance** to bring the system to a specific maintenance level.

15.3 Getting updates

The traditional way of getting updates is by asking your support center to ship you a tape with a specific fix. Alternatively, they may ship you one in response to a bug report or because you have a maintenance contract. For those connected to the Internet there is a more interesting alternative, the *fixdist* server. This is a system that can be used to find known fixes in a support database and to download fixes to your machine. At the time of writing only the US and a few other countries such as Germany have a *fixdist* server, but their number is growing. Contact your IBM representative to find your nearest server and whether this is a free service or for registered users only.

To use the US *fixdist* server, you have to obtain the *fixdist* client code from *aix.boulder.ibm.com* using *ftp* and then follow the included instructions. This server also contains a list of *fixdist* servers in other countries.

15.4 Collecting updates

If you have only one machine to worry about then it does not make much sense to collect updates on disk, but if you have to maintain many systems you probably want to build a PTF pool. Use either the *bffcreate* command, as in **bffcreate -qd /dev/rmt0.1 -t/your/ptf/pool all**, or **smit bffcreate** to transfer fixes to the disk. This will create PTF images in the directory you specify. The files are called *BFF* files for backup format file. To list the contents of one of these files you can use **restore -qTf filename**. You can also copy files to this directory from other tapes. Just make sure that you run the **inutoc** command in this directory after you have added fixes. It will create a file .toc in the current directory that contains a table of contents of the fixes in this directory. If you now export this directory with NFS, anyone can update their systems with the supplied PTFs, either by selecting single PTF files in the directory or, preferably, by selecting the directory itself. When selecting the directory, SMIT and the install tools will use the .toc file in the directory for the selection of available PTFs. If there is no .toc file, then selecting the directory will trigger the creation of the .toc file. This will not work well on NFS read-only mounted file systems. Make sure that you always run **inutoc** after adding new files. Automatic inclusion of prerequisite PTFs is only possible if one selects the directory. Selecting a PTF file does not give *installp* the information about the other available fixes.

If you want to know more about the contents of the .toc file, search in InfoExplorer for "Software Product Packaging".

15.4.1 Creating PTF tapes

Once you have a pool of PTFs, it is very easy to update machines over the network. But what about non-network-attached systems or machines in remote locations with little disk space? You can create your own PTF tapes from any PTF pool with the following script. It takes two parameters: the PTF directory where your collection is stored and the name of the tape drive that is to be used. The script assumes an 8-mm drive. For other drives you might need to adjust the block size. There is no provision for handling multiple tapes.

```
#!/usr/bin/ksh
# Script to generate a stacked AIX PTF tape from a PTF pool directory
# Assumes 8mm drive
# afx 5/95

LANG=C
PATH=/usr/bin:/usr/sbin

me=$(basename $0)
usage="usage:\t$me /ptf/directory tapename\n\t$me /aix/32/325+ rmt0"

if [[ $# -ne 2 ]] ; then
        echo $usage
        exit 123
fi

# Where are the PTFs?
PTFPOOL=$1
if [[ ! -d $PTFPOOL ]] ; then
        echo "$PTFPOOL is not a directory"
        echo $usage
        exit 123
fi
# Which tape should be used?
TAPEUNIT=$2
if [[ ! -n $(lsdev -Cctape -Savailable -l$TAPEUNIT) ]] ; then
        echo "$TAPEUNIT is not available"
```

```
        echo $usage
        exit 123
fi

id=$(id)
id=${id##uid=}
id=${id%%\(*}
if [[ $id != 0 ]] ; then
        echo "you must be root to run $(basename)"
        exit 123
fi

TMPDIR=/tmp/$me.$$.tmp
PTFLIST=$TMPDIR/ptflist
TAPE=/dev/$TAPEUNIT.1
TOC=$TMPDIR/tocfile
DD="dd bs=512 conv=sync"
mkdir $TMPDIR
cd $TMPDIR

# get a list of the PTFs in $PTFPOOL
touch $PTFPOOL/.toc > /dev/null 2>&1
if [[ $? = 0 ]] ; then
        echo "Generating PTF list..."
        inutoc $PTFPOOL > /dev/null 2>&1
else
        if [[ ! -s $PTFPOOL/.toc ]] ; then
                echo "$PTFPOOL has no .toc file and is not writeable"
                exit 123
        fi
fi
if [[ ! -s $PTFPOOL/.toc ]] ; then
        echo "There are no PTFs in $PTFPOOL"
        exit 123
fi
awk '/[a-zA-Z].* \{/ {print $1} ' $PTFPOOL/.toc > $PTFLIST

# Save old blocksize and set tape to 512
BLKSZ=$(lsattr -Fvalue -l $TAPEUNIT -a block_size)
if [[ $BLKSZ -ne 512 ]] ; then
        chdev -l $TAPEUNIT -a block_size=512 > /dev/null 2>&1
        if [[ $? -ne 0 ]] ; then
                echo "Could not change the tape block size to 512"
                exit 123
        fi
fi

typeset integer filecnt=3

echo "Creating TableOfContents file...."
echo "1 $(date +"%m%d%H%M%S%y") 1" > $TOC
for f in $(cat $PTFLIST)
do
        let filecnt=filecnt+1
```

```
        echo "adding $f"
        restore -qxf $PTFPOOL/$f ./lpp_name > /dev/null 2>&1
        if [[ $? -ne 0 ]] ; then
                echo "Error processing $f"
                exit 123
        fi
        sed "1,1s/[0-9]/1:$filecnt &/1" ./lpp_name >> $TOC
done
FILES=$filecnt
echo "TableOfContents completed"

# Rewind tape
tctl -f $TAPE rewind > /dev/null 2>&1

filecnt=3

echo "Writing dummy boot image..."
tctl -f $TAPE weof > /dev/null 2>&1
if [[ $? -ne 0 ]] ; then
        echo "Cannot write to tape, make sure it is not write protected."
        exit 123
fi
echo "Writing dummy bosinst image..."
tctl -f $TAPE weof > /dev/null 2>&1
if [[ $? -ne 0 ]] ; then
        echo "Error writing to tape"
        exit 123
fi

echo "Writing TableOfContents file..."
$DD if=$TOC of=$TAPE > /dev/null 2>&1
if [[ $? -ne 0 ]] ; then
        echo "Error writing to tape"
        exit 123
fi

# Read PTFLIST of files from $PTFLIST and write to tape
for f in $(cat $PTFLIST)
do
        let filecnt=filecnt+1
        echo "Writing file $filecnt of $FILES: $f..."
        $DD if=$PTFPOOL/$f of=$TAPE > /dev/null 2>&1
        if [[ $? -ne 0 ]] ; then
                echo "Error writing $PTFPOOL/$f to tape"
                exit 123
        fi
done

# Write EOF and rewind
tctl -f $TAPE weof > /dev/null 2>&1
tctl -f $TAPE weof > /dev/null 2>&1
tctl -f $TAPE rewind > /dev/null 2>&1

# Change tapedrive to old blocksize
```

```
[[ $BLKSZ -ne 512 ]] && chdev -l $TAPEUNIT -a block_size=$BLKSZ >
/dev/null 2>&1

echo "\ndone."
cd
rm -fr $TMPDIR
```

The script first tries to make sure that it has access to all the data and the tape device. It then generates a .toc file in the PTF pool directory. It then extracts the file names from the .toc file. The tape is set to a block size of 512 and a table of contents for the tape is generated. Two dummy images are written to the tape. The table of contents that was generated previously is then written to the tape as the third image, after which all the other images are written.

16

Security

Computer security means something different to everyone. The requirements range from none to paranoid. Before you start to change the system for security reasons first think about your in-house security policies. What do you allow, what do you disallow and what needs to be protected? Are the means for keeping a secure system more costly then recovering from security breaches? Security policies and methods that are overused will not necessarily give you a more secure system; they may even weaken the security. For example, it is better to have relatively simple password rules and forced changes only twice a year than having tight rules and frequent changes so that people start to write down their passwords. Once you have a clear security policy you can think about tightening systems. Most of the time you need protection not from clever outside crackers but from curious or disgruntled employees as well as simply protection from user errors.

There are people who believe that the less that is known about a system, the less vulnerable it is. This concept is called security by obscurity and is worthless. You cannot trust a system if you do not know its inner workings. You introduce many more problems in the area of user errors if you keep your users uneducated.

And then there is the myth that UNIX is one gigantic security hole. Although the system was never designed with security as a top priority, there is enough security in modern UNIX for most cases. AIX goes even one step further by including features that are usually only available in highly secure systems, such as access control lists, the trusted computing base and full auditing. AIX 3 provides all the C2 security features and some B-level additions as well. AIX 4 has even more security functions for password and log in control.

If you want to really dig into computer security you should read (*Computer Security Basics*, 29) and (*Practical UNIX & Internet Security, 2nd ed.*, 36). The first book explains the theories behind security levels (including C2 security classifications), whereas the second is a hands-on guide for implementing security means. In addition, there is an article on security in InfoExplorer (search for 'Security Threats'). Those who need firewall system to isolate their net from other networks such as the Internet should read (*Firewalls and Internet Security: Repelling the Wily Hacker*, 32) as well as (*Building Internet Firewalls*, 33).

In addition to the publications cited here, there are mailing lists and newsgroups on the Internet that you should follow if you are at all interested in security. The Internet can be a dangerous place to be, but you can also find many good security tools out there. Check out Appendix 2 for more specific pointers.

16.1 Basic security means

Do make backups! Most mischief done by security breaches that does not involve stolen information can be repaired by good backups. If you think that backups cost too much time, just calculate the time you need to restore your system to working order. It will be a lot more time than you can afford compared with the time you need to make backups. Do not rely on your backup and disaster strategy until you have tested it. Are your backup tapes readable? Do you store them somewhere far away from the machine so that they are not lost in case the building burns down?

16.1.1 Physical protection

Whatever type of software protection you use, physical access to the machine renders it useless. There is one exception – good encryption – but the *DES* option of the *crypt* command is available only on US systems because of some outdated export laws. Some countries even forbid you to use encryption. In addition, encryption is usually something you need to do actively. If you forget it there is no protection.

You do not even need to break open the system to access the data on the disks. On all RS/6000s apart from the 2xx models the external SCSI bus is always available. Only on the 2xx machines can it be disabled it by setting some jumpers on the motherboard. However, on some machines the port is protected by a lockable cover. If the key is available then there is no way of blocking an intruder, a simple boot in service mode is all it takes.

So if you need good system security, make sure the machine is in a controlled environment and the key is stored safely somewhere else. For normal operation the key lock should be in the "Normal" position; if it is in "Secure" it will not be able to reboot, which will disable the system in case of a crash or power outage.

16.1.2 Account management

The most common security problem is the account password. People tend to choose passwords that are easily guessable or writte them down in various places. When people start to write down passwords on those little yellow stickers that they put on the monitor you can forget the rest of your security strategy. Build up some awareness among the users so that such things do not happen. A good password should be memorizable but not guessable. It should have one or more non-alphabetic characters and utilize mixed case. It should have no relation to the user or the user's family, job, hobbies or account.

Password rules

The next thing is password rules. Here you get some help from AIX. As discussed on page 47, there are some rules you can specify for passwords. For a halfway tight system I would recommend the following entry in /etc/security/login.cfg on an AIX 3 system:

```
pw_restrictions:
        maxage = 8
        minage = 0
        minalpha = 5
        minother = 1
        mindiff = 3
        maxrepeats = 2
```

This will require a password change every 8 weeks but a password can be changed anytime; it needs at least five alphabetic and one non-alphabetic characters, it has to have at least three characters different from the previous password and it can contain a character only twice. Unfortunately, there is no direct way of specifying that a password needs a minimum length, which would allow more flexibility than specifying only *minalpha* and *minother.* A password should have at least six characters. Unfortunately, AIX, like any other UNIX, recognizes only eight characters in a password.

On AIX 4 the rules can be specified on a per-user basis and have been moved to /etc/security/user. Now they are not only on a per-user basis but are also more flexible. They are either specified in the default stanza or for each individual user:

```
maxage = 8
maxexpired = 4
maxrepeats = 2
minage = 0
minalpha = 3
mindiff = 3
minlen = 6
minother = 1
pwdchecks =
dictionlist = /usr/share/dict/words
histsize = 6
histexpire = 52
registry = files
```

The first new field is *maxexpired*, which defines the number of weeks after a password expiration during which a password will still be changeable. When this limit is also reached the account will be blocked. Or, in other words, an account that has not changed the password for *maxage* weeks will be disabled after another *maxexpired* number of weeks of inactivity. As we now have a *minlen* entry, the *minalpha* entry can be smaller, allowing more flexibility in the chosen passwords. Another new and interesting field is *pwdchecks*. If non-empty it should point to a program that validates the password. You could install any additional password checks you want to make here. See the sample on page 281.

The *dictionlist* stores a list of dictionary files against which a password is checked before it is accepted. If you have the text formatting services installed you could at least use /usr/share/dict/words. You can specify several dictionaries separated by comas. A good dictionary would be one of cracked passwords and terms specific to your site. The *histsize* is the number of old passwords against which a new one is checked to avoid early reuse of passwords. *Histexpire* specifies a number of weeks before an old password can be used. Those parameters work together: passwords in the history (up to *histsize*) are kept for *histexpire* weeks.

Finally, the *registry* tells the system from which user database it should authenticate the user. This is normally not used and can be used to integrate DCE-based authentication.

All the password control features of AIX 4 can be set with SMIT. Use **smit security** to access them or edit the files directly.

If you want to check the quality of your passwords you should get *Crack* from the Internet or some UNIX user group. This program uses dictionaries and a clever algorithm to detect the majority of simple passwords. Many passwords that people think are secure can be cracked. I suggest running *crack* regularly on large installations. In addition to the supplied dictionaries you should augment it with local dictionaries and non-English dictionaries. Of course, you need to trust the system administrator who is running it :-). As AIX uses shadow passwords, *crack* will not work with them. Use */usr/sbin/mrgpwd* (which is part of NIS) to create a traditional password file out of the AIX files so that *crack* can work on it. If you want to automate even further you could analyze *crack*'s output and set the ADMCHG flag for each user whose password was found.

Password expiration

AIX 4 will warn the user that the password needs to be changed if *pwdwarntime* is set to a non-zero value in days in the file /etc/security/user. Five days is usually sufficient. There is no advance warning when the system forces you to change your password on AIX 3. This might lead to badly chosen passwords. The following script will mail a warning to users 5 days in advance so that the password change can be done at a time when it is convenient for the user.

```
#!/usr/bin/ksh
# /usr/local/etc/pwdwarning
# Warn users that a new password will be requested by the system
# in $warndays
# afx 1/93
# this script depends on the format of /etc/security/passwd,
# /etc/security/login.cfg and the output of lsuser
# it checks the last password change for all accounts where
# login is enabled.
# This program needs to be run with root or security permission.
# Best put it in root's crontab.

# no one should read our files.
umask 177
PATH=/usr/bin:/usr/sbin

# Start warnings if forced change is at maximum $warndays away
typeset -i warndays=5
typeset -i day1=86400
typeset -i warn=$day1*$warndays

pw=/etc/security/passwd
logincfg=/etc/security/login.cfg

# get todays date in seconds from epoch for comparison
year=`date +%y`
day=`date +%j`
hour=`date +%H`
minute=`date +%M`
let today="(year - 70) * 365 * day1 + (day - 1) * day1 + hour * 3600 +
minute * 60 + (year - 69) / 4 * day1"

# get the password expiry period and convert it to seconds
typeset -i maxage=`fgrep "maxage = " $logincfg|cut -f3 -d" "`
let maxage=7*day1*maxage

# warning(id,lastlogin)
# send a warning to id if password is due to be changed within $warndays.
warning () {
```

```
        # calculated time where warnings start
        typeset -i wstart=$maxage+$2-$warn
        if [ $today -ge $wstart ]
        then
                # calculate time until password expires
                typeset -i w=$maxage+$2-$today
                # If it has not been expired days ago
                if [ $w -ge 0 ]
                then
                        # If in less than a day expired
                        if [ $w -le $day1 ]
                        then
                             message="Your password has expired."
                        # If forced change more than a day away
                        else
                             let w=w/day1
                             message="Your password will expire in $w days."
                        fi
                        echo $message | mail -s "Password expiry warning" $1
                fi
        fi
}

# List all users who are allowed to log in and have done so at least once
# For all the users found call the function warning with the username
# and the time of the last login
for u in `lsuser -a login time_last_login ALL|grep time_last_login|
cut -f1 -d\ `
do
        warning $u 'awk  "
                BEGIN          { found=0 }
                /$u\:/         { found=1;
                                 next;
                               }
                /.*lastupdate/{ if (found==0) next ;
                                 found = 0;
                                 print \\$3;
                                 exit 0;
                               }
        "  $pw '
done

exit 0
```

This script reads the names of all users who have ever logged in from the output of *lsuser* and then searches for the time of the last password change in /etc/security/passwd. The id of the user and the time of the last change are given to the function *warning*, which will calculate the remaining time for that user. If the password is expired or will be expired in the number of days specified at the beginning of the script then the user will get a warning via mail.

The numeric features of the Korn shell are used here extensively. This avoids forking of the *expr* command for calculations. All calculations are done in seconds relative to epoch. Epoch is the starting point for all time measurement under UNIX, 00:00 on 1 January 1970. In the in-line generated *awk* script the variable *$u* that is set up by the surrounding for loop is expanded by the shell so that we can search for the user. Any *awk* variable that starts with a '$' needs to be protected from the shell expansion, which is why *$3* is preceded by '\\'.

The output of the *awk* program, the time of the last password change, is used as the second parameter to the *warning* function. The function then calculates the remaining time until the next forced password change. If the user already has an expired password then no mail is sent otherwise we might fill up the mail spool space with useless warnings. If the time until the forced change is less than 1 day, the user receives a message indicating that the password has expired. Alternatively, if the user's password will expire within the warning period a message indicating the number of days until the password change is sent.

This script can be run out of root's *crontab* every weekday in the early morning for example. An appropriate entry would be

```
1 6 * * 1-5 /usr/local/etc/pwdwarning
```

As it is not possible to write setuid scripts on AIX, a script like this cannot be run by the user. The invocation via root's *crontab* is the easiest way to run it automatically for the users.

Expiring accounts

When using temporary accounts, for example for temporary staff, you should set an expiration date. If you forget to disable the account the system will do it for you. The expiration date for an account can be set via **smit chuser** or directly via **chuser expires=MMDDhhmmYY user**. You should also expire accounts that are used to install applications but are never actively used.

AIX 4 allows you to specify an automatic expiration period for unused accounts by setting *maxage* and *maxexpired*, which together form the expiration period of an account in weeks. This facility does not exist on AIX 3. The following script will do this for you on AIX 3.2.

```
#!/usr/bin/ksh
# /usr/local/etc/expire
# checking the time of the last log in for all users
# if a user has not been logged in for $expdays the account
# will be disabled, $admin gets a notification mail
# afx 1/93
# this script needs at least AIX 3.2
# it depends on the output of the lsuser command

# no one should read our files.
umask 077
PATH=/usr/bin:/usr/sbin

# who should be notified:
admin=root
# after $expdays days of non-usage the accout expires!
```

```
typeset -i expdays=80
typeset -i expiry=86400*$expdays

user=/etc/security/user
tmp1=/tmp/exp.tmp1.$$
tmp2=/tmp/exp.tmp2.$$


# list all users who are allowed to log in
lsuser -a login time_last_login ALL |grep "login=true" > $tmp1

# get all users who have logged in at least once with login date
grep "time_last_login" $tmp1|sed 's/login=true time_last_login=//'>
$tmp2

# get all users who have never logged in yet, set their login date to 0
grep -v "time_last_login" $tmp1 | sed 's/login=true/0/' >> $tmp2

# get todays date in seconds from epoch for comparison
year=`date +%y`
day=`date +%j`
hour=`date +%H`
minute=`date +%M`
let today="(year - 70) * 365 * 86400 + (day - 1) * 86400 + hour * 3600
+ minute * 60 + (year - 69) / 4 * 86400"

expdate=`date +"%m%d%H%M%y"`
exptoday=`date +"%y%m%d%H%M"`

# for each user found, check whether the account has not been unused
# too long
while read name last
do
    typeset -i min=$today-$expiry
    if [[ $min -gt $last ]]
    then
        x=`lsuser -c -a expires $name|tail -1|cut -f2 -d\:`
        x1=`echo $x|cut -c1-8`
        x2=`echo $x|cut -c9-10`
        x="$x2$x1"
        if [[ $x -le $exptoday ]]
        then
            # $name has already been expired...
            continue
        else
            chuser expires=$expdate $name
            mail -s "Expire user $name"  $admin <<- ENDOFMAIL
            The luser $name has been expired.
            The account has not been used for at least $expdays days.
ENDOFMAIL
        fi
    fi
done < $tmp2
```

```
rm -f $tmp1 $tmp2

exit 0
```

This script generates a list of users that are allowed to log in. Those accounts that are enabled but have never been used will assume a last login time of zero. Then the while loop reads from the generated list pairs of user id and last login time. This time is compared with the allowed maximum, and if a user has not logged in within that period the account will be disabled by setting the expiration date to the current date. The root user will be notified via mail. If an account is already expired, no message is generated, but you could send a reminder here. A less harsh version of the script would not expire the user right away but only notify the system administrator. If you prefer this do not use the *chuser* command in there. This script is also a good candidate for *cron*. I would run it every Monday morning for example:

```
1 3 * * 0 /usr/local/etc/expire
```

Login restrictions

In AIX 4 some features to restrict log ins have been added. The ability to restrict user log ins to certain ttys is already present in AIX 3. In addition, AIX 4 allows restrictions based on time as well as locking of ports and accounts after failed log in attempts. Three files are used to configure these functions. /etc/security/login.cfg and /etc/security/portlog are used to configure the port log in restrictions. The file /etc/security/user stores the account-based restrictions.

In /etc/security/login.cfg or via **smit login_port** the log in restrictions for specific ports can be set:

```
/dev/tty1:
    logintimes = !1-5:0800-1800
    logindisable = 3
    logininterval = 120
    loginreenable = 20
    logindelay = 10
```

With the above setup one *cannot* use the port /dev/tty1 during normal work hours from eight in the morning until six in the evening on weekdays (it is meant for the night shift only). If there are three invalid log in attempts within 2 minutes the port will be disabled. The port is available again after another 20 minutes. The time between login prompts will increase by 10 seconds for every failed attempt.

The file /etc/security/portlog stores the invalid log in attempts per port as well as the lock status. Each configured port (in login.cfg) will have a corresponding stanza here once a failed log in on that port has occurred. The attribute *unsuccessful_login_times* stores the times of the failed log in attempts since epoch. If *locktime* is –1 the port is locked, if it is 0 it is enabled, and any other value is the time of the last failed log in attempt.

When setting the user attributes either with **smit login_user** or by editing /etc/security/user you can set log in times as with a port. You can restrict the user from remote (*rlogin=false*) or local (*login=false*) log in and define valid ttys

(*ttys=/dev/tty1*). Initially this worked only for real ttys. AIX 4 also allows the specification of XDM logins by using the display name with the ':' replaced by '_' as in 'barolo_0' or '_0' instead of 'barolo:0' or ':0'. Check out the README files and InfoExplorer. I am still hoping that future versions will allow log in restrictions based on the name of the remote system. On the AIX 4 versions I was working with, it was necessary to explicitly allow */dev/pts* for network log ins if *!ALL* was used to disable all normal ttys (*ttys = !ALL,/dev/pts*).

You can also set the maximum number of failed log in attempts before the account is blocked via *loginretries*. Use **chuser account_locked=false userid** to re-enable the account.

Account configuration

With relaxed security users quite often have the current directory in their search path. This should be avoided when tight security is needed as it might open a hole for Trojan horses. The path should never include a directory that is writable by anyone, such as /tmp, for the same reason. The root user should never ever have the current directory in the search path (constructions such as '.' or '::' or a PATH ending with ':'). Even some system administrators use full pathnames for all commands always to avoid picking up a fake version. This, of course, assumes that *$IFS* is correctly set, else the shell will not use the whole pathname.

The home directory of a user is created with read access for the rest of the world by default. Change /etc/security/mkuser.sys to use more restrictive default permissions if needed. The *umask* defines the default access rights on files that a user creates. You can set a different default umask in /etc/security/user. You can change it for individual users when creating the account in SMIT or via the **chuser umask=077 userid** command. Users can change it themselves by putting the appropriate *umask* command in their profiles.

Preconfigured user ids and groups

When creating accounts the default group is *staff*. *Staff* has a group id below 100, which historically means that it is an administrative group. This has no effect on AIX, but you still might want to change the default group in /etc/security/mkuser.default to *usr*.

AIX comes preconfigured with some system ids. Preconfigured ids are usually a security hole, but on AIX this is not the case as the password is disabled by the * in the password field in /etc/passwd. They behave like any newly created id for which the root user has not yet set a password. You still might want to change their *login* and *rlogin* attribute to false and add them to /etc/ftpusers. There are two accounts that need special treatment here: the *guest* account and the *nobody* account. The *guest* id can be deleted (**rmuser -p guest**) as it is only included for reasons of historical compatibility. The *nobody* account is used by NFS, the Xstation manager and some other daemons. NFS uses *nobody* to map the root id on mounted file systems where no root access is given. The Xstation manager uses it for the kludged log in to another system. When using *xdm* and the *chooser* client there is no need for this rather ugly hack. Some of the daemons started via *inetd* will be run under the nobody id as well.

Logging root access

If you have several users that know the *root* password you should disable log in for root. This would force all access to the *root* account via the *su* command. Access via the *su* command is traced via /var/adm/sulog as well as the AUTH facility of *syslogd* and the auditing sub-system. This trace can be deleted by the person who used *su* to gain root access, but here it serves more as a trace for regular maintenance access then as a trace for security breaches. If you really want an unspoiled trace than you should send the *syslogd* output for AUTH to a direct attached printer. If only one person knows the root password and the console is in a secure environment it might also be a good idea to allow root log in only on the console. This can be done by **chuser rlogin=false ttys=/dev/tty0 su=false root** and adding root to /etc/ftpusers.

Logging failed log ins

If you want to check if there have been unsuccessful log in attempts, then you can have a look at the /etc/security/failedlogin file with the *who* command: **who -a /etc/security/failedlogin**. This file should be deleted occasionally as it grows without bounds. If someone tries to log in with an unknown user id it is logged not with the user id that was used but with a user id of UNKNOWN. This reduces the usefulness of the log but ensures that when a user enters the password instead of the login name the password will not be exposed to the system administrator.

In addition to this log, which is only accessible by root or members of the security group, every user that logs in via the network or a tty will be notified about the last successful and the last failed log in for that id by a short message after the display of the /etc/motd file.

AIX 4 (and AIX 3 with the latest updates) will also log all failed log in attempts via *syslog*. Check for messages from *tsm*, the terminal state manager (*tsm*, *login* and *getty* are all the same executable). Of course, you could also use the audit subsystem to log failed log ins in drastic cases.

Successful log ins are not logged by default, but this feature can easily be added with a one-line authentication method (see page 281 for details).

Checking accounts

The *grpck*, *pwdck* and *usrck* commands are quite helpful in checking the correctness of the security configuration of users and groups, but be careful when you execute them with the *-y* flag, as this could disable special-purpose user ids, such as the *nobody* account. Use the *-t* flag instead, which will prompt you before changing anything.

Limiting log ins with a custom authentication method

You can use a custom authentication method to control log in when needed. The following sample will allow only two concurrent log ins per user, but this method could also be used for other checks.

AIX supports two authentication methods, the primary and the secondary. Only the exit code of the primary method can be used to terminate log in attempts. But the primary method can itself consist of several methods.

First we need the check for multiple log ins. The following shell script is placed in /etc/security/maxlogin:

```
#!/usr/bin/ksh
# /etc/security/maxlogin
# Additional authentication method for AIX
# Controls maximum number of log ins per user
# Called by the login program
# needs to be configured as part of the primary authentication method
# afx 12/93

trap "" 1 3 4 6 8 13 15 17 21 22 30 31
PATH=/usr/bin

# Maximum number of log ins per user
Max=2
User="$1"

# no user set, exit with failure, terminate log in attempt
test "$User" = "" && exit 1

# Let's find out how often $User is already logged in and where
Terminals=`who | egrep "^$User "`
Current=`who | egrep "^$User " | wc -l`

# Exit with success if below maximum
test "$Current" -lt "$Max"  && exit 0

# Maximum has been reached, tell the user and sent a message to syslogd
logger -p auth.notice "$User tried to log in more than $Max times on
`tty`"
echo "\007"
echo "------------------------------------------------------------"
echo "  Only $Max simultaneous log ins are allowed for $User!"
echo "  You are already logged in on the following terminals:"
echo "$Terminals"
echo "------------------------------------------------------------"
echo
# Exit unsuccessful, terminate log in attempt
exit 1
```

The script sets some traps so that it cannot be interrupted. It checks whether it was given a parameter, the name of the user who wants to log in. If the number of log ins for that user has not yet been reached then the script exits with a return code of zero and allows the log in program to proceed. When the number of maximum log ins has been already reached, the script sends a message to the *auth* facility of *syslog* and tells the user that the maximum number log ins has been reached and on what terminals the user is already logged in.

This method now needs to be activated. In /etc/security/login.cfg we register the method as MAXLOG:

```
MAXLOG:
        program = /etc/security/maxlogin
```

For each user that will be checked by this method we have to modify manually the entry in /etc/security/user or change the primary authentication method via **smit chuser**. For example for user zaphod:

```
zaphod:
       admin = false
       auth1 = SYSTEM,MAXLOG
```

Now user zaphod can log in only on two terminals simultaneously. To activate that restriction for all user ids, you need to modify the default stanza. If you do so I suggest setting an explict *auth1* entry for root without this authentication method.

Logging all log ins with a custom authentication method

The secondary authentication method in AIX cannot be used to check log ins, but it can be used to do some more logging. Install the following *authlog* script in /etc/security if you want to log all log ins.

```
#!/usr/bin/ksh
# /etc/security/authlog: syslog all successful log ins

/usr/bin/logger -t tsm -p auth.info "$@ logged in from $(/usr/bin/tty)"
```

Then create a stanza in /etc/security/login.cfg:

```
AUTHLOG:
        program = /etc/security/authlog
```

If you now modify the *auth2* entry in the defaults stanza of /etc/security/user to use the AUTHLOG method, all log ins that use the terminal state manager (also known as *getty* and *login*) are logged through *syslog*.

The only exception to these logs is XDM/CDE. The graphical log in methods do not use *tsm*. If you want to log all connects through XDM-type log in methods you need to modify the Xsessions (see page 190) file to call the *logger* program, as in the above script.

Custom password checks on AIX 4

AIX 4 allows you to install your own password checker that will check passwords according to your policies. This is implemented through loadable modules into the *passwd* program. The following sample C code can be used as a starting point:

```
/* mypwck.c
 * Trivial sample program for the pwdchecks password exit in AIX 4
 * afx 4/95
 */

#include <stdio.h>
#include <stdlib.h>
#include <string.h>

#define BUFS 1024

int mycheck (char *,char *,char *,char **);

int mycheck (UserName, NewPassword, OldPassword, Message)
char *UserName;
char *NewPassword;
char *OldPassword;
char **Message;
{
        char *msg;
        msg=(char *)malloc (BUFS+1);    /* allocate message buffer */
        *Message = msg;             /* make it visible to the outside */
        strcpy(msg,"ran mycheck");      /* initialize just in case */
        if (strncmp(OldPassword,NewPassword,8) == 0) {
                strcpy(msg,"You should CHANGE your password!\n");
                return 1;
        }
        if (strncmp(UserName,NewPassword,8) == 0) {
                strcpy(msg,"You should not use your id for passwords!\n");
                return 1;
        }
        return 0;
}
```

This program is compiled with **xlc -D_ALL_SOURCE -e mycheck -o mypwck mypwck.c**. To install it simply copy the *mypwck* file to /usr/lib, then add the line *pwdchecks=mypwck* to all ids in /etc/security/user where you want the additional checks or just to the default stanza.

Once this program is installed, you can no longer copy a newer version to /usr/lib as AIX caches all dynamic loadable modules in memory. To get rid of any shared libraries currently installed in memory but not used, run the **slibclean** command. You can then replace the module in /usr/lib.

16.1.3 Managing groups

The group concept on AIX allows users to be in more than one group simultaneously, as in most other modern UNIX implementations. This means you can use groups to specify access rights to data much more easily than in traditional UNIX systems. You still have to use the *newgrp* command if you want to use a different default group to create files, but file access is checked against all groups of which a user is a member.

You should use groups for departments or special functions where several people need to access the same information. Do not overuse groups or you will create an administrative mess. You also get into trouble accessing older UNIX systems via NFS if you are a member of too many groups. If you try to access SunOS 4.x then you should be a member of eight groups at most. This might severely limit the usefulness of groups for you.

If you do not use the group *staff* as a default for creating new accounts you should change /etc/security/mkuser.default and set your default group there in the user stanza. You can include a complete group set there as well via the groups record.

Large systems might need group administrators. A group administrator is a user id that is allowed to change the membership of groups. The administrator also needs to be member of the security group. If we have a group of programmers that are members of the *hacker* group and the user id *guru* should be the administrator of that group, then we need to do the following:

(1) Create the group hackers: **mkgroup hackers**.

(2) Make the user *guru* the administrative user of this group: **chgroup admin=no adms=guru hackers**.

(3) Include the user *guru* in the security group: **chgrpmem -m + guru security**

(4) As soon as *guru* logs in again, the new group set is active and *guru* can add others to the hackers group. Initially this can be done by using *chgroup*, but to add a user to an existing group one needs to use *chgrpmem* or to list all members of the group with *chgroup* command.

If you share data in a group and you need a common directory then you can use the SGID bit on the directory to make sure that all files created in this directory will be owned by the group that owns this directory. Basically this sets the group automatically for you. The SGID bit is set via **chmod g+s directoryname**.

16.1.4 File access control

Most of the system's security is controlled by the permission bits for the objects in the file system. Although not as explicit as access control lists, UNIX permission bits allow you to specify enough different access modes to files and directories to make life complicated. Misunderstanding the effects of permission bits can have drastic side-effects on your security.

A list of the standard permission bits and their meaning on AIX is shown in Table 16.1.

Table 16.1 Permission bits on AIX.

Octal	chmod	ls -l	Object	Meaning
4000	u+s	`---s------`	Exec	Run with UID of owner on execution
		`---S------`	Dir	Ignored on directories
2000	g+s	`------s---`	Exec	Run with GID of group on execution
		`------S---`	Dir	Create files in this directory with the GID of the directories owner
1000	+t	`---------t` `---------T`	Exec	Ignored on executables, the VMM already caches text pages
			Dir	Files in this directory can be deleted only by the owner (link permission)
0400	u+r	`-r--------`	File	Readable by the owner, group or others
0040	g+r	`----r-----`	Dir	Accessible by the owner, group or others
0004	o+r	`-------r--`		
0200	u+w	`--w-------`	File	Can be written to by owner, group or others
0020	g+w	`-----w----`		
0002	o+w	`--------w-`	Dir	Files in the directory can be created or erased by owner, group or others
0100	u+x	`---x------`	File	Can be executed by owner, group or others
0010	g+x	`------x---`	Dir	Can be searched by the owner, group or others
0001	o+x	`---------x`		

The special *s* and *t* bits in Table 16.1 may show up as *S* and *T* when their corresponding *x* bit is not set. Some other UNIX systems support the setting of SUID bits on non-executable files to configure mandatory file locking for them. This is not supported on AIX.

Permission bits are checked from most to least specific, or in other words the permissions for the owner are checked before the group, which is checked before the other permissions. Thus, if one is not the owner of a file, but belongs to the group that owns the file, one cannot access the file if the group permissions do not allow access.

```
$ ls -l junk
-rwx---rwx   1 root     staff          13 Oct  6 09:04 junk
```

The above file is not accessible for members of the *staff* group. If one owns a file that has no access permissions for the owner the file cannot be accessed by the owner even if others could acces it.

```
$ ls -l junk
----rwxrwx   1 afx      staff           13 Oct  6 09:04 junk
```

The above file is not accessible for the user *afx* even if *afx* is in group *staff*.

After passwords, the next biggest threat is 'set uid' or *setuid* programs (SUID). They assume the user id of the owner or group of the program when invoked. They are used by crackers to keep back doors open or by ordinary users for convenience. The fewer *setuid* programs you install the better. AIX comes with quite a few of them already. They are normally used to delegate authority for single commands where it is not necessary to work with full root privileges, for example the *passwd* command. In contrast to older UNIX systems, the *setuid* feature does not work on shell scripts. It is technically not possible to make secure shell scripts so this feature was disabled. If you need to run *setuid* shell scripts, wrap them in a little C program that *exec*s them. A simple way to find all *setuid* and *setgid* programs is the following *find* command:

```
find / -type f -a \( -perm -4000 -o -perm -2000 \) -print.
```

SUID/SGID files outside of the system directory tree (/usr) are usually an indication of trouble. You should generate such a list after you have installed the system. Later you can compare the reference list with the current state of the system.

Sometimes old files stay around long after their owner has been deleted from the system. They may also indicate some intruder. You can find these files with

```
find / -nouser -o -nogroup -print
```

One typically finds files of deleted accounts in the mail spool directory (/var/spool/mail) for example.

The integrity of system files can be checked by *sysck* or *tcbck* commands. Security-relevant system files, devices and commands are listed in /etc/security/sysck.cfg. Any changes in these objects will be found when *tcbck* is run. You can integrate your own objects in here. This is especially useful when you add security-relevant files and commands to the system. For each object the following attributes are recorded here: owner, group, file mode, TCB attribute (the TCB is discussed in Section 16.4), links, size and checksum. To check these files, simply run **tcbck -n ALL**. You will get a few warnings on some devices at most on a vanilla system. With the ALL option only the files that are listed in /etc/security/sysck.cfg are checked. For a more complete check use **tcbck -n tree**. This will produce many warnings even on a vanilla system as the database records only the bare minimum of system-relevant files. However, the *tree* option will check the whole system. Any SUID or SGID program is suspicious for *tcbck*. If you really want to use this facility you need to add all the programs that need *setuid* bits manually via **tcbck -a file attributes** as there is no automatic update flag. On AIX 4 the *-l* flag will automatically add entries for devices listed on the *tcbck* command line.

UNIX needs a few directories that are world writable, such as /tmp and /var/tmp. On these directories the sticky bit is set. This disallows the deletion of files that are owned by other users. A file in a directory with the sticky bit set can only be deleted by the owner. You might find this useful if you need to create other world- or group-writable directories. The sticky bit is set via **chmod +t directoryname**.

Recursive chown

The *chown* command has a *-R* flag to change ownership of complete directory trees. Unfortunately, it contains a hidden security-critical side-effect as a result of some POSIX requirements. Using the *-R* flag makes *chown* follow symbolic links, or, in other words, if the superuser changes the ownership of a directory tree to a user and there is a symbolic link in it that points to a root-owned file then it suddenly belongs to the user.

```
$ id
uid=203(bad) gid=1(staff)
$ ln -s /etc/passwd
$ ls -la
total 56
drwxr-xr-x   2 bad     staff       512 Oct  6 09:21 .
drwxr-xr-x   6 bin     bin         512 Oct  6 09:21 ..
-rwx------   1 bad     staff      3025 Oct  6 09:21 .kshrc
-rwx------   1 bad     staff      1084 Oct  6 09:21 .profile
lrwxrwxrwx  1 bad    staff      11 Oct  6 09:21 passwd -> /etc/passwd
# id
uid=0(root) gid=0(system) groups=2(bin),3(sys),7(security),8(cron)
# chown -R bad /home/bad
# ls -l /etc/passwd
-rw-r--r--   1 bad     system      392 Oct  6 09:21 /etc/passwd
```

On AIX 4 there is an additional flag *-h* to get around this problem, but one still needs to be aware of the flag and use it. On AIX 3 you have to use the *find* command, as in

```
find /u/bad \( -type f -o -type d \) -print | xargs chown bad
```

to get around the problem.

16.2 Access control lists

If the standard means of specifying file access permissions are not sufficient for you then access control lists (ACLs) may be the solution. ACLs offer a finer granularity of file access permissions than the standard UNIX permission bits. ACLs can be used explicitly to grant or revoke rights for users and groups or specific combinations. Files that would be accessible based on the permission bits can be made inaccessible via ACLs and vice versa.

ACLs extend the permission bits with three fields:

permit permits a specific operation for users or groups.

deny denies a specific operation for users or groups.
specify specifies explicitly the access for users or groups.

Each of these fields can be set to read, write or execute just like the normal permission fields. Those additional fields are accessed together with the normal permission fields via the *aclget*, *aclput* and *acledit* commands. When using *acledit* the environment variable *EDITOR* should be set to the editor of your choice. Using *aclget* on a file produces output similar to that in Figure 16.1.

```
attributes:
base permissions
    owner(zaphod):  rw-
    group(staff):  r--
    others:  r--
extended permissions
    disabled
```

Figure 16.1 A file without ACLs.

In this file only the normal UNIX permission bits are in use – the extended attributes for the ACLs are disabled. The example Figure 16.2 shows the output of *aclget* on a file that uses the extended permissions.

```
attributes:
base permissions
    owner(zaphod):  rw-
    group(staff):  r--
    others:  ---
extended permissions
    enabled
    permit   rw-     u:artur
    deny     rwx     g:hackers
    specify  ---     u:boss,g:system
    permit   rw-     u:tricia,g:tv
```

Figure 16.2 A file with ACLs.

The base permissions are the same, but the extended permissions allow the user *artur* to read and write the file even though the base permissions would only have given read access if the user is member of the *staff* group. It makes no difference in which group *artur* is in – he has read and write access unless some other extended permissions would reduce that. Thus, if he were in the group *hackers* the following deny statement would override his permit statement. The extended permission fields are applied so that the least privilege is used, it does not matter in which sequence the statements appear. The user *boss* is denied access totally, but only if he or she is also a member of the *system* group. If *boss* is not a member of the *system* group the statement does not apply. Finally, the user *tricia* is granted read/write access, but only when also member of the *tv* group.

The above example shows that one can specify a great deal of detail when using ACLs. As soon as you maintain ACLs on more than a few files you could run into maintenance problems. For most systems a well thought out group scheme is more appropriate than the use of ACLs, but there are cases where they are the only solution.

There is no management tool for ACLs that would automatically force the use of ACLs or set a default ACL as *umask* does for normal permission bits. Each ACL has to be specified individually. It is very easy to lose an ACL accidentally through the *chmod* command. Every time *chmod* is used with an absolute numeric argument the extended permissions are disabled. You still see them when using *acledit*, but they are disabled and you need to set them to enabled again. So when using ACLs you should be very careful with *chmod* and only use it in the symbolic form, which will not harm ACLs.

If you use only AIX machines then ACLs even work across NFS. Unfortunately, there is no standard for ACLs as yet, so you cannot use them in heterogeneous environments.

Another limitation is backup. Only *backup* and *restore* will save ACLs – the other tools such as *tar*, *cpio* and *pax* do not archive the ACLs so you have to be careful about which tools you use for backup. As *mksysb* on AIX 3 uses *pax* for portability reasons, you cannot clone a system with ACLs or have a crash recovery via a *mksysb* generated tape that includes ACLs. AIX 4 again uses *backup*.

Another point to consider is the invisibility of ACLs when using commands such as *li* or *ls*. You can see them only when using *aclget* or *acledit* or by explicitly specifying the *-e* flag on *ls*, which will add an 11th column to the permission bits field that shows '–' for no ACL and '+' for files with ACLs. To find files on the system that have ACLs applied you can use the *-perm* flag on *find* with a not very well-documented argument: **find / -perm -200000000 -print**.

16.3 Auditing

The AIX audit subsystem allows you to trace security-relevant events like access to any object in the file system that you think needs monitoring. If you want to use auditing you should first check if it is legal to do so and whether you need to tell users that auditing is running. In some countries the laws define explicitly what is allowed to be audited and under what circumstances. Elsewhere, you may need to inform the workers representatives of the company before you start auditing or logging user activities.

The first thing you need to do is to decide what you want to audit. You can audit read or write access to any file you want to, and there are numerous other system activities that will generate audit events. You should think twice before you start auditing. It generates much data that needs to be analyzed before you can get anything useful out of it. Most sites will never need it. However, if you run a firewall system, for example, then auditing will be extremely useful for you.

Auditing works the following way. The kernel or other processes write via the *audit* system call audit records to the /dev/audit device. Auditing backends will read audit information from this device and format the auditing information according to user specifications. Auditing is available from programs that are programmed to use auditing and from global kernel services that perform auditing. The three most common operations on files, read, write and execute, can be audited without specific user programs, which the kernel does for you. Security-related programs and system calls have their own entries in the audit log and you can read these or ignore them according to your needs.

16.3.1 Audit configuration

The audit configuration files reside in /etc/security/audit. The file objects stores the names of files and devices that can be audited. The file events stores system calls and commands that can be audited. The events and objects that are configured in these files are grouped into classes in the file config. This file also specifies the auditing mode and which audit classes are used for which users.

Here is what the *objects* look like:

```
/etc/security/environ:
        w = "S_ENVIRON_WRITE"

/etc/security/group:
        w = "S_GROUP_WRITE"

/etc/security/limits:
        w = "S_LIMITS_WRITE"

/etc/security/login.cfg:
        w = "S_LOGIN_WRITE"

/etc/security/passwd:
        r = "S_PASSWD_READ"
        w = "S_PASSWD_WRITE"

/etc/security/user:
        w = "S_USER_WRITE"

/etc/security/audit/config:
        w = "AUD_CONFIG_WR"
```

A write, read or exec for an object generates an event. The general form of entries in this file is

```
object:
        x = "Execute_Event"
        r = "Read_Event"
        w = "Write_Event"
```

One minor limitation of objects is that you cannot use symbolic links as objects. It is necessary to specify the real file name or a file name that is a hard link. If you try to start auditing and you receive a message such as '** failed setting kernel audit objects **' you have probably specified a symbolic link or a missing file somewhere in your objects file.

For each type of object event detection you also need to have an entry in events. However, events also lists system calls and commands that produce auditing events together with their formatting specification:

```
auditpr:

* kernel proc events

*       fork()
        PROC_Create = printf "forked child process %d"

*       exit()
        PROC_Delete = printf "exited child process %d"

*       backup, restore
        BACKUP_Export = printf " %s "
        BACKUP_Priv = printf " %s "
        RESTORE_Import = printf " %s "

*       shell
        USER_Shell = printf " %s "

* objects (files)

*       /etc/security/environ
        S_ENVIRON_WRITE = printf "%s"

*       /etc/group
        S_GROUP_WRITE = printf "%s"

*       /etc/security/limits
        S_LIMITS_WRITE = printf "%s"

*       /etc/security/login.cfg
        S_LOGIN_WRITE = printf "%s"

*       /etc/security/passwd
        S_PASSWD_READ = printf "%s"

*       /etc/security/passwd
        S_PASSWD_WRITE = printf "%s"
```

This is only a short excerpt of the events file. For each auditing event there is a formatting string that specifies how the information will be printed when the audit data is analyzed. The general format of event entries is as follows:

```
Event_Name = printf "formatstring"
```

or

```
Event_Name = formatprogram arguments
```

For simple output the *printf* version is used. The *printf* string will receive one parameter for objects; more parameters are available on other events depending on how the event is created. If more than the simple printing of arguments is desired then you can install your own formatting program. Before your program sees the arguments specified here it will get the arguments *-i* and a number that specifies how many spaces you need to indent. You will not get any additional parameters.

There are two ways to collect audit data: either in bins or as a continuous stream. Bins have a limit on the amount of data that they can store and two bins are used alternately. When one is full the other one is used and vice versa. This has the advantage that audit data is finite but you might lose information this way. The other method is stream auditing, in which the audit data is sent to some filter that will emit an unlimited stream of audit information. You configure the type of auditing in the config file.

```
start:
        binmode = off
        streammode = on
```

This configures stream mode.

```
bin:
        trail = /audit/trail
        bin1 = /audit/bin1
        bin2 = /audit/bin2
        binsize = 10240
        cmds = /etc/security/audit/bincmds
```

The bin stanza configures the place for the bin files, the trail and the auditing backend. Note that the default place for these files in the /audit directory is in the root file system. You should configure it to use a directory in the /var file system or set up a dedicated file system instead to avoid problems with a full root file system if you want to use bin auditing.

```
stream:
        cmds = /etc/security/audit/streamcmds
```

This stanza tells the auditing system where to find the backend for the stream mode.

```
classes:
        general = USER_SU,PASSWORD_Change,FILE_Unlink,FILE_Link,
FILE_Rename
        objects = S_ENVIRON_WRITE,S_GROUP_WRITE,S_LIMITS_WRITE,
S_LOGIN_WRITE,S_PASSWD_READ,S_PASSWD_WRITE,S_USER_WRITE,AUD_CONFIG_WR
        SRC = SRC_Start,SRC_Stop,SRC_Addssys,SRC_Chssys,SRC_Delssys,
SRC_Addserver,SRC_Chserver,SRC_Delserver
        kernel = PROC_Create,PROC_Delete,PROC_Execute,PROC_RealUID,
PROC_AuditID,PROC_RealGID,PROC_AuditState,PROC_AuditClass,
PROC_Environ,PROC_SetSignal,PROC_Limits,PROC_SetPri,PROC_Setpri,
```

```
PROC_Privilege
       files = FILE_Open,FILE_Read,FILE_Write,FILE_Close,FILE_Link,
FILE_Unlink,FILE_Rename,FILE_Owner,FILE_Mode,FILE_Acl,
FILE_Privilege,DEV_Create
       svipc =
MSG_Create,MSG_Read,MSG_Write,MSG_Delete,MSG_Owner,MSG_Mode,
SEM_Create,SEM_Op,SEM_Delete,SEM_Owner,SEM_Mode,SHM_Create,SHM_Open,
SHM_Close,SHM_Owner,SHM_Mode
       mail = SENDMAIL_Config, SENDMAIL_ToFile
       cron = AT_JobAdd,AT_JobRemove,CRON_JobAdd,CRON_JobRemove
       tcpip = TCPIP_config,TCPIP_host_id,TCPIP_route,TCPIP_connect,
TCPIP_data_out,TCPIP_data_in,TCPIP_access,TCPIP_set_time,
TCPIP_kconfig,TCPIP_kroute,TCPIP_kconnect,TCPIP_kdata_out,
TCPIP_kdata_in,TCPIP_kcreate
```

Audit events are grouped together in classes for easier reference. You can configure your own classes to reflect your needs.

```
users.
             root = general
```

For each user there is a line that lists the audit classes. You can add users here manually or via **chuser auditclasses=ListOfClasses user**. To make sure that each user is audited you should modify /usr/lib/security/mkuser.default and include *auditclasses = "your,audit,classes"*. Each new account will then be audited automatically.

It is unusual for the standard configuration to suit your particular site so you will need to adapt all those files to your needs. In the shipped objects file there are only a few entries. Most sensitive configurations files that are not account related are absent. For the following initial list of files you should create entries in the objects file that look like

```
/etc/hosts:
       w = "CONFIG_WRITE"
```

Here are some of the more interesting files:

```
/etc/hosts, /etc/syslog.conf, /etc/aliases, /etc/bootptab,
/usr/sbin/skulker, /etc/environment, /etc/filesystems, /etc/exports,
/etc/hosts.equiv, /etc/hosts.lpd, /.rhosts, /etc/inetd.conf,
/etc/inittab, /etc/group, /etc/passwd, /etc/qconfig, /etc/rc,
/etc/rc.bsdnet, /etc/rc.net, /etc/rc.nfs, /etc/rc.tcpip,
/etc/services, /usr/local/etc/rc.local
```

This list is not extensive and you should, for example, add the UUCP configuration files when using UUCP. I even include a /.rhosts file even though it is empty. The audit subsystem can only audit existing files, therefore I create empty files for hosts.equiv or .rhosts files even if I do not use them. As most configuration files reside in /etc, a quick way to set up the audit objects is to use the find command, as in

```
find /etc -xdev -type f -print > /etc/security/audit/objects
```

and then use *vi* to reformat the file list into the correct stanza format with the following *vi* command:

```
:%s/$/:^M    w = "CONFIG_WRITE"/
```

To enter the '^M' in *vi*, press <CTRL-V><CTRL-M>. This command replaces line ends with a colon and adds a new line to each line of the file. This method will include a bit too much however. You should remove the *pid* files as well as /etc/utmp and other files that are written to regularly.

In addition to tracing modifications to specific configuration files you might also be interested in the execution of critical utilities, for example the *no* command, which changes the system's TCP/IP parameters. Enter the commands you are interested in into the objects file in the following way:

```
/usr/sbin/no:
        x = "CONFIG_EXECUTE"
```

After adding all those objects we need entries in events that tell the system what to do with CONFIG_WRITE and CONFIG_EXECUTE events. You should add the following lines to it:

```
* config file changes
        CONFIG_WRITE - printf "%o"
* execution of configuration utilities
        CONFIG_EXECUTE = printf "%s"
```

Now the auditing system knows about new objects and how to print the information about changes. Next we need to create a new class that allows the configuration of our new events. You could add the following to config under classes:

```
        config = CONFIG_WRITE,CONFIG_EXECUTE
```

And then edit the stanza for the root user and add the config class so that it looks like

```
        root = general,config
```

Any change of the config files by the root user will now be logged when using bin mode.

After all this configuration of auditing events we need to start up the audit system. Run **audit start**. If you receive a message saying something like 'failed setting kernel object events' then you have probably specified a symbolic link or a nonexistent file in the objects file. When you have configured auditing to use bins you can then have a look at the bins via **auditpr -v < yourbinfile**.

16.3.2 Stream auditing

I prefer stream auditing to bin auditing as all events can be immediately post-processed and sent on to some other programs, write-once media or a printing device. For stream auditing you need to configure streamcmds. In here you can select different classes and events, for example, and send the previously filtered output to some file or device. This will create a lot of output so a clever setup of the filter criteria is necessary. The following sample streamcmds file can be used as a starting point.

```
/usr/sbin/auditstream -c config | /usr/sbin/auditpr -v >
/var/audit/config.stream &
```

This will log all config events in /var/audit/config.stream. The *auditstream* command reads audit events from /dev/audit and passes them on to backend programs. If you do not specify a class to be extracted then all classes will be selected. By using the *auditselect* command you can restrict the entries further:

```
/usr/sbin/auditstream | /usr/sbin/auditselect -e "login == zaphod" |
/usr/sbin/auditpr -v > /var/audit/zaphod &
```

This entry will send all events that are generated by the user zaphod to a file. In this way you can have individual files for each audited user. The *auditselect* command allows the selection of audit records according to the contents of the fields of the audit record. You can select records based on combinations of events, commands, results, login and real id of the user, process and parent process id as well as time and date. Failed log ins, for example, could be selected by the following constraint: *"event == USER_Login && result == FAIL"*. To trace invalid login and *su* attempts directly to a dedicated printer you could use

```
/usr/sbin/auditstream | /usr/sbin/auditselect -e "(event == USER_Login
|| event == USER_SU) && result == FAIL " | /usr/sbin/auditpr -v >
/dev/lp1 &
```

You can have as many commands in the streamcmds file as you need as long as each one terminates with a '&'. You also have to make sure that each entry is on one continuous line.

16.3.3 Using a remote machine for audit record storage

Another method is to send the audit records to *syslog* for processing. This has the advantage that *syslog*, in turn, can send the records to another machine so that the audit data cannot be tampered with on the machine being audited. The following *awk* program is used to join the audit record and its tail information into one line. Note that lines are broken up for printing reasons. The *awk* command will not work if there is no output command after the '|' symbol.

```
#!/usr/bin/awk -f

# Script to send AIX audit records to syslog
# Entries are logged only every other line as AIX audit records
# are usually two lines long when configured fully.
# leading and trailing spaces are stripped
# afx 6/94
```

```
BEGIN {printf ("%24s %8s(%8s) %13s Status Prog (PID) PPID: tail\n",
      "Date","login","real","Event") |
                  "/usr/bin/logger -p local1.notice -t AUDIT "
      }
/^[A-Z]/ { # found a normal line
            line=1
      head=sprintf("%s %s %2s %s %s %8s(%8s) %15s %4s %s (%s) %s",
            $4,$5,$6,$7,$8,$2,$10,$1,$3,$9,$11,$12);
            next;
      }
/^[ \t]/  {         # lines that start with tabs and spaces are tails
            if (line==1) {
                  sub("^[ \t]*",""); # get read of leading whitespace
                  printf("%s: %s\n",head,$0) |
                        "/usr/bin/logger -p local1.notice -t AUDIT "
                  line=0
            } # no else path, this skips the original audit header
            next;
      }
```

The audit data is sent to *syslog* with the priority *notice* on the facility *local1*. This makes it easier for the receiving *syslog* daemon to keep the data separate from other *syslog* entries if desired. The above *awk* script needs to be run from the /etc/security/audit/streamcmds file:

```
/usr/sbin/auditstream -c config,mail,tcpip,cron,user |
/usr/sbin/auditpr -vhelRtcrpP | /etc/security/audit/tosyslog &
```

This file wants one-line entries and has been split here solely for printing reasons. I use many flags on *auditpr* to obtain a little more information. The print statements in the above script as well as the one in the analysis script further on depend on these flags.

To send the data to another *syslog* daemon on a remote machine the local *syslog* daemon should have something like

```
local1.notice        @remote.machine
```

in its /etc/syslog.conf file. The receiving machine can then get all the remote records in one file by using

```
local1.notice        /var/log/remote/remotehost
```

16.3.4 Analyzing audit output

Now that you have all this audit data in a *syslog* file what do you do with it? I suggest using a cron job to analyze it daily. All the data is archived and any interesting events are mailed to the administrator. I have a specific user id called *maint* that is set up for all kinds of maintenance tasks. The *maint* id cannot be used for log ins or *ftp* as it is only accessible via *su*. All the analysis programs reside in /home/maint/bin. In ~/maint the directories tmp and log are used for temporary data and log files respectively. The following audit script needs to be run by root because it restarts *syslogd*.

```
#!/usr/bin/ksh
# script to automatically process audit messages
# AFX 3/93
#
# this script is run out of roots crontab as it needs root permission to
# refresh syslogd
#

PATH=/usr/bin:/usr/sbin

# set $from to the host name of the monitored system which should
# also be the file name in /var/log/remote/
from=remotehost
MAINT=/home/maint

LogSource=/var/log/remote/$from
LoginLog=$MAINT/tmp/audit.$from.login
D=`date +"%y%m%d.%H%M.%S"`
LogFile="$MAINT/log/audit.$from.$D"

cp $LogSource $LogFile &&
      (cp /dev/null $LogSource && refresh -s syslogd > /dev/null)

# A very simple log in analysis
egrep "USER_|getty|tsm|PASSWORD|PORT" $LogFile |
      awk '{ printf("%s %s %s %s %s %s %4s %5s %s\n",
            $6,$7,$8,$9,$10,$13,$14,$15,$18); }' > $LoginLog

# if non-empty mail result, else mail no info
if [[ -s $LoginLog ]] ; then
      mail -s "Login trail from $from" root < $LoginLog
else
      echo "nothing" | mail -s "No login trail from $from" root
fi

compress $LogFile
chmod 440 $LogFile.Z
chown maint.audit $LogFile.Z
rm $LoginLog
exit 0
```

The script copies the *syslog* data to the log directory and truncates the *syslog* file. Then *syslog* is restarted. The log file is analyzed for login and related events. Any interesting events will then be mailed to root. Even if nothing was found, a message is sent to inform the root user that everything is fine. Finally, the log file is compressed to save disk space. (The log archive directory would be a good candidate for the AIX 4 compressed file systems, as in this case you can skip the compression step.)

This analysis is not very exhaustive. You have to find your own set of events that needs continuous monitoring. The above filter will give you an accurate trail of log ins, failed log ins and locked ports, which can be quite interesting on systems that allow remote dial-up access. Viewing all log ins and not only failed ones allows one to see whether a failed log in was directly followed by a successful one.

After you have set up the script, tell *cron* about it with the following *crontab* entry:

```
1 0 * * * /usr/local/etc/audit
```

This will run the script every night at 00.01.

16.3.5 Starting auditing

When you have finally configured auditing you need to start it via **audit start**. You stop auditing with the **audit shutdown** command. If you need to suspend and restart auditing temporarily then **audit off** and **audit on** can be used. The auditing configuration files are only reread when **audit start** is used. A good place to start auditing would be in /usr/local/etc/rc.local. The status of the auditing system can be checked by **audit query**.

Unfortunately, you cannot use the *watch* command while the audit subsystem is running. *Watch* allows you to trace the execution of a single program in terms of execs and file I/O, but it uses mechanisms that compete with the normal auditing. The *syscalls* command that comes with the performance toolbox for AIX 4 is a good alternative. Or you can use the trace script from page 345.

16.4 TCB and TCP

If you work in an environment where no one can be trusted, then the trusted communication path (TCP) is for you. In areas where terminals are publicly accessible the chance of being the victim of a Trojan horse is quite high, so this is a solution for these open terminals in the university. The TCP ensures that you are communication with the real login program. After log in you stay on the TCP and can be sure that you work only with untampered programs which are registered in the trusted computing base (TCB).

What is the TCP? It is basically a mechanism that ensures that you are dealing only with a trustworthy login program. When you log in at some terminal then you can press the so-called secure attention key (SAK), which will kill all processes on this terminal and start a secure and untampered login process for you. However, works only on direct tty and Telnet connections. X sessions are not affected. The SAK is handled by the low-level terminal driver, so it is not catchable by an application program. The SAK is hard coded to <CTRL-X><CTRL-R> for native terminals. After logging in via the SAK you can only execute programs that are marked as trustworthy in the TCB. The number of programs that are included by default in the TCB is very small. Not even *ls* is included here. It is necessary to extend the TCB according to your needs if you want to do real work while working under it. Alternatively, use the TCB only to ensure that your log in is safe and then exit it. There is a trusted shell (/usr/bin/tsh) that will refuse to execute any program that is not marked as trusted. And when you use the trusted version of *vi*, *tvi*, it will not even work on an *aixterm* because the terminfo file that describes the terminal is not in the shipped TCB.

How can you be sure that the TCB itself is trustworthy? When installing a new AIX system, all programs that are included in the TCB that come off the IBM-supplied tape are considered safe. During installation their integrity can be checked automatically to confirm that you have an untampered installation. The TCB consists of the kernel, a core set of configuration files and a few programs that alter either the kernel or the configuration files.

Two programs are used to maintain the TCB: *tcbck* and *chtcb*. With *tcbck* you can find potential problems in the TCB and fix some of them. The *chtcb* command is used to query, set or reset the TCB bit for specific files. You can find all programs that have the TCB bit initially set with the following command:

```
find / -perm -0100000000 -print
```

One of the main uses of the TCB is the TCP. This path ensures that there is no Trojan horse between you and the machine. The TCP is accessed by pressing the SAK on appropriately configured terminals if the user id is also configured for using it. When the SAK is pressed during a terminal session while you are already logged in you will be put into the trusted shell, a subset of the Korn shell. When you press the SAK while the login prompt is displayed you will get a new login screen. If you do not get a new login screen but the prompt of the trusted shell (tsh> or tsh#) then you know someone has run a Trojan horse on this terminal. You could then use various system commands (*who* and *last* for example) to find out who the evil-minded user was.

You need to do two things to configure the TCP for a user. First set the SAK attribute for the terminals where the SAK key should be available in /etc/security/login.cfg:

```
/dev/tty0:
        sak_enabled = true
```

Next configure the account to be on the trusted path. There are several values for the tpath attribute:

nosak	This is the default. No secure attention key.
notsh	The user can never be on the trusted path.
on	This enables the SAK for this user, but the user is not forced to stay on the TCP.
always	The user is always on the trusted path. A user that is configured this way will never be able to execute a program that is not in the TCB.

Use **chuser tpath=value user** to change the tpath attribute of a user.

You can only execute programs that have the TCB bit set while working in the trusted shell under the TCP. For most tasks this is a very limited environment. On educational systems where pranks are common it might be safer to execute *su*, *passwd* and other security-related commands only when working in the TCP. Apart from that I suggest using it only for ensuring that you do not deal with fake login programs.

To get a clean session without always being handicapped by the TCP, use the following sequence if the user is on the TCP but not forced to stay on it (*tpath=on*):

(1) Press the SAK at the login prompt to get a clean login program.

(2) Log in as usual.

(3) At the initial prompt enter the shell command to get to your regular shell.

You can use the TCP over the network as well. The *telnet* command has a subcommand to send a SAK sequence. In my opinion this is not very useful. If you need security in a networked environment then terminals that are so unsafe that Trojan horses can be installed should not exist. Network security itself is much weaker than system security, and you should only invest in drastic measures like the TCP if you can trust your network, which is rarely the case.

16.4.1 The shutdown user

A question that comes up regularly is 'How do I allow ordinary users to shut down the machine without giving them full root privileges?'. The easy answer on AIX is simply enter **sync;sync** and then switch the machine off; the file systems will survive it. Note that this applies to AIX but not to applications, for example databases, which need to be terminated properly. However, perhaps this is too easy and, though I have never had problems with this method (I do not run databases), your data is probably valuable to you and you should use the second approach, the 'shutdown user'. This is a special user id that shuts down the system when someone logs in with that id.

(1) Create a user called shutdown. Set the *su* capability for this user to false so that no other users can use the *su* command to get access to this user id, which would give them root privileges. Add the shutdown user to /etc/ftpusers to disable *ftp* access.

(2) Edit /etc/passwd. Change *uid* and *gid* of the shutdown user to 0. Set the last field to */usr/sbin/shutdown -F*, but then be sure never to execute the commands *grpck*, *pwdck* and *usrck* with the *-y* option as they assume that something like this entry is broken.

(3) Give this user id a password with the *passwd* command.

(4) Edit /etc/security/passwd and set the flags entry for the shutdown user to ADMIN. This will ensure that only the root user can change the password for shutdown.

(5) Remove the contents of /home/shutdown and set the owner to root and the permissions to 700.

(6) Log in as shutdown to test the command.

This works only because the shutdown script traps break signals, otherwise anyone could abort *shutdown* and gain access to root privileges. For most installations this solution can be considered secure enough, although I would never use it in places where really tight security is needed. By generating another user id that is basically an alias to root you automatically reduce the overall security of your system.

A better way of doing this and other maintenance tasks is the *sudo* program. It is again one of those utilities that you need to get from the Internet or some user group (see page 439). *Sudo* is a program that runs *setuid* root but allows access to only a limited number of functions for configured users. This, together with the log of actions it creates, is one of the better ways to delegate authority in cases where this cannot be done via groups or ACLs.

16.5 Lost root password

If you have lost the root password and need to break into the system, you need either a bootable tape, CD or, on AIX 3, the boot floppies. Put the key in service mode and boot from one of them. Either use the AIX 4 menus to get to a state where you are in the maintenance shell with mounted file systems or go to the AIX 3 maintenance shell and execute the *getrootfs* command to get to the file systems.

Edit the file /etc/security/passwd and remove the password for *root*. Then use the *passwd* command to set a new *root* password. Put the key back into normal mode, enter **shutdown -Fr** and you are back in action.

This section illustrates why physical security is a must if you want to have any security at all. Everybody who can access the system can boot it in service mode if they have the key. And when physical force is used even the key is not needed: one can break open the machine and connect the lock contacts manually. An RS/6000 is not a safe.

16.6 Lost key

The documentation that comes with your system tells you how you can order additional keys, but if you have lost the keys and the keytag you cannot get new keys – you need a new lock. Ask your IBM service engineers how to get a new one.

Now how do you get into service mode while waiting for new keys? Use the *bootlist* command. The system uses boot lists for the normal and service key positions. If you want to be able to boot from tape while the key is in the normal position you can do so after you set the bootlist: **bootlist -m normal rmt hdisk**. The system would try to boot from any tape before trying hard disks in normal mode with this boot list. You can also name specific devices to boot from, not just generic ones. This is quite useful when you have different operating system releases on several hard disks and you need to boot them alternately.

16.7 Limiting file system access by quotas

File system quotas allow you to specify the maximum disk space that a user or a group can allocate on a given file system. Typically, this facility is used to regulate students or colleagues who use up too much file space on critical machines.

Quotas introduce two limits on file system use: a hard limit and a soft limit. When a user exceeds the soft limit the system will warn the user that the limit has been exceeded. If the soft limit has been exceeded for too long, then the soft limit becomes a hard limit. The hard limit allows no more allocation of disk space.

You need to configure quotas for each file system individually. First modify the file systems stanza in /etc/filesystems to set the quota attribute, for example on the /home file system:

```
/home:
        dev    = /dev/hd1
        vfs    = jfs
        log    = /dev/hd8
        mount  = true
        check  = true
        vol    = /home
        free   = false
        quota  = userquota,groupquota
```

This would enable the /home file system for user and group quotas. Quota information is stored in the root of a file system in the files quota.user and quota.group. To initialize the quota system for all enabled file systems, the **quotacheck -a** command is used. Quotas are then activated by the **quotaon -a** command. You should put both commands in /usr/local/etc/rc.local so that quotas are activated automatically at system restart. Individual quotas are then specified with the *edquota* command. To edit the quota information for the user *zaphod* you can simply use **edquota zaphod**. It will place you in the editor specified by *$EDITOR* and you can edit the quota information. It will look similar to the following:

```
Quotas for user zaphod:
/home:blocks in use: 24, limits (soft = 0, hard = 0)
        inodes in use: 6, limits (soft = 0, hard = 0)
```

Blocks are 1 KB in this context. When the limit is set to zero, then there is no limit. If you set the hard limit to 120 and the soft limit to 100 then *zaphod* could use up to 100KB without any problems. After that the user would receive a warning message from the system every time new disk space is allocated. When 120KB is reached no more disk will be allocated. The user can stay above 100KB only for a grace period that defaults to 1 week. If the user does not drop below the soft limit within this period the soft limit will turn into a hard limit and no more allocation of disk space is possible.

The grace period can be changed by specifying the *-t* option for *edquota*. In conjunction with the *-u* flag the user grace period for all quota-enabled file systems is edited. When used with the *-g* flag, the grace period for groups on all quota enabled file systems is edited. You cannot specify grace periods on a user or group basis but only on a file system basis.

If you want to edit the quota for a specific group you have to use the *-g* flag as in **edquota -g staff**. It might become tedious to specify quotas individually for a large number of users or groups. The command **edquota -p master -u newuser** uses the quota information from the user id master to establish the quotas for the user id newuser.

Although quotas are available not only on the native JFS but also on NFS, the way in which quotas react over NFS are different. You might not get the error message you expect when exceeding the limits on a NFS mounted file system.

16.8 Automatic log in

Some people want to use the system for only one dedicated application. They do not want to work with log ins and other security barriers. If you are in that situation, you can create the file /etc/autolog containing a user name. After the next reboot the system will automatically start the log in shell for this user on the console without any authentication. Set the shell for this id to the application you want to run on the machine.

16.9 System security checklist

- **Do make backups!**
- Publish a formal security policy for the use of the system.
- Educate your users about the security methods and policies.
- Keep the system in a physically secure environment.
- Store the key safely away from the system.
- Do not allow accounts without passwords.
- Use non-trivial passwords.
- Activate the password rules in /etc/security/(login.cfg | user).
- Set expiration dates on temporary accounts.

- Do not allow shared or guest ids.
- Do not allow root to log in directly.
- Use groups to delegate authority.
- Use *grpck*, *usrck* and *pwdck* regularly.
- Customize /usr/lib/security/mkuser.default.
- Do not include the current directory in *$PATH*.
- Do not include world writable directories in *$PATH*.
- Always use the least workable privilege.
- Make user profiles and home directories read only for others or, preferably, inaccessible for anyone but the owner.
- Set a restrictive umask (077).
- Check for suspicious programs with **tcbck -n tree**.
- Set the sticky bit on world-writable directories such as /tmp.
- When leaving a terminal unattended for a while lock it via *lock* or *xlock*.
- Do not use *su* from the session of another user.
- Consider using the TCP when dealing with notoriously insecure terminals.
- Consider the auditing system on exposed machines.
- Change the permissions of tape and diskette devices when needed.
- Use *crack* (from the Internet) to check passwords.
- Use *tiger*, *cops* or *tripwire* (from the Internet) to perform health checks.
- Make sure you have the latest security PTFs installed.
- Carry out security audits.

16.10 Network security

There are people who think network security is an oxymoron when talking about TCP/IP. Unfortunately, they are basically right. Standard TCP/IP utilities do not use encryption when sending data over the network. And there are programs that allow unchecked access when configured appropriately. What makes matters worse is that it is relatively easy to spoof MAC and IP addresses or DNS host names.There are solutions on the horizon, but none is complete yet. The next release of the IP protocol, which will hopefully be available in commercial products by 1997, promises more security. However, in the current IP environment there are only a few solutions that are usable, and most of them do not cover the full heterogeneous range of IP products that one typically finds at a site.

Apart from AFS and DCE/DFS and some newer kerberized services (based on the Kerberos security model) all data goes on the wire unencrypted. This means that when I Telnet to a remote system the password I enter there can be read off the network with a sniffer or even the *iptrace* program (and *tcpdump* on AIX 4) that comes with AIX.

And even the security-minded DCE does not have a *telnet* program that sends password information encrypted over the network. You have to write your own kerberized *rlogin* program to achieve that level of security. All these secure file systems are only secure in the area of file sharing – they do not deal with remote log in.

16.10.1 Unauthenticated access

Tools such as *rsh*, *rlogin* or *rcp* can be configured such that they do not check for a password when accessing remote systems. This is done either via the .rhosts file in the home directory of an individual user (it must have mode 600) or globally via /etc/hosts.equiv. These files list hosts (and optionally user ids) that are trusted, a desireable feature if you can trust the remote machine and its administrator. But what if the remote machine is compromised? Your machine is the next victim without any defense. Unless you work in an environment where you can trust all other machines and can be sure they will not be compromised you should not use this mechanism.

A similar mechanism is in place for *ftp* and *rexec* except that they use the .netrc file in the home directory of a user that initiates the connection. The .netrc file stores the password for the remote system. Unfortunately, this is done in clear text.

If you want to remove the ability to use the .rhosts and hosts.equiv based programs then you only need to add the *-l* flag for the *rlogind* and *rshd* daemons in /etc/inetd.conf and then run **refresh -s inetd** (first run **inetimp** on AIX 3). This will, however, not inhibt the use of the /.rhosts file for root. If you also want to disable the use of .netrc files then you can run the **securetcpip** command, which will also disable the trusted host mechanism by creating the file /etc/security/config and adding the stanza

```
tcpip:
    netrc = ftp,rexec
```

in addition to completely disabling the *r** daemons.

16.10.2 Dangerous daemons

Some daemons that come with AIX open up more security holes when not properly configured. They are usually activated via either /etc/inetd.conf or /etc/rc.tcpip. Check the following daemons:

fingerd Although harmless in itself, this can be used to find out information about logged in users on a machine. It is deactivated by default. If security is particularly tight, keep it disabled.

ftpd — *Ftp* in itself is not a problem, but you cannot restrict *ftp* access via SMIT in the same way that you can restrict remote log in. Use the file /etc/ftpusers to list those users that are not allowed to access this machine with *ftp*. The debug mode of the *ftpd* daemon stores not only useful debug information but also the password of the user that connects via *ftp*, another good reason to use different passwords for different machines.

rexd — Together with NFS and the *on* command this daemon opens up an unblockable security hole. Make sure that it stays disabled.

rwhod — Provides information similar to *who* and *finger*. You should not activate it not only because it reveals the use of the system to other machines but also because it runs continuously and wastes resources. It is usually started out of /etc/rc.tcpip.

sendmail — Although essential for mail operation, *sendmail* is not without inherent problems. I cannot remember a year when no new *sendmail* security bug was discovered. Make sure that you always have the lastest *sendmail* fix on your system: IBM is quite quick in fixing these security problems, but you are responsible for obtaining the fixes. For extremely critical systems such as Internet gateways you might want to use the *smap* tool from the TIS toolkit (see page 439) as a front end to *sendmail*.

tftpd — Unless you need it for booting Xstations or diskless machines, you should not enable it. It allows unauthenticated access to the system. If you need to run it use /etc/tftpaccess.ctl to restrict the directories and files to which it has access. I suggest replacing the *-n* flag that allows write access with *-tv*, which will give you a bit of logging instead.

uucpd — The UUCP daemon for providing UUCP services over TCP/IP. It should stay deconfigured unless you really need it. UUCP is not one of the safest communications mechanisms with its clear text passwords in configuration files.

rusersd — Like *finger*, this allows remote queries about logged in users. In contrast to *fingerd* it is active by default on AIX if you configure NFS. It provides less information about a specific id than *fingerd* but answers to broadcasts that scan the whole local subnet.

16.10.3 Monitoring network security

Network security can be monitored by the auditing sub-system. If you configure auditing to include the *tcpip* class you will see all connections to the machine that come through *inetd* controlled daemons (see Section 16.3).

The other tool for monitoring network connections is *netstat*. Use **netstat -af inet** to see active TCP connections and all ports on which servers are listening. This not only shows you active conversations but also whether the system really listens only on those services that you have configured.

Checking the debug logs generated by *syslogd* will tell you about connections, file transfers with *ftp* (when using the *-l* option on *ftpd*), mail and other interesting things. For more logging I suggest getting the TCP wrapper (also called *log_tcp*) from a friendly Internet FTP server near you (see page 438). I use it on all our critical systems.

Although it has been greatly hyped in the press, SATAN is still a very useful tool for scanning your own network for security problems. See page 438 for a *ftp* server that has SATAN.

16.10.4 Turning off IP source routing

Any AIX machine can be used as a router. It also does IP source routing, which allows IP packets to be routed through machines that normally would not route the packet. If you want to use the machine as a firewall between two networks (as an Internet gateway for example) it is necessary to turn off routing and IP source routing. This is done with the following *no* commands at the end of /etc/rc.net:

```
/usr/sbin/no -o ipsendredirects=0
/usr/sbin/no -o ipforwarding=0
/usr/sbin/no -o nonlocsrcroute=0
```

On AIX 4 the *ipforwarding* option is off by default.

16.10.5 NIS

NIS, or yellow pages as it was called initially, is a way of managing distributed systems by replicating configuration files across the network. NIS has always been a security problem. To make matters worse it is not very well integrated with the password-managing mechanisms of AIX and thus the password configuration rules of AIX cannot be used.

Any NIS-serving machines should configure the file /var/yp/securenets. It contains the IP addresses of machines that are allowed to obtain NIS data from this system. It lists address masks and addresses. To allow only machines from the network 192.168.1 and the machine 192.168.10.15 access you would have the following lines in the file:

```
255.0.0.0         127.0.0.0
255.255.255.0     192.168.1.0
255.255.255.255 192.168.10.15
```

The first line must always be present as the machine would not be able to access its own daemons otherwise.

Without the /var/yp/securenets file any machine can get the encrypted passwords off the server. As there are plenty of people who use simple passwords, an attack with the freely available *crack* program has a high chance of success. However, even with this file machines within the NIS domain that is managed by this server can obtain the encrypted passwords by simply running **ypcat passwd**, the whole effect of shadow passwords is gone.

As NIS relies on remote procedure calls (RPCs), there is no reliable way to pass NIS traffic through a firewall. Anything you do to allow RPC traffic through a firewall compromises the function of the firewall.

Overall you should not run NIS when security is strict as there are more methods of abusing it than the ones mentioned here. Use DCE instead. It provides a Kerberos-based security mechanism that is not only more powerful but also a lot less breakable than NIS.

The NIS client systems can be easily tricked into using a fake server. AIX 3.2.5 introduced a change that by default does not allow use of the *ypset* command to tell the client about a new server. Use the *-ypset* (for all) or, preferably, *-ypsetme* (for the local host) options on the *ypbind* command line in /etc/rc.nfs to enable *ypset.*

16.10.6 NFS

NFS is a simple and cheap way to share file systems in a network, although it does have some security flaws. Unless it is used together with NIS there is no way to guarantee the uniqueness of a user id. A user *zaphod* on machine A might have the id 220 and a user *trillian* on machine B might also have the uid 220. When A mounts a file system from B then all files in this file system that belong to *trillian* will behave as if they belong to *zaphod.*

When using NFS you should use it only to export read-only information that is not classified. In this way you avoid the problems with the uid mapping. This, of course, is not always possible. When you need to export file systems for read/write access you should limit the number of hosts that have write access. Never export to *localhost* and always use fully qualified host names.

AIX, by default, allows mount requests from unprivileged ports. This can be turned off with one of the following *nfso* commands at the end of /etc/rc.nfs:

```
nfso -o nfs_portmon=1 (in AIX version 3 )
nfso -o portcheck=1   (in AIX version 4 )
```

Like NIS, NFS uses RPCs to communicate requests from clients to servers. This makes NFS unusable across packet-filtering firewalls.

If you need a distributed file system with good security you should look at DFS or AFS.

17

The boot process

Booting an AIX system is a bit different from booting a classical UNIX system. First of all, it is called initial program load (IPL) in IBMese.The RS/6000 loads a boot image from disk (or any other configured boot device) and then transfers control to it. In contrast to other systems, the AIX boot image is a compressed mini UNIX file system, containing the kernel and some initial programs, that is loaded into RAM. After a great deal of setup activity the RAM file system is discarded and the system runs off the real disk. Having a good understanding of the individual actions of the boot process can be very helpful in problem situations. The introduction of the PowerPC-PC systems has resulted in a new class of machines that run AIX but do some things differently from the RS/6000s. One of the major differences is the boot process. There is no LED status display, there is no key to select the boot mode and there are other internal differences. This chapter focuses on the boot process of the RS/6000, as most low-level deviations are very system specific (PowerPC-PCs are available not only from IBM but also from many other vendors as well), and on the high-level side one deals only with AIX.

17.1 How does the system boot?

The boot process can be divided into several steps:

(1) Initialize the hardware.

(2) Load the boot image and execute it.

(3) Configure devices.

(4) Start the *init* process.

(5) Run the commands in /etc/inittab.

The whole procedure is fairly elaborate and time-consuming, quite unlike other UNIX systems, but I must admit that I would rather wait for the tests and the dynamic configuration than run a system with unnoticed hardware problems or having to rebuild kernels after every parameter change. And most UNIX systems are run continuously anyway, being brought down only for hardware maintenance or major operating system upgrades.

Only when commands out of inittab are executed will you see messages on your screen. Until then, the 3 digit LED display keeps you informed about the process (assuming, you have a real RS/6000 and not just a PowerPC-PC). Each individual step has an LED code assigned that flashes by as a test or configuration method is executed. A displayed code that stays on the display or starts to flash regularly indicates trouble. Unfortunately, there is no single complete list of LED codes in the InfoExplorer database. The codes are spread over several articles. To add to the confusion the display is referenced as 'Three-digit display' in InfoExplorer. Search exactly for this string to find a list of articles about the display values: searching for 'LED' will not find all of the relevant articles. A very helpful booklet for interpreting LED codes in case of problems is (*Service Request Number Cross Reference*, 4). This booklet is updated regularly as new models of the RS/6000 are released. You should make sure to get the latest one each time you order a new type of system.

17.1.1 Hardware initialization

The various RS/6000 models contain hardware for self-test at power up. This self-test is called built-in self-test (BIST). It is run by chips on the I/O board and a special part of the CPU. The system will refuse to boot if a failure is found here. Trivial errors to check for in this case are loose cables and connectors as well as defective cards. The LED display will show a code in the range 100 – 199 during those tests. Not only will errors in the CPU or I/O boards cause the system to stop, but errors in the power supply will also terminate the boot process. On the bigger models even the operation of the individual fans for the hard disks are checked and the system refuses to boot if they do not work.

The second step is the execution of the power on self-test (POST). The individual steps of POST are indicated by LED codes in the range 200 – 299. In this step the non-volatile RAM (NVRAM), a battery backed-up memory and the state of the key switch are read. Apart from storing the boot list, the NVRAM contains device information and bit steering information for memory hardware defect correction. It can be reset by disconnecting the battery for half an hour when needed.

If the NVRAM does not point to a specific boot device or device list, all slots starting with the highest number are searched for a SCSI adapter with a boot device starting with SCSI id 0. Each of the devices found is checked for a magic number, a non-zero pointer to a boot image and a non-zero length of the boot image. If these conditions are met, control is transferred to the boot device. The built-in search strategy is shown in Table 17.1.

Table 17.1 Default boot device search order.

Key	NVRAM	Search order
Normal	Valid	Previous boot device, built-in scan, disk, CD ROM, tape, serial link disks, Token-Ring, Ethernet
	Invalid	Direct attached non-SCSI disk (on older systems only), built-in scan, service mode scan
Service	Valid	Diskette, CD ROM, tape, built-in scan, disk, serial link disks, Token-Ring, Ethernet
	Invalid	Diskette, CD ROM, tape, built-in scan, disk, serial link disks

Unfortunately, the boot device scan that is executed when the NVRAM is invalid does not always work. This leads to a system hanging with LED codes 223/229 or 222; remedies are discussed on page 315. If present in the NVRAM, a device extension code can be loaded to support a boot device that is not supported through the system read-only storage (ROS, IBMese for ROM). With this method any device could be used to boot the system once one has loaded its driver into the NVRAM.

Information about the current boot device can be obtained with **bootinfo -a**. The boot list for each key position can be changed with the *bootlist* command, for example **bootlist -m normal hdisk3 hdisk4** would tell the system to try to boot from hdisk3 first and from hdisk4 second when the key is in the normal position. One can also specify generic devices as in **bootlist -m service rmt hdisk**, which would try to boot from attached tapes before trying the disks when the key is in service mode.

The bootlist for the secure key position is not changeable by the *bootlist* command. Booting is always disabled in the secure key position.

Changing the bootlist for normal mode to specific hard disks allows you to switch your boot disk and keep several different versions of AIX on different disks. It is only necessary to install the different AIX versions on different disks and flip the boot list every time you want to change to the other version.

When working with PowerPC-PC systems the *bootlist* command will not work – boot from a service mode diskette or the ROM-resident setup to modify the boot list.

17.1.2 Loading the boot image

Once the boot image is found, it is loaded into memory. This compressed image is created by the *bosboot* shell script. It holds the kernel, optionally the kernel debugger, device configuration information and a RAM file system with all necessary commands to initialize the system.

Everything that is stored in the RAM file system is listed in a .proto file in /usr/lib/boot. The *bosboot* command uses these files as templates to create the boot image. To create a standard boot image on hdisk0 use the command **bosboot -d/dev/hdisk0 -a**. If you want to include the kernel debugger, add the *-D* flag.

When the boot image has been loaded, control is passed to some glue code that uncompresses and relocates the boot image. Then the kernels *main()* routine is called and the kernel is initialized. This point is marked by the LED display 299.

The kernel is now running off a RAM file system. It passes control to *init*, which is really not the *init* process but a simple shell (*ssh*). This shell is used only for system initialization. It does not need shared libraries. This simple shell executes the /sbin/rc.boot script twice, once for each IPL phase. It will then be replaced by the real *init* process which processes /etc/inittab. In the first phase the *restbase* command is executed. This will load the base custom configuration from the boot image. The LED shows 510. Then the configuration manager is invoked for phase 1. It will check the devices on the bus and activate them if they are needed in phase 1 and have already some device information in the database. The workings of the configuration manager are discussed in Section 18.4.2. When this step is completed all disks should be configured (at least when booting from disk) and the LED shows 511. The IPL control block is linked to /dev/ipldevice; usually this is a link to hdisk0.

The second phase is indicated by the LED 551 and starts by executing *ipl_varyon*, which will vary on the root volume group. After varying on the root volume group the initial paging space is activated. The root file system is checked with *fsck* and mounted. Next the /usr file system is mounted either locally or from a remote server. Volume group information from the RAM file system and the real root file system are merged and put in the real /etc/vg directory. The next step is to merge the device configuration from the hard disk with the device configuration information in RAM. This ensures that the major/minor numbers in /dev match the devices configured so far. If any updates need to be run, they are done so now.

At this stage we are ready to move the whole system to a real disk-based file system and to discard the RAM file system. First all disk-based file systems are unmounted and then remounted at their correct mount points. This step is indicated by the LED display 517. Once /usr is mounted the LED switches to 553 and the second phase is finished.

The simple shell exits and the kernel will respawn the real *init* process. Before doing so, it will destroy the RAM-based file system and return the memory to the system. The kernel also unloads all shared libraries. The real *init* now runs with real disk-based file systems and starts to execute the commands in /etc/inittab. The *brc* entry in inittab will be run, executing the third phase for rc.boot. Should /etc/inittab be missing, then *init* will try to execute /sbin/rc.boot directly. This avoids hung systems due to a missing inittab file.

On systems on which /usr is remotely mounted, the portmapper and the status daemon are started. Then /tmp is mounted. The root volume group is synchronized with mirrors when needed, and all lock files are cleared. Now the configuration manager phase 2 is run. This will complete the system configuration. All secondary devices are activated and the console screen is configured. The current base configuration database is saved to the boot image. This is the point at which you see the first message on the screen.

Now unused ttys are removed from inittab (ttys that are configured in inittab but not the ODM), the sync and error daemons are started and the LED display is cleared. The system checks for known configuration conflicts and missing devices. Then the system initialization is complete and *init* continues to process the other inittab entries. The next entry executed is *rc* for /etc/rc. Here all non-root volume groups are activated as well as all remaining paging spaces. All file systems are now checked with **fsck -fp** and minor problems will be fixed automatically, for example problems that can be corrected by replaying the JFS log. After that all file systems that have the *mount=true* option set in /etc/filesystems are mounted. The script executes a few more things, such as recovering files from *vi* crashes, and then exits. Finally, the other inittab entries for run mode 2 are executed and the system is ready for action.

17.2 Booting via the network

AIX 4 supports network boot through NIM. Section 14.2 discusses the details of NIM setup. Once the boot server has been set up the network boot process is like the normal boot process with some deviations.

The client system either uses a built-in *bootp* client to obtain boot information from the server or uses configured boot parameters. In the case of an old system that does not support network boots, a special diskette or tape can be created to allow a network boot. Once the boot parameters have been obtained, the boot code will use the TFTP protocol to load a boot image from the server. After having obtained the boot image the boot process continues as with a normal boot. In the case of disk or dataless systems the loaded boot image will NFS mount the required disks from the server.

During the network boot process LED values in the range 600 – 630 are displayed. Even values are NIM status indicators, whereas odd values are failure indicators. They are explained in (*AIX 4.1 Network Installation Management Guide and Reference*, 14).

Although there is no NIM for AIX 3, it uses the same method for disk and dataless clients, but, unlike AIX 4, it has no support for the creation of network boot diskettes or tapes.

17.3 Recovering from boot failures

There are various reasons for problems in the boot step. Loose cables, faulty hardware, full file systems, corrupted configuration information or an eventual bug can all cause the system to refuse to boot. Many of the software problems can be fixed from the maintenance shell. To get a maintenance shell put the key in service mode and boot from CD, tape or floppy disks (see Section 1.5 for details on the generation of boot floppies for AIX 3) and select the 'Start a limited function maintenance shell' or 'Access the root volume group' menu item.

On AIX 3 this will put you in a very limited shell. To get to the root volume group use **getrootfs**. Without any parameters it will tell you which disks are available. On most systems **getroofs hdisk0** will activate the root volume group and mount the basic file systems, but if you have more than one SCSI adapter then the hdisk0 in normal operation might be different from the hdisk0 in maintenance mode so get a listing of the available disks first. It will show you the bootable ones. In the following examples hdisk0 will be used. Some forms of boot failures do not even allow the mount of the file systems. Using the third form of *getrootfs*, **getrootfs hdisk0 sh**, will start a shell before mounting the file systems, but after the root volume group has been activated.

On AIX 4 you can choose from the menu whether or not to get a shell before mounting the file systems. This makes the above step somewhat simpler as the commands are hidden, but that is the only difference. The following hints all use the *getrootfs* command, which is not needed on AIX 4, but otherwise the steps are usually the same.

Whatever release you are on, the floppies, CD or tape that you use to boot the system in maintenance mode should correspond to the level installed on your system. When working with diskless or /usr clients the following steps are not very useful – they are for complete systems only. When a system hangs during boot the problem can usually be corrected with a bit of work unless it is a true hardware problem. As soon as you can access the normal file systems use **errpt** to see if the system experiences CHECKSTOPs. They are usually caused by defective hardware and you will need to contact IBM hardware support to fix them.

On AIX 4 you are prompted for the disk to activate, but on AIX 3.2 you can run **lqueryvg -Atp hdiskN | grep hd5** for each disk to find out which one has the boot logical volume hd5.

17.3.1 Invalid boot list or hardware problems

If the system is stuck at BIST (LED codes below 200), then you should check the hardware. LED codes in the range 200 – 299 can be caused by hardware or wrong configuration information. A steady LED code of 201 indicates hardware trouble with the system planar. Should you be able to boot the diagnostics disks or get into maintenance mode check the error log for CHECKSTOP entries. Should the system alternate between 223/229, 225/229, 221/229 and 233/235 or be stuck at 221, 222 or 721 you can try to clean up the default boot list as those errors indicate a missing boot device or the system ROM being unable to work with the configured boot device. If all cables and connectors are OK, go into maintenance mode and execute

```
getrootfs hdisk0
bootlist -m normal -i
sync;sync
```

Then turn the key to normal and reboot the system.

This will invalidate the boot list information about the previous boot device and the system will try to boot from the built-in boot list. If this still does not help, you can try to disconnect the NVRAM battery for half an hour and then boot again.

The problem may also have been caused by a full root or /tmp file system. Check the file systems with *df* before using *bootlist* to see if a little house cleaning can solve the problem, Section 6.4 might give you some hints.

17.3.2 Corrupted boot images

If the LED display on your system alternates between 201 and 299 or hangs on 517 then its boot image is probably corrupt. The LED sequences 888-103-207-299 and 888-103-208-299 may also indicate a corrupted boot image. You can try to generate a new boot image with the following commands in maintenance mode:

```
getrootfs hdisk0
syncvg -v rootvg
synclvodm -v rootvg
bosboot -d /dev/hdisk0 -a
sync;sync
```

Here *hdisk0* stands for the disk drive that contains your boot image. Then turn the key to normal and reboot the system. A corrupted boot image could be caused by a full / or /tmp file system during the *bosboot* run, therefore you should check the available space before running the *bosboot* command. See Section 6.4.

17.3.3 Corrupted file systems

If your system refuses to boot because of a corrupted file system in the root volume group, it may display LED 518. Use the AIX 4 menus to get to the root volume group without mounting file systems or use **getrootfs hdisk0 sh** on AIX 3.2 to access the root volume group without mounting the file systems. Then use *fsck* to repair the file system damage:

```
fsck -y /dev/hd1
fsck -y /dev/hd2
fsck -y /dev/hd3
fsck -y /dev/hd4
fsck -y /dev/hd9var
```

You should then run *fsck* on other file systems that you created yourself in the root volume group. Then **sync** twice and reboot. The *-y* option allows *fsck* to fix errors without asking.

If a file system cannot be fixed by *fsck*, then you will probably have to recreate it. In particular, if you receive the message that block 8 is damaged the chances are high that it cannot be fixed. This will work for all file systems but *hd4*, which would require a reinstall of AIX. If block 8 is readable but you get errors indicating that the file system is not recognized then you can try to copy a backup block of the superblock to block 1 with the command

```
dd count=1 bs=4k skip=31 seek=1 if=/dev/hdN of=/dev/hdN
```

where hdN is the file system in question.

Should you get errors indicating problems with the JFS log then you can create a new JFS log with the *logform* command. The default JFS log for the root volume group is on *hd8*. Reformat the log logical volume with **/usr/sbin/logform /dev/hd8**. Now try to *fsck* it again. If it does not work this time it needs to be recreated.

17.3.4 Varyon problems

The system displays code 551 when it starts to activate the root volume group. If it hangs there or hangs/alternates with 552, 554, 555, 556 or 557 then it has problems activating the root volume group. There are various reasons for these codes: a corrupted file system, a bad JFS log or a bad disk.

Boot in maintenance mode and try to activate the root volume group with the **getrootfs hdisk0** command on AIX 3 or the menu point to activate the root volume group and mount the file systems on AIX 4. If this succeeds, it is likely that the root or /tmp file system is full, /dev is missing or /bin does not exist. Make sure that / and /tmp contain some free space and /bin and /dev are OK. You should also check files in /etc for their integrity, especially /etc/filesystems. If everything looks fine try a normal boot.

If the *getroofs* step failed, you should reboot and use **getrootfs hdisk0 sh** instead or access the root volume group without mounting file systems on AIX 4. Use the steps outlined in Section 17.3.3 to repair the file systems. If they fail, then the ODM may be corrupted. It is possible to create a non-corrupted but stripped down version of the ODM. With this you will lose much device configuration information but you can get at least to the disk. The old ODM files will be saved so that they can be used to retrieve the lost information should the files still be usable. Here are the steps – they assume that the root volume group is active but that the file systems are not yet mounted.

```
mount /dev/hd4 /mnt
mount /dev/hd2 /usr
mkdir /mnt/etc/objrepos/bak
cp /mnt/etc/objrepos/Cu* /mnt/etc/objrepos/bak
cp /etc/objrepos/Cu* /mnt/etc/objrepos
/etc/umount all
exit
```

Now the system should be up with the file systems mounted and the mini ODM active. Find your boot logical volume and the disk it resides on with **lslv -m hd5**. Use the indicated hard disk to save the ODM configuration on the boot logical volume with **savebase -d /dev/hdiskN**. You then need to create a new boot image with **bosboot -a -d /dev/hdiskN**.

17.3.5 Problems with /etc/inittab

If the system hangs with LED 553 this could indicate problems with /etc/inittab, a full /tmp or / file system or that /bin has been removed. A missing shell or shell profile could also be the cause. Those errors are usually recoverable from the maintenance shell by simple cleanup operations. Run **getrootfs hdisk0** on AIX 3 or use the menus of AIX 4 to get to the root volume group with mounted file systems and use **df** to see if any of the file systems are full. Check the following files and links for correctness: /bin, /etc/inittab, /etc/environment, /bin/sh, /bin/bsh, /etc/fsck, /etc/profile and /sbin/rc.boot.

17.3.6 Problems with the console

Should your system hang with a code of c31 then it has problems accessing the console device. Either it is not properly configured or a device on one of the integrated serial ports makes the system think there is a console even although there is none. Remove all non-terminal devices (plotters, modems, wrap plugs) from the serial ports, turn on all terminals connected to the native serial ports and try a reboot. If you see this code on a system that has a direct attached console but no serial terminals, you probably do not have the necessary device driver for the graphics card or the console configuration is damaged. Go into the maintenance shell, activate the root volume group and use **smit chcons** to set up the console. If you do not have the right drivers loaded, this will not help you. If you can identify the missing driver on the operating system CD or tape you now can load it, create a new boot image and see if the system comes up correctly. Otherwise, you will need to call support for the new driver. This usually only occurs if you try to use newly announced hardware with code that is not yet up to date.

17.3.7 Hanging on LED 581

Some systems seem to hang forever on LED code 581 when booting. They will eventually continue, but this may be long after your patience has been exhausted. The LED code is displayed when the configuration manager runs /etc/rc.net to configure TCP/IP into the kernel. Should the system have problems accessing the network then it might hang there until some time-outs kick in. In most cases it has problems with name service. A very typical case is a system that acts as a name server. It tries to access the name server for its own host name configuration but the named daemon will be started only much later when /etc/rc.tcpip is run. The system will wait quite some time before it gives up trying to access the name server.

On AIX 4 the workaround is to set *NSORDER=local,bind* in /etc/rc.net and /etc/rc.tcpip to search the /etc/hosts file first and have all necessary hosts for booting configured in there. The search order defined with *$NSORDER* will be kept by all daemons started from those files. The other method is to create a temporary /etc/netsvc.conf file at the beginning of /etc/rc.net and then remove it at the end of /etc/rc.tcpip. This will allow you to change the lookup order after starting the daemons. The contents of /etc/netsvc.conf would be *hosts=local,bind*.

Other network problems might also lead to a long hang on LED 581. LAN network cards or interfaces might have problems – check the error log and see if the interfaces are up and running once the system finally comes up. If NIS is used and the network cannot be accessed the system will most certainly have problems here.

18

Coping with the ODM

Configuring devices for a traditional UNIX system usually means specifying which drivers are to be linked in the kernel, re-linking the kernel, making entries in the device directory and modifying several other configuration files. It is very easy to make mistakes in this rather tedious process. In any case, your average end user does not want to see those details. In addition, parsing ASCII configuration files is not a very efficient method. AIX tries to get around all this by using a binary database for the configuration information, which is then used by the dynamic kernel. The database is called the object data manager (ODM). It consists of a database access API and command line interface programs which interact with the database files in various directories. Although it simplifies many things compared with traditional methods, it also makes things more complicated for experienced UNIX system administrators as they need to learn new ways of configuring the system. Because of its binary nature the ODM is less easy understood by looking at it than standard ASCII configuration files. Those two problems have created an aura of mysticism around the ODM. The following chapter is meant to remove this aura and show you how simple the ODM really is.

18.1 The purpose of the ODM

The ODM was designed to maintain system and device configuration as well as vital product data (hardware and software release levels). It is extensible and can accommodate user-designed databases. Access to the ODM is via some form of object model, but I think this is just the current buzzword, for me it is a simple database.

All device configuration in the ODM is rule driven as far as possible to make it easy to extend the system. Apart from the device configuration you will find the history of installed software as well as hardware levels and all the SMIT menus in the ODM. And various subsystems use the ODM partly or wholly to store their configuration data.

18.2 The structure of the ODM

The ODM database used by AIX consists of files spread over several directories. The first is /usr/lib/objrepos and the second is /etc/objrepos. All the files from /usr/lib/objrepos are accessible in /etc/objrepos via symbolic links. The two directories are necessary to separate shareable and non-shareable parts of the configuration. In addition, there are database files in /usr/share/lib/objrepos that store information about the installed software. Objects in the ODM can have associated programs or methods, which usually reside in /etc/methods.

The databases in /etc/objrepos contain the actual configuration, often called customized objects, whereas /usr/lib/objrepos contains default configuration or predefined objects. Anything that changes the configuration of the machine usually changes the databases in /etc/objrepos.

ODM object classes are files with fixed size records. Each record is a C structure. Objects are records in the database. Object classes are described via object descriptors. Those descriptors are either C language primitives or links to other object classes or methods, which are actually the pathnames of programs. Figure 18.1 shows how these things look like.

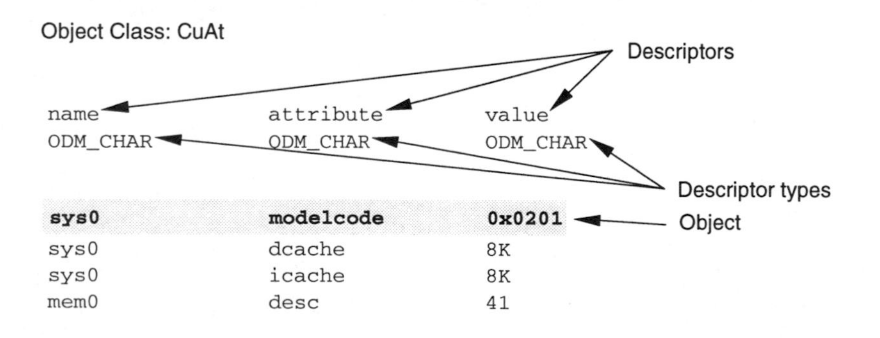

Figure 18.1 A sample from an ODM database.

As you can see, it is simply a database with different names. The database (object class) *CuAt* has records (objects) which consist of three fields (descriptors) – name, attribute and value – all of which are of the type (descriptor type) ODM_CHAR. The commands that access the ODM use the environment variable *ODMDIR* to find the right directory. It is initially set to /etc/objrepos in /etc/environment.

18.3 Accessing the ODM

Most of the time you will not directly access the ODM. All these high-level commands for system configuration will do this for you. However, there are times when direct access is quite useful to work around problems. If you start to experiment with the ODM you should do this on a copy, not the original. Create a copy of the ODM files with **cp -r /etc/objrepos /tmp** and tell the ODM commands to use this copy with **export ODMDIR=/tmp/objrepos**. Now you can experiment safely without risking your system configuration.

The following list of commands can be used to access the ODM:

odme You can edit ODM files with this full-screen editor on AIX 3, but its user interface is awkward at best and it is very easy accidentally to modify a file with it. Some people think that it should have never been shipped as there are numerous reports of databases being accidentally destroyed with it. AIX 4 finally comes without it.

odmcreate The *odmcreate* command takes a description of an object class and creates the object class as well as the necessary .c and .h files to access the object class from C programs. If you do not need the C files you can skip them via the *-c* flag. The input file looks like some C structure definitions that describe the objects in the new class.

odmget Running *odmget* with only a class name as a parameter will list the complete class in a stanza format. If you want to list only specific records you can specify a search criterion with the *-q* option. It can include logical operators and the keyword *like* together with wildcards. To see all attributes of the *sys0* device in the customized attributes database (*CuAt*) you could use **odmget -q"name=sys0" CuAt**. Compare this with the output of **lsattr -El sys0** and you will find some interesting differences. All those values that are not displayed with the *lsattr* command have their *nls_index* set to zero as there is no description in the message catalogues for this attribute. To list all of these entries use a combined search criterion, as in **odmget -q"nls_index=0 and name=sys0" CuAt**. If you only want to know about any entries in this database that have something to do with caches, a query such as **odmget -q"attribute like *cache*" CuAt** will list only the cache attributes in this database.

odmadd

This command allows you to add data to the ODM. The object class has to exist already before this command can be used. It takes one or more input files and adds their objects to the object classes that are referenced in the files. The input format for *odmadd* is a stanza format like the following:

```
CuDvDr:
        resource = "devno"
        value1 = "12"
        value2 = "1"
        value3 = "rmt0"
```

Using this stanza in the input file for **odmadd inputfile** would add one record to the *CuDvDr* (customized device driver) object class. Because you have to specify the object class in the input file you can add data to several classes with one input file. This command adds only to the object class – existing records are not changed.

odmchange

When you want to change objects in the database that match certain criteria you can use this command. It will replace all objects that match the search criteria with the objects given in the input file. For example, if you want to change the *CuDvDR* class entries for the *rmt0* tape you could use **odmchange -oCuDvDr -q"value3=rmt0" rmt0.change**. This would use the changes that are in rmt0.change on all records that match the criteria *value3=rmt0*. To create the initial changes file you should use the *odmget* command as this command is very picky about the format of the input file and you may easily miss something by accident.

odmdelete

Use *odmdelete* to delete entries in an ODM database. To delete all entries for *rmt0* in *CuAt* the command **odmdelete -oCuAt -q"name=rmt0"** would be used. Be careful when using this command. If you forget to specify the criteria, all the entries in the object class are deleted. Even if all entries are deleted, the object class still remains.

odmdrop

This is the command to remove a complete object class, including its definition, without any checks. It will finish the work that *odmdelete* has started, but you do not need to run *odmdelete* first, as *odmdrop* does not care whether there are still objects in the class.

odmshow If you want to see the underlying definition of a database use *odmshow*. It will display the C structure that makes up the object. In addition, it displays the number of entries in the database and the offset of the data from the beginning of the file.

savebase *Savebase* is a special command that copies the device customization information (all those *Cu** classes) to the boot device. It writes this information directly to /dev/hd5 without the need to call *bosboot*.

restbase The inverse of the *savebase* command. It is used during the first part of the boot process to set up the customized part of the ODM from the initial configuration in the boot image. This command is not meant to be executed on a normal running system.

18.4 System configuration with the ODM

The following section is meant as an overview for those readers who want to understand the basics of the ODM device configuration. A much more detailed description can be found the in the device driver books (*AIX Version 3.2 Writing a Device Driver*, 9) and (*AIX Version 4.1 Kernel Extensions and Device Support Programming Concepts*, 7).

18.4.1 Device configuration in the ODM

Device support is implemented in various object classes in the ODM. Those object classes contain the default devices and their configuration. The names of predefined classes all start with *Pd*.

PdDv This class contains predefined devices. All devices that are directly supported by AIX can be found in here. In addition, there are a few generic devices for disks, printers and tapes so that one can attach non-IBM equipment to the machine. If you want to integrate new unsupported devices then this and the other two predefined object classes need to be updated with information about the new devices. Here is the entry for generic disks in this database:

```
PdDv:
        type "= "osdisk"
        class = "disk"
        subclass = "scsi"
        prefix = "hdisk"
        devid = ""
        base = 1
```

```
has_vpd = 1
detectable = 1
chgstatus = 0
bus_ext = 0
fru = 1
led = 1825
setno = 57
msgno = 8
catalog = "devices.cat"
DvDr = "scdisk"
Define = "/etc/methods/define"
Configure = "/etc/methods/cfgscdisk"
Change = "/etc/methods/chgdisk"
Unconfigure = "/etc/methods/ucfgdevice"
Undefine = "/etc/methods/undefine"
Start = ""
Stop = ""
inventory_only = 0
uniquetype = "disk/scsi/osdisk"
```

The entry defines the type *osdisk* (for other SCSI disk) in the disk class. If it were an IBM disk, it would have a type that reflects the disk name or capacity. The subclass is used to relate this device to other devices when needed. Any instances of this device would have a name that starts with hdisk, as specified by the prefix entry. If this were a Micro Channel card, then the *devid* would be set to its unique card id. The base attribute is set to 1 as it is a device that can be part of the minimum base configuration for the boot phase. It is assumed that the system can read device identification data from the disk, and therefore *has_vpd* is set. The detectable flag says that this device can be automatically detected. The disk is not a bus extension and is a field-replaceable unit. When it is configured by the configuration manager the LED will show the hexadecimal representation of 1825 (721_H). The string that describes this device for a command such as *lsdev* is number 8 in set 57 of the devices.cat message catalogue. In contrast to other message catalogs, this catalog is stored in /usr/lib/methods. The device driver for this device can be found through the *scdisk* entry in the *DvDr* object class. It has no start or stop methods and the define, unconfigure and undefine methods are generic – only the configure and change methods are specific for SCSI devices. As it is a real device not one that is there for reference purposes only, the *inventory_only* flag is 0. The unique name of this device type for the *PdDvLn* and *PdAt* classes is *disk/scsi/osdisk*.

PdAt

This database stores predefined attributes for the devices in the *PdDv*, for example the above other SCSI disk would have attributes in this class that can be found under the unique type *disk/scsi/osdisk*. Use **odmget -q"uniquetype = disk/scsi/osdisk" PdAt** to list them. The attributes for SCSI disks are not very interesting for most people so let's look at the Ethernet adapter:

```
PdAt:
        uniquetype = "adapter/mca/ethernet"
        attribute = "xmt_que_size"
        deflt = "30"
        values = "20-150,1"
        width = ""
        type = "R"
        generic = "DU"
        rep = "nr"
        nls_index = 10
```

This entry describes the transmit queue size attribute. It has a default value of 30 and can be set in the range 20 – 150 with an increment of 1. If the attribute describes I/O addresses, then the length of the I/O area would be set with the width field. The type field tells us that this is a standard regular attribute. It is displayable and user configurable according to the generic field. It is a numeric range according to the rep field when displayed and the description for it can be found in message 10 in the message catalog specified for this device. Any value that can be displayed and changed by the user can also be listed via *lsdev*. For the transmit queue size of the Ethernet adapter the command would be **lsdev -Rl ent0 -axmt_que_size**.

PdCn Connections between devices are stored here. This database is used to make sure that devices are not modified while other devices still need them.

The information from the above classes is used to generate device instances with customized data in several classes for customized devices. The names of these classes start with *Cu*.

CuDv You will find one record for each device here, for example the SCSI adapter on a model 220 has the following entry:

```
CuDv:
        name = "scsi0"
        status = 1
        chgstatus = 2
        ddins = "pscsidd"
        location = "00-00-0S"
```

```
        parent = "sio0"
        connwhere = "14"
        PdDvLn = "adapter/sio/pscsi"
```

The *name* of the device is the instance name that can be found in the /dev directory. If there are several devices of the same type then the system assigns sequential numbers for them automatically. The *status* flag shows the state of the device. In this case it is available. The *chgstatus* flag indicates changes after the system boot. The *ddins* entry defines the device driver for this device. It corresponds to a driver name in the *PdDv* object class. The *location* code specifies where the device is located. In this case it is on the planar board. It can have up to four parts: the CPU or drawer number, then the I/O channel number, then the device on the I/O planar and then the device on the specific adapter. The *parent* is the device that is the parent of this device. A parent device is configured before this device and calls this devices configuration method when the configuration manager is run. The *connwhere* attribute is the link to the connection of the parent device. The *PdDvLn* entry specifies which entry in the predefined device link database contains the predefined device information.

CuAt

If a device contains customizable attributes then they are stored in here. For example, the tape device *rmt0* on my machine has three entries in here which describe the customizable attributes of the device: two for the density settings and one for the SCSI reserve/release support. These are the attributes that are different from the default ones in *PdAt*. If an attribute is not found in *CuAt* then its default value from *PdAt* is used by the system. Each attribute in here looks as follows:

```
CuAt:
        name = "rmt0"
        attribute = "density_set_2"
        value = "17"
        type = "R"
        generic = "DU"
        rep = "nr"
        nls_index = 13
```

First the name of the device instance is specified, then the name of the attribute and its current value. The attribute type specifies the meaning of the attribute value; in this case it is simply some regular attribute with no special meaning. The generic entry specifies whether the attribute is displayable 'D' and whether the user can change the value 'U'. The rep attribute specifies the format in which the attribute is displayed by commands such as *lsattr*. The nls_index finally points to a message in a message catalog where an NLS description of the attribute can be found.

CuDep This class lists device dependencies. For each device that has dependencies there is one entry for each of its dependent devices, for example the *inet0* device has a dependency on the *en0* Ethernet interface:

```
CuDep:
        name = "en0"
        dependency = "inet0"
```

CuDvDr This class stores the connections between the device, the device driver and the device major and minor number.

```
CuDvDr:
        resource = "devno"
        value1 = "16"
        value2 = "3"
        value3 = "fd0"
```

In this case the value1 is the device major number and value2 is the device minor number; value3 is the name of the device instance.

```
CuDvDr:
        resource = "ddins"
        value1 = "pscsidd"
        value2 = "11"
        value3 = ""
```

In this case the value1 field points to the name of the device driver in the *PdDv* class. The value2 is the device major number and value3 is unused.

CuVPD This database contains device specific vital product data such as EPROM release numbers and other information required for maintenance. The **lscfg -v** command uses this information.

Each of the devices in this database has five to seven methods (programs) attached that are used to create, delete and configure various states of the device as shown in Figure 18.2. Methods are stored in /usr/lib/methods. They are not meant to be run from the command line in normal operation. They are called from high-level commands or the configuration manager.

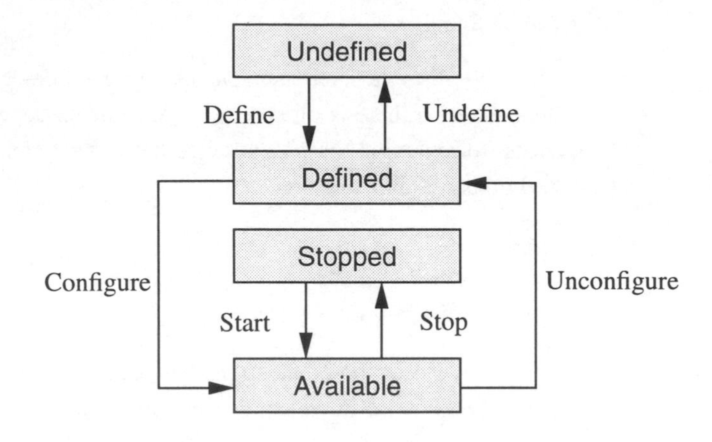

Figure 18.2 Device state table.

The device configuration methods are:

Define The define method is used to set the device interfaces in relation to the rest of the system and make some initial configuration decisions so that the device driver can access the device. Micro Channel devices select their interrupts or memory ranges via this method. Information from the predefined databases is taken in this method to create a specific device instance. After this method has been run for a device it is usually in the defined state. The define method can be invoked via *mkdev*.

Configure The configure method loads the device driver in the kernel and sets up the interfaces to the other parts of the system. It uses information from the predefined and customized device databases. This method is responsible for creating the necessary entries in the /dev directory. After this method has been run for a device it is usually in the available state. To move a device from the defined to the available state you could use **mkdev -l rmt0**, for example if the tape has been turned on after the computer.

Unconfigure Unloads the device driver if no other instances of a device references it and sets the device back to the defined state. It is run by *rmdev*.

Undefine The undefine method removes specific device instances from the customized device database. It is run when a device is deleted, for example *rmdev* when called with the *-d* flag.

Change The change method is used to change attributes of the device. It is usually called from commands such as *chdev*.

Stop This method is used to stop a device temporarily. It is only used on some pseudodevices and not on true hardware devices.

Start The start method is used to resume after the stop method has been invoked.

18.4.2 Using the configuration manager

All of the above databases and methods are used by the configuration manager (*cfg-mgr*), which is responsible for running the define and configure methods at the right time to activate and configure all devices in the system. In addition to the above databases, it uses the *Config_Rules* object class to determine in which sequence devices need to be activated. Each entry consists of a phase in which the rule has to be run, a sequence number which defines the position in the activation sequence within the phase and a boot mask that defines whether the rule is applicable to the current boot method. There are three phases: phase 1 is run when the mini AIX out of the boot image is run; phase 2 runs later in normal mode, and phase 3 runs instead of phase 2 when the key is in service mode. An entry in the *Config_Rules* class looks like this:

```
Config_Rules:
        phase = 1
        seq = 2
        boot_mask = 0
        rule = "/etc/methods/deflvm"
```

This stanza tells the configuration manager to run the definition method for the logical volume manager as the second method in boot phase 1 independent of the boot device.

Whenever you change the configuration rules for phase 1 you need to execute the *bosboot* command to update the boot image with the changed classes and methods.

Figure 18.3 shows the configuration manager and the objects it works with. Whenever the configuration manager executes a method to define a device it returns the names of its children that need to be defined. The configuration manager then runs the appropriate methods for those devices. This is repeated until each device specified in the initial rule and all its children are completely configured. The define methods are used by the configuration manager to set up the interfaces to the various devices. For Micro Channel cards they find the correct memory ranges, interrupt levels and I/O memory ranges via the *busresolve* subroutine. These settings are then set in the POS registers of the cards and in the *CuAt* database. The configure methods will use the information from the *CuAt* later to access the devices.

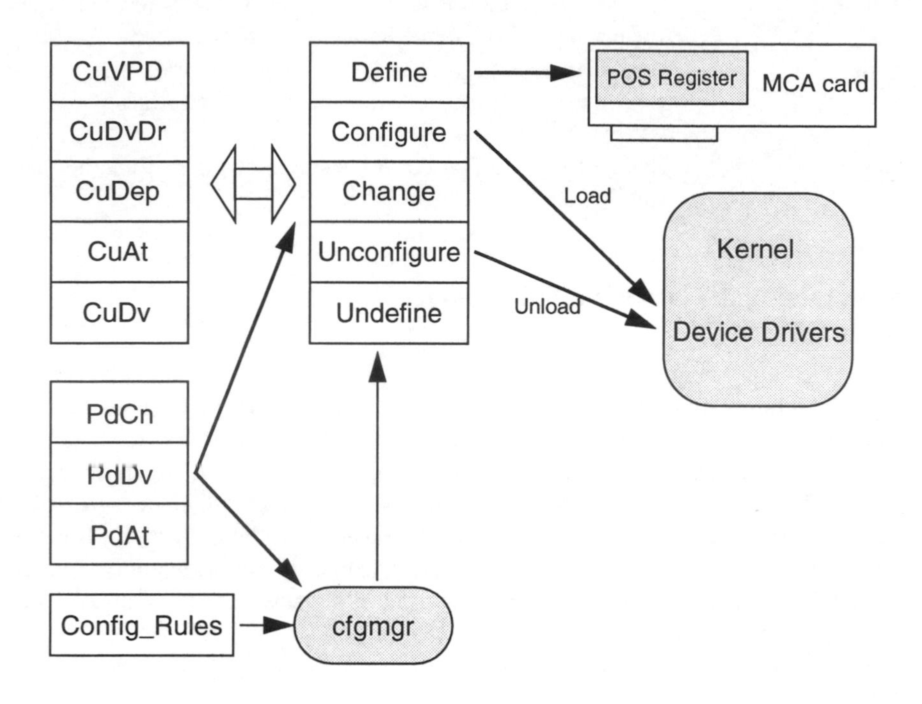

Figure 18.3 Devices and the configuration manager.

18.4.3 Cloning configurations with *rda*

AIX contains a program that makes it relatively easy to clone ODM configurations. It is called *rda* for *r*ecover *d*evice *a*ttributes and at the time of writing it is unfortunately undocumented, even on AIX 4. It hides in /usr/lpp/bosinst and is used for cloning systems via the backups created with *mksysb*. It extracts configuration information from ODM classes and creates shell scripts that can be used to recreate this information. It is usually run as part of the *bosmain* script during the installation to merge old configuration information with what is now on the system.

```
rda [-a attributefile] [-c prefix] [-d devicefile] [-p ODMpath]
    [-s scriptname] [-e] [-R] [-r] [-x]
```

-a The file specified with *-a* is the output *CuAt* stanza file. It defaults to ./CuAt.sav. It contains the stanzas for the device attribute configuration

-c Search prefix for the old *CuDv* and *CuAt* classes. Only objects that have this prefix are considered. If no prefix is specified then the wildcard '*' is used.

-d Specifies the output *CuDv* class stanza file. It defaults to ./CuDv.sav.

-e Extracts only. Do not create commands to recover devices and configuration. It will only create the stanza files.

-p Pathname of the old ODM (defaults to /etc/objrepos).

-R Relaxes the configuration determination criteria. This is used for cloning when devices are at different locations.

-r Only recovers device and configuration information. It uses the files created with the *-e* option to build the shell script that is specified with the *-s* option. It does not look at the ODM itself.

-s Filename for the shell script that is created. If none is specified the script is sent to *stdout*.

-x Runs the shell script that is created with the *-r* and *-s* options.

To generate a cloning script for the ODM configuration on a master machine you could use **rda -rs clone**. Have a look at the generated script and modify it if necessary. Then run it on other machines and – hey presto – they are configured alike. The more elaborate way would be to use *rda* to create the *CuDv* and *CuAt* information on the master then use them as input for *rda* on the clone and use the *-R* flag when creating the script.

If you have to maintain a large number of machines then *rda* is the key to cloning their configuration automatically via the network.

18.5 Other ODM databases

There are databases in the ODM other than just those needed for the device configuration. Information about the installed software, SMIT menus, diagnostics information, configuration of daemons and more can be found in the ODM.

Installed software

The information about installed software is spread over three directories, each containing the same files, which store only the LPP information that is relevant to this part of the directory tree. In /etc/objrepos the information about the root part of the LPP is stored. In /usr/lib/objrepos the *usr* part can be found and the shareable part is in /usr/share/lib/objrepos. All the files are linked via their *lpp_id* entries.

lpp Stores the names of the installed LPPs.

history This class stores the information about who installed what when and which updates.

product Stores fix information, pre/co-requisites and supersedes.

inventory Lists the files that belong to an LPP.

The system resource controller

The system resource controller (SRC) stores its configuration in the ODM classes *SRCnotify, SRCodmlock*, *SRCsubsvr* and *SRCsubsys*. Use *odmget* on *SRCsubsys* to see in detail all the daemons that are configured in the SRC. By modifying this class directly, characteristics such as the *stdout* connection for a subsystem or daemon can be changed.

Inetd configuration on AIX 3

The internet super daemon *inetd* reads its configuration from the *InetServ* class instead of using /etc/inetd.conf on AIX 3. To update the class when inetd.conf or /etc/services has been changed you need to run **inetimp**. If you look at the object class you will find the same information as in the flat file. I have yet to find a reason why the configuration for *inetd* was moved into an ODM object class. Fortunately, on AIX 4 we no longer need to bother with it.

SMIT configuration

SMIT stores its configuration and menus in various ODM classes: *sm_cmd_hdr* for the commands, *sm_cmd_opt* for the command options, *sm_menu_opt* for the menu structure and *sm_name_hdr* for premenu selectors.

19

Monitoring, tuning and troubleshooting

Usually tuning means getting better performance out of a system. You might use it to minimize the resources you need to perform a given task or get the maximum performance out of a system, which is not necessarily the same. Tuning the system itself and tuning in a networked environment present two different problem areas. A third one is application tuning when you have access to the source code and are willing to optimize it for a given architecture.

Tuning might also be troubleshooting; in my experience this is true in at least 70% of all performance-related problems. Your performance might be bad because of defects or misconfiguration in the system. The key to successful tuning is to understand what the problem is and its cause. If you start playing around with system parameters without knowing what you are doing you will most likely make matters worse as the defaults are already trying to give a reasonable overall performance. Alternatively, you may end up with one aspect highly optimized while the rest of the system does not perform at all. So monitoring the system becomes a key to understanding where changing parameters might be useful.

There is an excellent IBM book on those topics that you should read. The AIX tuning bible (*Performance Monitoring and Tuning Guide*, 3), which is also included in InfoExplorer. The following sections will give you only a rough indication of the areas of interest and the most important rules of thumb on tuning.

19.1 System monitoring

To tune the system you need to identify your bottlenecks and troublespots first. Numerous tools come with AIX for this purpose. In addition to standard UNIX monitoring tools such as *sar* you will find several AIX additions, most notably those in /usr/lpp/bosperf on AIX 3. Unfortunately, these tools are unbundled in AIX 4 and you have to purchase the performance agent part of the Performance Toolbox/6000 for an additional fee. You should play around with these tools on your system to get a feeling for what is normal and what their output means for you. If you do not and then have to work with them in a stress situation you do not know whether they indicate real trouble or merely strange side-effects.

In addition, there are various ways of checking the system for errors, such as the *errpt* command or *syslog* output, which should be checked for possible troublespots. Many daemons and applications have debug flags that will trigger debug output either to a file or to *syslog*. Be sure to deactivate them again after testing. You do not want your file systems to fill up because of a forgotten debug file that grows forever.

In addition to the tools mentioned here, an optional graphical monitoring system available on AIX 3 allows you to monitor not only local but remote systems. Have a look at the AIX Performance Toolbox/6000. It not only gives you a real-time graphical display of the workload of a machine but also allows you to set up alarms for critical situations. On AIX 4 you have to purchase the toolbox anyway to obtain the commands that were included in /usr/lpp/bosperf on AIX 3.

Although AIX 4 ships with fewer low-level performance-monitoring commands, it comes with a new high-level tool set that can help you detect problems long before they become critical. The performance diagnostic tool (PDT) helps you to detect developing troublespots with an automated daily system analysis.

In addition to the AIX commands for system monitoring, there is a free program called monitor that gives a very good overview of the systems resource use. It can be found on the Internet at *ftp.funet.fi:pub/unix/AIX/rs6000/*.

19.1.1 The error log

When in trouble, check the error log first. Use **errpt** to see a quick summary of recent entries or **errpt -a | more** for more details. The output of *errpt* without any options contains a time stamp in the format MMDDhhmmYY, which looks a bit odd at first. Here is a short sample of the simple *errpt* output:

```
ERROR_ID TIMESTAMP  T CL RESOURCE_NAME  ERROR_DESCRIPTION
2BFA76F6 0101200894 T S  SYSPROC        System shutdown by user
9DBCFDEE 0101201194 T O  errdemon       Error logging turned on
C14C511C 1231204993 T H  scsi0          ADAPTER ERROR
9DBCFDEE 0101140794 T O  errdemon       Error logging turned on
```

The error id is an identifier for the type of error. You can select specific error type in the *errpt* output with the *-j* flag. The T field tells you whether it is a temporary error (T), a permanent error (P) or an unknown error (U). The CL field specifies whether it is a Hardware (H) or a Software (S) error or a log entry (O). The resource name is the name of the hardware or software component that generated the error, and finally there is a short description. Although the error log may contain much information, it provides no analysis for hardware errors – you have to use the *diag* command to do this.

You should check the error log regularly to obtain advance warnings, for example the entry above for the SCSI adapter is only temporary. However, if you have plenty of them, there is a problem somewhere on your SCSI chain that may lead to lost data some day. For example, you can find entries in the error log about memory scrubbing when the memory subsystem has detected bad bits in the memory hardware or entries about bad block reallocation on the disks. Some forms of network problems will also generate entries here. You can even include your own entries with the *errlogger* command.

If you find too many entries in the log you should check the various flags of *errpt*, which allow you to limit the output to a range of days (*-s*, *-e*), to specific error ids (*-j*), to specific resources (*-N*,*-R*) or a class (*-d*) or type of errors (*-T*) as well as to exclude specific error ids (*-k*). If you no longer need the error log it can be truncated to a certain number of days with *errclear*. To erase all entries completely use **errclear 0**.

Some forms of error log entries will contain a block of hex data that is not too informative. The *diag* command can be used to analyze these entries. Run **diag**, then follow the menus 'Service Aid', 'Hardware Error Report Service Aid', and 'Display Error Analysis Detail' to get a log with the decoded data.

19.1.2 *ps*

For many performance related problems a simple check with *ps* may already reveal the source. AIX is shipped with a *ps* command that implements both the BSD and the System V options. Check out the available options – there are plenty of them.

Interesting things to check for in the *ps* output will be the top memory and CPU users. Unfortunately, the AIX version of *ps* does not sort its output according to these criteria as does the BSD version. Use **ps aux | tail +2 | sort -k 1.15,1.19nr** as a quick workaround to sort the output by CPU usage. I use this command quite often, and so I have set up an alias for it (see Section 23.4.3). A great deal of detail can be learned from *ps* depending on the command line options. The ones I use most often are shown in Figure 19.1 and Figure 19.2.

With **ps vg** (Figure 19.1) you can see not only CPU and memory consumption, but also paging activity and the status of processes. Use **ps -uUserId** to see processes of a specific user and **ps -tTTYname** to see processes associated with a specific terminal. Another way of looking at processes is **ps -eal** as shown in Figure 19.2.

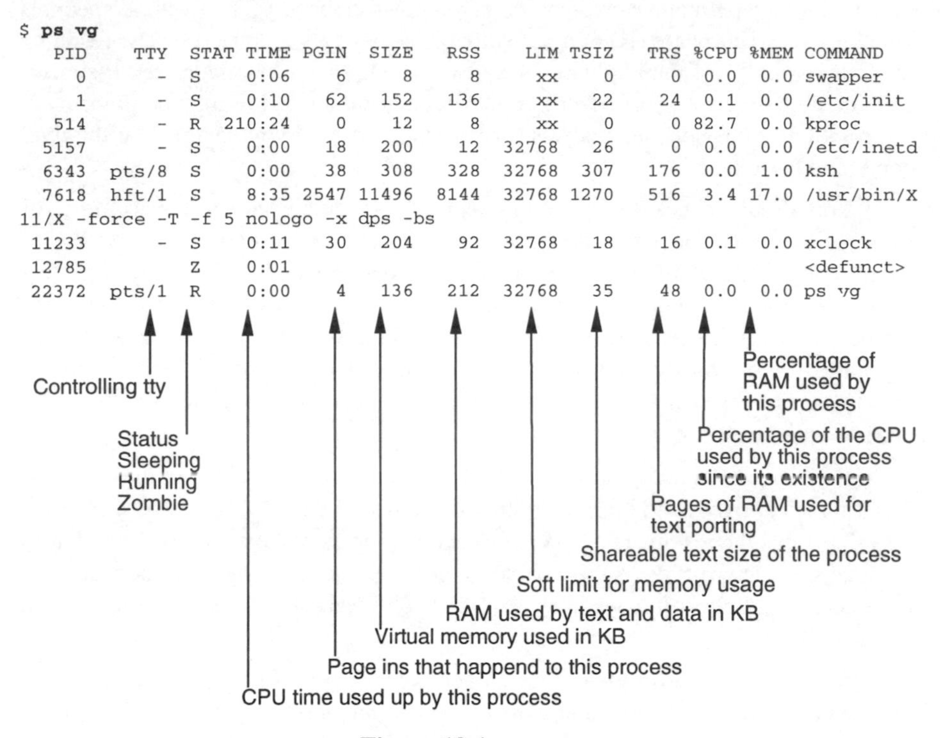

Figure 19.1 **ps vg**.

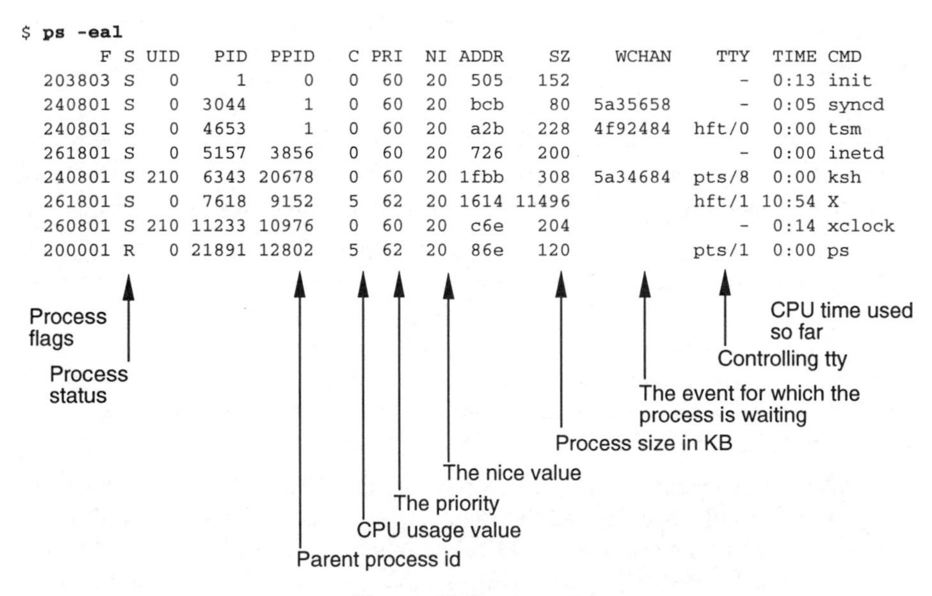

$ ps -eal
F S UID PID PPID C PRI NI ADDR SZ WCHAN TTY TIME CMD
203803 S 0 1 0 0 60 20 505 152 - 0:13 init
240801 S 0 3044 1 0 60 20 bcb 80 5a35658 - 0:05 syncd
240801 S 0 4653 1 0 60 20 a2b 228 4f92484 hft/0 0:00 tsm
261801 S 0 5157 3856 0 60 20 726 200 - 0:00 inetd
240801 S 210 6343 20678 0 60 20 1fbb 308 5a34684 pts/8 0:00 ksh
261801 S 0 7618 9152 5 62 20 1614 11496 hft/1 10:54 X
260801 S 210 11233 10976 0 60 20 c6e 204 - 0:14 xclock
200001 R 0 21891 12802 5 62 20 86e 120 pts/1 0:00 ps
Process flags
Process status
CPU time used so far
Controlling tty
The event for which the process is waiting
Process size in KB
The nice value
The priority
CPU usage value
Parent process id

Figure 19.2 **ps -eal**.

The flags (F) are documented in InfoExplorer. This bit field can tell you a lot about the state of a process when needed, but it takes some time to decipher it. The process status is the same as with the BSD version. The CPU usage value tells you whether the process is CPU intensive (high values) or not. It shows up non-zero only for active processes, as it is divided by 2 every time the scheduler runs. The lower the priority value shown here the higher the process's priority is. The average process usually runs at priority 60. The *nice* value is added to the process priority value to calculate the priority for the next run of the process. The higher it is, the lower the priority will be. The process size is the complete size of the process, not just the real RAM used currently. The WCHAN column identifies an event the process is waiting for if it is not running. Finally, the time column tells you how much CPU time the process consumed so far.

There are some processes in the process listing (depending on the *ps* options) that are not real processes but so-called kernel processes, a kind of subsystem in the kernel. Use **ps -k** to list them. Usually you will find one of these *kprocs* (on AIX 3 it has the PID 514, on AIX 4 it is 516), which eats up a great deal of CPU time. This is the wait process. Anytime the operating system has nothing to do, the wait process is run. The architecture of AIX requires that at least one process is always running. It has the lowest possible priority (127) so that it does not interfere with working processes.

The AIX 4 kernel supports threads, and *ps* has been changed to show them as well when using the *-m* flag together with *-o THREAD*. For most processes you will see only one thread as threaded applications are still rare.

19.1.3 *sar*

This is the system activity report. It can report on various aspects of the system performance. In its simplest form you can take a look at the CPU utilization over a specific interval. To see five samples of CPU usage with an interval of 1 s use **sar 1 5**.

```
AIX rhino 2 3 000043994100 06/06/93

12:49:17    %usr    %sys    %wio   %idle
12:49:18      11      32       0      57
12:49:20       7      49       0      44
12:49:22       9      38       0      54
12:49:24       6      36       0      58
12:49:25       9      34       0      57

Average        8      38       0      54
```

You can see the system was not very busy in the above *sar* output. It never had to wait for I/O and was idle more than half of the time. The next *sar* output comes from a *sar* run while running *make*:

```
13:01:18    %usr    %sys    %wio   %idle
13:01:20      61      33       4       2
13:01:22      46      40       5      10
```

```
13:01:24        59        38        0        4
13:01:26        58        40        0        2
13:01:29        28        44        0       28

Average         51        39        2        9
```

The system was busier then. It had to wait a little for the disks to deliver the data initially; later there was no waiting for the disk, presumably because all the files were already in memory and no further disk access was needed. At an even later stage all files were in memory and the system was fully busy on the CPU. The *wio* and *idle* columns showed zero.

Usually a UNIX system is not always completely busy, so if your *idle* column shows mostly zero while *wio* is also quite low you have a CPU-bound load on the system. This may be normal as some programs consume any available CPU time, no matter how fast a CPU you have. Interpreters are especially known for this. A system that does not sit idle is in itself not yet a problem. It is only if the responsiveness of the system is also poor that you know that it is probably too small for your needs or you have a badly behaved application. Use the *ps* command to see which programs use the most CPU time.

If you want to record CPU utilization over a long period of time then the report can be logged to a file with the *-o* flag and later redisplayed with the *-f* flag.

Showing the CPU utilization is not the only purpose of *sar*. When used with the *-A* flag it will give you more information: about I/O, context switches, forks, execs and more. Have a look at the man page for more details. If you want more than current snapshot information, I suggest activating the *sar* entries in the cron table of the *adm* id. Use **su - adm -c crontab -e** to remove the comment characters. All the *sar* analysis options can then be used on the generated data in /var/adm/sa/sa01.

Whereas *sar* gives you information about everything, there are some dedicated tools that sometimes will give you information in a more understandable way.

19.1.4 *vmstat*

The *vmstat* shows you memory and CPU utilization. It displays its output concurrently with the data acquisition process. To see the system activity for 5s with a 1-second reporting interval use **vmstat 1** 5 (Figure 19.3).

Beware that the first line of *vmstat* output always reports the statistics since system startup. The *procs* column tells you the number of runable and blocked processes. Blocked processes are waiting for some resource such as a disk transfer. The *memory* column informs you about allocated virtual and free RAM memory pages (each page is 4KB). You will notice that the free list (*fre*) is not necessarily what you think it should be. Pages are not given back to the free list until needed. In particular, when the system uses large amounts of memory for I/O caching, then these pages are given back only when the free list is getting empty. The sum of the *avm* and *fre* column do not need to add up to the real memory size of the machine.

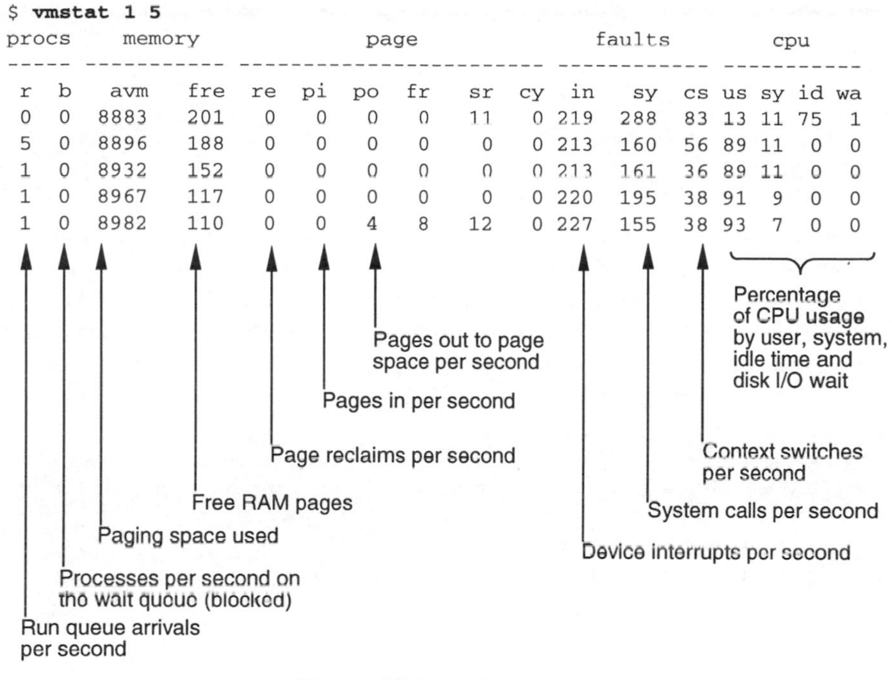

Figure 19.3 Using *vmstat*.

The *pi* column shows you how many pages were paged in within the current interval, this includes program pages paged in from the file system. *Po* shows the pages that are paged out (which should be a low number on a well balanced system) and *fr* the pages that are freed by the memory manager. If any of these numbers apart from *pi* which might be just program loading are not close to zero the there are processes fighting for memory. The *faults* columns tell you how many interrupts (*in*), system calls (*sy*) and context switches (*cs*) occurred per second during the sampling interval. Here you have to develop your own measures for normal. You should use *vmstat* on a nearly idle system and then later on a more loaded system so that you can see what is normal in your environment. Anything that deviates radically from your average might be a pointer to problems. The *cpu* columns show you the CPU utilization as seen previously with the *sar* command.

If the paging numbers are high and the *fre* column is close to zero then you should either reduce the number of memory-hungry programs or buy more memory. It is very likely that your system is memory constrained.

If the number of contexts switches is a magnitude higher than usual then you might have too many processes on the machine. However, it is more likely that some processes are competing for a resource and have reached a state of deadlock. If this happens you should see a number of processes in the blocked column. A possible solution to this problem might be to change the scheduler's time slices, as shown in Section 19.2.1.

You can also specify up to four physical volumes when running *vmstat*. This will then display the average block transfers per second in the interval for those disks, which is quite helpful when you want to correlate the memory statistics with I/O.

19.1.5 *svmon*

In /usr/lpp/bosperf on AIX 3 or when installing the performance agent on AIX 4 you will find another useful tool for checking the memory utilization of an AIX system: *svmon*. It offers a much more detailed view on the use of memory than *vmstat* or *sar*. If you run it without parameters it will tell you how much real memory and paging space is used as well as how much memory is used for mapping files and the number of pages that are pinned in memory (Figure 19.4).

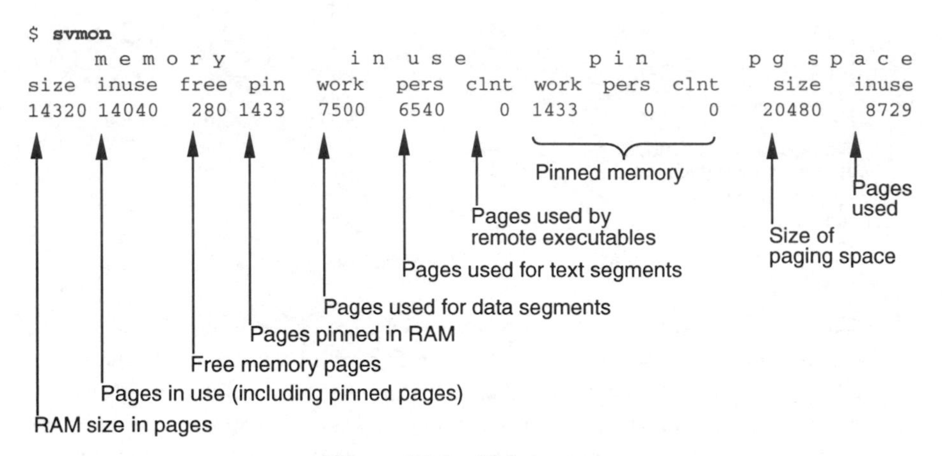

Figure 19.4 Using *svmon*.

This tells you that the system has 56MB of real memory (14320x4KB) and 14040 pages of it are used by the system. Of those 14040 pages, 7500 are used for working storage of programs including 1433 pinned pages. The remainder of the used memory, 6540 pages, is used to memory map files. Of the 20480 pages of paging space, only 8729 are used.

If you now want to have a closer look at the memory utilization you can run **svmon -P**. This will emit a list of processes and their memory use. For each process you see the segments that are used and how many pages are used in those segments. This is what you get for the *man* command for example:

```
Pid:   16125
Command:   man

Segid  Type  Description        Inuse  Pin  Pgspace  Address Range
 10a2  pers  /dev/hd2:23349         2    0        0  0..1
 7a2f  pers  /dev/hd2:68219         1    0        0  0..0
```

```
4809   work   shared library       1057    0    1759    0..1834 : 65471..65535
bb17   work   private                40    2      32    0..100 : 65403..65535
 aa1   pers   code,/dev/hd2:12442    42    0       0    0..41
```

The process has five segments in use: one for its code, one for its data, one for shared libraries, one for the message catalogue, and one for the data file. The numbers listed after the file system device are the i-node numbers of the files.

19.1.6 iostat

Another way to monitor disk I/O is via *iostat*, which also reports terminal I/O. Using *iostat* without any parameters gives you a summary of statistics since system start up. With the *-d* and *-t* options you can specify disk or terminal statistics only – the default is to display both. Using an interval and a count parameter will show you the accumulated statistics first and then statistics for the interval specified as in Figure 19.5 and Figure 19.6.

```
$ iostat -d 5 2
Disks:        % tm_act      Kbps      tps     Kb_read    Kb_wrtn
hdisk0           0.5         1.4      0.2     199971     240728
hdisk1           0.1         0.3      0.0      23993      77970
hdisk2           0.0         0.1      0.0      16691        188
cd0              0.0         0.0      0.0          0          0
hdisk0           0.0         0.0      0.0          0          0
hdisk1           0.0         0.0      0.0          0          0
hdisk2           0.0         0.0      0.0          0          0
cd0              0.0         0.0      0.0          0          0
```

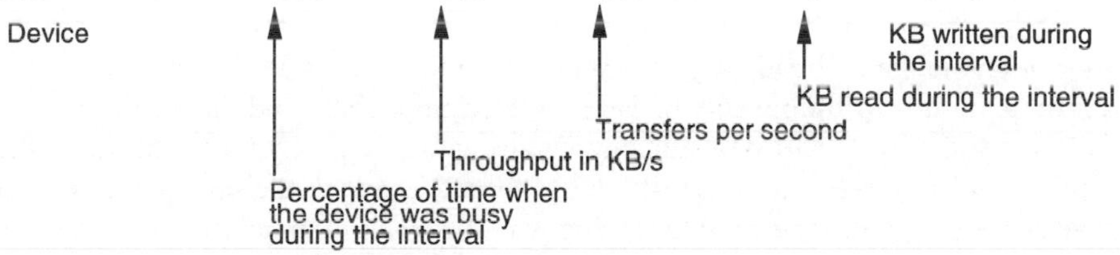

Figure 19.5 Using *iostat -d.*

The first interval is really the accumulated statistics since system start up; only the second interval corresponds to the disk I/O during the specified interval of 5 s. In the disk statistics you see the time each drive was active (*%tm_act*), the number of kilobytes transferred per second, the number of I/O requests per second as well as the number of kilobytes read or written. The I/O statistics reported by this command include all disk I/O including paging. If you have several disks and notice that one is much more active than the others, you should try to distribute your data better over the disks. The *filemon* command is very helpful for finding the exact files.

```
$ iostat -t 5 2
tty:   tin        tout   cpu:   % user     % sys      % idle     % iowait
       0.1        9.0           14.2       4.4        81.0       0.4
       0.0       32.3            0.2       0.6        99.2       0.0
```

Characters written to ttys and ptys

Characters received on ttys and ptys

Figure 19.6 Using *iostat -t*.

As with the disk statistics, the first entry is the statistics since system start up. The *tin* and *tout* columns show you the total number of characters read or written by all ttys and ptys. The percentage statistics in the tty row are the usual CPU use statistics plus the percentage of time wasted on waiting for I/O to complete.

19.1.7 *filemon*

Filemon is a tool to analyze file I/O in a running system. It gives you I/O statistics on file, file system and disk use. Like various other tools on AIX, it is a front end to the system trace facility. On AIX 4 it is part of the performance agent package. If you have an I/O-constrained program then you can use *filemon* to determine which file accesses take the most time. As it also records the use of paging space and the JFS log you get a very good picture on where the I/O really happens. You can use *filemon* to analyze disk use and use the results to improve the spread of your file systems over disks.

By default only activity that is started after starting *filemon* is recorded. The recording ends with the *trcstop* command. By using the *-u* flag you can start up *filemon* and include already active processes in the monitoring. For an initial test, run **filemon -o/tmp/fm.out -O all**. This will start up *filemon* and the resulting trace will be written to /tmp/fm.out, including all reports. Once you have finished the application use **trcstop** to terminate the trace and generate the output file. If you have already generated a trace file directly with the *trace* command you can use it as an input to *filemon* with the *-i* flag, which is very convenient if you want to monitor several aspects of a running application. If you want to see more than just the top 20 files in the report you have to use the *-v* option.

19.1.8 *fileplace*

Once you have found critical files with the *filemon* command you can check their placement and fragmentation with the *fileplace* utility, which is also part of the performance agent on AIX 4. Using **fileplace -v /unix** on my system reveals the following:

```
File: /unix  Size: 1626875 bytes  Vol: /dev/hd2 (4096 byte blks)
Inode: 10592  Mode: -r-xr-xr-x  Owner: root  Group: system

  Logical blocks
  --------------
  11044-11051                     8 blks,     32 KB,    2.0%
  11053-11283                   231 blks,    924 KB,   58.0%
  unallocated                     1 blk,       4 KB,    0.3%
  11284-11399                   116 blks,    464 KB,   29.1%
  13987-13990                     4 blks,     16 KB,    1.0%
  16564-16575                    12 blks,     48 KB,    3.0%
  169700-169715                  16 blks,     64 KB,    4.0%
  171331-171334                   4 blks,     16 KB,    1.0%
  171355-171360                   6 blks,     24 KB,    1.5%

  397 blocks over space of 160317:  space efficiency = 0.2%
  8 fragments out of 397 possible:  sequentiality = 98.2%
```

Although it is fragmented in only eight fragments, they are far apart (397 blocks in a range of 160317). Fortunately, the /unix file is not read that often by AIX. If you find a data file whose blocks are this far apart it is time to think about reorganization. Unfortunately, there is no command in AIX 3 that will do this for you. If you have a file system in which many files are fragmented it is necessary to back it up, remake the file system and restore the files to get rid of the fragmentation. On AIX 4 a new *defragfs* command can defragment the files in a file system. This assumes that your file system itself is not fragmented. A fragmented file system can be reorganized with the *reorgvg* command, as discussed on page 90.

If you use the *-p* flag then *filemon* will also display the physical blocks where the file resides, not just the logical blocks. The unallocated blocks above are an effect of sparse files in UNIX. Blocks that are compeltely empty in a file are not really allocated on disk, but if you read the empty blocks, you will read zeros. They are created by seeking several blocks past the end of the file and then writing to it. The space inbetween never gets allocated on disk.

19.1.9 *rmss*

Use *rmss* to simulate smaller memory sizes (part of the performance agent on AIX 4). Much simpler than removing memory boards the *rmss* command allows you to block memory so that the system cannot use it. Either set the simulated memory size in megabytes with **rmss -c size** or run a command under control of *rmss* with various memory sizes, as in **rmss -s startsize -f stopsize -d increment -n iterations command**. In this form the command is run several times for each memory size and the resulting run times as well as some page in information are written to rmss.out. If you prefer a different output file use the *-o* flag. When not using the iterative form of the command you should reset the memory size with **rmss -r** after your tests.

If you are developing software on a well-equipped machine you should always try to run your application in a memory-limited environment to determine the effects on your application before your customers see it.

Of course, you should use the previously mentioned monitoring tools while running your application in the memory-constrained environment so see the secondary bottlenecks that are created by memory starvation.

19.1.10 System trace

Should the high-level analysis tools fail to give you enough hints you can always resort to running *trace* directly, but be prepared to deal with copious output. The system trace records a flow of time-stamped system events that contain a very detailed view of the system activities. If you use just *trcrpt* to view the trace the amount of data is overwhelming. Unless you have a good understanding of how AIX or UNIX operating systems in general work you will have a hard time understanding the unfiltered trace report. Usually one uses other tools (*netpmon*, *filemon*) to analyze the trace or selects only a small number of trace hooks that are included in a system trace. Although *trace* records a huge number of events, the overall overhead is only 5% as *trace* only gathers data in a pinned memory buffer and any other processing is done after the trace proper.

The easiest way to run *trace* is via **smit trcstart**. Use the <F4> key to select the trace hooks of interest to you. You can run trace on an alternate, singular or circular buffer. This and the size of the trace buffer defines how much data you can gather before the trace terminates or data is overwritten. However, instead of setting a large default trace buffer by default you should first check your application's memory requirements. The trace buffer is in memory and will be flushed only to disk when full, depending on the type of trace mode selected. The default log file on AIX 3 is in the /usr file system, which is not a very good choice – use something like /var/tmp/trcfile instead.

After finishing the application you want to trace, use **trcstop** to terminate the trace and flush the buffers to the log file. You then have to run *trcrpt* to generate a human-readable file from the trace data. Depending on the *trcrpt* options you can have a more or less verbose output. I usually prefer to run *trcrpt* with the options *-O pid=on,ids=on,exec=on*, as these show the process ids associated with the events and the processes started during the trace.

If you want to use the system trace to gather your own statistics you can set up templates for the *rmap* utility to filter and analyze the trace data on AIX 3. It is no longer supported on AIX 4. The output of *rmap* will still be voluminous, but probably more meaningful for you. To be able to use *rmap* you need to do some work first. You have to set up a configuration file for *rmap* that describes what you want to analyze in the trace. See /usr/lpp/bosperf/samples/sample.conf for a sample configuration file. In addition to its configuration file, *rmap* also needs an input file that is generated with **trcrpt -r > trace.file** from the original trace data. Another file that is needed is a name address mapping table for the kernel, which can be generated with **trcnm > trace.namelist**. Those two files have to be named in *rmaps* configuration file. Now you can run *rmap*, using the configuration file as a parameter. The output will still be massive; if possible use a wide window to view it.

If you develop your own software and want to use the system trace for tracing your application without the overhead of *printfs*, there are facilities to do this. This is especially useful for drivers that are time constrained. Apart from the information in InfoExplorer you should check (*AIX Version 3.2 Writing a Device Driver*, 9) which has some examples of how to use trace hooks in your own application.

19.1.11 A simple trace frontend

Often, the above trace methods are overkill. When trying to find out why a program does not run I usually just want to see its file access attempts and a few more details. This happens sufficiently often to make it worthwhile doing it with a script like the following one. It traces either everything during the execution of the program or only the program itself, depending on the name with which it is called. Using *traceone* will result in a log that includes only the trace program and no other processes that are executing concurrently. Any other name will include other processes, which may be interesting in case of forks. The number of trace hooks checked is very small and should be sufficient for simple checks. It takes care of some AIX3/4 differences automatically.

```
#!/usr/bin/ksh
# traceone/traceall: A very simple trace frontend
# when called as traceone it reports only about the program
# being traced. With any other name (traceall) it reports about
# all processes that run while the traced program is executed.
# afx 12/94

ME=`basename $0`
if [[ $# -lt 1 ]] ; then
        echo "usage:\n$ME program [arguments ... ]"
        exit 123
fi

# Define the hooks you are interested in (Hint: check smit trace)
FILE_HOOKS="107,12E,130,15B,163,19C"
SYSCALL_HOOKS="101"
KERNEL_HOOKS="134,135,139"
HOOKS="$FILE_HOOKS,$SYSCALL_HOOKS,$KERNEL_HOOKS"

# Options for trace formatting
REPORT_OPTS="ids=off,exec=on,pid=on,svc=on,pagesize=0,timestamp=3"

# AIX 3 and AIX 4 react slightly different.
# AIX 3 does not understand the -x flag on trcrpt
# AIX 3 seems to ignore the ids=off option.
AIXVERSION=`uname -v`
```

```
if [[ $AIXVERSION -eq 3 ]] ; then
      REPORT_FLAGS="-v"
else
      REPORT_FLAGS="-v -x"
fi

# We only want to see our program not tons of other junk
WANTED=`basename $1`

logfile=/tmp/$ME.$WANTED.out

# now start the trace
trace -a -d -j $HOOKS
trcon
$*
trcstop

# Keep older trace files just in case
[[ -f $logfile ]] && mv $logfile $logfile.$$

if [[ "$ME" = "traceone" ]] ; then
      trcrpt $REPORT_FLAGS -O $REPORT_OPTS > $logfile.tmp
      if [[ $AIXVERSION -eq 3 ]]
      then
            (head -12 $logfile.tmp
            egrep "^[0-9][0-9][0-9] $WANTED" $logfile.tmp ) > $logfile
      else
            (head -12 $logfile.tmp
            egrep "^$WANTED" $logfile.tmp ) > $logfile
      fi
      rm $logfile.tmp
else
      trcrpt $REPORT_FLAGS -O $REPORT_OPTS | egrep -v "^trace" >
$logfile
fi

echo "Check $logfile for the trace report"
```

The above script can be easily adapted to specific traces by setting the correct trace hooks. You could, for example, set only the networking-related hooks when trying to monitor a program that has communications problems.

19.1.12 Tracing system calls on AIX 4

AIX 4 has a new command that comes with the performance toolbox to trace only system calls. In contrast to the other low-level trace tools, this command does not rely on the system trace facility. Either you can trace a single program with **syscalls -x yourprogram** or you can start the trace with **syscalls -start** and then see either statistics with **syscalls -c** or a time-stamped trace of the system calls with **syscalls**

-t. To stop the trace and print a summary use **syscalls -stop**. Use the *-o* flag to direct the lengthy output to a file.

19.1.13 Using the performance diagnostic tool on AIX 4

To start the PDT use **/usr/sbin/perf/diag_tool/pdt_config**. Define a mail address where you want the reports to arrive, set a severity level (I suggest 2 initially) and start the logging. This will put a few entries in the crontab of *adm*. During the normal working week, two data collection processes will be run. And on every weekend a weekly summary will be generated. You will need to tell PDT about hosts, files and directories that it should monitor. From there on the process usually does not need any further attention: simply check the generated reports for things that you see as critical. PDT checks for unbalanced resource usage, for files that grow too much, changes in the workload, hot items in the error log and a few more items.

You need to tell PDT about the files and directories it should monitor by adding them to /var/perf/cfg/diag_tool/.files. I suggest the following initial list:

```
/var/adm/
/var/spool/qdaemon/
/tmp/
/var/tmp/
/etc/
/dev/
```

If you are dependent on other hosts on the network, then creating /var/perf/cfg/diag_tool/.nodes with the host names will instruct PDT to monitor their *ping* response times.

PDT needs to hold a history of collected data for trend analysis. By default the old records are kept for 35 days. Should this be too long or to short for you, you can change the file /var/perf/cfg/diag_tool/.retention.list to reflect your needs.

To get a report directly you can use **/usr/sbin/perf/diag_tool/pdt_report**, which will send a current report to *stdout*. This works only after PDT has run at least once.

19.2 System tuning methods

19.2.1 The scheduler

The AIX scheduler can be adjusted by the *schedtune* program. You might need to compile it first on AIX 3, where it can be found in /usr/lpp/bos/samples. On AIX 4 check /usr/samples/kernel. The AIX 4 version does not contain the necessary includes, so you have to live with the executable provided. With *schedtune* you can change scheduler parameters at runtime, and these changes will be cleared at the next reboot. If you find useful settings for your system then run *schedtune* in rc.local.

You can change the average time slice of the scheduler via the *-tN* parameter. The system uses 0 for N as the default on AIX 3; on AIX 4 it is 1. Setting N to any other value will change the maximum number of clock ticks between dispatches of processes. Usually the scheduler dispatches processes once per clock interrupt (roughly every 10ms), so the maximum time a process can be active before the dispatcher tries to dispatch another one is 10ms. With some applications this might lead to poor throughput when several processes wait for a shared resource and the one that has it does not have enough time to do its job and release it again. Another example of where it might help is in the case of heavy interactive use of a database. The user's I/O will usually give them a more favored priority so that the database cannot complete its work. This again results in a sluggish user interaction.

Other parameters of *schedtune* allow you to set the delay before retrying a failed *fork()*, to set the delay after thrashing before a process gets into the run queue again and to set how long a process has to be able to run before being suspended again.

The rule of thumb for adjusting the values is to try and experiment while a real workload is executed: their effects are very much application dependent. Using the wrong values can make your system very slow – remember to use **schedtune -D** to get back to the system defaults when you are stuck.

19.2.2 The memory manager

In */usr/lpp/bos/samples* you can find the source to the *vmtune* command on AIX 3. On AIX 4 check /usr/samples/kernel for the *vmtune* executable. This allows you to change the characteristics of the virtual memory manager (VMM) by modifying the parameters for the page replacement algorithm. Like *schedtune*, *vmtune* is a command that one should not play around with unless one knows what is really going on. It directly modifies the behavior of the virtual memory manager and the defaults are usually OK for most applications. For the few exceptional case you can set the following parameters:

minfree (*-f*) The minimum number of free pages. If the number of pages drops below this limit then the VMM will try to steal pages.

maxfree (*-F*) The maximum number of free pages at which the VMM will steal memory.

minperm (*-p*) The minimum number of pages (in percent of available real memory) available for permanent pages (file caching). When this limit is reached the VMM starts to steal pages from computational memory.

maxperm (*-P*) The maximum number of pages (in percent of available real memory) that can be used to map persistent storage into memory. Lowering this value will favor computational memory.

minpgahead (*-r*) The minimum number of pages to read ahead when accessing persistent storage (file systems).

maxpgahead (*-R*) The maximum number of pages to read ahead when accessing persistent storage (file systems).

Using *vmtune* without any of the above options will show you the current values. As *vmtune* has no defaults option you should record them first.

When would you want to change the parameters for the VMM? If you run a modern database application the user's private segments may be quite large. When a large number of users are running this application the system might seem to react sluggishly, even though the CPU is not fully busy but there is page in activity. Reducing *maxperm* would tell the VMM to steal pages preferably from persistent storage (another term for data in file systems) and not from computational memory. This will, of course, have a negative effect on file access as the number of pages available for caching will be reduced. Increasing *minperm*, in contrast, would favor caching of permanent storage, which is rarely desired.

If you have a very bursty workload then you might want to adapt *minfree* and *maxfree*. Sudden requests for memory that cannot be handled with the small minimum free list (the default on a 64 MB system is 120) will cause too much activity of the VMM as it needs to steal pages until *maxfree* is reached. Increasing *minfree* and *maxfree* might help in this case.

Changing *minpgahead* and *maxpgahead* to lower values could be beneficial when the sequentiality of the files read by the prime application is very low. Enlarging them further might be too costly for most file access however.

19.2.3 The disk I/O subsystem

Optimization of disk access

After checking the results from *filemon* and *fileplace* you might want to reorganize your disk layout. As mentioned already on page 71, you should try to spread the disk activity over as many disks and SCSI adapters as possible for optimum performance.

If you have several large files that are accessed by the same application, try to keep them on separate disks. Use separate disks for the application and the application data. Try to spread your paging space over several disks and avoid multiple paging spaces on one disk. On AIX 4 consider striping. Putting /var and /tmp on a separate disk from your data will help if you have an application that uses these file systems for temporary files. You might want to put the log logical volume for the logical volumes of a volume group on a separate disk from the data logical volumes to reduce the overhead of the journal. You might even consider buying a third party solid state disk for this if you are performing many writes to the disk.

Optimizing file caching

The only thing you can do to optimize the file cache on AIX is to buy more memory. Since AIX uses as much memory as available (in fact up to 80% of the real memory) for mapping files to memory, so the only way of increasing the cache for files is to buy more memory. Of course, you could try to steal memory from the working storage of the rest of the system by using *vmtune*, but this would probably hurt the overall performance even more.

High I/O load versus interactive response

You should investigate in I/O pacing when you have a high I/O load on the system together with interactive use. Large batch jobs with a lot of I/O or routine copying of large files may queue up a lot of data for the disk. When you, as an interactive user, also want to access this disk you must wait until those requests are satisfied. Setting the high- and low-water marks for the I/O buffers will slightly slow those large I/O jobs and greatly improve the interactive feel of the system.

You can influence the disk I/O pacing of the system by changing the *maxpout* and *minpout* parameters of the *sys0* device (use **smit chgsys** or *chdev*). These values control the number of outstanding page writes to an individual file. Any process that tries to write to a file that already has the high-water mark or more pages queued up for a file will be put to sleep. It will be awakened when the number of writes in the queue again falls below the low-water mark. A page in this context is a standard 4KB page. The default setting is off, and both values are set to zero. You can change these values in SMIT when you run **smit chgsys**.

A good initial recommendation for a fair balance is 8 for *minpout* and 17 for *maxpout*. If you want to favor interactive I/O even further you might try using *maxpout=9* and *minpout=6* Of course, you need to experiment with these values to adjust them to your environment. One should use a value of 4*x+1 for *maxpout* because an asynchronous write occurs on the fifth page write request. Applications that do write with buffers greater than 4KB are less suspect to the control of I/O pacing.

19.2.4 ttys

The serial ports that are available for the RS/6000 allow a wide range of connectivity options, but they are not necessarily optimized for all of them. Most of the add on cards are assumed to handle real terminals with interactive users. Using them for PostScript printers or high-speed data acquisition requires different defaults. Here are a few factors that will influence the performance and the CPU load of the ttys:

- If possible do not use *echo* to process the input when running raw mode applications. Use **stty -echo < /dev/ttyX** to turn it off or set *-echo* permanently when configuring the port with SMIT.

- If output translations are not needed for raw mode applications or file transfers, turn off *opost* with **stty -opost < /dev/ttyX** or set *-opost* permanently when configuring the port with SMIT.
- Increasing the *vmin* time of a tty (not available on the native ports) will reduce the CPU use for large data transfers. The default is 4, but can be set up to a maximum of 255, which should be used for applications that transfer large amounts of data. This is the minimum number of bytes that should be received when a read is successful.
- Setting *vtime* (not available on the native serial ports) to a value greater than zero will prevent eternal blocks on read. On the 128-port adapter it should be set to zero to offload the POSIX line discipline to the adapter, freeing the CPU from this task.

19.3 Analyzing the network

AIX comes with a suite of utilities that help you with this task. You should familiarize yourself with them and use them regularly on different systems so that you get a feel for what is normal and what is not. If you look only at pathological cases and never see a healthy system you might misinterpret the data from these tools.

When working with a network, the number of potential troublespots rises dramatically. The networking hardware itself and the interaction between various protocols and processes can be additional problem areas. Here are a number of tools that help you to analyze what might have gone wrong where:

errpt	Use this first to check for hardware problems. It is also discussed in Section 19.1.1.
ping	See if you can reach the remote machine.
traceroute	Find out where the connection is broken.
host	Does name service work?
nslookup	Where is the problem in the name service?
spray	Allows you to test UDP broadcasts.
rup	Shows you machines that are on-line locally.
netstat	See various statistics and counters.
ifconfig	See the state of an interface.
arp	Checks and modifies the ARP cache.
iptrace & ipreport	Traces IP packets to and from a host.
tcpdump	Another packet-tracing tool available on AIX 4.
rpcinfo	Checks whether certain RPC services are available.
trace	Traces parts of the system.
nfsstat	Displays NFS statistics.

netpmon Analyzes network use by process.
ndb Undocumented network debugger to analyze sockets and *mbufs*.

The following sections will show you how to use these tools and what you can learn from their output.

19.3.1 *errpt*

The *errpt* command is discussed in Section 19.1.1. It rarely gives you direct hints on network problems unless you have hardware trouble. Excessive token ring errors are often generated by machines with the wrong ring speed: TOK_BEACON2 and TOK_ESERR are the error labels that you would probably see in this case. In addition, you may find Ethernet errors when someone uses the wrong terminators on the yellow wire or the wrong type of coaxial cable has been used for thin-wire Ethernet connections. On X.25 connections you may sometimes see some entries for reset packets, but depending on the quality of your X.25 network supplier, they may be normal.

If the errors in the error report indicate hardware problems you should run the *diag* command to determine if hardware problems really exist. My experience has been that this rarely occurs and that most of the errors are due to some form of misconfiguration. My favorite case is plugging a 4MB machine into a 16MB ring. This will slow the network to a crawl.

19.3.2 *ping*

Not only can *ping* be used to see if you can contact a remote machine, it also has some options that help you to see in more detail what is going on. Should you have trouble with name service use the *-n* option to avoid name resolution. In this case *ping* will use only numbers.

Apart from just trying to *ping* an address or a host name you can see the route a packet has traveled by using the *-R* option. This works only if the destination is reachable. Another limitation is the space in the packet for the information gathered by the record route option. Only nine hops can be stored, so the *-R* option is not very useful when checking distant systems. Using *ping* in this way will record all interfaces passed both ways so that you get two entries for each router in between.

The *ping -R* output in Figure 19.7 shows the path from rhino via the router cabernet, which has two interfaces, to the machine baroloe and back. Although only three machines are involved there are already six entries.

```
# ping -R baroloe -c 1
PING baroloe: (9.23.2.12): 0 data bytes
8 bytes from 9.23.2.12: icmp_seq=0 ttl=253
RR:      cabernetg (9.23.13.7)
         cabernete (9.23.2.7)
         baroloe (9.23.2.12)
         cabernete (9.23.2.7)
         cabernetg (9.23.13.7)
         rhino (9.23.13.11)

----baroloe.ak.munich.ibm.com PING Statistics----
1 packets transmitted, 1 packets received, 0% packet loss
```

Figure 19.7 Using *ping -R*.

Not all systems support the record route option of *ping*. By default, *ping* sends packets until interrupted by <CTRL-C>. You can limit the number of packets sent with the *-c* option, which makes *ping* more usable in shell scripts for example.

If you have trouble with truncated packets because of broken fragmentation you can find the troublespot by specifying a packet size on the *ping* command line. Usually the packets that *ping* sends are only 64 bytes long. This is much smaller than the MTU sizes that are typically in use. Try setting the packet size to something that is equal to your MTU size (1500 or 4096 for example) if you think you have a problem here. Then *ping* all points in the connection and see where it does not return.

When checking connections with *ping* you should bear in mind that *ping* packets are ICMP packets. Normal TCP/IP connections use UDP or TCP packets. This might trigger different behaviors at packet-filtering routers that are used for firewalls for example.

On older systems (for example on AIX 3.1) it is possible to *ping* broadcast addresses. AIX 3.2 does not respond to broadcast ICMP messages. This is according to the recommendations in the RFCs, but it might be confusing for people who are used to a different behavior. On AIX 4 the response to broadcast *pings* can be turned back on with **no -obcastping=1**. For some types of tests the *rup* command may be used instead, but this assumes that the *rstat* daemon is available on the remote systems.

Ping -f allows testing with high packet frequencies. It floods the network with packets without delay and has a nice visual feedback for dropped packets. For each packet sent a dot is printed. For each packet received a backspace is sent to the terminal. The more dots you see, the more packets are dropped. As this puts some stress on the network the *-f* option is accessible only by root.

19.3.3 *traceroute*

Traceroute is the ultimate route-checking tool. In most cases it allows you to see exactly where the path is broken.

Traceroute sets a small ttl (time to live) and sends packets to an invalid port number. The ttl value is increased after the three packets that get sent to a gateway. When a gateway receives the packet it decrements the ttl. When the ttl reaches zero the packet is not forwarded and an ICMP "Time Exceeded" message is sent back to the originating machine. *Traceroute* displays one line for each gateway from which it receives such messages. As three packets are sent per gateway, there should be three times at the end of the line. The final destination will send back an ICMP "Unreachable Port" message because *traceroute* uses invalid port numbers to get exactly this message. With that message *traceroute* knows it has reached the destination. *Traceroute* records interfaces only one way: compare the *traceroute* output in Figure 19.8 with the *ping -R* output in Figure 19.7.

```
# traceroute baroloe
traceroute to baroloe (9.23.2.12), 30 hops max, 40 byte packets
 1  cabernetg (9.23.13.7)  58 ms  37 ms  41 ms
 2  caberneti (9.23.13.8)  42 ms  41 ms  43 ms
 3  baroloe (9.23.2.12)  43 ms  42 ms  42 ms
```

Figure 19.8 Using *traceroute.*

In contrast to the limit of nine entries in the record route table of *ping -R*, the default number of hops that *traceroute* can follow is 30. This could be extended even further with the *-m* option.

When you see only '*' instead of responses, then you have hit a system that is down or a system that does not support *traceroute*, such as SNALINKs on older VM TCP/IP systems. Exclamation marks usually point to routing loops in a gateway.

As implementations of TCP/IP vary greatly the exact output of *traceroute* is not necessarily an exact display of the problem. The only thing you can be sure of is that the machine shown properly last in the list should be examined for its routing to the destination. This assumes that the display of *traceroute* has shown you a correct route so far.

As *traceroute* is UDP based, it is handled quite different from *ping* through gateways. Be sure to use both if you are in doubt. If you have trouble with name service use the *-n* option to avoid name look ups.

19.3.4 *host*

The quickest check for a working name resolution is to compare the output of **host ip-address** and **host host-name**. If they differ your name service is broken.

AIX 3.2 and 4.1 up to 4.1.3 have only a very simple version of the *host* command. AIX 4.1.4 finally has the *host* command from BIND 4.9.3. It is available under the name *hostnew*. For many purposes it is as good as *nslookup*. Try the *-a* option which will list all DNS resource records and if you want even more information add the *-n* option. See Figure 7.9 and Figure 7.10.

19.3.5 *nslookup*

There are plenty of things that you cannot check with the *host* command but can with *nslookup*. With it you can query everything that a name server knows.

Use **set type=any** to see more than just the address mapping or **set type=mx** to see mail exchange records. The *ls* command allows you to list complete domains, the *server* command to query specific servers and the debug options to see how your queries are processed. Use **set debug** and **set d2** to follow the query process. When trying to list a domain and specific servers, use the *server* command to set the name server that *nslookup* uses. It defaults to the server listed in /etc/resolv.conf.

Owing to the quirks of DNS, the *nslookup* command needs a different syntax for reverse name resolution checks of networks. It wants addresses in the form used to specify them in the name server configuration. To query the network 193.12.14, for example, you would use 14.12.193.in-addr.arpa instead of the address written in the usual way. This syntax is only needed for network queries. Simple reverse name resolution works as expected.

If you use *nslookup* often with the same options then setting them in ~/.nslookuprc might be useful – I usually have *set type=any* in there.

When checking a local server it might be easier to see what is wrong by dumping the server's database to /var/tmp/named_dump.db (use **kill -INT `cat /etc/named.pid`**). If you see entries with duplicate domain names in the dump then there is a terminating dot missing for this entry in the configuration file.

19.3.6 *spray*

The *spray* command works in a similar way to the *ping -f* command. It sends out packets as fast as it can and then displays statistics about the process. In contrast to *ping*, it uses RPC messages (in UDP packets) and not ICMP packets by default. It needs an RPC daemon to collect the packets at the other machine (*sprayd*). With the *-i* option it can use ICMP messages instead of RPCs.

As the RPC calls go to a higher level than ICMP messages, a comparison of both will tell you how much overhead the remote system has when reacting to RPC calls. Compare the two examples in Figure 19.9.

```
# spray ouzo
sending 1162 packets of lnth 86 to ouzo ...

        789 packets (67.900%) dropped by ouzo
        389 packets/sec, 33514 bytes/sec
# spray -i ouzo
sending 1162 packets of lnth 86 to ouzo ...

        36 packets (3.098%) dropped by ouzo
        770 packets/sec, 66233 bytes/sec
```

Figure 19.9 Comparing *spray* with RPC and ICMP packets.

You can see that there are fewer ICMP packets dropped than RPC packets. The remote machine cannot respond fast enough to the RPC requests.

The above test is quite unrealistic however. RPC messages are usually not generated as fast as *spray* does it without any delay in between. So far I have found no system that does not drop packets when *spray* is used to generate RPC messages without a delay. Adding a delay of only 1 ms between RPC calls makes a big difference (Figure 19.10).

```
$ spray ouzo
sending 1162 packets of lnth 86 to ouzo ...

        853 packets (73.408%) dropped by ouzo
        28 packets/sec, 2457 bytes/sec
$ spray ouzo -d 1
sending 1162 packets of lnth 86 to ouzo ...

        no packets dropped by ouzo
        161 packets/sec, 13907 bytes/sec
```

Figure 19.10 Using *spray* with a delay.

A normal machine should be able to handle *spray* with a delay of 1 ms without dropping any packets. If it still drops packets then either the queues for TCP/IP or the device drivers are too small, the machine is too slow or too loaded or there are problems on gateways in between the systems.

Many network parameters have an influence. If the sending machine is faster than the remote, high drop rates can easily result. Use *spray* both ways to see the differences. Check *netstat -i* on the machines for input and output errors and use the other tools described in this chapter for further analysis.

Use the *-l* parameter to set different packet lengths when going across a gateway to determine the effects of fragmentation and MTU. Figure 19.11 shows the result of going via Ethernet (MTU 1500) to a remote Token-Ring (MTU 4096).

It can be seen that fragmentation takes up enough time to drop packets. If you do not specify a count with the length *spray* will send as many packets as necessary to transfer 100KB in total. Thus *spray* sent only 25 and 100 packets in the example in Figure 19.11.

```
$ spray mickeymouse -d 1 -l 4000
sending 25 packets of lnth 4000 to mickeymouse ...

        7 packets (28.000%) dropped by mickeymouse
        1 packets/sec, 7137 bytes/sec
$ spray mickeymouse -d 1 -l 1000
sending 100 packets of lnth 1002 to mickeymouse ...

        no packets dropped by mickeymouse
        434 packets/sec, 435075 bytes/sec
```

Figure 19.11 Running *spray* over a gateway.

19.3.7 *rup*

Rup is a simple command that queries other hosts for their uptime and load average. It does this via RPC broadcasts on all interfaces if no host is specified. Any machine that should reply to a *rup* query needs the *rstatd* daemon configured in /etc/inetd.conf. It is useful to find out whether the name service and the interfaces work in one command. In addition, it indicates how long the machines have been on line and whether they are busy.

If you see lines without host names but hexadecimal host numbers then you know you have a name service problem. If you know that a host is reachable directly via two different interfaces and you do not see two lines in the *rup* output for this host then one of the interfaces on this machine or on the remote machine has problems.

19.3.8 *netstat*

Netstat shows statistics, sockets and routing tables. Its various invocations give you the maximum possible information about the network configuration. On all of its options that involve network addresses or host names you can specify the *-n* option to avoid name look up should you have trouble with name service. I make it a habit always to use the *-n* option. In particular, when displaying routing tables, it is more meaningful as you get a clearer picture with numbers than with names.

netstat -a

This displays the state of all sockets. To see only the active internet sockets you can further add *-f inet* to the commandline. Figure 19.12 shows an abridged sample.

```
$ netstat -af inet
Active Internet connections (including servers)
Proto Recv-Q Send-Q  Local Address      Foreign Address     (state)
tcp        0      0  barolo.2278        chablis.domain    TIME_WAIT
tcp        0      2  barolo.login       chablis.1023     ESTABLISHED
tcp        0      0  barolo.ftp-data    chablis.1030     ESTABLISHED
tcp        0      0  barolo.ftp         chablis.1029      CLOSE_WAIT
tcp        0      0  *.6000             *.*                   LISTEN
tcp        0      0  *.1027             *.*                   LISTEN
tcp        0      0  barolo.1600        *.*                   LISTEN
tcp        0      0  *.writesrv         *.*                   LISTEN
tcp        0      0  *.fontserv         *.*                   LISTEN
tcp        0      0  *.telnet           *.*                   LISTEN
tcp        0      0  *.ftp              *.*                   LISTEN
udp        0      0  *.ntalk            *.*
udp        0      0  *.1088             *.*
udp        0      0  *.1087             *.*
udp        0      0  *.tftp             *.*
```

Figure 19.12 Sample **netstat -af inet** output.

Recv-Q and *Send-Q* show you whether there is data in the socket buffers to be delivered. The port number or the corresponding name from /etc/services is appended to the machine names in the address field. Services that have * as a source or a destination are listening servers. The last field shows the current status of the socket:

LISTEN The endpoint has been opened locally and is waiting for a connection request. This is typical of TCP-based servers that are not started with *inetd*.

SYN_SENT The endpoint has been opened and has sent a connection open request to a remote endpoint.

SYN_RCVD The endpoint has both received and sent connection open requests and is now waiting for a confirming ACK.

ESTABLISHED A connection is established and data can flow in either direction. This is the normal state of a connection.

FIN_WAIT_1 Received a close from the local user and is waiting either for a close request (FIN) from the remote endpoint or an ACK of the FIN request already sent.

FIN_WAIT_2 Waiting for a FIN from the remote endpoint.

CLOSE_WAIT A connection close (FIN) request has been sent from the remote endpoint and is waiting for a corresponding close from the local user. Data from the local user will still be sent over the connection.

LAST_ACK Sent and received a connection close, ACKed the remote close (FIN), and waiting for the last ACK from the remote endpoint.

CLOSING Waiting for the ACK from the remote endpoint.

TIME_WAIT Waiting a time interval to ensure that the remote endpoint has received the ACK of its close request.

CLOSED No connection, but the endpoint exists (probably from a UDP open).

netstat -i

This invocation of *netstat* (Figure 19.13) tells you how many packets have been transmitted over an interface so far as well as the number of accumulated errors. It also shows you the MTU that is really configured for an interface. Using *lsattr* on the interface might not give you the correct result as it takes the value out of the ODM, which does not necessarily need to be in synch with the device as ODM attributes can be set for the next reboot.

```
$ netstat -i
Name  Mtu   Network  Address    Ipkts  Ierrs Opkts  Oerrs Coll
lo0   1536  <Link>               57958     0  57958     0    0
lo0   1536  127     localhost    57958     0  57958     0    0
en0   1500  <Link>             1522347     0 148655     0    0
en0   1500  9.23.2  baroloc    1522347     0 148655     0    0
tr0   4096  <Link>              544157     0 313149     0    0
tr0   4096  9.23.4  barolo      544157     0 313149     0    0
```

Figure 19.13 Using **netstat -i**.

The collision column is always zero on AIX 3 because the Ethernet device driver does not report the collision statistics back to the system. If you find any errors here, use the other options of *netstat* to find out more about the probable causes. Possible reasons for input errors are:

- Bad packets because of screwed up routers or hardware problems.
- Bad checksums, which might point to a host sending corrupted data.
- Not enough space on the driver's input queue to keep up with the number of packets coming from the network.

Possible reasons for output errors are:

- The driver is not capable of putting the packets out to the network as quickly as it receives them from IP.
- There are hardware errors on the net.

netstat -I

Use **netstat -I interface interval** for a concurrent display of packet and error counts for a specific interface. When using the *-I* option (Figure 19.14), the first line gives the accumulated numbers and the subsequent lines show the numbers for the specified interval.

```
$ netstat -I tr0 1
   input     (tr0)       output           input    (Total)      output
 packets  errs  packets  errs colls  packets errs  packets  errs colls
  544310     0   315546     0     0  2125437    0   522426     0     0
       4     0      538     0     0        6    0      539     0     0
       0     0      560     0     0        3    0      561     0     0
       1     0       69     0     0        2    0       70     0     0
       0     0        0     0     0        1    0        1     0     0
^C
```

Figure 19.14 Using **netstat -I**.

netstat -m

Netstat -m reveals memory statistics about the use of the *mbufs*. This command has quite different output on AIX 3 and AIX 4 as the network buffer memory management has been greatly changed. The AIX 4 output is shown in Figure 19.15 and the AIX 3 output in Figure 19.16.

Although the AIX 3 *mbuf* pool has already been used for more than just socket buffers, the output of **netstat -m** never really showed it. As shown in Figure 19.15 you get a very detailed statistic on AIX 4. In addition, the traditional *mbuf* tuning is no longer needed since AIX 4 has a self-tuning *mbuf* pool. The only thing you can do is change the size of the pool and turn on some trace hooks.

On AIX 3 (Figure 19.16), the number of used pages (clusters) should not approach the number of mapped pages too closely or else the *mbuf* manager *netm* needs to change the allocation, and this will cost CPU time. The mapped pages line tells you how many clusters are in use and how many clusters are allocated in the pool at any moment (*netstat* refers to clusters as mapped pages).

```
# netstat -m
11 mbufs in use:
0 mbuf cluster pages in use
2 Kbytes allocated to mbufs
0 requests for mbufs denied
0 calls to protocol drain routines

Kernel malloc statistics:

By size        inuse    calls failed    free   hiwat   freed
32               406     1344      0     362     640       0
64                48      182      0      16     320       0
128              130     2840      0      30     160       0
256              146   149665      0      46     384       0
512               13     3777      0      19      40       0
1024               3      704      0       5      20       0
2048               0      961      0       2      10       0
4096               2     1959      0       7     120       0
16384              1       33      0      14      24       7

By type        inuse    calls failed  memuse  memmax    mapb
mbuf              13   148755      0    3328    9216       0
mcluster           0     5364      0       0   16384       0
socket           128      784      0   18656   20384       0
pcb               91      453      0   14400   16320       0
routetbl           5        5      0     896     896       0
ifaddr             5        5      0     576     576       0
mblk              54     2409      0    9344   10112       0
mblkdata           3     2358      0    1536    8704       0
strhead           11       37      0    3232    5952       0
strqueue          21       68      0    5376    9984       0
strmodsw          15       15      0     960     960       0
strsyncq          27      168      0    2880    5248       0
streams          369      990      0   20928   33312       0
kernel table       2        2      0   40960   40960       0
temp               8       67      0    6400  524288       0
```

Figure 19.15 Checking *mbufs* with **netstat -m** on AIX 4.

```
$ netstat -m
278 mbufs in use:
        29 mbufs allocated to data
        3 mbufs allocated to packet headers
        93 mbufs allocated to socket structures
        122 mbufs allocated to protocol control blocks
        17 mbufs allocated to routing table entries
        11 mbufs allocated to socket names and addresses
        3 mbufs allocated to interface addresses
16/104 mapped pages in use
485 Kbytes allocated to network (27% in use)
0 requests for memory denied
0 requests for memory delayed
0 calls to protocol drain routines
```

Figure 19.16 Checking *mbufs* with **netstat -m** on AIX 3.

Memory allocated to the network should not be above 90%. If you are too close to the limit you might not have enough memory to respond to peak requests. Increase the *mbuf* space (*thewall*) if you are getting close to or over 90%.

If 'requests for memory denied' is not zero either you do not have enough memory or the pool is extremely fragmented and the *mbuf* manager *netm* is working hard to allocate memory. You should increase the memory pool (*thewall*) and perhaps pretune the *mbuf* pool by adjusting *lowmbuf*, *lowclust* and *mb_cl_hiwat* as described in InfoExplorer. Usually every request that is denied results in a dropped packet.

netstat -r

The routing table is displayed with this option. I suggest always using *netstat -rn* to avoid name service problems and to achieve a better understanding of the network addresses involved.

More is displayed than just the IP routing table, but the only useful information for us at the moment are the entries in the IP routing table (Figure 19.17).

```
$ netstat -rn
Routing tables
Destination     Gateway         Flags  Refcnt Use      Interface
...
default         9.23.2.24       UG          0     1088  en0
9.23.2          9.23.2.12       U           3    36796  en0
9.23.3          9.23.2.253      UG          0     6137  en0
9.23.4          9.23.4.120      U           7   315481  tr0
9.23.10         9.23.4.198      UG          0        0  tr0
9               9.23.2.9        UG          0        0  en0
9.23.13         9.23.2.7        UG          3    95305  en0
127             127.0.0.1       U           1        5  lo0
127.0.0.1       127.0.0.1       UH          2    56360  lo0
...
```

Figure 19.17 Checking the routing table with **netstat -rn**.

The lines with only a U (up) flag refer to local interfaces, whereas flags that include a G (gateway) refer to gateways and flags that include a H (host) refer to host routes. In addition, entries with a D (dynamic) are entries generated by ICMP redirects and those with a M (modified) have been modified by a ICMP redirect.

Check the destination addresses to see if they fit the netmask you are using; something like the following line is wrong:

```
9                  9.23.2.9       UG           0          0  en0
```

Although the above entries are all for subnets of the class A network 9, there is one entry that points to net 9 only. This is usually an error and the routing of the machine will be confused. In this particular case it was generated by a buggy *routed* daemon. If gateways are listed here but you cannot reach them directly, something is probably wrong.

The reference count shows the sum of all connections (TCP) in use. The use column shows how many packets in total have passed through this interface so far. Unfortunately, **netstat -rn** does not display networks with a trailing zero. If, for example, you add a route to net 9.23.0 you will see only 9.23 in the routing table:

```
9.23                 9.23.7.1          UG           0           0  en0
```

netstat -s

This displays protocol statistics for all TCP/IP protocols. It shows fragmentation, retransmissions, routing errors, errors resulting from garbled packets, hardware errors and more. You can limit the display with *-p* if you want to display only a single protocol and not all protocols. The following samples are from a machine that is on Token-Ring and Ethernet. It has routing enabled but is not an official router.

netstat -sp ip

In Figure 19.18 errors in packets would indicate hardware trouble either in a network card in one of the machines on the network or in the cabling. 'Fragments dropped' points to duplicate frames, *mbuf* shortages or network transmission problems. 'Fragments dropped after timeout' points to CPU load or *mbuf* shortages: The driver could not read all the frames. It might also be the case that a router is causing trouble somewhere on the net. 'Packets not forwardable' and 'redirects sent' suggest routing problems (see *netstat -rn*). AIX 3 shows you somewhat less than the above output. The most interesting entry that AIX 3 is missing is 'ipintrq overflows', which points to an *ipqmaxlen* that is too small. Use *no* to increase it. To check the interrupt queue on AIX 3 it is necessary to use *crash* (see page 384).

```
ip:
        42604 total packets received
        0 bad header checksums
        0 with size smaller than minimum
        0 with data size < data length
        0 with header length < data size
        0 with data length < header length
        0 with bad options
        0 with incorrect version number
        0 fragments received
        0 fragments dropped (dup or out of space)
        0 fragments dropped after timeout
        0 packets reassembled ok
        42604 packets for this host
        0 packets for unknown/unsupported protocol
        0 packets forwarded
        10 packets not forwardable
        0 redirects sent
        38026 packets sent from this host
        0 packets sent with fabricated ip header
        0 output packets dropped due to no bufs, etc.
        0 output packets discarded due to no route
        0 output datagrams fragmented
        0 fragments created
        0 datagrams that can't be fragmented
        0 IP Multicast packets dropped due to no receiver
        0 ipintrq overflows
```

Figure 19.18 The output of **netstat -sp ip** on AIX 4.

netstat -sp icmp

The statistics in Figure 19.19 are updated mostly by running *ping* in normal operation. Unless the statistics show bad packets everything should be fine.

```
icmp:
        1 call to icmp_error
        0 errors not generated 'cuz old message was icmp
        Output histogram:
                echo reply: 168
        0 messages with bad code fields
        0 messages < minimum length
        0 bad checksums
        0 messages with bad length
        Input histogram:
                echo reply: 1420
                echo: 169
        168 message responses generated
```

Figure 19.19 The output of **netstat -sp icmp** on AIX 4.

netstat -sp tcp

The following lines in Figure 19.20 are the most interesting ones:

```
1101 duplicate acks
277 completely duplicate packets (2234 bytes)
```

Either a slow network (WAN) or some local networking problems that cause delays.

```
722 out-of-order packets (127344 bytes)
```

Problems because of varying transmission times (WAN).

```
28599 embryonic connections dropped
```

Routing problems, usually one-way routes.

```
874 retransmit timeouts
```

Lost connections: sporadic or permanent network failures.

```
531 keepalive timeouts
```

Keepalive packets sent because of timeouts, you might need to adapt the keepalive option with the *no* utility.

```
tcp:
     263464 packets sent
          129326 data packets (31508207 bytes)
          79 data packets (39718 bytes) retransmitted
          97397 ack-only packets (94118 delayed)
          4 URG only packets
          166 window probe packets
          4707 window update packets
          31785 control packets
     300163 packets received
          121246 acks (for 31513560 bytes)
          1101 duplicate acks
          0 acks for unsent data
          157137 packets (42662949 bytes) received in-sequence
          277 completely duplicate packets (2234 bytes)
          7 packets with some dup. data (44 bytes duped)
          722 out-of-order packets (127344 bytes)
          4 packets (1 byte) of data after window
          1 window probe
          194 window update packets
          13 packets received after close
          0 discarded for bad checksums
          0 discarded for bad header offset fields
          0 discarded because packet too short
     29506 connection requests
     659 connection accepts
     1568 connections established (including accepts)
     30241 connections closed (including 4 drops)
     28599 embryonic connections dropped
     112925 segments updated rtt (of 141596 attempts)
     874 retransmit timeouts
          0 connections dropped by rexmit timeout
     0 persist timeouts
     531 keepalive timeouts
          79 keepalive probes sent
          160 connections dropped by keepalive
```

Figure 19.20 The output of **netstat -sp tcp**.

netstat -sp igmp

The *igmp* statistics on AIX 4 refer to multicasts (Figure 19.21). They are only meaningful if one has configured the machine to react to multicast addresses.

```
igmp:
        0 messages received
        0 messages received with too few bytes
        0 messages received with bad checksum
        0 membership queries received
        0 membership queries received with invalid field(s)
        0 membership reports received
        0 membership reports received with invalid field(s)
        0 membership reports received for groups to which we belong
        0 membership reports sent
```

Figure 19.21 The output of **netstat -sp igmp** on AIX 4.

netstat -sp udp

UDP errors in **netstat -s** (Figure 19.22) indicate hardware problems that garble packets. They also show you broadcast packets that were seen but not accepted because no services were configured to accept them.

```
udp:
        2990 datagrams received
        0 incomplete headers
        0 bad data length fields
        0 bad checksums
        1 dropped due to no socket
        1790 broadcast/multicast datagrams dropped due to no socket
        0 dropped due to full socket buffers
        1199 delivered
        174 datagrams output
```

Figure 19.22 The output of **netstat -sp udp** on AIX 4.

netstat -v

Each adapter has different statistics associated with it. These are displayed with *netstat -v*. A full description of all the values is not available, but looking at the technical reference for the adapter in question is usually helpful. In addition, there are the include files in /usr/include/sys: tokuser.h, entuser.h, x25user.h, soluser.h and fddiuser.h. The sample output in Figure 19.23 is for AIX 3. On AIX 4 the statistics displayed are somewhat more comprehensive.

A few of the more interesting values:

Max Transmits queued

This should always be less than the transmit queue size (*xmt_que_size*) otherwise the queue is likely to be overrun.

```
ETHERNET STATISTICS (en0):
Hardware Address: 02:60:8c:2f:00:bd
Transmit Byte Count: 14770684.0 Receive Byte Count: 208651683.0
Transmit Frame Count: 215558    Receive Frame Count: 1723176
Transmit Error Count: 0         Receive Error Count: 0
Max Netid's in use: 7           Max Transmits queued: 13
Max Receives queued: 0          Max Stat Blks queued: 0
Interrupts lost: 0              WDT Interrupts lost: 0
Timeout Ints lost: 0            Status lost: 0
Receive Packets Lost: 0         No Mbuf Errors: 0
No Mbuf Extension Errors: 0     Receive Int Count: 1723175
Transmit Int Count: 215559      CRC Error Count: 0
Align Error Count: 0            Recv Overrun Count: 0
Packets Too Short: 0            Packets Too Long: 0
No Resources Count: 0           Recv Pkts Discarded: 132976
Xmit Max Collisions: 0          Xmit Carrier Lost: 0
Xmit Underrun Count: 0          Xmit CTS Lost Count: 0
Xmit Timeouts: 0                Parity Errors: 0
Diag Overflow Count: 0          Execute Q Overflows: 0
Execute Cmd Errors: 0           Host side End of List Bit: 0
Adpt side End of List Bit: 0    Adapter pkts to be uploaded: 1723176
Adapter pkts uploaded: 4972583  Start receptions to adpt: 0
Receive DMA timeouts(lock up): 0
```

Figure 19.23 The output of **netstat -v** for an Ethernet adapter on AIX 3.

Max Receives queued

This should always be less than the receive queue size (*rec_que_size*) otherwise the queue is likely to be overrun.

Receive Packets Lost

The *ipqmaxlen* might be too short.

No Mbuf Errors

Problems in the *mbuf* management. Check low- and high-water marks as well as *thewall*. Check **netstat -m** for more information. If the *mbuf* values are OK you may want to check the receive queue length: *rec_que_size*.

No Mbuf Extension Errors

Problems in the *mbuf* management. Check low- and high-water marks as well as *thewall*. Check **netstat -m** for more information. *Netm* might be thrashing.

Packets Too Short, Packets Too Long

Indicates hardware problems in cabling or other machines. Check *errpt*.

No Resources Count

May indicate an *mbuf* problem or queues that are too small.

Recv Pkts Discarded

This might point to an *ipqmaxlen* that is too short or receiving garbage.

Parity Errors

Probably hardware problems on the wire.

Receive DMA timeouts(lock up)

An EC level mismatch between driver and hardware or a broken hardware might show up here.

netstat -D

On AIX 4 there is a new *netstat* option *-D* that will tell you in detail at what point in the path on the system packets are dropped. This helps tremendously when trying to find the exact location of bottleneck.

Note that you also see the localhost interface in Figure 19.24. As Ethernet adapters usually do not have any loopback capability, the local interface is used.

```
Source                        Ipkts              Opkts     Idrops     Odrops
----------------------------------------------------------------------------
ent_dev0                      11370               3747          0          2
                ------------------------------------------------------------
Devices Total                 11370               3747          0          2
----------------------------------------------------------------------------
ent_dd0                       11370               3747          0          0
                ------------------------------------------------------------
Drivers Total                 11370               3747          0          0
----------------------------------------------------------------------------
ent_dmx0                      11371                N/A          0        N/A
                ------------------------------------------------------------
Demuxer Total                 11371                N/A          0        N/A
----------------------------------------------------------------------------
IP                            12668              12668          0          0
TCP                            5370               4521          0          0
UDP                            7298                448          0          0
                ------------------------------------------------------------
Protocols Total               25336              17637          0          0
----------------------------------------------------------------------------
lo_if0                         1414               1510         96          0
en_if0                        11371               3746          0          0
                ------------------------------------------------------------
Net IF Total                  12785               5256         96          0
----------------------------------------------------------------------------
NFS/RPC Client                    0                N/A          0        N/A
NFS/RPC Server                    0                N/A          0        N/A
NFS Client                        0                N/A          0        N/A
                ------------------------------------------------------------
NFS/RPC Total                   N/A                  0          0          0
----------------------------------------------------------------------------
(Note:  N/A -> Not Applicable)
```

Figure 19.24 The output of **netstat -D** for an Ethernet adapter on AIX 4.

19.3.9 *ifconfig*

This shows the current status of an interface. Here you can see the netmask, whether the interface is up or down and what type of interface it is. LAN interfaces usually have the BROADCAST and NOTRAILERS flag set. WAN interfaces should have the NOARP and maybe POINTTOPOINT flags set. The samples in Figure 19.25 are for Ethernet and X.25.

```
$ ifconfig en0
en0: flags=2000063<UP,BROADCAST,NOTRAILERS,RUNNING,NOECHO>
        inet 9.23.2.12 netmask 0xffffff00 broadcast 9.23.2.255
$ ifconfig xt0
xt0: flags=e1<UP,NOTRAILERS,RUNNING,NOARP>
        inet 192.35.65.55 netmask 0xffffff00
```

Figure 19.25 Checking interfaces with *ifconfig*.

Ifconfig is usually more accurate than *lsattr* as the ODM can be updated without updating the real device. Here are the most common flags:

UP The interface is usable. This is toggled with the up/down/detach options of *ifconfig*.

BROADCAST The interface is a broadcast interface. Broadcasts can be sent over this interface. This should be available only over a LAN. Some third-party vendors sell WAN solutions that have the broadcast flag set in the interface. This can lead to routing troubles or problems with daemons that want to broadcast information.

NOTRAILERS Do not use trailer encapsulation. This is the usual default. Only some very old UNIX systems still use this outdated method.

RUNNING The interface is active. Toggled with the up/detach option

NOARP The ARP protocol is disabled on this interface. This is typical of a WAN in which the hardware addresses are hardcoded in the configuration instead of dynamically fetched via ARP broadcasts.

POINTTOPOINT This is a point to point interface. PPP, SLIP, SNALINK, ISDN, X.25 should have this flag set.

SIMPLEX The interface cannot see its own broadcasts (typical for Ethernet). This flag is only visible with AIX 4.

MULTICAST If this option is set on AIX 4, the interface supports IP multicasts.

19.3.10 *arp -a*

The ARP cache of the machine can be displayed or modified with the *arp* command (Figure 19.26). All machines that one has recently communicated with are usually listed in the ARP cache.

```
$ arp -a
chablis.ak.munich.ibm.com (9.23.4.2) at 10:0:5a:4f:d7:36 [token ring]
cardhu.ak.munich.ibm.com (9.23.4.65) at 10:0:5a:4f:ec:da [token ring]
cabernete.ak.munich.ibm.com (9.23.2.7) at 8:0:5a:1:9e:b6 [ethernet]
duke2.tmsc.munich.ibm.com (9.23.2.253) at 2:60:8c:2e:a1:79 [ethernet]
tinto.ak.munich.ibm.com (9.23.2.24) at 0:dd:1:8:20:db [ethernet]
```

Figure 19.26 Checking the ARP cache with **arp -a.**

Should the ARP cache list incomplete or wrong entries, then one usually has problems with defective hardware or software in the network. Try deleting the entries with **arp -d hostname** and then *ping* the machine in question to get the cache updated.

In addition to the entries displayed here, the network adapter has a non-accessible one-entry cache to avoid excessive look ups when exchanging several consecutive packets with another machine.

19.3.11 *iptrace & ipreport*

The *iptrace* program traces packets on an interface to a file. Its output can be converted to human-readable form via the *ipreport* utility. One needs to be familiar with the TCP/IP protocols to be able to understand fully the trace generated by these programs. However, even if you do not know all the inner details of the TCP/IP protocols you can get valuable information out of the trace. Try running it for a few sample tests, such as pinging another host to familiarize yourself with it.

In contrast to a general-purpose network sniffer tool, you can only trace IP packets to and from the host the trace is running on when using AIX 3 or Token-Ring on AIX 4. The generated output might still be overwhelming. You can limit the number of packets traced by specifying which ports and source/target machines are to be traced. Use the following sequence of commands for a trace:

(1) Run iptrace: **iptrace -a -i en0 /tmp/ipt.**

(2) Run the problem application.

(3) Kill the *iptrace* process.

(4) Run *ipreport*: **ipreport -rns /tmp/ipt > /tmp/ipr.**

Be sure to limit the packets you trace if you do not want to be flooded with packets that you do not want to read. In the above example the *-a* flag excluded all ARP packets. ARP packets, in particular, can become irksome when you do not want to investigate ARP problems as there are usually many ARP broadcasts on larger networks.

If you want to trace the connection with only one machine, use *-d* (destination) or *-s* (source) together with *-b* (both) to filter out the other packets. You can specify the protocol with the *-P* flag and the port to trace with the *-p* flag when necessary. On AIX 4 the *-e* flag allows promiscuous tracing if the interface supports it (Ethernet does so, but not Token-Ring). The *-rns* flags for *ipreport* make the output more readable and generate NFS statistics if any NFS packets are found in the trace.

Iptrace and *ipreport* do not offer a real-time display like *etherfind* on a Sun or *tcpdump* on AIX 4. They are more efficient as the expensive post-processing and decoding of the data do not interfere with the trace. However, a real-time trace is sometimes necessary. A make-do workaround for AIX 3 is available:

```
mknod /tmp/iptrace p
ipreport -rns /tmp/iptrace
iptrace -i en0 /tmp/iptrace
```

This creates a pipe called /tmp/iptrace. The *ipreport* process reads from it while the *iptrace* process writes to it – not 100% real time but the closest you can get with those tools. On AIX 4 you can also use the *tcpdump* command for a real-time trace.

Many protocols have clear text messages associated. Use *iptrace* to monitor *tftp*, for example, when you have trouble booting diskless machines or Xstations.

Most IP-based services such as *ftp* or *telnet* will show their clear text passwords when analyzed with *iptrace* or other network-monitoring tools.

19.3.12 *tcpdump*

The Berkeley *tcpdump* utility was added to AIX with version 4. In contrast to *iptrace/ipreport*, it can output packets immediately, but it also supports record and playback of traces. Whereas *iptrace* can only filter on interface, ports and hosts, *tcpdump* can filter on more complex expressions that analyze the packet headers. The *tcpdump* command will not print the packets contents, only header information, unless *-x* is specified, which will dump packets in hexadecimal.

For a quick check running **tcpdump -I** will show you all packets seen on the first configured interface.

19.3.13 *rpcinfo*

With *rpcinfo* you can check which RPC services are made available by a host and whether the portmapper daemon is running on the machine (Figure 19.27). *Rpcinfo* tries to contact the portmapper daemon on the local or a remote machine to find out which services are registered at this server. When used without a machine name parameter the local host is queried. Should the portmapper have problems, *rpcinfo* will fail.

```
$ rpcinfo -p
   program vers proto   port
    100000    2   tcp    111  portmapper
    100000    2   udp    111  portmapper
    100001    1   udp   1025  rstatd
    100001    2   udp   1025  rstatd
    100001    3   udp   1025  rstatd
    300004    1   udp    740
1080231175    1   udp   1027
```

Figure 19.27 Listing available RPC services with **rpcinfo -p**.

You will always find the portmapper listed. When using NFS you will find the mount program and lock daemons listed here as well. All these RPC programs are registered by their program number. The port is dynamically assigned by the portmapper apart from the one used by the portmappers itself (port 111). There are three different versions of the *rstatd* daemon available, one for each revision of the protocol. The last two lines in the output in Figure 19.27 are generated by the licence daemon for FrameMaker.

Should *rpcinfo* on the local machine report only the portmapper but you have configured more than that, check the local host interface (*lo0*) – it might be down.

19.3.14 *trace*

The system *trace* can be used to monitor network activity as well. Check out Section 19.1.10 for more information on *trace* as this section will discuss only the networking-relevant parts.

```
DISPATCH IDLE PROCESS
resume     IDLE
         I/O INTERRUPT
         slih tokdd [9815 usec]
         return from slih [46 usec]
         slih i_offlevel [53 usec]
tokdd ID: rDAT     d1=00180000 d2=00000000 d3=00000000 d4=00000052
receive  interrupt tok0 count=0052
MBUF m_get canwait=M_DONTWAIT type=MT_DATA callfrom=013ECF90
MBUF return from m_get mbuf=05567300 dataptr=0556731C
NETIF_TOK ie5_netintr (entry)  ifp=0147F780, status=0
NETIF_TOK ie5_recv (entry)  m=05567300, ifp=0147F780
NETIF_TOK ie5_recv (rtn)
NETIF_TOK ie5_netintr (rtn)
tokdd ID: rNOT     d1=00180000 d2=00000001 d3=05567300 d4=00000052
enque kernel data  tok0 mbuf=5567300 count=0052 channel=0001
set on ready queue telnetd 31423
dispatch telnetd
```

Figure 19.28 Receiving one packet and passing it on to *telnetd*.

When using *trace* for network activity one needs to select the right trace hooks to avoid being swamped by irrelevant data, for example **trace -j'211 212 213 214 215 216 218' -a** would trace the NFS subsystem. Use *trcstop* to stop the trace and *trcrpt* to display the collected data.

Sockets can be traced with hooks 252 and 253. *Mbufs* can be traced with hook 254. Network errors are on 251 and the interfaces are from 255 to 259. The TCP/IP debug hook is 25A and there are some interesting DMA trace hooks as well.
Figure 19.28 shows a very much abridged and edited excerpt of the reception of a packet for the Telnet daemon. A packet is received by the Token-Ring card, which generates an interrupt. The driver puts the packet into an *mbuf* and queues it for IP. IP passes the *mbuf* on to the proper socket for *telnetd* and *telnetd* gets scheduled to run.

I suggest using either *netpmon* if available (AIX 3 or Performance Toolbox /6000 on AIX 4) or the *traceall* script on page 345 with the network trace hooks added. The easiest way to obtain a list of currently available trace hooks is via **smit trace**.

19.3.15 *nfsstat*

Nfsstat is used to display NFS statistics. It shows you RPC information as well as NFS server (Figure 19.29) and client (Figure 19.30) statistics.

```
$ nfsstat -s

Server rpc:
calls      badcalls   nullrecv   badlen     xdrcall
1916391    0          0          0          0

Server nfs:
calls      badcalls
1416799    5
null       getattr    setattr    root       lookup     readlink   read
0  0%      277882 19% 1679   0%  0  0%      444811 31% 37765   2% 420762 29%
wrcache    write      create     remove     rename     link       symlink
0  0%      21170   1% 368   0%   299   0%   67   0%    3   0%     0  0%
mkdir      rmdir      readdir    fsstat
21   0%    7  0%      140449   9% 71511   5%
```

Figure 19.29 Checking an NFS server with **nfsstat -s**.

The following points should be checked:

badcalls > 0 RPC requests are rejected. This might be because of authentication problems (user in too many groups, accessing an exported file system as root or secure RPC problems).

nullrecv is not zero NFS requests are not arriving fast enough to keep all the *nfsd* daemons busy. You have probably configured too many of them.

symlink > 10% If there are too many *symlink* calls (> 10%) you might want to mount the directories and files that are symbolically linked elsewhere because your clients are wasting time as they have to process several stats on the server to get to a file.

getattr > 50% If there are too many *gettattr* calls (>50%) then some caches on the clients may be improperly configured. Check where they deviate from the defaults (for example the *noac* option).

null > 1% When null is greater than 1% you may have an automounter running with timeouts that are too small. (Null calls are used by the automounter to find servers.)

```
# nfsstat -c

Client rpc:
calls     badcalls    retrans     badxid      timeout     wait        newcred
65667     2           10          0           12          0           0

Client nfs:
calls     badcalls    nclget      nclsleep
48770     2           48770       0
null      getattr     setattr     root        lookup      readlink    read
0  0%     8085 16%    1  0%       0  0%       23915 49%   0  0%       14205 29%
wrcache   write       create      remove      rename      link        symlink
0  0%     140  0%     1  0%       0  0%       0  0%       0  0%       0  0%
mkdir     rmdir       readdir     fsstat
0  0%     0  0%       1528  3%    895  1%
```

Figure 19.30 Checking an NFS client with **netstat -c**.

On a client the following points are the most interesting ones:

Badcalls > 0 RPC calls on soft-mounted file systems may be timing out. Should you try to access a crashed server then the number will rise. During normal operations this number should be constant. If not, check the time-out values (*timeo* and *rtrans*) on the mount options.

retrans Retransmits are very expensive. If this number is increasing check your system for other networking errors.

badxid If there are timeouts and bad xids, then the server handles client requests that have been retransmitted as well as the original requests. Change your timeouts on the mount.

timeout Either the network has problems delivering the packets to the server or the server is too slow to handle the requests.

wait If wait is non-zero then a call had to wait on a busy client handle.

Use other tools to check your network when you see problems here. If they find nothing you might need to get faster machines at least at one end.

The *-z* option of *nfsstat* can be used to reset the statistics when needed.

19.3.16 *netpmon*

Netpmon is a front end to the system *trace* that allows easy monitoring of CPU use and network throughput per interface, process or file. It makes it very easy to discover network hogs and other bottlenecks. It comes as standard with AIX 3; on AIX 4 you have to purchase the Performance Toolbox /6000 to get it. To run a trace with *netpmon* use the following sequence:

(1) Start a trace with verbose output: **netpmon -o /tmp/netp.out -v**.

(2) Run your test program or whatever you think causes the trouble.

(3) Stop the trace and generate the report in /tmp/netp.out with **trcstop**.

You will get several pages of detailed statistics. All processes running during the test interval and their CPU and network use are recorded. All device drivers and interrupt handlers used during that period are recorded. The number of packets and bytes per remote host and device are listed as well as the real NFS block sizes used.

19.3.17 *ndb*

This program is neither documented nor supported, but it is quite useful for those who program at the socket interface. It allows you to list current socket and *mbuf* structures in the kernel. It is not very useful for the average network administrator as one needs to know a lot about TCP/IP internals, but anyone who develops network applications might benefit from it.

19.4 Network tuning options

Network tuning can happen on different layers. The first is the underlying networking hardware. Although Ethernet is cheap and widely available, it does not perform well under high load and its maximum packet size is fixed at 1500 (1492 on IEEE Ethernet). Token-Ring, on the other hand, operates at a higher speed, can be configured for much larger packets and performs better under high loads but is not as widely available; in addition, the cabling for small networks may be more expensive. Another option is FDDI, which is even faster, but this needs large packets for good performance and its cabling is even more expensive. ATM is just appearing and it will hopefully become widespread and deliver the promised data highway. On the WAN side there is SLIP, PPP, X.25 and ISDN, all of which suffer from slow network speeds and small packets sizes or even fragmented packets.

Above the hardware are parameters that you can change in the device drivers, such as the queue sizes between the driver and the IP support. Above that are the IP and UDP/TCP layers, which offer many changeable parameters such as *mbuf* memory or socket buffers. And then there are the parameters that can be changed in the application via *setsockopt()* if you have access to the source.

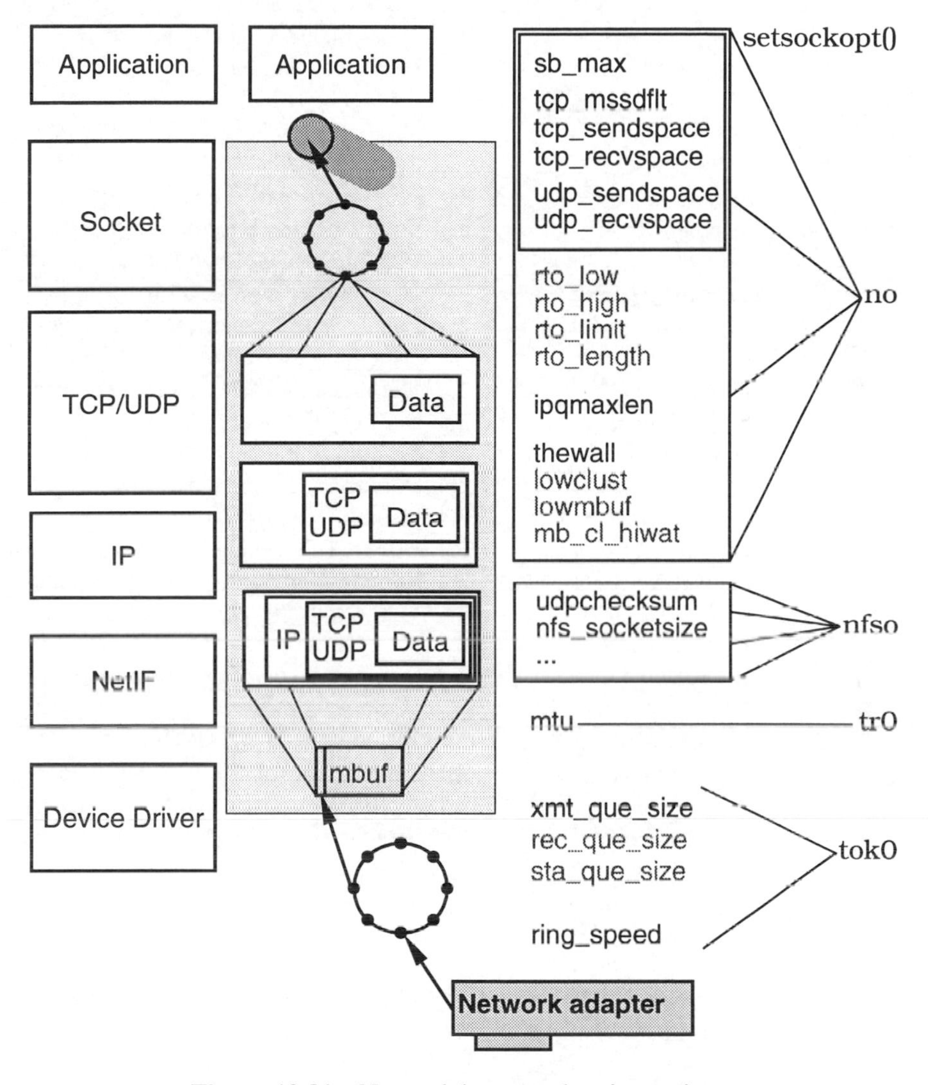

Figure 19.31 Network layers and tuning options.

Table 19.1 TCP/IP tuning options.

Location	Option	Rel.	Use
Device *tok0*, *ent0*, ...	*xmt_que_size*	3,4	Transmit queue length in packets in the device driver
	rec_que_size	3	Receive queue length in packets in the device driver
	sta_que_size	3	Status queue length in the driver
	ring_speed	3,4	The speed of the Token-Ring LAN, 4MB or 16MB
IP interface *tr0*, *en0*, ...	*mtu*	3,4	Maximum packet size for the device
no	*lowlust*	3	Low-water mark for *mbuf* clusters
	lowmbuf	3	Low-water mark for *mbufs*
	thewall	3,4	Maximum size of *mbuf* pool
	mb_clust_hiwat	3	*Mbuf* cluster high-water mark
	net_malloc_police	4	Enables checks and traces of network memory allocation
	sb_max	3,4	The maximum size of a socket buffer
	tcp_sendspace	3,4	Default TCP send buffer size
	tcp_recvspace	3,4	Default TCP receive buffer size
	udp_sendspace	3,4	Default UDP send buffer size
	udp_recvspace	3,4	Default UDP receive buffer size
	rfc1323	3,4	Allows TCP socket buffers > 64KB
	ipqmaxlen	3,4	Maximum packets on IP input queue
	rto_low, rto_high, rto_limit, rto_length	4	TCP retransmission parameters
	tcp_mssdflt	3,4	Default message size for routed TCP connections
	subnetsarelocal	3,4	Toggles *tcp_mssdflt* usage
nfso	*nfsudpcksum / udpchecksum*	3, 4	Toggles use of UDP checksums for NFS
	nfs_chars / nfs_socketsize	3, 4	Sets the size of the NFS socket buffer
	nfs_gather_threshold	3,4	Maximum size of sleeping write
	nfs_duplicate_cache_size	4	Request cache for retransmission avoidance
	nfs_server_base_priority	4	The base priority for NFS daemons
	nfs_dynamic_retrans	4	Allows NFS to adjust retry parameters and block sizes automatically
	nfs_iopace_pages	4	Number of dirty pages that will be flushed by the client in one operation

Figure 19.31 (page 375) should help you to understand where in the path of the data received via the network the various options are in effect. All of the options need to work together. Changing one without considering the impact on other parts could remove one bottleneck by creating another. The following sections will help you to understand where those options are useful and in Section 19.3 you will find the tools to examine the effects generated by changing the options. Table 19.1 (page 376) gives a rough overview about the variables that you can change in the networking area.

Before you start to experiment with all these variables you need to know where it makes sense to change them. The following pages will show you where it makes sense to adapt those options to your environment. Most new AIX releases that I have used included additional options to the *no* and *nfso* commands, so check InfoExplorer and the README files (*info* usually lags behind) – there might be more useful options for you.

19.4.1 Adapter queues

The adapter queues sit between the communications subsystems and the network adapters. Although they are usually big enough for simple TCP-based services such as Telnet, their values are too small for the heavy UDP traffic that is found on NFS servers or diskless machines.

xmt_que_size This is the transmit queue between IP and the adapter. Outgoing frames are buffered here until the adapter can accept it and put it onto the network. There is one queue per adapter and its default length is 30. One should set it to the maximum.

rec_que_size This is the receive queue between the adapter and IP. Incoming frames are buffered here until the proper communications protocol can accept it and put it into *mbufs*. There is one queue per adapter and protocol and its default length is 30 on AIX 3. This is no longer tunable on AIX 4.

sta_que_size The status queue size. There is one queue between adapter and each communications protocol and its default length is 5. In comparison with the receive and transmit queues, the size of this queue is less critical. This is no longer tunable on AIX 4.

When checking the networking subsystem with *netstat -v* check if the values for 'Max Transmits queued' and 'Max Receives queued' approach the values that are set for *xmt_que_size* and *rec_que_size*. If they do, it is time to increase the queue sizes. In or out errors in the output of **netstat -i** or **netstat -I** also point to queues that are too small.

Use *chdev* on the adapter devices, as in **chdev -l ent0 -axmt_que_size=150**, to change the values for a specific adapter. The maximum value can be found with

lsattr -Rl ent0 -axmt_que_size. As this can be done only on an inactive device, use **ifconfig detach en0** first to deactivate the associated Ethernet interface. After changing the option use **ifconfig en0 up** and **chdev -l en0 -astate=up** to reactivate it. Or use the *-P* option on *chdev* and reboot the system.

19.4.2 The MTU

The MTU (message transfer unit, the maximum frame size on the network) has a large influence on the achievable throughput of a network. Whereas you are stuck with a limit of 1500 on standard Ethernet, you can increase it much further on Token-Ring and FDDI, for example. Large MTUs are good for file sharing and other forms of bulk data transfer, but when used on a slow medium such as X.25 or SLIP they will have a negative influence on interactive applications such as Telnet.

On a 16MB Token-Ring I suggest using an MTU of 4KB. A larger MTU, such as 8500, will give you slightly better NFS performance at the cost of higher CPU use. All the tests I have performed so far indicate 4KB as the ideal MTU for Token-Ring, but you should do some tests yourself to see which MTU gives you the optimum performance for your needs. The IBM tuning documents recommend 8500KB, so that one can transfer one NFS I/O request in one packet for example.

When using gateways between different LAN topologies with different MTUs you have to be aware of the fragmentation that will occur. When sending packets from a LAN with a 4KB MTU to a LAN with a 1500-byte MTU the gateway will fragment the packets and the final receiver has to reassemble the fragments to obtain the original packet. This is very costly. Try using static routes with the correct MTU if possible so that fragmentation is avoided. The *-mtu* option of the route command can be used for this. All machines on a physical network should have the same MTU configured. Although the RS/6000 will work with misconfigured MTUs on a LAN, the cost in terms of performance may be high.

When using WAN interfaces (SLIP, PPP, ISDN) the MTU on both sides of the connection has to match otherwise you will be able to *ping* the remote machine but applications with larger packets such as *ftp* will fail. Use *ping* with larger packet sizes to detect problems based on mismatched MTUs.

19.4.3 Mbuf pool configuration

Mbufs are memory buffers that are used to transport data in between the network device drivers and the application. They also hold most other networking queues, buffers and routing information. There is one *mbuf* pool in the system that is used by all communications subsystems such as TCP/IP, SNA and STREAMS on AIX.

The design of the *mbuf* subsystem changed drastically between AIX 3 and 4 as AIX 4 uses *mbufs* for much more than AIX 3. The following *mbuf* tuning discussion applies to AIX 3, AIX 4 has a self-tuning *mbuf* pool. The only things you can change are its maximum size (*thewall*) and additional checks (*net_malloc_police*).

In addition, AIX 4 has *mbufs* of many different sizes, not just ordinary *mbufs* and clusters like AIX 3. Use **netstat -m** to see them and to which subsystems they are allocated.

Within the pool there are two types of *mbufs*: small ones that are usually just called *mbufs* and clusters which are groups of small *mbufs* put together. Small *mbufs* hold 256bytes and clusters hold 4KB. Small *mbufs* are usually used to hold small packets or packet headers, whereas clusters are used for things that are bigger than 256 bytes and contain only data.

Like *mbufs*, clusters can be chained. Header information is always stored in *mbufs*. Clusters are then linked to *mbufs* that hold their header information.

The *mbuf* pool is managed by the kernel process *netm*, which tries to maintain a minimum number of free buffers at all time. The size of the *mbuf* pool and the high- and low-water marks for the clusters can be adjusted on-line with the *no* command. The *lowmbuf* and *lowclust* options are used to set the lower limits. When the number of free buffers drops below these values then the expansion of the number of buffers is scheduled for the *netm* kernel process. The next time *netm* is dispatched the buffer areas will be enlarged. This, of course, can be done only as long as there is enough free space for *mbufs*. This limit is defined by *thewall*. If the system hits *thewall* then it will start to drop packets. If the number of free clusters is larger than *mb_cl_hiwat* then *netm* will release some of the clusters back to the *mbuf* pool memory (Figure 19.32).

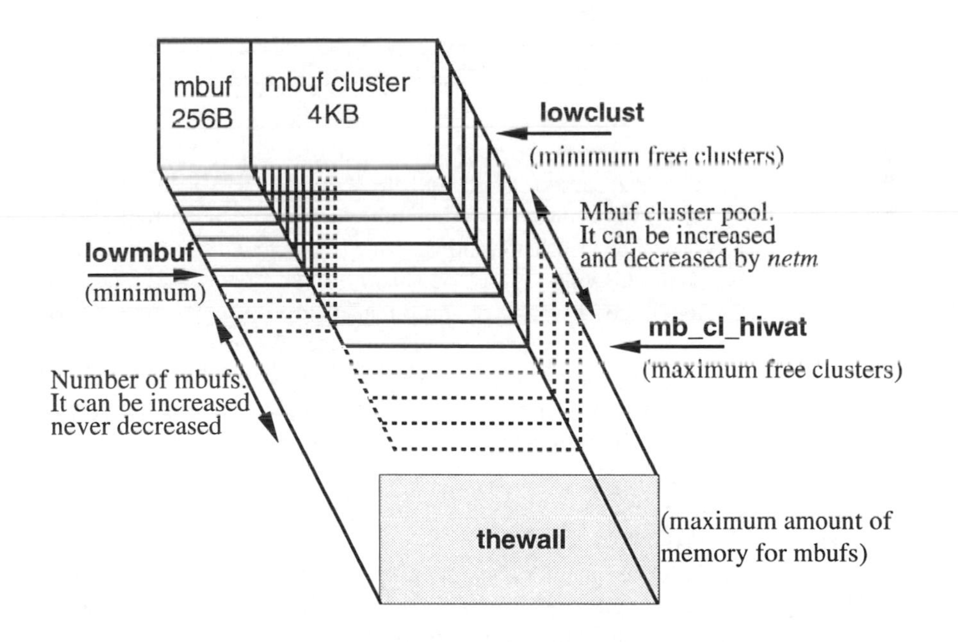

Figure 19.32 The *mbuf* pool.

Usually not all *mbuf* memory is used by *mbufs*. The *netm* kernel process sets up only a part of the pool memory for *mbufs*. The allocation is changed in the running kernel by reaching the thresholds given by *lowclust*, *lowmbuf* and *mb_cl_hiwat*. The less *netm* needs to adjust, the faster the *mbuf* handling is. Select those thresholds very carefully!

lowclust The low limit on free *mbuf* clusters on AIX 3. When this limit is reached, the *mbuf* allocator will try to expand the number of *mbuf* clusters until at least *lowclust* free *mbuf* clusters are available. This should be adjusted together with *lowmbuf* as most clusters have a *mbuf* associated to store a header.

lowmbuf The low limit on free *mbufs* on AIX 3. When this limit is reached, then the *mbuf* allocator will try to expand the number of *mbufs* until at least *lowmbuf* (small) *mbufs* are available. This number should be always higher than two times *lowclust* as most clusters have a small *mbuf* associated and small *mbufs* are often used for other small items.

mb_cl_hiwat When the number of free clusters reaches this value on AIX 3 then any freed clusters (released by applications) above that number will be returned to the *mbuf* pool. This should be always at least greater than two times *lowclust* to avoid *netm* thrashing.

net_malloc_police If non-zero, the size of a trace buffer for *net_malloc()* and *net_free()* is specified. A non-zero trace buffer will activate the trace hook HKWD_NET_MALLOC and some additional error checking on the *mbuf* handling will be enabled. Use it when you suspect *mbuf* handling problems on an AIX 4 system.

thewall The maximum amount of *mbuf* pool memory available. The size is specified in KB and the default is 2MB on AIX 3, or much more on AIX 4, depending on the installed memory. If you change other options that affect *mbuf* usage be sure to adapt this value as well. If *vmstat* shows more paging after you increased *thewall* you might need to consider buying more memory or rethink the *mbuf* allocation. When changing the value *maxmbuf* of the *sys0* device then the boot default for *thewall* is changed. Any *no* command entered after booting the system that changes *thewall* will override the setting of *maxmbuf*.

Use */usr/sbin/no* to set these values at the end of /etc/rc.net so that they are also activated at the next reboot.

The *mbuf* pool is pinned memory, so any change in pool size affects the system's memory use. The default pool size should be sufficient for most machines. Increasing it will take away RAM from the rest of the system. Decreasing it might cripple the network.

It pays to be careful when modifying the values as it is very easy to set parameters in a way that will have a negative impact on the system's throughput. If *netm* (which runs at a very high fixed priority) has to perform much *mbuf* reallocation, then the system's throughput will be hurt because *netm* uses the CPU too often. If the size of the *mbuf* pool is too small then packets will be dropped. If the area is too large it steals pinned memory from the system, which may cause more paging in applications as they have less real memory to work with.

InfoExplorer has an article on *mbufs* under the heading 'tuning the mbuf pools'. It explains how to set up the values for the *mbuf* allocation so that the activation of *netm* in the running system is minimized.

It is usually only heavily loaded servers that need *mbuf* tuning. Your average machine comes with a reasonable enough configuration to satisfy the requirements. As long as **netstat -m** does not reveal any problems such as denial of memory requests or the number of mapped pages in use being close to the number of pages available, there is no need to fiddle with *mbuf* parameters.

In addition to heavily loaded servers you may find WAN gateways with a heavy *mbuf* use. If they get data from the LAN very fast they need to buffer it before sending it off to the much slower WAN. All the buffering is done in *mbufs*.

19.4.4 Socket buffers

TCP as well as UDP uses socket buffers to queue data between IP and the application. The size of these buffers can be set by each application individually with the *setsockopt()* library routine. Under TCP the size of the socket buffer is used to calculate the window size for TCP streams. Under UDP the application has to manage that buffer itself. In either case it is highly recommended that the application sets the buffer to a value that takes into account the type of network and the MTU as well as the load that will be sent via the socket.

If the application does not use *setsockopt()* to optimize the socket buffer allocation it will get the system-wide defaults which might not be optimal for this particular application.

Setting send and receive space does not really allocate memory, but it sets the limits on the *mbuf* usage per socket. The number of permissible *mbufs* is calculated from the send/receive spaces.

sb_max This is the limit of all the socket buffers allocated to a particular socket. The socket buffers are used to copy data from user space into kernel space and back. When this limit is exceeded, the sending process blocks until the buffer use drops as a result of data being set by the TCP or UDP layer. It should be greater then the TCP/UDP send and receive spaces.

tcp_sendspace, tcp_recvspace The default buffer size for TCP sockets when no other size is specified by *setsockopt()*. This is basically the window size (buffer/MTU) as it determines how much data can be buffered before an ACK needs to be received. It should always be a multiple of (the MTU minus the TCP/IP packet header) and be a multiple of 4KB (the systems memory page size). It should be less than or equal to *sb_max*. The maximum size for those buffers is 64KB unless the *rfc1323* option is set to 1. Using higher values is useful for networks such as FDDI that work best with large MTUs.

udp_sendspace, udp_recvspace, nfs_chars, nfs_socketsize The default buffer size for UDP sockets when no other size is specified with *setsockopt()*. This is basically the window size (buffer/MTU). This area is used for buffering as the TCP spaces, but the windowing has to be done by the application as UDP itself does no ACKs. It should always be a multiple of (the MTU minus the UDP/IP packet header). NFS is a heavy user of these buffer spaces, but to decouple the NFS requirements from the rest of the system the NFS socket buffer space is set via *nfso* options and not *no* options (*nfs_chars* on AIX 3, *nfs_socketsize* on AIX 4). However, if one makes them too large, then NFS might queue up too much data for the remote side to accept quickly. This would then lead to a degradation of the overall NFS throughput. The maximum for these options is set by *sb_max*.

As with the other available tuning options, I recommend changing them only slowly and carefully while monitoring the effect on the network. Do not set larger values hastily. Making them too large may introduce latency problems on applications that do not send large amounts of data for example.

Use */usr/sbin/no* to set those values at the end of /etc/rc.net so that they are activated at the next reboot as well. The NFS paramters need to be set in /etc/rc.nfs with */usr/sbin/nfso*.

19.4.5 TCP retransmissions

On AIX 4 the retransmission algorithm for TCP connections can be modified. This can be useful if a very fast machine talks to slow systems or a slow WAN link is used. Each TCP packet needs to be confirmed by an acknowledging packet. If the packet containing the acknowledgement does not arrive on time, the original packet is retransmitted. When a fast server talks to a slow client there may be more retransmits than needed. Four parameters can be used to change the algorithm that determines whether a packet is resent. The following code describes their relationship:

```
TCP_BACKOFF(x) = x+1 >= rto_limit ? rto_high : rto_low << (shifts *
x / rto_limit)
```

The shifts variable is calculated as the number of bitwise shifts from *rto_low* to *rto_high*. The first retransmit is sent after *TCP_BACKOFF(0) * N*. (N is an internal constant). The next retransmit will occur after *TCP_BACKOFF(1) * N*. This continues up to *TCP_BACKOFF(rto_length-1) * N*.

In most cases one would not want to change those parameters. Only if **netstat -sptcp** shows large numbers of duplicate ACKs and duplicate packets should you start to modify them.

19.4.6 NFS options

The *nfso* command can be used to change several NFS-specific options. As with the *no* command you should be careful when changing these and if you want to set the new values permanently put the commands to do it at the end of /etc/rc.nfs. Use **nfso -a** to see the currently active values.

nfsudpcksum (AIX 3), updchecksum (AIX 4) Toggles the use of UDP checksums. The default is to use checksums. One can disable the generation of checksums to achieve higher throughput at the cost of risking incorrect packets.

nfs_chars (AIX 3), nfs_socketsize (AIX 4) This sets the size of the UDP socket buffer for NFS. Use this instead of changing *udp_sendspace* and *udp_recvspace* if you want to optimize NFS throughput.

nfs_duplicate_cache_size The NFS server caches requests to detect duplicates. This variable controls the cache size. It can only be increased in a running system. It is initially set to 1000, but can be increased up to 10000. Use it on very fast servers.

nfs_dynamic_retrans This parameter toggles the dynamic resizing of packets and changes in the timeouts for retransmissions. If set to 1 (the default) then the NFS client can retransmit packets with smaller read/write packets to overcome the limitations of a bad communications channel. The actual values for retransmissions and packet sizes are calculated from the response times.

nfs_server_base_priority Normally *nfsd* processes run with standard AIX priorities. When this parameter is non-zero, then it is used as the base priority from which the priority of the NFS daemons is calculated by the scheduler.

nfs_iopace_pages NFS clients often buffer quite a lot of pages before they get flushed to the server. With this parameter you can set the limit on the number of pages being flushed at a time. It defaults to 32 pages but can be set anywhere from 1 to 65536. Decreasing it may improve interactive performance, whereas increasing it could make large I/O operations faster.

nfs_gather_threshold The maximum size of writes that can be kept before they need to be written to disk.

19.4.7 Various other network options

There are many more network options that can be set. The number of options available with the *no* command increases with every AIX release, although only a few of them are performance related. Check out InfoExplorer and the README files on the latest list of available options. Here are some that may be useful.

ipqmaxlen This is a limit to the number of datagrams queued inbound between the net interface and the IP layer. When this limit is reached, no more inbound packets are accepted. When this happens the inbound packets are dropped. This limit applies to the system as a whole.

On AIX 3 there is only one way to check for overflows. You have to use *crash*:

```
# crash
> knlist ipintrq
        ipintrq: 0x01471c48
> od 01471c58
01471c58: 00000000
> quit
```

Get the address of *ipintrq*.
Add 10_H to the address.
Dump the new address with *od*.
If it is non-zero you have overruns.

On AIX 4 you can check for IP queue overflows with **netstat -sp ip**.

Increasing *ipqmaxlen* preallocates more memory out of the *mbuf* pool. If the queue is too long, then the system can get a great deal of UDP traffic from the net very quickly, but later on IP has to deal with it. The IP code might not be able to handle this fast enough.

rfc1323

When using FDDI, ATM or other high-bandwidth connections, this may improve throughput when set to 1. The RFC 1323 describes additional TCP options that extend the usual TCP windowing facilities to support larger window sizes.

tcp_mssdflt

When establishing TCP connections to systems via a router then AIX, by default, uses a TCP message size that is very small (*tcp_mssdflt*). Use the *subnetsarelocal* parameter when working in a subnetted environment so that TCP does not use the *tcp_mssdflt* segment size for remote connections or set *tcp_mssdflt* to a value that corresponds to your MTU size minus packet headers (40 bytes). The other method of avoiding small TCP segments is to use the *route* command with the *-mtu* option if possible. Like the MTU, the *tcp_mssdflt* should be set to the same value on both sides of the connection.

19.5 Application monitoring

When analyzing and tuning applications for which you have access to the source, some more tools are available. The classic UNIX profilers *prof* and *gprof* can be used if the application is compiled with the appropriate flags (*-p*, *-pg*), but they do modify the generated code. To profile an application without any object code modification you can use the system trace in the form of the *tprof* utility. On AIX 4 *tprof* is in the optional performance agent package; it comes as standard with AIX 3.

19.5.1 *tprof*

Tprof is a profiler that uses some hooks of the system trace to generate a profile of a running program without program modification – you need only include symbol information in the executable by compiling it with *-g*. The system trace output is processed by some scripts that relate the trace data to the source. As *tprof* does not modify the program but collects data externally, the resolution of *tprof* is not as fine as that of other profiling tools. Samples are taken only every 100th second (this time unit is refered to a tick). This is the price you have to pay for running an untampered executable. For each source file in the executable you will receive a trace file that shows you how many ticks a source line has been executed. Program parts that have not been visited often will quite often show no ticks at all. I used *tprof* on an executable from a Motif application. The executable contained code for the function *ParsePixels* from a source file called xpmread.c. *Tprof* generates a trace file for it called __t.ParsePixels_xpmread.c. The trace file contains only the code lines together with a tick counter, not the definition of variables:

```
647      6              for (y = 0; y < height; y++) {
648      -                  xpmNextString(data);
649      7                  for (x = 0; x < width; x++, iptr++) {
650     10                      int idx = colidx[xpmGetC(data)];
651      -
652      -                      if (idx != 0)
653      -                          *iptr = idx - 1;
654      -                      else {
655      -                          XpmFree(iptr2);
656      -                          return (XpmFileInvalid);
657      -                      }
658      -                  }
659      -              }
```

Only three lines of the above fragment contain tick counter values – they have been executed often enough to be found in the sampling by *trace*.

In addition to the profiling output, *tprof* also gathers some process statistics for the time during which the process was run. The program I used *tprof* on was called Mosaic. A file generated by *tprof* is `__Mosaic.all`, showing the ticks used on this and other processes during the profiling run in addition to the summary of ticks used in the functions of Mosaic itself. This file can be created even without compiling the source with *-g* – it will still have a list of subroutines and the ticks used in them. The output of *tprof* can be huge. To make it easier to find the hotspots, files starting with `__h.` are created for the source files in which the most ticks where spent. These files contain only the interesting lines, so you do not need to wade through thousands of lines of traces to find the items that need further investigation.

You can use *tprof* even if you do not want to trace a specific program, for example **tprof -ksex sleep 60** will generate a listing of the running processes during the next 60s and their CPU consumptions in ticks in the file `__prof.all`. It will also include a list of the system calls that occured during this interval and how often they happened. This is very useful in identifying bottlenecks.

19.6 Application tuning

There are many things that can be done to tune an application. Depending on your interest in optimizing it for a given architecture, the cache design, the CPU type as well as structuring of code and I/O can be considered. The compiler can be used to do some of the optimizations automatically; others have to be done by the programmer. I suggest always using *xlc* instead of *cc* as the ANSI mode is more limited in terms of allowed tricks, which in turn allows the compiler to optimize better as it does not assume that the programmer performs hidden tricks.

19.6.1 Compiler options

Here are a few compiler options that should be used for optimum performance:

-O (-O2)
This should always be used. Compiling for a superscalar processor without the optimizer is nonsense – the CPU and compiler are a team that can achieve a good performance only when combined.

-O3
This optimization level is very aggressive and can lead to wrong code under special circumstances. In particular floating point exceptions, the sign of zero and precision side-effects based on the ordering of variables are influenced by this option. To get most of the *-O3* optimization but without the above side-effects, the additional option *-qstrict* should be used. However, one can also improve *-O3* by using *-qhot* to allow more optimizations, such as additional unrolling techniques.

-Q=N
Tells the compiler to inline functions that are N lines or less. This works only if *-O* is also used.

-qarch=[com|pwr|pwrx|ppc]
Tells the compiler to generate code for common mode (*arch=com*) for all processors, which is the default, or for the classic Power architecture (*arch=pwr*) or for the Power 2 architecture (*arch=pwrx*) or for the PowerPC architecture (*arch=ppc*). Using this option can result in code that runs only on the architecture for which it was compiled. It will use instructions available only on the specified architecture, which can result in better performance. Floating point-intensive code on the Power 2 architecture will probably benefit most from the *arch=pwrx* option, whereas single precision floating point-oriented programs will see the biggest benefit from *arch=ppc* on a PowerPC system.

-qtune=[pwr|pwrx|601]
Using *-qtune* will tell the compiler to optimize for a given processor architecture, but it will not use architecture-specific instructions. This affects mostly instruction ordering and data placement. The code will run on all systems, but it will run even better on the one for which it has been optimized.

The compiler supports many more options, but the above ones have the biggest performance impact.

19.6.2 Compiler pragmas

In addition to the command line options, there are compiler *#pragma* statements. Those can be inserted in the source to give the optimizer a few hints that make its job easier and will result in better optimization. The following *#pragma*s should be used if possible:

disjoint

```
#pragma disjoint (a,b)
```

This tells the compiler that a and b are not aliases for each other. As C allows the programmer to have pointers to anything and two pointers can easily reference the same memory location, the compiler has to be careful when trying to optimize variable access. The disjoint pragma allows a much more aggressive optimization. The compiler option *-qassert=[typ|allp|addr]* can be used to achieve a similar effect on a per file basis. There is also a *-qdisjoint* option that works similarly to the *#pragma* statement, but I suggest using pragmas in the file itself, as the command line option is rather cryptic.

isolated_call

When using

```
#pragma isolated_call a
```

the compiler assumes that function a does not modify any global variables or have other side-effects. Only function returns and pointers passed by reference are assumed by the compiler.

19.6.3 String and memory operations

The *xlc* compiler supports the inlining of string/memory operations, some of which can even be directly mapped to CPU instructions. When using the include file string.h the compiler automatically generates fast inline code for most of the *str*()*, *mem*()* functions as well as for *index()* and *rindex()*.

In addition, you can speed up memory operations by coding in a way that allows you to use fixed-length strings. This is because you can substitute *mem*()* operations for *str*()* operations as the *mem*()* functions do not check for null termination by examining every single byte but operate on fixed-length memory regions.

19.6.4 Some coding hints

For certain data types and coding styles better optimization is performed by the compiler. If possible, you should make it easier for it to perform its job.

Use unsigned characters wherever possible, this is best achieved by the compiler option *-qchars=unsigned*. Although *int*s take up more space, they are easier to process than *char*s or *short*s, so use *int* whenever possible. Access to local (auto) variables helps the optimizer, so use local variables instead of global variables when possible. If you really need to use global variables and have more than one access to it, copy it to a local variable if possible as access to local variables is faster than to global variables.

Memory access patterns also have a great influence on the program execution time. You should try to keep frequently referenced data or code together as much as possible. If you jump between different parts of the code that are spread far apart, the code needed next might have been paged out in the meantime because of another process that needed memory. The same applies to data: frequently referenced data should be in the same memory page if possible. Although accessing a memory page that is not in the cache is costly compared with a memory page in the cache, the penalty for accessing paged out memory locations is higher by a factor of 1000. The following rules should be followed for structuring code and data.

Never *malloc()* more memory than needed. Your own program might not notice it, but the pages have to be stolen from other processes first. (Early versions of the AIX linker typically exhibited this behavior.) Do not use *calloc()* unless required as it will touch all pages immediately.

When data structures need to be initialized, try to do so immediately before using them. If they are initialized at the beginning of the program but only used much later, they will have been paged out meanwhile.

When using very large data structures infrequently so that memory can be freed in between, think about using the *disclaim()* call to give it back to the operating system. *Free()* will only mark the memory as reusable for your own process.

Keep rarely needed code out of the modules that are frequently used so that the compiler (actually the linker in this case) can put it somewhere else. A typical example is error handlers that do not really need to be in the main code.

19.6.5 Compiler invocation

For simple syntax tests I suggest compiling without optimization as this will speed up compile time quite a bit. If your program is ANSI C compliant, then the *xlc* invocation of the compiler is slightly faster than the *cc* method.

By adapting /etc/xlC.cfg (/etc/xlc.cfg on AIX 3), you can set up different compiler invocations. See the samples on page 402 for more details on custom compiler invocations

20

Running AIX in a non-US English environment

As the computer market outside the US is much bigger than the US market you will find many things in AIX that help it to adapt to different language environments. International language support (ILS) is a key feature of AIX. It supports a wide variety of environments ranging from the European Latin-derived ones to Arabic and Asian. As I do not have access to any of the environments that require more than just clean 8 bit support, this chapter is limited to the single-byte character set world in western Europe. However, the basic mechanisms are the same for all the environments.

20.1 Customizing AIX for non-US English environments

AIX allows you to define cultural conventions, such as collating order or currency symbols, message texts and keyboard mapping, independently of each other. Although I am one of those who need this flexibility for an optimal work environment, it can be somewhat confusing for others. I typically work with a German keyboard but use locale definitions for US English, classic UNIX messages and fonts in the ISO 8859-1 encoding.

As AIX 4 no longer includes everything and the kitchen sink automatically during the installation one may end up without the necessary file sets for the desired locales. Find out if **smit keyboard** will allow you to select the keyboard support for the languages you need. If it does not, you need to install the missing file sets.

20.1.1 The locale: cultural conventions

What are the cultural conventions one can specify? The term locale is used to group all the language and cultural conventions of a country together. Use the command **locale** and you will see the following options, which are all specifiable individually as environment variables.

LANG Usually one needs to set only this environment variable (the system-wide default is set in /etc/environment). The other locale options will inherit their value from it if not set by individual environment variables. Typically one would set this to *de_DE* in Germany or *en_US* in the USA.

LC_COLLATE This variable defines the collating rules and thereby also the sorting order. Setting it to *de_DE* would specify string comparison and sorting according to the German rules with characters in the ISO code page.

LC_CTYPE Defines the handling of single characters, for example when using the POSIX locale "C" character functions like *isalpha()* assume only 7 bit characters and 8 bit characters are treated as non-printable characters.

LC_MONETARY Although not used by AIX itself, applications that are language sensitive use this setting for the treatment and display of monetary values.

LC_NUMERIC The properties of numeric values are defined here, for example the decimal point, which is a "," in Germany but a "." in the US.

LC_TIME Time and date formatting is controlled by this variable, for example

```
$ LC_TIME=en_US date
Sat May 20 20:17:13 CEST 1995
$ LC_TIME=de_DE date
Sa 20 Mai 20:17:17 1995
```

LC_MESSAGES The messages of the operating system and language-sensitive applications are controlled by this variable. As I prefer classic UNIX messages, I keep this set to "C". Unfortunately, a few commands will not display enough information with this setting. For example *lsdev* will not include any description of the devices as these are stored in message catalogs that will not be consulted in a "C" environment on AIX 3.

Whereas AIX 3 needed manual conversion of the delivered message catalogs from PC850 to ISO, AIX 4 ships both of them. The language selected at the initial installation will trigger the loading of message files with the correct code pages automatically.

Programs that search for their messages will do so according to the setting of *$LC_MESSAGES* or *$LANG* and the *$NLSPATH*. The "%L" in *$NLSPATH* is set to the language specified by *$LC_MESSAGES*. For example, the default *$NLSPATH* on AIX 4 will be expanded from */usr/lib/nls/msg/%L/%N:/usr/lib/nls/msg/%L/%N.cat*, to */usr/lib/nls/msg/en_US/%N:/usr/lib/nls/msg/en_US/%N.cat* if *$LANG* is *en_US*.

LC_ALL If set, this variable will override the others, including *$LANG*.

AIX 4 introduced yet another environment variable, *LC__FASTMSG*. This variable is used to control access to message catalogs. If it is set to true then only built-in messages will be consulted in a C/POSIX environment. Otherwise, the system would try to access a message catalog even for those locales.

To see the available locales on the current system use the command **locale -a**, which will list all the installed locales. On an AIX 4 system that has support for Germany loaded you will see the following output:

```
C
POSIX
de_DE
de_DE.ISO8859-1
```

The C and POSIX locales are equivalent. The German locale is available only for the ISO8859-1 code pages in this case. On an AIX 3 system the output was:

```
de_DE.ISO8859-1
De_DE.IBM-850
en_US.ISO8859-1
En_US.IBM-850
```

Here the locale support included also the PC 850 code pages, which are compatible with the PC world. Typically one sets only the name of the locale without the code page. The code page is indicated by the first letter of the *$LANG* setting. As you can see, *de_DE* would be for the ISO code pages and *De_DE* for the PC 850 code pages. For *en_US*/*En_US* the distinction is practically meaningless as US English does not have any 8 bit characters.

The code page defines where the characters are placed in the character set. The English-speaking world and most of the rest of Europe can live with the ISO 8859-1 code page or the PC 850 code pages if compatibility with PCs is more important than compatibility with other UNIX systems.

20.1.2 Fonts

No matter what locale and code page you choose, the fonts that you use need to match this locale. Full font names under X will have the encoding in their name, for example

```
-ibm--medium-r-medium--20-140-100-100-c-90-ibm-850
-ibm--medium-r-medium--20-140-100-100-c-90-iso8859-1
```

Both names refer to the same font (in this case it is Rom14 as it is commonly known on AIX), but with a different encoding. On the native console display you can use **smit font** to set up the fonts. Under X you can use the X configuration files, as shown in Section 11.2.5 to set up the right fonts. You can use *xfontsel* to select the X fonts or use the *custom* program or the customization utility that comes with CDE to set up the fonts. They all allow you to select the code page explicitly.

20.1.3 The keyboard

One of the major items that needs to be set up is the keyboard. Unless you use an ASCII terminal that knows about only one keyboard, you have to tell the system what your keyboard looks like. Use **smit keyboard** to set up the system keyboard mapping.

When running X, then you need to set up an additional keyboard map in the X server with the *xmodmap* command. this is typically done in the X profiles as described in Section 11.2.1.

The standard keyboard maps can be found in /usr/lib/nls/loc; the X maps are in /usr/lpp/X11/defaults/xmodmap.

20.2 Interoperability with other systems

Most UNIX systems today use ISO code pages. The PC world still uses mostly the IBM PC code pages. Then there are, of course, the IBM mainframe EBCDIC code pages and a few other, more exotic, code pages. What you use on AIX depends very much on which environment you work in and what application support is available. Well-written applications are code page independent, but these are unfortunately rare. It may therefore be necessary to carry out some testing before you decide whether you use PC or ISO code pages. This assumes central Europe; in China the choices would be quite different. AIX 3 assumes PC 850 by default, whereas AIX 4 uses ISO 8859-1 as the default code page.

Quite often people use PCs as X servers and run programs on AIX that use the PC as a display. Most of the time it is easier to set up the PC to use the fonts from AIX via a font server (see Section 11.2.9) than to tweak X applications that have been written with ISO code pages in mind to use PC code pages.

If you need to convert text files from one code page to another, then you can use the *iconv* utility that comes with AIX. To convert a text from PC850 to ISO8859-1 the command would be

```
iconv -f IBM-850 -t ISO8859-1 < text.pc850 > text.iso
```

Converting a text from a German ENCDIC mainframe to ISO code pages could be done with

```
iconv -f IBM-273 -t ISO8859-1 < text.ebcdic > text.iso
```

There is however, one problem converting from EBCDIC to ISO or ASCII: line endings. EBCDIC files use a record structure to specify line boundaries, whereas the ASCII world uses line end characters. Thus, the conversion might be less than perfect. The converters and translation tables for *iconv* are in /usr/lib/nls/loc/iconv and /usr/lib/nls/loc/iconvTable.

When telnetting to an IBM mainframe (using *tn3270*), you will need to tell the *telnet* client the code page that is used on the host. To set it up for a German host use **RM_HOST_LANG=IBM-273**.

20.3 Programming for an international environment

When programming in an international environment, the application needs to be aware of many details. To tell the system libraries as well as the X and Motif libraries that you want to run with support for more than just the 7 bit ASCII character set, then you need to call the *setlocale()* subroutine at the beginning of your application. This will automatically trigger the correct behavior of library routines such as *isalpha()* and the correct display of ILS data in Motif text widgets.

To use the user-defined locale, the *setlocale()* subroutine should be called in the following way: **setlocale(LC_ALL, "")**. This will set all locale information according to what the user has specified with the environment variables described previously. See InfoExplorer for more details.

20.3.1 Shell scripts

When programming shell scripts one is always vulnerable to the setting of *$LANG* that was chosen by the user. This can greatly change the output of some commands, for example

```
$ echo "7 8.9" | LANG=de_DE awk '{print $1+$2}'
15
$ echo "7 8,9" | LANG=de_DE awk '{print $1+$2}'
15,9
$ echo "7 8.9" | LANG=en_US awk '{print $1+$2}'
15.9
$ echo "7 8,9" | LANG=en_US awk '{print $1+$2}'
15
```

It is therefore highly recommended that *$LANG* is set explicitly to C or some other consistent value in shell scripts that are used by more than one user, as each user can set the environment variables that define the locale in a different way.

20.4 ILS and benchmarks

International language support has its costs. Using message catalogs instead of built-in messages does not necessarily speed up programs and taking account of language properties when performing string comparisons or numeric conversions also costs CPU time. Quite often AIX gets poor results in benchmark tests, especially for shell scripts. For example, the command **sort -r /usr/dict/words | wc** will take about 1.8 s when *$LANG* is set to *C* or *en_US* on a 250 with AIX 3.2.5. However, as soon as *$LANG* is set to *de_DE* the time more than doubles to 4.2 s. On AIX 4 the difference is less drastic, but it still takes longer to run in a German than in a POSIX environment.

So if you benchmark systems, be sure to set the locale definition to equivalent values on all systems, otherwise the results are not comparable.

21

AIX memory management and other tidbits

Several questions regarding AIX memory and process management crop up regularly. In particular, processes being killed by the PSDANGER signal and the mysterious kprocs 514 and 516 are often a puzzle for those familiar with other UNIX systems. These mysteries, as well as the way in which AIX allocates process ids, are discussed in this chapter.

21.1 The malloc story

21.1.1 Memory allocation and paging space

Memory is allocated to processes with the *sbrk()* system call. This memory is then managed with the *malloc()* family and *free()*. As long as this memory is not touched, no paging space/real memory is allocated for it, thus allowing programs to allocate very large data structures and still consume little real storage. An example would be the use of sparse matrices when one wants to use large matrices for ease of programing in which only a few elements are ever referenced. In some scientific programs it is not uncommon to *malloc()* memory chunks that are larger than the paging space.

As long as not all pages of this memory are touched, this will work. However, when the program suddenly needs really to use memory/paging space for the pages that have not been used so far, then a shortage of memory can cause problems. The program trying to access the already allocated memory usually does not know about this situation. It, as well as other programs, will get the SIGDANGER signal. Programs that do not have a signal handler registered for SIGDANGER can be killed by a SIGKILL, which might follow shortly after this signal to free memory resources.

This, in turn, leads to some particularly nasty trouble as memory-hungry processes will get killed first. The standard X server on AIX is a prime candidate for this as it does not have a SIGDANGER handler and can therefore kill your whole X session when paging space is getting short.

There is an environment variable, *PSALLOC*, that when set to *early* will force allocation of paging space for a process even if its memory pages have not yet been touched. Some AIX applications would need an incredible amount of paging space when this variable is set, as they use compiled in tables that are very large but usually consume no real storage as long as the pages are not really used. The X server is a prime example of this strategy – it would consume more than 250MB with early allocation.

To monitor the paging space situation, a process can check the available memory by using the *psdanger()* function.

A nice way to kill the system is to run **wc /dev/kmem**, which will try to really allocate the memory for all the arrays in the kernel. The result is that the kernel eats up all memory.

21.1.2 Different malloc styles

Since AIX 3.2 introduced a new malloc algorithm there have been many complaints that programs which ran well previously do not run since the switch to AIX 3.2. The problem here is not the *malloc()*, but always faulty program (or library) code.

AIX 3.1 used a fast, but very inefficient algorithm to allocate memory. It always allocated chunks of memory in powers of 2. Thus, if you needed 230 bytes of memory, you would have always been allocated 512 bytes. As many programs need much larger memory areas, you can imagine how wasteful this is.

AIX 3.2 introduced the so-called Yorktown *malloc* which has been used by IBM's mainframe operating system for years. This algorithm is just slightly slower, but much more efficient as memory requests are rounded up to the nearest 16 byte boundary and not to the next power of 2.

The problem with the new *malloc* is that program errors that were hidden by the overallocated memory of the old *malloc* scheme are now exposed. Once you overwrite the boundary of allocated memory anything can happen, from rather benign segmentation violations to totally unexplainable program behavior in unrelated parts of the code.

A quick check to determine whether there is really a problem with access to unallocated memory is to run the program with the environment variable *MALLOCTYPE=3.1*. Should the program work with that setting but fail otherwise it is time to find out if all calls to *free()* are matched by *mallocs* and whether there is any memory access beyond the allocated boundaries. Use freeware or commercially available debugging *malloc()* routines to find the error. The *mallopt()* function can be used from within programs to control the memory allocation algorithm if necessary.

21.1.3 Giving memory back

One can call *free()* as often as one wants in a process, still the memory will not be given back to the system but will stay in the memory pool allocated to the process. When working with dynamic memory in a constrained environment, try to use the *disclaim()* call to give memory back to the operating system. When *disclaim()* is called, pages that have been freed so far are given back to AIX.

21.2 Shared libraries

On AIX all the system libraries are shared. If you want to know which shared libraries a given executable uses, you can use the *dump* command, as in **dump -H /usr/bin/vi**, which will also tell you the library search path of the executable. On AIX 3 you can find more tools to analyze the use of shared libraries in /usr/lpp/bosperf. On AIX 4 these tools come with the optional performance management package. The utility *genkld* will tell you about currently loaded shared library objects. To obtain a listing of the shared objects loaded by different programs *genld* can be used. Use *genkex* to display all the loaded kernel extensions.

Even after all programs that used a specific shared library have terminated, the shared library still stays cached in memory. To clean up this cache use the *slibclean* command.

21.3 Process management

21.3.1 Kernel processes

AIX 4 finally has kernel threads – AIX 3 did not have them although some thread-like process management in the kernel was required even in older versions. Kernel processes (*kprocs*) were introduced to fulfil that need. They are processes in the kernel that, although not as lightweight as threads, still have far less context switching overhead than normal UNIX processes. Use the *-k* flag on the *ps* command to see them. Unfortunately, they are not listed by name – they just show up as *kproc*. Among them are the *swapper*, the network memory manager (*netm*), the wait process and the scheduler.

21.3.2 The wait process

The design of AIX and the POWER/PowerPC CPUs mandate that there is always one process running; it is called the wait process. This leads to the constantly reoccurring question: "Why does one kernel process take up all the CPU time?" The answer is that machines are always idle at least some of the time and then the wait process gets scheduled. It always runs at the lowest possible priority and will therefore never interfere with your working processes, but it can be quite confusing for the uninitiated. On AIX 3 the process id is always 514 and is usually listed as a *kproc* (kernel process). On AIX 4.1 the process id is 516. Use the *-k* flag for *ps* to see them.

21.3.3 How are process ids allocated?

Classic UNIX systems allocate process ids in a linear fashion. Most still use a 16 bit number for process ids. It takes quite some time for the process ids to be recycled. This is not so on AIX. Here process ids are 32 bit numbers that are a combination of a process slot and a generation count. The generation count is an 8 bit number (bits 24 – 31 of the process id) that is incremented for each new process. Each process has a process slot that is identified by the bits 7 – 23 (the leading bits 0 – 6 are not used at the moment) of the process id. As each process slot would occupy pinned memory if used, AIX tries to minimize the number of process slots used by reusing them as much as possible. Therefore process ids reappear much more quickly on AIX and the numeric relationship between a father and the child processes is not so easy to decipher. The aggressive reuse of process slots would generate reappearing process ids much too quickly. This is where the generation count comes in: it makes sure that process ids do not reappear too quickly.

22

Compiling software for AIX

This chapter mainly gives tips for porting free software that is found on the Internet, but the tips should be useful for anyone porting to AIX.

Compiler options that deal mainly with performance or adaptations to the different Power architectures can be found in Section 19.6.

There are two strategies for porting software:

(1) Make it run and don't worry about any minor details.

(2) Make it compile cleanly in a strict environment.

The first strategy is chosen by many. It is only necessary to use the *bsdcc* definition that enables you to compile nearly any old code. I use this option for minor tools when I am in a hurry, but it can be more costly because of hidden bugs and other subtleties.

The second strategy involves more work as it may be necessary to adapt not only the makefile but also source files. This is the preferred strategy for production-quality code. It will give you a less bug-ridden and possibly even faster code as it utilizes the ANSI features of the compiler and the inline string subroutines that take advantage of the processor's string operations. In any case you should read /usr/lpp/xlC/README.C on AIX 4 or /usr/lpp/xlc/bin/README.xlc on AIX 3 for up-to-date information on the C compiler. The compiler configuration file name has changed between AIX 3 and 4. First it was /etc/xlc.cfg and now it is /etc/xlC.cfg. I use both names intermixed in this chapter; pick the one that applies to your release – they are very similar.

22.1 Using *bsdcc*

The following has been documented on AIX 3 in /usr/lpp/bos/bsdport. On AIX 4 there does not seem to be a similar example, but the method still works. In there a BSD compatible compiler is defined. This amounts to generating a new name for the compiler via **ln /usr/bin/xlc /usr/bin/bsdcc** on AIX 3 or **ln -s /usr/lpp/xlC/bin/xlC /usr/bin/bsdcc** on AIX 4 and a new stanza in /etc/xlC.cfg or /etc/xlc.cfg. Put the stanza in Figure 22.1 in the C compiler configuration file.

```
* old BSD compatible CC
bsdcc:use       = DEFLT
      crt       = /lib/crt0.o
      mcrt      = /lib/mcrt0.o
      gcrt      = /lib/gcrt0.o
      libraries = -lbsd, -lc
      proflibs  = -L/usr/lib/profiled
      options   = -H512,-T512,-qlanglvl=extended,-qnoro,-ma,-D_BSD,
-D_NONSTD_TYPES,-D_NO_PROTO,-bnodelcsect,-U__STR__,-U__MATH__
```

Figure 22.1 The definition of *bsdcc* in /etc/xlc.cfg on AIX 3.

On AIX 4 you can skip the *-H* and *-T* options. Note that the options line has to be really one line! Instead of using *cc* you now can use *bsdcc* with many predefined flags that let you compile heaps of old code. Most utilities that I have obtained from the Internet were compilable this way, but you will always have the nagging feeling that there may be some very strange bug lurking in the code that is not discovered because all checks are turned off. The AIX 4 compiler will also complain that the internal symbols *__STR__* and *__MATH__* have been undefined. Both are used to trigger inline code instead of library code, but this often clashes with source code that defines string and math functions on the fly instead of using the proper include files.

22.2 Compiling all sources

The clean way to compile all programs is to use a fully ANSI-compliant C compiler. ANSI C gives you a much better C environment as it performs parameter type-checking for function definitions and more to prevent the kind of accidental errors that one makes so easily in C. Unfortunately, many of the common library functions that are used under UNIX are not included in ANSI C. You need to access yet another standard for them, POSIX. To access the prototypes for POSIX-compliant library routines one needs to set *-D_POSIX_SOURCE* on the compiler command line. And there is, of course, X/Open which also has some additions. To include all of these functions you should define *_XOPEN_SOURCE*.

You may sometimes run across a problem when the compiler thinks a function or definition is missing altogether but you know that it is in the system includes, for example the definition of *O_DELAY* in fcntl.h. This happens because there are usually more things in a standard UNIX C library than are defined by either ANSI C, POSIX or X/Open. If you include *-D_ALL_SOURCE* on the compiler command line or in /etc/xlc.cfg then these definitions in the include files are also accessible. To make life easier you need to define only the highest of them and then include standards.h, which defines all of the others. The other easy solution, of course, is to modify the *xlc* definition in the compiler configuration file.

When you start compiling older software with the ANSI compiler you will usually get errors for redeclared identifiers. Either bracket them with '*#ifndef _AIX*' or remove them altogether if you feel radical. This, of course, assumes that you then use the right include statement to get to the system-supplied prototypes.

22.3 Useful default defines

The C compiler sets some defines by default so that you can see on what machine you are running. See /etc/xlC.cfg for standard defines. You will find *-D_IBMR2* there for the hardware platform (the RS/6000 is IBM's second RISC machine), *-D_AIX* for the operating system and then something like *-D_AIX32* for the release. Unfortunately, there is no default define for AIX 4 – the *_AIX32* define is present there as well. However, the compiler defines its own version number when using the AIX 4 version. This is not available on AIX 3, so one can check for the *__xlc__* macro to find out whether one runs on AIX 3 or 4.

In addition, there are some internal defines. Usually the compiler defines *__STR__* so that the inline string instructions of the processor are used. When using the ANSI version, *__STDC__* is also defined (triggered by setting *-qlanglvl=ansi*, which is the default for *xlc*). The *__MATH__* define triggers some inline math functions.

22.4 Typical problems

There are some very common pitfalls that can be circumvented very easily by knowing the cause.

22.4.1 Missing terminal definitions

There are programs that compile without any problem on AIX and then complain that they do not know how to access the terminal. Usually they link with *-ltermcap*. AIX does not really support the *termcap* library, but it has a fairly complete *terminfo* library. If you run into this problem, link with *-lcurses* instead of using *termcap*. The curses library has a *termcap* emulation that will use the *terminfo* database.

AIX 4 adds an additional potential problem as it only installs a minimum set of terminal definitions by default. You have to install the missing ones yourself.

22.4.2 Duplicate definitions

There is still a great deal of code that assumes an old UNIX system with missing or incorrect header files. Those programs usually have some form of external function definitions in the source files. You either can bracket all these definitions

```
#ifndef _AIX
char *strcpy();
#endif /* not _AIX */
```

or you can compile the troublemaker with *-D_NO_PROTO*, which will undefine all prototypes in the AIX header files. You might also need to add *-U__STR__* to your compiler command line because of the definition of the internal string routines. Another typical error message that has the same origin is ‘Parameter list cannot contain fewer...’.

22.4.3 Where is *alloca*?

Some programs have functions that use *alloca()* to allocate memory on the stack. This memory is freed automatically when the function is left. This routine is not very portable and its use is discouraged, but it works on AIX if you tell the compiler that you want to use it. You can do so by having a pragma at the beginning of your source file, such as:

```
#pragma alloca
```

This will tell the compiler that you want to use *alloca()* and it will use an internal function for it – there is no library function for *alloca()*. The other method of telling the compiler about it is to use the *-ma* flag on the compiler command line.

22.4.4 MIT X libraries, *imake* and *xmkmf*

When trying to link programs that need X Consortium libraries such as libXaw.a, libXau.a libXmu.a and others you might not find them in the MIT/consortium standard places. Check out /usr/lpp/X11/Xamples/lib and read Section 11.4. In principle, everything is there, and it is only necessary to compile the examples and create some symbolic links to access them in more standard places. See /usr/lpp/X11/Xamples/README for instructions on compiling the Xamples.

The *imake* and *xmkmf* utilities are also there – check out /usr/lpp/X11/Xamples/config and /usr/lpp/X11/Xamples/util/scripts on AIX 3. AIX 4 already has them in /usr/bin/X11.

22.4.5 Generating full core dumps

Should a program dump its core because of some segmentation violation or other errors, then only a partial core dump is created. If you need a full core dump, then the *SA_FULLDUMP* flag needs to be set when calling *sigaction()*.

22.4.6 What is deadbeef?

When analyzing memory dumps or tracing programs one occasionally comes across hexadecimal numbers that sound like real words. One example is $deadbeef_{16}$, which is typically the contents of a freshly initalized register that the program has not yet modified. Another one is $badfca11_{16}$, which can be found after trying to call a function whose address is wrong.

22.5 The AIX linker

The AIX linker is quite different from those that are normally found on UNIX systems. Linking on AIX is easy in most cases – the linker does the right thing. But this has a price. In this case it is memory. The linker needs very large amounts of memory compared with others. You can get around this by incremental linking; however, if your *ulimits* are the problem, you can increase them via the *ulimit* command (or your system administrator can do it for you). In some cases the paging space might need to be increased. If you run into this problem you may get errors such as 'binder killed by signal 9', 'paging space low' or 'BUMP error'.

For normal programs the order of libraries is not important. All libraries and object modules are read into memory and the linking is carried out in one run. You should specify each library only once on the commandline, otherwise you slow down the linking process.

22.5.1 Shared libraries

Most of the libraries that come with AIX are shared. The linker will not include the library code in the executable by default, only some glue to resolve the references at program load time. The advantage of shared libraries is saved memory. The code is held in memory only once, no matter how many programs use it.

22.5.2 Linking non-shared

In a few cases shared libraries are a problem and you will want to link non-shared. Either because you want to be sure that the end user has a specific library level linked or because you know that the program will be the only one that uses the library and only one instance of the program is run at any given time and you want to save a few cycles from the dynamic relocation. You can link libc.a static for example:

```
cc -o prog -bnso -bI:/lib/syscalls.exp obj1.o obj2.o ... objn.o
```

This will tell the linker to link non-shared. If you have your own libraries that you want to link statically you have to use the following procedure:

```
ld -r yourobject.o -oyourlib.o -bnso
cc -o yourprog someobject.o yourlib.o
```

First you create a non-shared object library then you link it to your other objects. This sample will link all libraries shared apart from the one you explicitly added unshared.

22.5.3 Creating shared libraries

Shared libraries cannot contain undefined symbols. You must resolve all the references in a shared library. This means that you need to link in libc.a, for example, when creating a normal shared library as most programs will need functions from libc.a.

The following sample assumes two source files: one with no external references (subself.c) and one with references to libc.a (subext.c). For each of those files you need an export file that lists the exported symbols.

subself.c

```
int addint(int a, int b)
{
        return a + b;
}
```

subext.c

```
#include <stdio.h>

void printint(int i)
{
        printf("Result: %d\n", i);
}
```

subself.exp

```
#!
addint
```

subext.exp

```
#!
printint
```

usesub.c

```
main()
{
        printint( addint(40,2) );
}
```

The following commands will build your libshared.a and compile/link the program main to use it. The *-lc* on the command line for generating the *subext* library is needed because *subext* references *printf* from libc.a.

```
1$ cc  -c subself.c
2$ ld -o subselfshr.o subself.o -bE:subself.exp -bM:SRE -T512 -H512
3$ cc  -c subext.c
4$ ld -o subextshr.o subext.o -bE:subext.exp -bM:SRE -T512 -H512 -lc
5$ ar r libshr.a subselfshr.o subextshr.o
6$ cc -o usesub usesub.c -L: libshr.a
7$ usesub
Result: 42
```

The above sample gives you only a very quick tour of this subject. Please also read what InfoExplorer has to say about the *ld* command.

22.5.4 Relinking executables

You can relink final executables and exchange changed objects. This has the advantage that you do not need to link your executable completely anew when changing only one module. This works only on non-stripped executables of course. For example:

```
1$ cc -o prog prog1.o prog2.o prog3.o
2$ cc -c prog2.c
3$ cc -o prog.new prog2.o prog
```

In step 1 the program is completely linked. Now you can recompile one of its modules and then relink the executable like in step 3.

You may want to perform incremental linking if you are working on a very large executable with large libraries. You can prelink several libraries into object modules. This is done in the following way:

```
1$ cc -c prog1.c prog2.c prog3.c
2$ ar cv libprog.a prog1.o prog2.o prog3.o
3$ ld -r -o libprog.o libprog.a
4$ cc -o someprog someprog.c libprog.o
```

First you create your library out of object files as you would normally. Then you create a prelinked object file with the *-r* flag of *ld*. This prelinked object module is much faster in linking when creating the final executable than normal library modules. This works by resolving all internal references within the library in the prelinked object module. Anything that could be resolved in the first linking step does not need to be done in the final step and saves time.

22.5.5 AIX-specific tools for object files

In /usr/lpp/bosperf on AIX 3.2 there are some tools that help you to anaylze executables and the currently running kernel. On AIX 4 these tools are part of the performance toolbox, which must be purchased separately.

genkex Generates a list of currently loaded kernel extension drivers.

genkld Generates a list of currently loaded shared objects.

genld Generates a list of shared objects for each currently running process.

stripnm Generates a name list similar to the output of *nm* but from stripped executables.

23

Other useful utilities and tips

In this chapter you will find various tidbits that would not fit anywhere else in the book. If you have a problem that is not covered elsewhere, have a look in here – you may find a useful hint.

23.1 Common questions and answers

This section lists common problems and their solutions. There are many minor problems that people tend to stumble across. This is my 'answers to frequently asked AIX and UNIX questions'. This section does not, however, cover anything that has been discussed in previous chapters.

23.1.1 Restoring libc.a from tape

Occasionally people manage to remove the shared C library from the system, after which no new processes can be started as all processes on the system depend on it. Now is the time to dig out a system backup tape or distribution CD to fix this problem. Boot from the backup medium and follow the release specific commands below.

Restoring libc.a on AIX 3.2

Get into the maintenance shell and run **getrootfs hdisk0 sh**. If you are not sure whether *hdisk0* is your boot disk, run **getrootfs** without parameters first. The *sh* parameter will run a shell before mounting the file systems, which is necessary to run with the libc.a of the backup medium instead of trying to use the non-existent one on disk. Now follow the steps below.

```
tctl -f/dev/rmt0 rewind
tctl -f/dev/rmt0.1 fsf 3
chdev -l rmt0 -a block_size=1024
mount /dev/hd2 /mnt
pax -rvf/dev/rmt0.1  -s"/usr/mnt/" ./usr/ccs/lib/libc.a
umount /mnt
exit
```

Now the system will mount the file systems and you can run a normal *shutdown* command.

Restoring libc.a on AIX 4

On AIX 4 use the menu options to get to a maintenance shell without mounting the file systems. Then run the following commands:

```
tctl -f/dev/rmt0 rewind
tctl -f/dev/rmt0.1 fsf 3
mkdir /mnt/usr
mount /dev/hd2 /mnt/usr
cd /mnt
restbyname -xqf/dev/rmt0.1 ./usr/ccs/lib/libc.a
sync;sync;reboot -q
```

23.1.2 Full-screen applications and remote connections

If you access curses applications (applications that use the curses library to handle the terminal) over a network connection you might run into problems with function keys. Terminals send escape sequences for function keys. Each key sends the ESC character and some other characters. Applications or curses need to be able to distinguish between a single <ESC> key and function keys that start with the ESC character. If you are directly logged in, this is not usually a problem. The delay between pressing the <ESC> key and the next character is easily distinguishable from an ESC sequence, in which the delay is much smaller. When accessing the application over the network or via a modem, this distinction is blurred. Curses-based applications can be adapted by setting the environment variable *ESCDELAY* to some value in milliseconds. Depending on the speed of the network I suggest starting with a value of 2000 and increasing it if necessary. Vi, SMIT and HCON are typical applications that use the curses library and can be adapted to network connections with *ESCDELAY.*

23.1.3 Temporary file names in shell scripts

Many people use the process id in shell scripts to create temporary file names. This might lead into problems on an AIX system as AIX recycles process ids more often than other UNIX systems (see Section 21.3.3). This makes certain process operations more efficient. In C programs the *tmpnam()* or *tempnam()* library calls could be used to generate temporary file names. In shell scripts I suggest using a combination of process id and date/time to get around this problem. For example

```
tmpfile=/tmp/`basename $0`.tmp.$$.`date +%Y%m%d%H%M%S`
```

23.1.4 Killing zombies

Zombies are processes that are finished but whose status information still occupies a process slot. You can see them in the *ps* output as *<defunct>* entries. Those processes hang around in the system until their parent process checks the exit status of the child process. If the parent is already gone, the child will be reparented to *init* and *init* will never really check the exit status of the adopted children. They cannot be killed by the *kill* command – they will only go away after a shutdown or after they have been reaped by a cleanup procedure of *init*, but this takes quite a while.

23.1.5 Where is the kernel?

Occasionally someone deletes /unix. On some systems this is reason for panic, but not on AIX. The kernel of the running system is in the boot image created by the *bosboot* command. The /unix file is used only to generate new boot images and to deliver kernel symbol information to commands such as *ps* or *crash*. And even /unix is not the real kernel, it is just a symbolic link to the file in /usr/lib/boot that is the real kernel. On AIX 3 it is simply called unix; on AIX 4 it might be unix_up or unix_mp, depending on whether the system is running on a uniprocessor or multiprocessor hardware. Should you accidentally delete the real kernel, you can restore one from your backup tape with the mechanisms shown in Section 13.1.

23.1.6 Where did the program crash?

When a program dumps core one often does not know which program it was and where exactly it died. Using *dbx* on the core file will tell you which program created the core file when complaining that there is no program matching the core image. If you have an executable compiled with *-g* you might find out where the program crashed with the *where* subcommand. Simply copy both the executable and the core file into one directory and run *dbx* on the executable and use the *where* subcommand.

23.1.7 Where did the system crash?

When the system crashes, the kernel dump can be analyzed with the *crash* command. The location of the dump is slightly different on AIX 3 and 4. On AIX 3 you need to use *dd* to copy the dump from /dev/hd7 to the file system. On AIX 4 the core file that was dumped to the paging space should be available in /var/adm/ras. If you do not run *crash* on the system that generated the dump you need a copy of /unix as well. /unix is needed to resolve the memory addresses in the dump into meaningful locations. Then run **crash /unix /yourdumpfile**. This should be done in an *aixterm* window with an active scroll bar. Some of the *crash* commands have endless output.

Use the *crash* subcommand **proc -r** to see all the processes that were runable when the system crashed. Then use **trace -k** to see in which kernel function it crashed. These two checks are usually the only things one can do without a deeper understanding of the kernel. From there on it is a job for the people in the AIX support center.

23.1.8 Reviving your keyboard on AIX 3

Should you unplug your keyboard from a running system then it will be unusable after you plug it back in. If you still can log in from a remote system or the keyboard is at least halfway working (most of the time only <SHIFT>, <CTRL> and <ALT> are screwed) then you can run **/usr/lpp/diagnostics/da/dkbd** which will reset the keyboard. This works only on AIX 3 however.

23.2 Less well-known known AIX commands

There are quite a few AIX commands that go unnoticed because nobody knows them. Some of them might even be undocumented. Check out the following list and see if you find something new and useful.

hdf [[[file] start] length] Dumps data in hexadecimal and ASCII, a welcome change over *od*. On AIX 4 this command is no longer available.

li This command lists files and directories like the *ls* command, but with the *-O* flag it can be used to restrict the output to only executables (**li -Ox**) or files (**li -Of**) or devices (**li -Ocb**). This is much easier than piping the output of *ls* through *awk*. It has a few more interesting options that make it superior to *ls*, such as *-S* for the sort order. On AIX 4.1 it is in the *bos.compat.cmds* file set and we are threatened with its complete removal.

showled number Displays codes in the machine's LED display. The number is treated as a decimal representation of a three-digit hexadecimal number. Or you can use hexadecimal notation by prepending the number with 0x. This command resides in /etc/methods.

23.3 Shell programming hints

Shell scripts can make life much easier, and here are some hints that should make programming the shell easier. All of them are geared towards the Korn shell. Anyone who really wants to get the most out of the Korn shell should read (*The New Korn Shell*, 41).

The Bourne shell would allow a more portable version of the scripts as the Korn shell is not yet available on all UNIX versions, but the aim of this chapter is not portability but efficiency on AIX.

Shell scripts should always start with *#!/usr/bin/ksh* in the first line. This will tell the kernel explicitly to execute the Korn shell and use this file as an input file for it. The *#!/program/to/execute* notation can also be used for other type of scripts. You can set other shells or *awk* here depending on the script language.

Command line parameters can be added to this line, for example *-x* would start the shell in trace mode so that you can see which commands are executed in the shell script. If you want to send all output of the script to a trace file you can execute the script with standard out and standard error redirected to a file as in

```
yourscript > /tmp/script.trace 2>&1
```

Standard out is redirected to /tmp/script.trace and standard error is tacked onto standard out. Sometimes one cannot start the script explicitly, but it is still possible to get a trace by putting the following at the beginning of the script:

```
exec > /tmp/script.trace 2>&1
```

After this line, all output to standard out and standard error is sent to /tmp/script.trace.

Redirecting all output to a file has the disadvantage that the script's progress cannot be monitored. Using the *tee* command provides a workaround:

```
yourscript 2>&1 | tee /tmp/script.trace
```

Note that the redirection of standard error is now before the pipe to the *tee* program – it would not work as intended if it were appended to the command. As *tee* uses buffered I/O the output might be slightly delayed.

When using the *-x* flag to trace program execution, line numbers can be quite helpful. The environment variable *PS4* can be set up to show line numbers during script traces. I export *PS4='$0.$LINENO+ '* in my ~/.profile to see the line numbers and the script name when *-x* is active.

If you do Bourne shell programming then you will often exec *grep*, *sed* and *awk* for things that can easily be handled in the Korn shell itself. The ${} parameter expansion functions in the Korn shell are very powerful functions for string manipulation. Using several of those is more efficient than calling *sed* or *awk*. As the Korn shell supports arithmetic with *(())* and the *let* command, the external *expr* command is no longer needed, saving another costly exec.

Quite often one needs simple menus in scripts. The Korn shell has the select statement to make this easier. For example

```
#!/usr/bin/ksh
PS3="Choose a number: "
select i in "First Choice" "Second Choice" "Third Choice"
do
    echo $i
done
```

Typically one uses *[ ]* or *test* for expression evaluation in shell scripts. The Korn shell *[[ ]]* compound command replaces these obsolete functions. Its expression syntax is a superset of the old test command with the addition of pattern matching. One now can use [[*x* = *pattern*]] instead of just [[*x* = *string*]]. For example

```
[[ $(tty) = *pts* ]] && echo "running on a pty"
```

Note that the pattern is not enclosed in quotes.

Command substitution with the 'command' syntax can get rather complex when special characters or environment variables are used in the command. The $(command) syntax that the Korn shell offers is usually easier to understand as evaluation of parameters is more consistent with the rest of the shell syntax.

If you try to do string comparisons in the Bourne shell, it gets a bit tedious to take care of the case of the string. The Korn shell uses assignment attributes to specify the case of the string like in **typeset -l lower=$Anystring**. To force the contents of a variable to upper case use *-u*. Other parameters for *typeset* that are used for justification are *-L* (left), *-R* (right) and *-Z* (zero fill). When using *-i* to make a variable an integer variable you can specify different bases. Apart from that it is not really necessary to tell the Korn shell about the type of the variable.

23.4 Some home-grown shell scripts and functions

After working for a while with any operating system one starts to amass a collection of home-grown or copied macros and commands. The following collection has not necessarily been invented by me – it grew out of self-made and copied functions.

23.4.1 To which lpp/file set does a file belong to?

Quite often one wonders where a file on AIX comes from. To which LPP on AIX 3 or file set on AIX 4 does it belong? The following script will answer this question. It is based on a *whichlpp* script that Mickey Coggins posted to comp.unix.aix.

```
#!/usr/bin/ksh
# to which file set/lpp does a specific file belong to?
# afx 12/94
# Based on a script by Mickey Coggins
#

export LANG=C
ME=`basename $0`

if [[ -z $1 ]] ; then
    echo "usage: $ME [path|filename]     "
    exit 123
fi

for f ; do                    # for all objects on the command line
    b=`basename $f`
    found=0
    for ODMDIR in /etc/objrepos /usr/lib/objrepos
/usr/share/lib/objrepos
    do
        if [[ $b != $f ]] ; then
            stanza=`odmget -q"loc0 = $f" inventory`
        else
            stanza=`odmget -q"loc0 like */$f" inventory`
        fi
        [[ -n $stanza ]] && found=1
        stanza=`echo $stanza`     # converts all newlines to spaces
        while (( ${#stanza} > 1 )) # As long as stanza is not empty
        do
            # stanza contains one or more entries
```

```
            # take the rightmost one
            tmpstanza=${stanza##*inventory:}
            lpp_id=${tmpstanza#*lpp_id = }
            lpp_id=${lpp_id%% *}
            rname=${tmpstanza#*loc0 = \"}
            rname=${rname%%\"*}
            hlinks=${tmpstanza#*loc1 = \"}
            hlinks=${hlinks%%\"*}
            slinks=${tmpstanza#*loc2 = \"}
            slinks=${slinks%%\"*}
            name=`odmget -q"lpp_id = $lpp_id" lpp`
            name=${name#*name = \"}
            name=${name%%\"*}
            if [[ ${rname#*inst_root/} = $rname ]] ; then
                echo "lppname: $name"
                echo "  location: $rname"
                [[ -n $hlinks ]] && echo "  hard links: $hlinks"
                [[ -n $slinks ]] && echo "  soft links: $slinks"
            fi
            # chop off the last entry in the list
            stanza=${stanza%inventory:*}
        done
    done
    if [[ $found -eq 0 ]] ; then
        if [[ $b != $f ]] ; then
            echo "Couldn't find "$f" with an exact search."
            echo "Try entering simply "\"$ME $b\"
        else
            echo "Couldn't find "$f" in the inventory."
        fi
    fi
done
```

The script scans the ODM inventory to find the LPP index to which the file belongs. It then uses the LPP index to get the LPP name out of the *lpp* ODM class. This has to be done for each ODM location. Installation support entries (those with inst_root in the pathname) are skipped.

23.4.2 Killing processes by name

The following shell function will kill processes by name. It will kill all processes that start with the names given on the commandline. Optionally, one can specify a signal before the process names.

```
# This is a real neat function that will kill commands.
# Thanks to MAC :-)
function zap {
case "$1" in
    "") echo "Usage: $0 [-SignalName | -SignalNumber] ProcessName"
        return 1
        ;;
```

```
    -*) SIGNAL=$1
        shift
        ;;
     *) SIGNAL=-15
        ;;
esac

PROCESSNAMES=""
while [ $# -gt 0 ]
do
    PROCESSNAMES=" $1|$PROCESSNAMES"
    shift
done
PROCESSNAMES=${PROCESSNAMES%\|}

PIDS=`ps -e | awk "/ $PROCESSNAMES/"'{print $1}'`
if [ -z "$PIDS" ]
then
     echo "No process with name $PROCESSNAMES."
     return 1
fi
echo "Sending signal $SIGNAL to \"$PROCESSNAMES\", pid $PIDS"
kill $SIGNAL $PIDS
}
```

23.4.3 Various ways to list processes

The following examples are on one line; they have been wrapped for the layout.

List the top 10 CPU users

On AIX 3:

```
alias pstop='echo "USER       PID %CPU %MEM   SZ  RSS    TTY STAT    STIME
TIME COMMAND";ps aux|tail +2|sort -k 1.15,1.19nr|head'
```

On AIX 4:

```
alias pstop='echo "USER       PID %CPU %MEM   SZ  RSS    TTY STAT    STIME
TIME COMMAND"; ps auxw|tail +2|sort -k 1.16,1.20nr|head'
```

List the top 10 memory users

On AIX 3:

```
alias psmem='echo "USER       PID %CPU %MEM   SZ  RSS    TTY STAT    STIME
TIME COMMAND";ps aux|tail +2|sort -k 1.20,1.24nr|head'
```

On AIX 4:

```
alias psmem='echo "USER       PID %CPU %MEM   SZ  RSS    TTY STAT    STIME
TIME COMMAND"; ps auxw|tail +2|sort -k 1.21,1.25nr|head'
```

Grepping for processes

```
function psg {
    ps -eaf|egrep -v "egrep -i $*" |egrep -i "$*"
}
```

23.4.4 Disk and file system information

Here is a script that will list all the disks and volume groups on the system as well as their relationship. By default, it will list all information. When options are used, only the information selected by the options will be listed. The options select disk/vg relationships (*-d*), unallocated disks (*-u*), file systems (*-f*) or logical volumes without file systems (*-l*).

```
#!/usr/bin/ksh
# diskinfo
# script that displays interesting points about disks and file systems
# afx 4/95

export LANG=C
export LC_MESSAGES=en_US

DoPV=0
DoFS=0
DoLV=0
DoNA=0

if [[ $# -ge 1 ]] ; then
        for opt
        do
                case $opt in
                -d)     DoPV=1
                        ;;
                -f)     DoFS=1
                        ;;
                -l)     DoLV=1
                        ;;
                -n)     DoNA=1
                        ;;
                *)      echo "Unknown parameter $opt"
                        echo "Usage:\n$(basename $0) [-d][-f][-l][-n]"
                        echo " -d: disks and volume groups"
                        echo " -f: file systems"
                        echo " -l: logical volumes without file systems"
                        echo " -n: unallocated disks"
                        exit 1
                        ;;
                esac
        done
else
        DoPV=1
        DoFS=1
```

```
        DoLV=1
        DoNA=1
fi

echo "Disk report for $(hostname -s) (machine id $(uname -m))\n"

disks=$(lspv | egrep -v None | cut -f1 -d\  )

[[ $DoPV -eq 1 ]] && {
        echo "Disks and Volume groups"
        echo "                          Physcal partitons"
        echo "VG          PV      size  used  free Location    Description"
        for d in $disks
        do
                (lsdev -Cl $d; lspv $d ) |
                awk '/Available/   {d=$1;loc=$3;
                                desc=substr($0,index($0,$4));
                                next}
                        /VOLUME GROUP/      {vg=$6;next}
                        /PP SIZE/           {sz=$3;next}
                        /FREE PP/           {free=$3;next}
                        /USED PP/           {used=$3;next}
                        END {printf("%-12s %-8s %4d %5d %5d %-12s %s\n",
                                        vg,d,sz,used,free,loc,desc)}
                '
        done
        echo ""
}

[[ $DoNA -eq 1 ]] && {
        lspv | egrep None > /dev/null
        if [[ $? -eq 0 ]] ; then
                echo "Unallocated physical volumes:"
                for d in $(lspv | egrep None | cut -f1 -d\  )
                do
                        lsdev -Cl $d
                done
        else
                echo "No unallocated physical volumes"
        fi
        echo ""
}

(( ($DoLV+$DoFS) >= 1 )) && {
echo "Volume Group Disk     LV            LPs   Distribution        Mount
point"
for d in $disks
do
        vg=$(lspv|awk "/$d/ {print \$3}")
        ( echo "$d $vg"
                [[ DoFS -eq 1 ]] && lspv -l $d | tail +3 | egrep " /"
                [[ DoLV -eq 1 ]] && lspv -l $d | tail +3 | egrep -v " /"
        ) | awk '{  if (NR==1) {
                                disk=$1
```

```
                        vg=$2
                } else {
                        printf("%-12s %-8s %-12s %-5s %-15s %s\n",
                                vg,disk,$1,$2,$4,$5)
                }
        } '
done
echo ""
}
```

24

Other sources of information about AIX

AIX has been on the market for quite some time so there are not only IBM publications about it. Apart from other books about AIX and some magazines that focus on AIX and the RISC System/6000 there is also that ocean of information, the Internet.

24.1 IBM publications

Most IBM publications are available in both hard- and soft-copy form. All AIX documentation can be obtained in paper form. Standard system documentation comes on-line in InfoExplorer format or for the CDE help system. Redbooks are also available in Bookmanager/read format. This is another IBM on-line viewing system that is optionally available for AIX.

Redbooks are so called because they are really red. These are books that are written not by the professional authors who write the standard documentation but by field support people. They are usually written in a different style from the normal books and contain many useful real life hints. And they are fun to write as I know from experience ;-}

24.1.1 Recommended IBM publications

There are many more IBM publications than the ones listed here. These are the ones that I have found to be the most useful. The order numbers listed here are general ones that do not indicate a specific release. For example, publication GG24-1234 might have two releases, GG24-1234-00 for the initial one and GG24-1234-01 for the newer one.

1 *AIX and Related Products Documentation Overview*
SC23-2456
You should receive this with your system. It contains a description of IBM and third-party literature about AIX.

2 *Problem Solving Guide*
SC23-2204

3 *Performance Monitoring and Tuning Guide*
SC23-2365

4 *Service Request Number Cross Reference*
SA23-2629
Not as detailed as the *Problem Solving Guide*, but a good reference for the LED codes and part numbers.

5 *Hardware Technical Reference: General Information*
SA23-2643

6 *Hardware Technical Reference: Options and Devices*
SA23-2646

7 *AIX Version 4.1 Kernel Extensions and Device Support Programming Concepts*
SC23-2611

8 *Kernel Extensions and Device Support Programming Concepts*
(AIX 3 only) SC23-2207

9 *AIX Version 3.2 Writing a Device Driver*
GG24-3629

10 *AIX Version 4.1 Writing a Device Driver*
SC23-2593

11 *AIX Version 4.1 Tech Ref V5: Kernel and Subsystems*
SC23-2618

12 *AIX Version 4.1 Tech Ref V6: Kernel and Subsystems*
SC23-2619

13 *AIX Version 4.1 Software Problem Debugging and Reporting for the RISC System/6000*
GG24-2513

14 *AIX 4.1 Network Installation Management Guide and Reference*
SC23-2627

15 *AIX Storage Management*
GG24-4448

16 *Keeping Your RISC System/6000 Up in a Down Economy / Managing AIX V3 for Availability*
GG24-3648

17 *AIXwindows Desktop Handbook*
GG24-4451

24.1.2 IBM on-line support

There are various forms of on-line support from IBM depending on the type of support contract you have. Contact your IBM representative or the business partner from whom you bought the system.

If you are on the Internet check out IBM's servers. Use *http://www.ibm.com/* as a starting point. Especially interesting are *http://www.austin.ibm.com/* for AIX-related topics and *ftp://aix.boulder.ibm.com* for updates.

If you need to get the Internet e-mail address of an IBMer, send e-mail to *nic@vnet.ibm.com*. In the body of the message you can include several queries with the *whois* command, which understands wildcards. For example

```
echo "whois Siegert" | mail nic@vnet.ibm.com
```

would probably find my e-mail address. There is a limit of 25 answers per requester per day. The VNET.IBM.COM gateway is not the only Internet gateway that IBM has, but as it is the biggest one the chances of finding an address there are pretty high.

24.1.3 The TechLib CD

In addition to the normal InfoExplorer CD there is also an enhanced version that contains information from IBM internal support systems. The TechLib CD comes with how-to articles from IBM's HONE system and bug reports and workarounds from IBM's RETAIN system. The CD is accessed via InfoExplorer like the standard documentation on CD. I consider it a must for anyone who deals seriously with AIX.

Unfortunately it is not available in all countries. If you cannot get it directly from IBM, contact the company that creates the CD:

The TDA Group
IBM AIX Technical Library/6000
PO Box 1360
Los Altos, CA 94023-1360
Phone: 800-551-2832 (US or Canada)
International: +001-415-948-3140
Fax: +001415-948-4280

24.2 The Internet

The Internet contains various resources dealing with AIX. If you are not connected yet, get connected! Any computer professional will benefit greatly from Internet access – I could not do my job without it.

On-line discussions regarding AIX can be found in the news group *comp.unix.aix*. An archive of this group is located at *http://www.thp.Uni-Duisburg.DE/cuaix/cuaix.html*. There is an FAQ (frequently asked questions) file which is archived at *ftp://rtfm.mit.edu/pub/usenet/news.answers*, or look at the hypertext version at *http://www.cis.ohio-state.edu/hypertext/faq/usenet/aix-faq/top.html*.

There are various FTP archives that cater for AIX users. The most prominent ones are *ftp://aixpdslib.seas.ucla.edu/pub* and *ftp://ftp.uni-stuttgart.de/sw/rs_aix32*.

Appendix 2 includes a wider selection of interesting resources on the Net, including useful tools.

24.3 Other publications

I have not read all of the publications listed here, please review them yourself before buying.

24.3.1 AIX-specific books

18 *AIX Version 3*
Michael Abel
te-wi Verlag 1994
ISBN 3-89362-253-7
This book is currently only available in German. It is most useful for beginners and those who are not very UNIX literate. There is also a version on AIX 4 from the same author.

19 *Power RISC System/6000: Concepts, Facilities, Architecture*
Dipto Chakravarty
McGraw-Hill 1994
ISBN 0070110476

20 *PowerPC: Concepts, Facilities, Architecture*
Dipto Chakravarty/Casey Cannon
McGraw-Hill 1994
ISBN 0-07-0111928

21 *AIX Companion*
David L. Cohn
Prentice-Hall 1994
ISBN 0-132912201

22 *AIX for RS/6000: System & Administration Guide*
J. DeRoest
McGraw-Hill 1994
ISBN 0-07-0364397

23 *IBM RS6000 AIX System Administration*
William C. Hollicker
Prentice-Hall 1996
ISBN 0-134526163

24 *The Advanced Programmer's Guide to AIX 3.x*
Phil Colledge
McGraw-Hill 1994
ISBN: 0-07-707663-x

24.3.2 AIX-specific magazines

25 *AIXpert*
IBM Corporation
Mail Stop 36
472 Wheelers Farms Road
Milford, CT 06460
Fax: 203-783-7669

26 *AIXtra*
IBM Corporation
NCM Enterprise
PO Box 165447
Irving, TX 75016-9939
US phone: 1-800-678-8014
Fax: +001-214-518-2507

27 *RiSc World*
PO Box 399
Cedar Park, TX 78613
Fax: 512-331-3900

28 *RS/Magazine*
PO Box 3272
Lowell, MA 01853-9876

24.3.3 General UNIX books

Some of these books can also be ordered from IBM. Check the documentations overview that comes with your system for a list of books that are orderable through IBM.

29 *Computer Security Basics*
Deborah Russel & G.T. Gangemi Sr.
O'Reilly & Associates 1991
ISBN 0-937175-71-4
This is not a technical book but one that explains the general principles.

30 *DNS and Bind*
Paul Albitz & Cricket Liu
O'Reilly & Associates 1992
ISBN 1-56592-010-4
IBM: SR28-4970
Unless you are already a DNS guru, this is for you if you need to work with DNS.

31 *Essential System Administration, 2nd ed.*

Æleen Frisch
O'Reilly & Associates 1995
ISBN 1-56592-127-5
My favourite book on UNIX system administration in heterogeneous environments; includes AIX specifics.

32 *Firewalls and Internet Security: Repelling the Wily Hacker*

William R. Cheswick & Steven M. Bellovin
Addison-Wesley 1995
ISBN 0-201-63357-4
The best source on firewall principles.

33 *Building Internet Firewalls*

D. Brent Chapman & Elizabeth D. Zwicky
O'Reilly & Associates 1995
ISBN 1-56592-124-0
The firewall implementation bible.

34 *Managing NFS and NIS*

Hal Stern
O'Reilly & Associates 1991
ISBN 0-937175-75-7
IBM: SR28-4968
Somewhat Sun-centric but nevertheless quite good.

35 *Managing UUCP and Usenet*

Tim O'Reilly & Grace Todino
O'Reilly & Associates 1992
ISBN 0-937175-93-5
IBM: SR28-4960
If you need to work with UUCP, get it.

36 *Practical UNIX & Internet Security, 2nd ed.*

Simpson Garfinkel & Gene Spafford
O'Reilly & Associates 1996
ISBN 1-56592-148-8

37 *Sendmail: theory and practice*

Frederik M. Avolio & Paul A. Vixy
Digital Press 1995
ISBN 1-55558-127-7

38 *TCP/IP Illustrated, Vol. 1*
W. Richard Stevens
Addison-Wesley 1994
ISBN 0-201-63346-9
A very good explanation of the protocols with real-life examples.

39 *TCP/IP Network Administration*
Craig Hunt
O'Reilly & Associates 1992
ISBN 0-937175-82-X
IBM: SR28-4853

40 *TCP/IP Running a Successful Network*
K. Washburn & J.T. Evans
Addison-Wesley 1993
ISBN 0 201 62765 5
A very good explanation of UNIX networking topics.

41 *The New Korn Shell*
Morris I. Bolsky & David G. Korn
Prentice Hall 1995
ISBN 0-13-182700-6

Appendix 1

The file tree layout of AIX

The AIX 3.2 file tree layout is a result of the advent of diskless and dataless systems. The classical UNIX file tree layout is not suited to sharing parts of the operating system across machines. Like Solaris, System V.4 or OSF/1, the AIX file tree tries to keep machine-specific parts, common executables, dynamic data and machine-independent data in different file systems to make it easier to share them. Compatibility with a classic UNIX file tree is maintained by more than 1000 symbolic links on AIX 3. Thus, if you use the old-style pathnames you will usually find what you are searching for, but for each access you pay a small performance penalty as the system needs to follow the symbolic link. I suggest setting up all your programs and profiles to use the new locations. You may achieve some increase in speed in shell scripts that execute many utilities.

AIX 4 tries to reduce the number of links (there are no more links to executables out of /etc by default – you need to install yet another file set *bos.compat.links* to get the links), and future versions will have even fewer symbolic links for compatibility. Although this appendix explains the file system layout, it does not explain the underlying file or disk management system. Please refer to Section 6.1 for details about disk management and to Section 6.2 for details on the file systems.

Figure A1.1 shows an abridged tree of the main directories and file systems. A complete tree would be beyond the scope of this appendix. Use **li -ROd** / to obtain a tree of all real directories on your system. On an AIX 4 system the *li* command can be found in the *bos.compat.cmds* file set; on AIX 3 it is available by default.

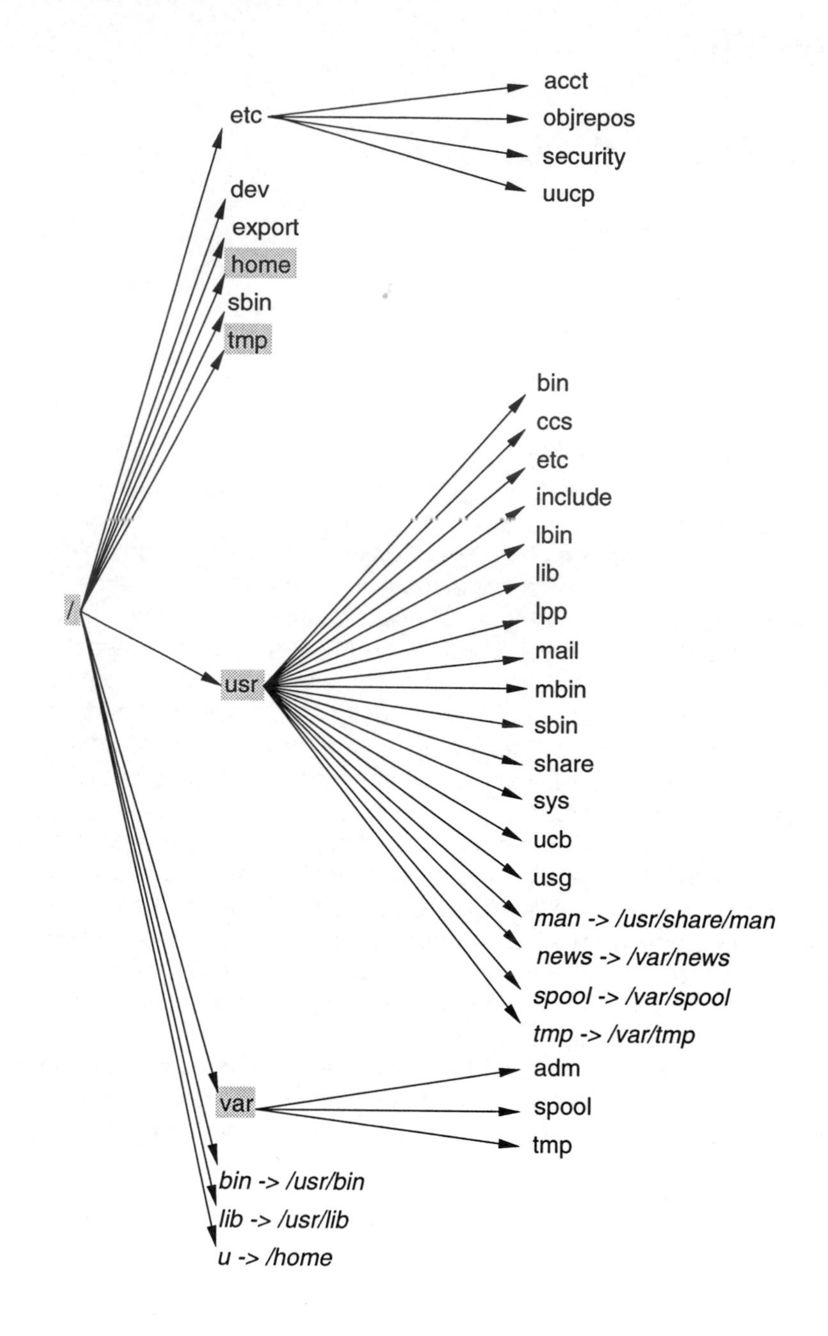

Figure A1.1 The file tree layout of AIX.

1.1 The main directories

Now where do you find what in this file tree layout?

/bin This is no longer a directory but a symbolic link to /usr/bin. Do not put /bin and /usr/bin in your $PATH as this will search /usr/bin twice.

/etc Here all machine-specific configuration data is stored. Configuration files that were previously found in /usr/lib, for example, can now be found here or in subdirectories of /etc. System administration executables are no longer stored in here. Most of them can be found in /usr/sbin. You should omit /etc from your $PATH. On AIX 3 there are still many links to the executables in this directory. They are no longer present on AIX 4, but can be installed via a compatibility option (*bos.compat.cmds* file set). So far I have found no need to install them.

/export Used as the root directory for file systems for diskless systems. It should be deleted and recreated as a separate file system if you intend to use it.

/home The home directories for users are set up in here by default. There is still a symbolic link from /u to /home for compatibility with older AIX systems. This is a separate file system. It is usually a good idea to delete it and recreate it on a separate disk if there are many users on the system.

/lib This directory has been replaced by a link to /usr/lib.

/sbin Things needed for booting the system and mounting /usr that are not found in the boot image.

/tftpboot Boot images for NIM managed systems on AIX 4. It should be deleted and recreated as a separate file system.

/tmp Still the main temporary directory and a separate file system.

/usr The place where all executables are stored; this is a separate file system.

/var All dynamic data such as log and spool files are stored in here. This is another separate file system. Read Section 6.4 to see the files that reside in here and tend to grow quickly.

1.1.1 The /usr file system

The /usr file system contains everything you need to run the system:

/usr/bin All ordinary executables. This should be first in your *$PATH*.

/usr/ccs Additional C development tools. They are usually accessed via symbolic links from /usr/bin. Even if you do not do any development work, this tree is needed since it stores libc.a. This is a shared library that is used by all programs shipped with AIX. If you remove it your system is dead.

/usr/include All the include files.

/usr/lib All libraries or symbolic links to the libraries and a few non user commands. It also stores architecture-dependent databases.

/usr/lpp This is where all application programs shipped by IBM are installed. It is analogous to /opt on System V systems.

/usr/mbin Multibyte executables on AIX 3. If you do not run with multibyte character sets then it can be removed to save a few bytes if space is tight. See Chapter 20 for more details. It is no longer present on AIX 4 as AIX 4 ships only the multibyte versions of these tools.

/usr/sbin Commands for system administration or internal non user-accessible sub-systems such as UUCP – usually all the executables that were found in /etc or /usr/etc in older systems.

/usr/share Architecture-independent data and libraries such as the man pages or the *terminfo* database.

/usr/spool Various spool files. This is no longer a direcory but a symbolic link to /var/spool.

/usr/sys/inst.images Install images on preloaded systems. This is one of the default places that SMIT offers as a choice when installing new software or updates. It is empty if you do not have a preloaded system.

/usr/tmp This is no longer a directory but a symbolic link to /var/tmp.

/usr/ucb This is for Berkeley compatibility. Some commands, such as *install*, work different in the Berkeley version. If you are used to BSD UNIX you should put this directory first in your *$PATH*.

1.1.2 The /var file system

The /var file system stores all the files that grow, spool files and some configuration data.

/var/adm	Contains accounting data and the *su* log. Error reporting tools use /var/adm/ras for the error log.
/var/news	System news is stored here, this is known as /usr/news on older systems.
/var/preserve	*vi* crash recovery files are stored here.
/var/spool	The replacement for the classic /usr/spool.
/var/tmp	The replacement for the classic /usr/tmp.
/var/spool/cron	Spool area for *cron* and *at* jobs.
/var/spool/lpd	Stores print requests from remote systems.
/var/spool/mail	The system's mail boxes.
/var/spool/mqueue	Temporary mail queue files.
/var/spool/qdaemon	Spool space for the queueing system.
/var/spool/uucp	Spool space for the UUCP subsystem.
/var/spool/uucppublic	Public directory for UUCP.
/var/spool/writeserv	Working directory for the *writesrv* daemon.

Appendix 2

Resources on the Internet

The Internet offers solutions to many problems. In this vast sea of information there are some tools that are indispensable on a UNIX system. The following collection of mailing lists, servers and tools is highly recommended. I would not be able to do my work without them.

2.1 Mailing lists

To join a mailing list, one usually sends a message to one of the request addresses below. Some of the mailing lists, such as the firewalls mailing list, have so much traffic that it is impossible to follow them when intermixed with regular mail. Check out the *slocal* command that comes with the *mh* mail handler or use the *filter* program that comes with the *Elm* freeware mailer to separate mailing list traffic from your regular e-mail.

Austin security alerts — The AIX lab in Austin provides security alerts via a mailing list. Send a mail message to *security@austin.ibm.com* to subscribe.

bugtraq — Discussion of security-related bugs. This is a full disclosure list or, in other words, exploit scripts to check for holes will also be posted. Subscribe with
echo "add Your@address" |
bugtraq-request@crimelab.com

CERT — The Computer Emergency Response Team (CERT) will send out security alerts to registered parties. Send a mail to *cert@cert.org* to subscribe. Other countries might have their own CERT groups. Ask CERT in the US about groups in other countries that they know about when subscribing here.

Firewalls — The firewalls mailing list discusses all kinds of firewall issues. Subscribe with
echo "Subscribe Firewalls" |
mail Majordomo@greatcircle.com

The above list represents only a minute part of the available lists out there, but so far these have been the most important ones for me.

2.2 Newsgroups

Although there is only one AIX-specific newsgroup, there are many more that are worth following. The ultrashort minimal list that I suggest here is less than 1‰ of what is out there. Which groups you follow will depend on your own requirements.

comp.answers — This newsgroup collects FAQ files. FAQs are answers to frequently asked questions. I suggest collecting FAQs on all topics that you are even remotely interested in. They provide a quick source of help in many problem situations.

comp.security.unix — UNIX-specific security issues.

comp.unix.aix	AIX-related discussions.
comp.security.announce	CERT announcements.
comp.security.misc	Various other computer security-related discussions.

2.3 Useful free code on the Internet

There are vast FTP and WWW archives out on the Internet that contain extremely useful code. Most of the code is copyright protected but can be used freely. When using such code please make sure to read and understand the licensing terms that come with the code. You also need to be aware that it comes with no warranty and that you are completely on your own when you use it. You should be also aware that when you import such code it might have hidden security problems or bugs that can compromise your system. You should only import source code that you can read and inspect yourself. Nevertheless, most of the Internet and most UNIX systems nowadays would not work without code that originally came this way. As long as one is aware of the limitations and inherent problems, the utilities listed here can be extremely helpful.

The following list represents only a glimpse of what is available. I consider most of them indispensable tools for system administrators.

COPS
ftp://ftp.cert.org/pub/tools/cops
Computer Password and Oracle System, a system security checker. Very old but still usable. Needs some adaptation to be fully usable, but provides interesting reports on any UNIX system. Check out both the shell/C version and the Perl one with the recursive checks.

Crack
ftp://ftp.cert.org/pub/tools/crack
A password cracker. Use it regularly to see if you have real stupid passwords on the system. Use the *mgrpwd* command from NIS to get the AIX passwords into a format that Crack understands (Crack wants standard UNIX passwordfiles that contain the encrypted passwords as input files).

Elm
ftp://ftp.uu.net:/networking/mail/elm
My favorite e-mail program. It is simple to use and powerful enough to handle most requirements.

Emacs
ftp://prep.ai.mit.edu:/pub/gnu/
The father of all programmable editors. Probably the most powerful editor that you can get freely on any UNIX system. Easier to use than *vi* and much more flexible, including X support, e-mail and more.

GNU-Zip
ftp://prep.ai.mit.edu:/pub/gnu/
A very efficient compression program. It compresses much

better than the standard *compress* program. Files with the ending .gz on FTP servers have usually been compressed with GNU-Zip. I rarely use the standard *compress* command any-longer.

GhostScript *http://www.cs.wisc.edu/~ghost/*
GhostScript is a freely available PostScript interpreter. It offers more functionality than the *showps* command that comes with AIX.

ISS *ftp://ftp.gatech.edu/pub/security/iss/*
Scans network ports to detect which ports systems listen on. ISS also tries to exploit some trivial holes, but these are fixed even on a standard AIX system.

Log_TCP *ftp://ftp.win.tue.nl/pub/security/*
Also known under the name TCP-wrapper. Access control for network daemons. A very useful little critter that sits between a daemon and the net. It allows access only to configured systems. Rejected access attempts can trigger custom programs and alerts. It is very useful for protecting systems in in-house networks. Unfortunately, it works only for TCP-based daemons that are started by *inetd*, but most services fall into that class anyway. I suggest installing it on all your servers – it is worth it just for the log information alone.

lsof *ftp://vic.cc.purdue.edu/pub/tools/unix/lsof*
Lsof is a utility that lists open files. Very useful to find out which process or user has which files or sockets open.

MD5 *ftp://ftp.cert.org/pub/tools/*
A secure checksum method. The standard UNIX/AIX *sum* program can be tricked. The MD5 algorithm is much more reliable.

monitor *ftp://ftp.funet.fi/pub/unix/AIX/RS6000/*
Monitor is a program that displays process and performance data on any ASCII screen or window. It is indispensable for quick overviews of system performance.

Mosaic *ftp://ftp.ncsa.uiuc.edu/Mosaic/*
The classic graphical Web browser.

Perl *ftp://ftp.netlabs.com/pub/outgoing/perl5.0/*
A very useful language. It combines the functionality of the Korn shell programming environment with *awk*, *sed*, *egrep* and low-level system access, for example a sockets interface. More and more tools from the net depend on Perl.

SATAN *ftp://ftp.win.tue.nl/pub/security/*
Currently the hottest network scanner (at least according to the press). Although not much more intelligent than the rest, its

easy user interface (via WWW) and open architecture make it the number one network scanner. Written by the guys who made COPS and Log_TCP. It requires Perl as it is written mostly in Perl.

SOCKS

ftp://ftp.nec.com/pub/security/socks.cstc/
The SOCKS server and library source code. You might need it to create your own socksified clients or a socks server for a firewall.

ssh

http://www.cs.hut.fi/ssh
A secure remote shell implementation with encrypted data transfer. It can even be used to encrypt X traffic over the network. Because of US patents and some strange cryptography laws in some countries it cannot be used legally in all countries.

Strobe

ftp://suburbia.apana.org.au:/pub/users/proff/original/
Currently the fastest TCP port scanner. Use it to see which TCP services are active on a remote system. Use it to scan your own systems before the bad guys do it.

SUDO

ftp://ftp.cs.colorado.edu/pub/sysadmin/utilities/
Sudo is a tool that allows normal users to execute specific programs with root privileges without having to pass the root password around. In addition, it logs all access. Very useful to implement operator-type ids.

Tiger/TAMU

ftp://ftp.tamu.edu/
A very useful system security checker from the Texas A&M University. It is so small that it can be run from a read-only floppy on AIX but it provides a great deal of useful output. It has a very open architecture that allows easy integration of custom checks. It is my preferred system security checking tool.

TIS toolkit

ftp://ftp.tis.com/pub/firewalls/toolkit/
A firewall toolkit from Trusted Information Systems. It has access control lists for *inetd*-controlled services like the *wrapper* plus proxy daemons and a *sendmail* replacement. It forms the basis of many DIY firewalls.

Tripwire

ftp://ftp.cs.purdue.edu/pub/spaf/COAST/tripwire/
A system integrity database and checking methods. A mix between COPS and the TCB that comes with AIX.

xv

ftp://ftp.cis.upenn.edu/pub/xv/
Displays images in many formats on screen. It can be used for image modifications, format conversions and to grab images from the screen. This program is shareware and the author requests a minimal registration fee.

Appendix 3

Undocumented LVM commands

There are some undocumented LVM commands that are not meant to be used directly. They are called by the high-level LVM commands, which are quite often shell scripts. Usually you should never need to use them and you are on your own if you get into trouble with them. They do not do much error checking and you will certainly lose your data if you make errors with these commands.

Do not play with these commands unless all other means have been exhausted. They can render your system useless without recovery if you make the slightest mistake!

On the other hand, there are times when you are out of business without them. For example I once moved the contents of my *rootvg* from one disk to another via *extendvg* and *migratepv* and then forgot to release the old disk with *reducevg*. I then made further mistakes and ended up with a non bootable system because LVM still thought that my *rootvg* had two disks. A simple call to *ldeletepv* got me out of that trap where *reducevg* was no longer working. I still had to remove some erroneous information about the old disk from the ODM, but that was easy – I just searched for the PVID of the old disk in the CuAt database (**odmget -q "value like *theoldPVID*" CuAt**) and removed them with *odmdelete* or replaced them with the appropriate PVID (via *odmchange*) for the new disk. When attempting to perform such tricks one should know the ODM files to avoid problems. Read Section 18.3.

The following list is not exhaustive but it might give you an indication of how to continue when the high-level commands fail. Quite often they are simply versions of the high-level command that work with obscure id strings instead of easily remembered device names. These id strings can be seen with *lslv*, *lsvg* or *lspv* for example; they are also shown when you use *getrootfs* without parameters from the maintenance shell on AIX 3.

lchangepv -g VGid -p PVid [-r RemoveMode] [-a AllocateMode]

This is the low-level command that is called by *chpv*. The *-r* flag is the same as the *-v* flag of *chpv* and the *-a* has the same meaning in both commands.

lresyncpv -g VGid -p PVid

This command is used to resynchronize stale physical partitions according to what is defined for logical partitions. It turns off the stale bit in the physical volume state information.

ldeletepv -g VGid -p PVid

This command allows you to delete physical volumes from the VGDA if *reducevg* no longer works because the mapping between a disk name and the PVid is no longer available.

lquerypv -p PVid [-g VGid | -N PVname] [-scPnaDdAt]

Other LVM commands use this command to query physical volumes. The meaning of the flags is as follows:

- *-s* Shows the physical partition size.
- *-c* Shows the state of the physical volume.
- *-P* Shows total number of physical partitions.
- *-n* Shows number of allocated physical partitions.
- *-a* Shows attributes described above.
- *-D* Shows number of VGDAs on physical partition.
- *-d* Shows the physical partition map.
- *-A* Same as "*-a*" but also shows physical partition map.
- *-t* Include field names in output.

linstallpv -N PVname -g VGid [-f]

This is used to install/add a physical volume in a volume group. With the *-f* flag you can install the physical volume in a volume group even if it appears to still be a member of another volume group.

lchangelv -l LVid [-s MaxPartitions] [-n LVname] [-M SchedulePolicy] [-p Permissions] [-r BadBlocks] [-v WriteVerify] [-w mirwrt_consist]

Changes various attributes for a logical volume, such as the name, maximum number of partitions, scheduling policy, permissions, bad block relocation, write verify, and mirror write consistency. This command is the low-level equivalent of *chlv*, which in turn is the backend for *chfs*.

- *-l* ID of logical volume to change, where *LVid=VGid.MinorNum*

-s New maximum number of partitions for the logical volume. Changes the maximum size attribute of the logical volume but does not actually change the current space allocation.

-n New logical volume name.

-M If *SchedulePolicy* equals 1, then schedule policy is sequential, else if *SchedulePolicy* equals 2, then schedule policy is parallel.

-p If *Permissions* equals 1, then logical volume is read–write, else if *Permissions* equals 2, then logical volume is read-only.

-r If *Relocation* equals 1, then bad block relocation is enabled, else if *Relocation* equals 2, then bad block relocation is not enabled.

-v If *WriteVerify* equals 1, writes to the logical volume are verified, else if *WriteVerify* equals 2, writes to the logical volume are not verified.

-w If *MirrorWriteConsistency* equals 1, keeps consistency on, else if *MirrorWriteConsistency* equals 2, keeps consistency off.

getlvcb [-acefilLmnrstuxyAPTS] lvname

This is the command that lets you snoop around in the logical volume control block. It returns the control block information for logical volume *lvname*. The information that is displayed is controlled by the following options:

-a Returns intra-policy field.

-c Returns copies field.

-e Returns inter-policy field.

-f Returns file system label field.

-i Returns logical volume identifier field.

-l Returns lvname field.

-L Returns label field.

-m Returns machine id field.

-n Returns numlps field.

-r Returns relocatable field.

-s Returns strictness field.

-t Returns type field.

-u Returns upper bound field.

-x Returns date/time created.

-y Returns date/time modified.

-A Returns all of the control block fields.

-P Returns the stripe width (AIX 4).

-T Prints tag field with all output values.

-S The first physical partition on the last disk of a stripe (AIX 4).

putlvcb [-a intrapolicy] [-c copies] [-e interpolicy] [-f fslabel] [-i lvid] [-L label] [-r reloc] [-n numlps] [-S ssize] [-O swidth] [-s strict] [-t type] [-u upperbound] [-N] [-v vgname] [-x vgautoa_on] lvname

The *putlvcb* command writes the control block information into block 0 of the logical volume *lvname*. Only the fields specified are written. *Putlvcb* can be used to write a new control block or update an existing one. Apart from *-N* each of the following options writes to an already existing logical volumes control block. This command should be used with extreme caution.

-a intrapolicy	The intra-physical volume allocation policy.
-c copies	The copy allocation values.
-e interpolicy	The inter-physical volume allocation policy.
-f fslabel	The file system label field / file system name.
-i lvid	The logical volume identifier.
-L label	The label field.
-n numlps	The number of logical partitions for lvname.
-r reloc	The relocation policy.
-s strict	The strictness allocation policy.
-t type	The logical volume type.
-u upperbound	The upperbound allocation policy.
-v vgname	The volume group name.
-x vgauto_on	The volume group *auto_on* value.
-N	This option indicates that a new logical volume control block is being written. If this flag is not set then a control block must already exist on the logical volume to be updated.
-S ssize	Sets the stripe size (AIX 4).
-O switdh	Sets the stripe width (AIX 4).

getlvodm [-a lvdescript] [-b LVid] [-B lvdescript] [-c LVid] [-C] [-d vgdescript] [-e LVid] [-F] [-g PVid] [-h] [-j pvname] [-L vgdescript] [-m LVid] [-p pvdescript] [-P] [-r LVid] [-s vgname] [-t VGid] [-w VGid] [-u vgdescript] [-y LVid] [-G lvdescript]

Displays logical volume data values from the ODM. The *getlvodm* command gets logical volume data from the configuration database and writes it to *stdout*. The information that is displayed is controlled by options. The descriptors *lvdescript*, *vgdescript*, or *pvdescript* can be either ids or a names (for example *lvdescript* can be *hd1* or 0000000012345678.1).

-a lvdescript	Returns the logical volume name for logical volume *lvdescript*.
-b LVid	Returns volume group name for logical volume *LVid*.
-B lvdescript	Returns the label for the logical volume *lvdescript*.
-c LVid	Returns the logical volume allocation characteristics for the *LVid* logical volume. The following charac-

teristics are returned (in the same order):
type value, intra-policy value, inter-policy value, upperbound value, strict value, copies value, reloc value.

-C	Returns all configured physical volumes.
-d vgdescript	Returns the major number of the volume group *VGid.*
-e LVid	Returns the logical volume name for logical volume *LVid.*
-F	Returns all the free configured physical volumes.
-g PVid	Returns the physical volume name for the physical volume *PVid.*
-G lvdescript	Returns the stripe size of the specified logical volume.
-h	Returns the list of volume group names known to the system.
-j pvdescript	Returns the *VGid* for the physical volume *pvdescript.*
-l lvdescript	Returns the logical volume identifier for logical volume *lvdescript.*
-L vgdescript	Returns the list of logical volume names and logical volume identifiers for volume group *vgdescript.*
-m LVid	Returns the file system mount point for logical volume *LVid.*
-p pvdescript	Returns the physical volume identifier for physical volume *pvdescript.*
-P	Returns a list of all configured physical volumes, their pvids (if applicable) and the name of the volume group they belong to (if applicable).
-r LVid	Returns the *reloc* value for the logical volume *LVid.*
-s vgname	Returns the volume group state for volume group *vgname.* 0 = varied off. 1 = varied on with all PVs. 2 = varied on with missing PVs.
-t VGid	Returns the volume group name for the *VGid.*
-u vgdescript	Returns the auto-on value for the volume group *vgdescript.*
-v vgdescript	Returns the volume group identifier for volume group *vgdescript.*
-w VGid	Returns the *pvids* and *pvnames* for the volume group *VGid.*
-y LVid	Returns the type for logical volume *LVid.*

putlvodm [-a intra-policy] [-B label] [-c copies] [-e inter-policy] [-l lvname] [-n newlvname] [-r relocatable] [-s strict-state] [-t type] [-u upperbound] [-y

copyflag] [-z size] [-S ssize] LVid putlvodm [-o auto-on] [-k] [-K] [-q state] [-v vgname] VGid
putlvodm [-p VGid] PVid
putlvodm [-V VGid]
putlvodm [-L LVid]
putlvodm [-P PVid]

The *putlvodm* command reads data from the command line and writes it to the appropriate configuration database class fields. The command line options specify what information is being written to the configuration database. Use this command with extreme caution. The following options apply to logical volume *LVid*:

-a intra-policy	Sets the intra-policy (m, e, or c).
-B label	Sets the label field.
-c copies	Sets the copies field (1–3).
-e inter-policy	Sets the inter-policy (m, x, or p).
-l lvname	Adds a new logical volume *LVid*.
-L LVid	Removes logical volume *LVid* data.
-n newlvname	Sets the logical volume name to *newlvname*.
-r relocatable	Sets the relocatable flag (y or n).
-s strict-state	Sets the strict-state (y or n).
-t type	Sets the type (example: jfs).
-u upperbound	Sets the upperbound (1–32).
-y copyflag	Sets the copy flag.
-z size	Sets the number of partitions (1–20000).
-S ssize	Sets the stripe size (AIX 4).

The following options apply to volume group *VGid*:

-o auto_on	Sets the *auto_on* flag (y or n).
-k VGid	Locks the volume group.
-K VGid	Unlocks the volume group.
-q state	Sets the *auto_on* flag: 0 = varied off. 1 = varied on with all PVs. 2 = varied on with missing PVs.
-v vgname	Adds a new volume group *VGid*.
-V VGid	Removes volume group *VGid*.
-p VGid	Adds the physical volume *PVid* to the VG.
-P PVid	Removes the physical volume *PVid* from the VG.

lresynclv -l LVid

Synchronizes all copies of all logical partitions in a logical volume and turns off its stale bit.

lcreatelv -N LVname -g VGid -n MinorNumber [-M MirrorPolicy] [-s MaxLPs] [-p Permissions] [-r Badblocks] [-v WriteVerify] [-w mirwrt_consist]

Creates a logical volume in a volume group. This is the backend for *crlv*.

ldeletelv -l LVid

Deletes a logical volume which must be closed. The LVM maps on the physical volumes are updated. It is called by *rmlv*.

lquerylv -L LVid [-p PVname] [-NGnMScsPRvoadlArtwb]

Prints information about a logical volume such as name, *VGid*, maximum size, mirror policy, mirror write consistency policy, state, current size, physical partitions size, permissions, bad block relocation policy, write verify policy, whether or not the LV is closed, and the logical partition map. This is the low-level version of *lslv*.

-N Selects logical volume name.

-G Selects associated volume group id.

-n Selects maximum number of logical partitions allowed in the LV.

-M Selects the logical volume mirror policy.

-S Selects the logical volume current state.

-c Selects current size in logical partitions.

-s Selects the physical partition size in the logical volume.

-P Selects the permission attribute of the logical volume.

-R Selects the bad block relocation attribute of the logical volume.

-v Selects the write verify state of the logical volume.

-o Selects the open/close state of the logical volume.

-a Selects all static attributes of the logical volume, that is *NGnMScsPRvo*. If this flag is combined with any other flags (except -*A*), the other flags are ignored.

-d Selects the logical partition map (dynamic attributes) of the logical volume.

-l Selects the long format of output (valid with *-d* and *-t* flags).

-A Selects all attributes of the logical volume.

-r Selects the output in *lreducelv* format.

-t Include tags/labels in the query output.

-w Selects the mirror write consistency state of the logical volume.

-b Returns the stripe exponent ($2^{stripexp}$=stripe size).

lextendlv -l LVid -s Size Mapfilename

Increases the size of a logical volume and/or adds copies for logical partitions. The logical volume is extended by the number of physical partitions given with the *-s* flag or by the physical volumes specified in the map file name. The map has an entry for each partition to be allocated in the Logical Volume. Each entry is a triplet containing a physical volume id, a physical partition number, and a logical partition number.

lreducelv -l LVid -s Size Mapfilename

Reduces the size of a logical volume and/or removes copies of logical partitions by either the number of logical partitions given with the-*s* flag or by exact physical partitions specified with the *Mapfilename* parameter.

lresynclp -l LVid -n LPnumber

Synchronizes all copies of a logical partition and resets the stale bit for them.

lmigratepp -g VGid -p SourcePVid -n SourcePPnumber -P DestinationPVid -N DestinationPPnumber

Moves the contents of a physical partition from one physical partition to another.

lvaryoffvg -g VGid [-f]

Varies off the volume group and removes any LVM data structures for this volume group from the kernels.

lvaryonvg -a VGname -V MajorNumber -g VGid [-ornpft] Filename

Varies on the volume group by reading the VGDA and creating the appropriate LVM data structures in the kernel. The command needs either a volume group major number or a list of physical volumes in *Filename* or via *stdin*.

- *-o* When not set, then the volume group can be opened, otherwise it can be used only for maintenance commands.
- *-r* Automatic resynchronization of stale logical and physical volumes in the volume group will be performed.
- *-n* The volume group will be varied on if a quorum exists even if one of the names of the physical volumes is missing.
- *-p* the volume group will be varied on if a quorum exists even if one of the physical volumes is missing.
- *-f* The volume group is forced vary on even if there is no quorum.
- *-t* Include tags and labels in the output.

lcreatevg -a VGname -V MajorNumber -N PVname -n MaxLVs -D VGDescriptorSize -s PPSize [-f] [-t]

Creates all the data structures in the kernel and on disk for a new volume group and adds the physical volume to the volume group. The *-f* flag can be used to force the creation even if it appears that the physical volume belongs to another volume group. The *-t* flag will include tags and labels in the output.

lqueryvg [-g VGid | -p PVname] [-NsFncDaLPAvt]

Prints out information about a volume group such as maximum number of LVs, physical partition size, number of free physical partitions, number of LVs, number of PVs, total number of VGDAs, and ids and states for each LV and PV.

- *-N* Shows maximum number of LVs.
- *-s* Shows physical partition size.
- *-F* Shows number of free PPs.
- *-n* Shows number of LVs.

-c Shows number of PVs in VG.
-D Shows total number of VGDAs in VG.
-a Shows attributes described above.
-L Shows logical volumes in VG.
-P Shows PVIDs and states in VG.
-A Shows all attributes above.
-v Shows VGID for a given physical volume name.
-t Include field names in output.

lqueryvgs [-NGAt]

Prints out the number of volume groups in the system and the VGIDs and major numbers of all varied on VGs.

-N Total number of volume groups known to system.
-G Shows all VGIDs and major numbers.
-A Shows all attributes above.
-t Include field names in output.

logredo [-n] filename

Replays the log for a file system so that file system tables are consistent with what has actually been written to disk before a system crash. This is performed automatically at system start up when needed.

logform device

Formats the specified log logical volume. This will erase the current file system transaction log. It is quite helpful should the JFS transaction log be corrupted. In this case the only remedy is to boot the system from maintenance mode and reformat the log logical volume.

Glossary

AES
Application environment specification. The definition of the OSF/1 operating system interfaces.

AIX
Advanced Interactive Executive. IBM's name for its UNIX operating systems.

APAR
Authorized problem analysis report. Another term for an officially recognized bug report. Usually the result of a PMR.

BGP
Border Gateway Protocol. A routing protocol to exchange routing information between routers.

BIND
Berkeley Internet Name Daemon. Another name for *named*, then name service daemon.

BIST
Built-in self-test.

bluespeak
Slang for IBMese, the strange language used in IBM documents.

BOS
Base Operating System. The core of the operating system.

BSD
Berkeley Software Distribution. The source of the BSD UNIX.

CDE
Common desktop environment. The graphical user interface introduced by COSE.

COSE
Common open software environment. An attempt to standardize operating systems.

DASD
Direct access storage device. An IBM term for a hard disk.

DCR
Design change request. Another word for a faint hope that something will change.

EPOCH
The date when time starts for UNIX: 1 January, 1970 at 00:00. All dates are kept internally as seconds since EPOCH.

Fileset
The POSIX term for an installable set of files. Used in AIX 4 terminology instead of LPPs and options.

FIPS
Federal information processing standard. A US government-only standard that AIX conforms to (FIPS 151-2).

ICMP
Internet control message protocol. An IP protocol to transport diagnostic and error messages.

ILS
International language support. Formerly NLS or national language support, the ability to run a system with support for various cultures.

IPL
Initial program load. Bluespeak for booting a system.

load module
Another term for executable file.

LP
Logical partition. Maps to one or more physical partitions (PP) on the disk.

LPP
Licensed program product. A name for an individually installable or orderable program.
LV
Logical volume. The term used by AIX for logical disk partitions.
LVM
Logical volume manager. The disk management components in AIX.
mbuf
A memory buffer used in the networking subsystem. It is 256 bytes on AIX 3, various sizes on AIX 4.
MES
Miscellaneous equipment specification. Basically this is an enhancement to a current product. It contains fixes and enhancements such as an LPP but also new products if ordered.
MTA
Mail transfer agent. The program that does mail delivery; on AIX this is *sendmail.*
MTU
Maximum transfer unit. The largest frame size on a network.
MUA
Mail user agent. The program used to read and send mail.
NIM
Network install manager. The tool to boot, install and update AIX 4 systems via the network.
NVRAM
Non-volatile RAM. A small CMOS memory that is powered by a battery. It stores configuration options that are needed to boot the system.
ODM
Object database manager. A simple database that stores various configuration details on AIX.
OSF
Open Software Foundation. An organization that was originally founded to counter the AT&T–Sun Microsystems coalition to control UNIX. Known mostly through the OSF/Motif user interface libraries.
OSPF
Open shortest path first. A very good routing protocol for dynamic routing.
page
The unit of memory used by the memory management subsystem. This is 4KB on AIX.
PMP
Preventive maintenance package. A collection of bug fixes and enhancements for already installed programs. It does not contain complete products.
PMR
Problem maintenance record. A problem that has been reported to the support organization.
POSIX
A portable operating system standard that AIX conforms to (ISP/IEC 9945-1).
POST
Power on shelf test. The built-in tests that are executed by an RS/6000 when the system is powered on.
PRPQ
Programming request for price quotation. Sometimes you can get non-official unsupported utilities and drivers as PRPQs from IBM.
PP
Physical partition. The unit of real storage used in partitioning disks.
PTF
Program temporary fix. A bug fix.
PTX
Performance Toolbox/6000. A collection of useful performance

tools. Optional for AIX 3, absolutely necessary on AIX 4 as some tools have been unbundled from the OS and moved into the PTX distribution.

PV
Physical volume. Another term for hard disk used in AIX.

ROS
Read only storage. ROM in normal computer terms.

SIPO
System installation productivity option. An installable/bootable tape in normal language.

SMIT
System management interface tool. A menu driven interface to system management commands.

SOM
System object model. IBM's object-oriented enabling technology.

SPOT
Shared product option tree. The directory tree under which file systems and images for diskless machines or NIM clients are kept.

SSU
Subsystem update. An update for a specific group of files on AIX 3.2.

tty
An ancient typewriter telex terminal. Used to name terminal interfaces on UNIX because of historical reasons.

UCB
University of California at Berkeley. Also found in pathnames such as /usr/ucb for BSD utilities.

USG
UNIX Support Group. The people at Bell Labs from which the original UNIX came. Sometimes found in path names such as /usr/usg.

UUCP
UNIX to UNIX copy program. The original name of some simple but efficient utilities to network UNIX systems via serial lines and modems. Today one refers to them often as BNU (Basic Network Utilities).

VPD
Vital product database. This is a database that stores information about the installed hard and software on a system.

VSM
Visual system management. A suite of tools to do basic system management tasks with drag, drop and a few more mouse clicks.

X/Open
A vendor consortium standard for open operating systems.

XPG
X/Open portability guide (AIX conforms to XPG4).

Index

Symbols

A

B

C

D

E

F

G

H

I

K

L

M

N

O

P

Q

R

S

T

U

V

W

X

Y

Z